NARRATIVE SYNTAX AND THE HEBREW BIBLE

BIBLICAL INTERPRETATION SERIES

VOLUME 29

NARRATIVE SYNTAX AND THE HEBREW BIBLE

Papers of the Tilburg Conference 1996

EDITED BY

ELLEN VAN WOLDE

BRILL
LEIDEN · NEW YORK · KÖLN
1997

This book is printed on acid-free paper.

Library of Congress Cataloging-in-Publication Data

Narrative syntax and the Hebrew Bible : papers of the Tilburg conference 1996 / edited by Ellen van Wolde.
p. cm. — (Biblical interpretation series, ISSN 0928-0731 ; v. 29)
Includes bibliographical references (p.) and indexes.
ISBN 9004107878 (cloth : alk. paper)
1. Hebrew language—Syntax—Congresses. 2. Narration in the Bible—Congresses. 3. Bible. O.T.—Language, style—Congresses.
I. Wolde, E.J. van. II. Series.
PJ4707.N36 1997
221.4'4—dc21 97-28704
CIP

ISSN 0928-0731
ISBN 90 04 10787 8

PRINTED IN THE NETHERLANDS

CONTENTS

INTRODUCTION

Seventy-two Hebraists and Biblical scholars met at the Tilburg conference on Narrative Syntax and the Hebrew Bible in October 1996 to study syntax. A blue sky and trees in bright autumn colours, visible through the glass wall of the conference room, formed the backdrop to their activities. A season of transformation, outdoors as well as indoors. The trees in the park show their changing colours: the oak shining in red, the maple in yellow and the beech in coppery colours, all dominated by the chestnuttree with its full yellow-brown crown; the holmoak shows, on the other hand, no readiness for change, and the fir and pine remain green "forever". Inside the conference room Biblical Hebrew syntax appears to be in a period of transition, too. The eminent scholars know their own stages of development. The person with the brightest colour of change has been one of the first to change his view. Some begin later and reveal their own coloration. Others still represent the evergreen and show a slight dislike for the colour alteration of the more changeable minds.

During the summer of Biblical Hebrew grammar all scholars concentrated on morphology and on the temporal and aspectual values of the verb forms, and restricted this morpho-syntax to the sentence boundaries. An increasing need was felt for a text-syntactic study: the traditionally oriented Biblical Hebrew word- and sentence-based grammar was criticised as inadequate. The predominant green colour turned out to differentiate itself in manifold autumn-colours: text-syntactic studies of the Biblical Hebrew verbal system appeared, in which morphological forms were analysed in their different narrative functions. Various studies of the contextual and communicative aspects of syntax were made. Biblical Hebrew word-order was studied afresh. Models inspired by pragmatics, discourse analysis and cognitive linguistics were developed. A spectrum of narrative syntaxes became perceptible. Traditional Hebrew grammar sometimes rejected these new approaches or at other times criticised its lack of analytical foundation and its eclectic range of biblical texts.

Summer or autumn, it was time for a discussion. Not only theoretical argumentations, but also practical analyses needed to be examined. Six scholars acquainted with the field were asked both to present a paper on their theories and ideas of the Hebrew syntax and to lead a workshop in which the consequences of their insights are shown in the syntactic analysis of Exodus 19–24 or 1 Samuel 1, two notoriously difficult narrative texts. Both kinds of contributions are collected in this volume, which explains the differences in style, in the number of footnotes and discussions in the theoretical articles on the one hand and the workshop papers on the other.

The articles differ in breadth of treatment and topic. However different they may be, in the end one may discover, surprisingly, a certain convergence. In the beginning, twenty years ago, Biblical Hebrew narrative syntax arose as a reaction to the traditional sentence-syntax, as if the one had to exclude the other. The articles in this volume tend to hold a less exclusive, more inclusive view. Verb forms, word-order and other syntactic features function at more than one level: in the clause and the sentence, in a hierarchy of clauses or textual units, in a story. A combination of a morpho-syntactic study at the sentence level and a text-syntactic approach should be made. From this point onwards the scholars concentrate on different levels.

Joosten explicitly elucidates an inclusive approach. Following Benveniste, who described the different levels of words which are composed of phonemes, but are themselves integrated into sentences (phonemes are not integrated in sentences), Joosten defends the distinction between verb forms functioning at the level of the sentence, and sentences integrated into a textual unit. Therefore, according to Joosten, verb forms are not integrated into a text; sentences, however, are. Joosten himself consequently focusses mainly on the verbs and their temporal, aspectual and modal functions in a sentence, and does not enter into detail concerning the textual arrangement of the sentences. Joosten's position is similar to Muraoka's on the one hand, and to Talstra's on the other: his work on the sentence-level is similar to Muraoka's approach, his acknowledgement of the integration of sentences into a larger unit corresponds to Talstra's hierarchical arrangement of clauses.

Talstra systematically builds up his elements: he starts with the morphological forms in the clauses, distinguishes grammatical clause types, lists the morphological and lexical correspondences between clause constituents in two clauses, the syntactic marking of paragraphs and the set of actors in a text, and consequently arranges the related constituents into a hierarchy of clauses, thus unfolding the coherence in a text. He very systematically elaborates the thesis defended by

Joosten: the relation of the elements occurs at one level, while the integration takes place at a higher hierarchical level. He explains this both at a theoretical and a practical level in his workshop paper. Although Van der Merwe is more generally descriptive in his articles and seems less interested in defending his own position, his choices seem to be close to Talstra's. He starts with the forms of the verbs and other words in clauses, and consequently proceeds to their discursive functions.

Alviero Niccacci starts at the sentence level too, and concentrates first on the verb forms and the place of the verb in the clause. He describes a theory of two sentence types, with either a verb form in first-place position or a verb form in second-place position. At the text-level he makes a distinction between "historical-narrative texts" and "direct speech texts". Thus he is able to describe the basic syntactic structures of Biblical Hebrew narrative and the functions of the verb forms in these structures. Niccacci considers the Hebrew verb form and the word-order in a clause as the indicators of their function in the prose text, either indicating the main line of action or the interruption of this main line. At the same time he acknowledges the tense aspects of the distinct verb forms both in the sentence and at the textual level, i.e. in the historical narrative and direct speech.

Muraoka differs markedly from Niccacci, as he begins and ends with the morphological form at the sentence level, meticulously analyzing the differences in form. He carefully argues on the basis of these forms within sentence boundaries, in order to prove or disprove the alleged final function of the Biblical Hebrew syntagm <*waw* + volitive verb form>. Generally speaking, one might say that they represent the extremes of the scale: Muraoka being on the morphological end of the scale, summarized as "from verb form to function in the sentence", and Niccacci on the functional end of the scale, which can be summarized as "from textual function to verb form".

These papers are preceded by two general and introductory articles, which do not present a theoretical model but elucidate the backgrounds of the actual developments; no workshop was presented in combination with these introductions. In the first article Van der Merwe gives an overview of the recent developments in Biblical Hebrew linguistics. He shows what necessitated a new approach to the study of Biblical Hebrew, and presents the trends in Biblical Hebrew narrative syntax. In the second article Van Wolde concentrates on recent developments in general linguistics and pragmatics which show tendencies very similar to the approaches in Biblical Hebrew narrative syntax. She relates the research of form and function to that of linguistic motivation and states that Biblical Hebrew narrative syntax has to deal with the question of "why" a certain form is used in a specific clause or textual context. These two introductory articles are intended to clarify the background to the discussion, and therefore the book starts with them.

The preparation of a conference and of its proceedings require much time and money. Both were made possible by the financial support of the Tilburg Faculty of Theology, the Netherlands School for Advanced Studies in Theology and Religion (NOSTER), the Netherlands Royal Academy of Sciences (KNAW), the Netherlands Organization of Scientific Research (NWO: SFT), the Radboudstichting, the Mr. Paul de Gruyter Stichting and the Sormanifonds. I am most grateful for the help of people without whom this project could not have been successfully completed. In the first place I wish to thank Drs. Yvonne van den Akker-Savelsbergh, my right hand in the preparation and actualization of the conference. Without her the organization would have been too arduous a task, not an agreeable one, as it turned out to be in the end. In the editing of this book I have received indispensable help of Drs. Ron Pirson and Cynthia Lieshout. And last but not least my gratitude goes to the lecturers and contributors to this volume, as well as to those who attended the conference: they all make syntax of Biblical Hebrew a stimulating field of research.

AN OVERVIEW OF HEBREW NARRATIVE SYNTAX

Christo H.J. van der Merwe
(Stellenbosch)

1. *Introduction*

The primary aim of this paper is to provide a bird's eye view of Hebrew narrative syntax. It serves two purposes: (1) to introduce exegetes who are not familiar with recent developments in Biblical Hebrew linguistics with an understanding of what prompted this type of study, its problems and how it has developed, in particular as far as the Biblical Hebrew verbal system is concerned, and (2) to advance communication between Biblical Hebrew grammarians who are involved in this field. I envisage to accomplish this goal by answering the following questions

— What necessitated this new approach to the study of Biblical Hebrew?
— What prompted this type of approach to the study of Biblical Hebrew?
— What are the major trends, if any, that could be identified in this type of approach to the study of Biblical Hebrew?

For the purpose of this paper, I will regard narrative syntax as an approach to the study of Biblical Hebrew that investigates grammatical phenomena not merely within the scope of sentences, but also within larger text units. In my follow-up paper I will, however, scrutinize some of the implications of these and other labels that are attached to the study of linguistic phenomena beyond the boundaries of the sentence and/or the study of language use.

2. *What necessitated a new approach to the study of Biblical Hebrew?*

There are certainly a number of factors that could have played a role in this regard. I would like to elaborate on only one of the most important ones.

— *Our knowledge base of Biblical Hebrew grammar has been restricted by the moulds in which it was transmitted in Western circles.*

The eleventh century is regarded as the golden era of Biblical Hebrew grammar. In those days Arabic-speaking Jewish scholars in Spain debated issues of Biblical Hebrew grammar even at big public venues. When these scholars and their students were later driven out of Spain, much of their knowledge was disseminated throughout Europe. Unfortunately the Latin mould of European grammar provided a very restricted framework for the wealth of Biblical Hebrew grammatical knowledge brought over by these Jewish grammarians. The reason was that the European schools regarded grammar, rhetoric and poetics as three different language sciences, in contrast to the Arabic model that regarded rhetoric and poetics as part and parcel of the grammar of a language. When Christian scholars started to dominate the study of Biblical Hebrew in the sixteenth century, they, of course, did so in terms of their narrow view of grammar. The tragedy was that Jewish scholars then lost all interest in the study of Biblical Hebrew and consequently Biblical Hebrew grammar was cut off from its only "living" tradition, viz. that tradition which survived in the Rabbinical circles. In this process much of what they knew about Biblical Hebrew rhetoric sank into oblivion. Two centuries later when Jewish scholars returned to the scene, the European model had already been so deeply entrenched that they too accepted it as the norm. Furthermore, until the beginning of the twentieth century the study of the forms of words, their history and the comparison of words dominated the study of language in European circles.[1]

Most Biblical Hebrew grammars were not out of step with the linguistics of their day. The grammars of Bauer and Leander (1922) and Bergsträsser (1929), which lack a syntax, the relatively short syntax of Gesenius-Kautzsch-Cowley (1910) and the meager syntax in most introductory grammars published up to the 1970s on Biblical Hebrew, are good examples in this regard. This led to a state of affairs in which we know a fair amount about Biblical Hebrew morphology, but relatively little about its syntax[2] and less about the conventions that determined the use of words and sentences in order to communicate.

[1] This section is based on Waltke and O'Conner (1990: 31–40). For a slightly different typology of the Arabic linguistics, cf. Fleisch (1994: 164–184).

[2] The following two factors could also have played a role in this regard: (1) According to Loewe (1994: 120–121) "A striking lacuna in the substantial body of Jewish

3. *What prompted this type of approach to the study of Biblical Hebrew?*

In a recent study (Van der Merwe 1994: 15) three possible reasons were identified why Biblical Hebrew grammarians have since the 1970s no longer been satisfied with the traditional sentence-based approach to grammar. These reasons concern the fields of grammar, exegesis and translation:

> (1) the influence of modern linguistics with its insistence that linguistic categories and levels of description will be defined in terms of explicitly stated criteria;
>
> (2) discontent with the historical-critical exegetical methods which led to more text-immanent approaches that again revealed the inadequacies of traditionally orientated Biblical Hebrew word- and sentence-based grammars; and
>
> (3) the movements in Bible translation to translate the sense rather than the words of an utterance. . . . The need for tools to understand the use of Biblical Hebrew exposed the too-narrow base (i.e., the sentence) of traditional grammar.

Apart from these internal factors that could have prompted a new approach to the study of Biblical Hebrew, an external factor, viz. *two major paradigm shifts in the study of language since the beginning of this century* could also have played a role in these regards. The first was a shift from attempts to trace the historical development of forms or meaning, which we could call *historical linguistics*, to one that demonstrates how all the forms and meanings are interrelated at a particular point in time in a particular language system, which could be labeled *structuralistic linguistics*. One of the main contributions of structuralism to the study of language is without doubt the pivotal role it assigned to these *distributional* criteria. Two main lines of thought developed in structuralistic linguistics, viz. *functionalism* and *generativism*. Basic assumptions of most developments in the *latter* are:

---

linguistic philological literature . . . is the almost complete disregard of syntax, despite the sensitivity of some of these grammarians to nuances and their syntactic indications when they were themselves commenting on the biblical text". (2) Although closer investigations of theoretical frame(s) of reference of the syntaxes of König (1897), Gesenius-Kautzsch-Cowley (1910), Joüon (1923) and Brockelmann (1956) are still wanted, according to Leitner (1984: 212), most sentence-based traditional grammars have their roots in the German linguistics of the early nineteenth century.

— The sentence is the largest unit of grammatical description.
— The syntactic structure of language can be described without recourse to semantic considerations.
— The syntactic component of a language is one of three organizational units within a grammar. The other two are the phonological and semantic units. Each constitutes an autonomous innate mental module.

A feature shared by the *functionalist* movement (in opposition to generativism) is the following:
— The structure of utterances is *determined by the use* to which they are put and the communicative context in which they occur.[3]

Although it is generally acknowledged today that there is indeed a good deal of arbitrariness in the grammatical structure of language systems and that a hard-line functionalist view is untenable, there is also a strong awareness of a growing number of observations about language that cannot be explained without recourse to contextual concepts. Moreover, the value of distributional criteria when applied to language use beyond the boundaries of the sentence has its limitations. This state of affairs contributed to a second paradigm shift in the study of language this century. Mey (1993: 20) describes it as follows: "The 'pragmatic turn' in linguistics can thus be described as a paradigm shift by which a number of observations are brought to the same practical denominator. Basically the shift is from the paradigm of theoretical grammar (in particular, syntax) to the paradigm of the language user".

The above-mentioned factors certainly did not only prompt the narrative syntactic approaches to Biblical Hebrew. In Van der Merwe (1994: 15) I argue that the latter approaches are part of a larger movement in the study of Biblical Hebrew that gave rise to

— revisions of traditional descriptions of Biblical Hebrew grammar, e.g. Joüon-Muraoka (1991) and Waltke and O'Connor (1990).
— an entire re-evaluation of existing grammatical knowledge in terms of a new look at all Biblical Hebrew data, e.g. Richter (1978–1980), Schweizer (1981) and Talstra (1987: 95–105).
— attempts to treat specific problems in terms of units or entities

[3] For a brief outline and comparison of the functionalism and generativism, cf. Lyons (1981: 224–235).

bigger or other than the sentence, e.g. Niccacci (1990), Bandstra (1992: 109–123), Buth (1994: 138–154 and 1995: 77–102), Andersen (1994: 99–116) and Longacre (1994: 50–98) to mention a few.

Studies from a narrative syntactic point of view are overwhelmingly part of the third group mentioned above.

4. *Trends in narrative syntax*

4.1 *Introduction*

As I mentioned earlier, the main focus of this overview of narrative syntax will be studies of the Biblical Hebrew verbal system conducted from this point of view. In order to put the latter studies in perspective, I will commence with a few remarks on (1) some of the main problematic issues of the Biblical Hebrew verbal system and (2) how they have been treated traditionally. Although Muraoka's revision of Joüon could strictly speaking not be regarded as a narrative syntactic approach to the Biblical Hebrew verb, some of his revisions[4] imply that he too considered contextual factors in his description of Biblical Hebrew linguistic phenomena. This, and, of course his contribution to this conference, necessitate a discussion of his views in the second part of this section. In part three solutions to some of the problematic aspects of the Biblical Hebrew verbal system from the point of view of narrative syntax will be discussed. Also, the views of Joosten, a participant of the conference, will be briefly summarized, even though they do not concern directly this new approach.

[4] Muraoka revised substantially Joüon's section on the word order of verbal clauses. Most of the views put forward in his dissertation of 1969, that was revised in 1985, are incorporated in Joüon-Muraoka (§ 155). Most significant is the fact that he reverses the view of Joüon that the unmarked word order in Biblical Hebrew is Subject-Verb. He states: "The statistically dominant and unmarked word-order in the verbal clause is: Verb-Subject". He, however, lists a number of cases (with reasons) where a marked construction does not express emphasis (a concept that he scrutinized in Muraoka 1969 and 1985). One of which is "to indicate the absence of sequence" (§ 155n). Joüon-Muraoka is without doubt cast in the mould of traditional grammar, in particular as far as verbal conjugations are concerned. However, one may argue that Muraoka's revision of Joüon's section of word order reflects a closer look at the context of a clause than was the custom in most traditional grammars, e.g. Muraoka (1985: 5) remarks "the question of word order cannot be properly treated without examining separately each of the different levels or style, or more exactly, the different literary genres found in the corpus concerned".

4.2 *The problem of the Biblical Hebrew verbal system*

The problem of Biblical Hebrew conjugation resides mainly in questions concerning the semantic value of the oppositions, on the one hand, *qatal-yiqtol*, and on the other hand, *wayyiqtol-w^e^qatal.*[5] More recently questions concerning the function of the *(w^e^)x-qatal—(w^e^) x-yiqtol* forms also come into play. Many solutions from various angles have been put forward, in particularly during the last two centuries.[6] The early Jewish grammarians assigned a tense value to the *qatal-yiqtol* opposition (i.e. past vs. future).[7] Since the second half of the nineteenth century it was argued that the Biblical Hebrew verbal system should be characterized as aspectual (i.e. either in the sense as "different ways of viewing the internal temporal constituency of a situation"[8] or in the sense of the opposition "complete(d) vs. incomplete").[9] The latter point of view is the one found in most Biblical Hebrew grammars of the twentieth century.[10]

As far as the *wayyiqtol-w^e^qatal* opposition is concerned, the early Jewish grammarians merely considered the *waw* as converting the tense of the *yiqtol* and *qatal* following it, hence the term the *waw-conversive*. Many modern scholars advanced the view that the *wayyiqtol-w^e^qatal* forms continue the aspect or tense of a preceding verbal form, hence the term the *waw-consecutive*. Recently, the term, the *waw-relative* was coined in order to convey the fact that the verb with the *waw-relative* represents "a situation subordinate to that of the preceding clause, either as a (con)sequence or as an explanation of it".[11]

With advances in the study of other Semitic languages, numerous attempts were made to explain the Hebrew verbal system from a historical-comparative point of view. Despite the fact that many of the views put forward by some had also in the meanwhile been refuted by others,[12] it is on account of among others these studies that

[5] Cf. McFall (1982: xii).

[6] Cf. Mettinger (1974: 64–84), McFall (1982), Waltke and O'Connor (1990: 343–361) and Endo (1993: 1–30).

[7] Cf. This view is still held by some prominent Jewish scholars like Blake and Blau, cf. Ljungberg (1995: 84).

[8] Cf. Comrie (1976: 3).

[9] Cf. DeCaen (1996: 129–151) for a critical assessment of the introduction of the concept "aspect" in describing Biblical Hebrew verbal forms.

[10] Cf. Endo (1993: 1–19). For an overview of recent developments, cf. Hendel (1996: 152).

[11] Cf. Endo (1993: 15) and Waltke and O'Connor (1990: 525).

[12] Cf. Waltke and O'Connor (1990: 496–501) and Endo (1993: 11–19).

— the necessity of distinguishing between short and long forms of the *yiqtul* is relatively widely acknowledged (the reason being that Biblical Hebrew originally had a *yaqtulu*, signifying the present-future and the iterative past, and a *yaqtul* form, signifying the jussive mode or preterite action, but the *yaqtul* and *yaqtulu* forms have largely fallen together when the *yaqtulu* lost its final *u*)[13] and
— the possibility that the Biblical Hebrew verbal system has two independent systems, viz. an indicative system that may be aspectual and/or temporal and a modal system, is nowadays hotly debated, alongside the question whether the position of the verbal form in a sentence could also serve as a marker of modality.[14]

4.3 *Revisions of traditional descriptions of Biblical Hebrew grammar*[15]

Muraoka in Joüon-Muraoka § 111 acknowledges the importance of distinguishing between the form and function of the verbal forms, hence he speaks of *qatal, yiqtol, w^eqatal* and *wayyiqtol* forms which have perfect, future, inverted perfect and inverted future meanings respectively. His two semantic labels, perfect and future, the shortcomings of which he is well aware of, reflect his view that Hebrew "temporal" forms express at the same time *tense and modes of action*—the latter he

[13] Cf. Waltke and O'Connor (1990: 501) and Buth (1992: 91–105).

[14] Cf. Rainey (1988: 35–42) and the discussion of Rainey's views in Endo (1993: 16–17), Revell (1989: 1–37) and DeCaen (1995). According to Buth (1992: 103), a scholar who incorporates many of the Simon Dik's functional grammatical views in his description of Biblical Hebrew, "Hebrew has four verb forms which reflect two separate parameters: tense aspect and thematic continuity".

[15] According to Endo (1993: 21) "the waw-conversive/inductive theory of Philip Gell (1818), S.R. Driver (1874), etc. which is taken up by G.K.C. (§ 49), T.O. Lambdin (1971), etc. may be considered as one of the pioneer attempts in the light of 'discourse', since this approach is concerned with the thread of discourse rather than with isolated clauses". Also the theories of Michel (1960), Hoftijzer (1974) and Loprieno (1980) who all take the syntactic relationship between clauses into consideration, he regards as approaches of this kind. Waltke and O'Connor (1990) fully acknowledge the necessity of studying Biblical Hebrew beyond the boundaries of the sentence, but "resisted the strong claims of discourse grammarians" because they believe the grammatical analysis of Hebrew discourse is still in its infancy (Waltke and O'Connor 1990: 55). This may be one of the reasons why their syntax contains no section on Biblical Hebrew word order. According to Endo (1993: 15) their view to consider "weQATAL and waYYIQTOL as relative verbal forms ('waw-relative') that 'represent a situation subordinate to that of the preceding clause, either as a (con)sequence or explanation of it' because of the force of the conjunction (i.e. 'and' of succession)" is similar to that of Joüon-Muraoka § 117–119. For a critical stance toward Waltke and O'Connor, cf. Dawson (1994: 24–28).

also wrongly refers to as aspect. However, he does not believe that aspect in the sense of the opposition pair completed vs. incomplete action "explains the choice of tenses in Hebrew adequately" (§ 111f). He does not deny its existence in an earlier stage of the language. His choice of the semantic labels "inverted perfect" and "inverted future" implies that he maintains a view of the *waw conversive*, even although he remarks "it may be assumed that the *wayyiqtol* is not identical with *yiqtol*" (§ 117b). The latter remark is explained by his acknowledgment that this state of affairs should be understood in the light of two different forms underlying: on the one hand, *wayyiqtol* and *yiqtol* short forms, and, on the other hand, *yiqtol* long forms (§ 117c).[16] He provides reasons why he avoids the terms *waw conversive* and *waw consecutive* (§ 117a (1)). Perhaps relevant to the purposes of this paper is his remark: "Because of its (i.e. Waw inversive, CvdM) first and main use which is to express succession in time, Waw inversive can, *a potiori*, be called *Waw of succession*, in contrast to *modal Waw* or *final-consecutive Waw* of the indirect volitive moods" (§ 117a).

4.4 *Attempts to treat specific problems in terms of units or entities bigger or other than the sentence*

In terms of our definition of narrative syntax a range of specific problems could come into play here that (1) could not be solved by sentence-based grammars, e.g.
— aspects of the Biblical Hebrew verbal system (cf. the problems referred to above),
— questions on the function of Biblical Hebrew word order (What is marked word order in Biblical Hebrew? What is the function of marked word order? Is only one type of function involved? Are different levels of linguistic description involved? What criteria should be used to determine a particular function? How should postverbal word order in Biblical Hebrew be understood?)

or (2) questions that are normally not considered in sentence grammars, e.g.
— Why are split constituents used in Biblical Hebrew texts, and does the different syntactic patterns mark one or other type of meaning?

[16] According to Muraoka § 117c (1) it is remarkable that Joüon's view in this regard needed no revision.

— Why do references to participants in a Biblical Hebrew narrative in some cases appear to be *overspecified* while in other cases they appear to be *underspecified* for speakers of modern Indo-European languages?
— How should macrosyntactic markers and discourse particles be treated?

I have elaborated elsewhere on attempts to solve some of these problems.[17] Significant of most of these attempts is that, apart from the fact that distributional criteria were used to identify functional categories, no particular theoretical frame of reference is dominant. However, most of those that address problems concerning the verbal system from a narrative syntactic point of view, could be related to theoretical concepts introduced by Harald Weinrich (1971, 1978: 391–412). Even Longacre (1992: 177) who developed his own discourse grammatical approach to Biblical Hebrew, acknowledges "Insofar as this (*i.e. his discourse perspective on the Hebrew verb*, CvdM) is a textlinguistic approach to the structure of the verb in Biblical Hebrew, my approach is similar to that of W. Schneider . . . with which I am acquainted via E. Talstra's review. . . ." Before a discussion of Schneider, the first Biblical Hebrew grammarian to use the views of Weinrich in an attempt to understand the use of Biblical Hebrew verbal forms and sequences, a few remarks on Weinrich may help to better understand Schneider, and for that matter Niccacci and Talstra who also acknowledge their indebtedness to Schneider. In the rest of this section I will then first treat the way in which, on the one hand, Niccacci developed and, on the other hand, Talstra suggested the ideas of Schneider should be developed. Secondly, I will discuss briefly the contributions of Eskhult, Endo and Joosten. Because Longacre addresses the problem of the verbal systems from a much different angle than his above-mentioned remark may imply, I will treat his views in my second paper.

4.4.1 *Weinrich*

Taking into account the following aspects of Weinrich's work may be helpful if one tries to better understand developments in Biblical Hebrew narrative syntax:

— Weinrich argues from a structuralist point of view, using mainly distributional criteria for his study of several modern European languages (Talstra 1992: 270).

[17] Van der Merwe (1994: 13–49).

— For him "syntax describes all the grammatical signals in a text that produce a preliminary sorting of the world. To these signals belong personal and demonstrative pronouns and the verbal forms" (Talstra 1992: 270).[18]
— Of the verb forms that produce a preliminary sorting of the world, "some . . . refer to the actual situation of communication; others to acts of facts outside the domain shared by speaker and listener" (Talstra 1992: 271); hence his distinction between a *discursive* and a *narrative* mode of communication, referred to as the orientation of a speaker ("Sprechhandlung").
— A verbal system, however, has two further basic oppositions, viz. text relief: *background vs. foreground*[19] and perspective: *prior, simultaneous or after the actual communication* (Talstra 1992: 272).

4.4.2 *Schneider*

The primary aim of Schneider's grammar was to serve as a handbook for an introductory course in Biblical Hebrew. Therefore he does not present this new model for describing Biblical Hebrew (narrative) syntax as such in his grammar. Talstra (1978: 168–175, 1982: 26–38 and 1992: 269–297) investigated Schneider's theoretical assumptions, and it is on account of his studies that I would summarize Schneider's most pertinent ideas as follows:

— Schneider distinguishes between narrative and discursive communication. The former is signaled by *wayyiqtol* and the latter by *yiqtol* and *q^{e}tol* forms of the verb.
— The use of *wayyiqtol* and *yiqtol* is not determined by time reference or verbal aspect but by the orientation of the speaker/narrator.
— The main line or foreground of a narrative is built by *wayyiqtol* forms of the verb and its background by *qatal* forms. The latter occurs mostly in *w^{e}x-qatal* clauses. He calls them *compound nominal clauses* because they do not primarily describe actions, but situations. They are used to refer to background information or mark the beginning or end of a story-line. He does not provide criteria for distinguishing between these two types of uses.
— The foreground of a discursive text is built by *yiqtol* or *q^{e}tol* forms of the verb and the background by *qatal/w^{e}qatal* forms. However, he

[18] I assume that one should read "narrative syntax" in stead of "syntax".
[19] Cf. the way in which Hopper (1979) explains this opposition, as quoted by Endo (1993: 22–23).

does not indicate the exact relationship between *yiqtol* and *q^{e}tol* and *w^{e}qatal* forms, in particular "which of them mark the main line of argumentation in a direct speech text" (Talstra 1992: 282).
— When background in a narrative is involved, *qatal* forms provide a past and *yiqtol* forms a future perspective. Background of a discursive orientation uses *w^e(x-)qatal* for a past, *qatal* for a zero and *w^{e}qatal* for a future perspective relative to the point in time the actual communication took place.
— The speaker orientation of a text may often change. This shift from narrative to discursive and vice versa is signaled by a "shift of tense", e.g. from *wayyiqtol* to *yiqtol* or *q^{e}tol.*

Talstra (1992: 276) came up with the following illuminating diagram (which I modified a little bit) in order to explain Schneider's application of Weinrich's ideas.

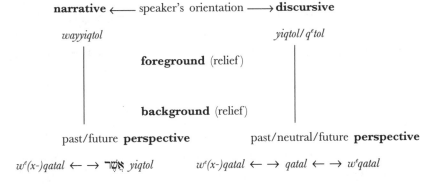

narrative ←— speaker's orientation —→ **discursive**

wayyiqtol | *yiqtol*/ *q^{e}tol*

foreground (relief)

background (relief)

past/future **perspective** | past/neutral/future **perspective**

w^e(x-)qatal ← → אֲשֶׁר *yiqtol* | *w^e(x-)qatal* ← → *qatal* ← → *w^{e}qatal*

4.4.3 *Niccacci*
According to Niccacci (1995: 111), Schneider inspired his own theory via the detailed reviews of his grammar by Talstra (1978: 168–175 and 1982: 26–38). It is impossible to do full justice to all the finer nuances of Niccacci's views here, firstly, due to a lack of time and space, secondly, due to the fact that Niccacci tends to operate with idiosyncratic, and often confusing, labels for the categories he uses. I am often not certain whether I understand him correctly. I will concentrate on those areas where he represents a development of Schneider.

— Niccacci (1994a: 132) also distinguishes between, according to his terminology, two "genres", viz. narrative and discourse (= discursive). The latter he also refers to as "direct speech" in order to avoid ambiguity with the concept "discourse analysis". This direct speech, however, must not be confused with "'direct reported speech' (i.e. quotation)". According to Niccacci, his direct speech also indicates indirect speech as "when an author comments in different ways upon the story he is narrating" (1994a: 119). The latter, also referred to as comment, is a mixed category, "an intrusion of direct speech" into narrative. "When commenting on the event he is narrating, the writer uses the same verb forms as in direct speech, although not all of them nor with the same temporal value" (1994a: 133). Niccacci furthermore distinguishes between historical and oral narrative (or report in the form of a quotation) on account of the distinctive verb forms they display, viz. *wayyiqtol* beginning a historical narrative and a *qatal* or *x-qatal* form beginning an oral narrative. How the relationship between direct speech and oral narrative should be understood is not clear to me.

— In *narrative*, foreground (he also refers to it as the main line of communication) is built by means of *wayyiqtol* forms and background (or subsidiary line of communication) by means of *w*^{e}*x-qatal*, *w*^{e}*x-yiqtol* (mostly for habitual or repetitive action), *w*^{e}*qatal* (also mostly for habitual or repetitive action) or simple nominal sentences.

— In *direct speech* the forms that build the foreground and background may differ in accordance with the temporal axis that is involved,[20] e.g. in the axis of the future *w*^{e}*qatal* indicates foreground and *w*^{e}*x-yiqtol* background. In the axis of the present, a simple nominal sentence may indicate foreground or background.

— The position of *yiqtol* forms may point to the mood that is involved, viz. jussive/volitive or indicative. The jussive normally occupies the first position in the sentence although it may also take the second position. The indicative *yiqtol*, in contrast, normally takes the second position in the sentence (*x-yiqtol*).

— According to Niccacci Biblical Hebrew does have tenses. In the foreground the verb forms have fixed temporal reference, i.e. tenses. However, in the background a relative temporal reference is involved. "Aspect, in the sense of mode of action (*Aktionsart*), is, then a legitimate category of the Hebrew verbal system" (1994a: 129).

— Niccacci also calls clauses in which the verb does not occupy the first position, i.e. *(w*^{e}*)x-qatal* and *(w*^{e}*)x-yiqtol*, *"compound noun clauses"*. At the sentence level, the x element may be emphasized, "it means

[20] Cf. Niccacci (1995: 116–120).

it is the predicate, or the new information" (1994a: 122). However, emphasis is not involved in every compound noun clause. In some cases the compound noun clause may "on the broader level of the text" have "the function of making the sentence as a whole dependent on another" verbal sentence. "the marked structure is used as a sign of subordination" (1994a: 123).[21] However, in some cases this marked structure may have both an emphasizing and subordinating function (1994a: 126). How exactly one should identify those cases that have both an emphasizing and subordinating function is not clear to me; neither how a non-emphasized marked structure should be described at the sentence level?
— According to Niccacci biblical narratives could be analyzed according to the verb forms used (1994b: 175).

4.4.4 *Talstra*

The most basic assumptions of Talstra's work[22] could be summarized as follows:

— The main problem Tastra wants to address is the fact that we know so little about: (1) Biblical Hebrew syntax and (2) the conventions that determine its use in order to communicate (or to put it differently, how Biblical Hebrew clauses are organized to form texts).
— Given the fact that we do not have living speakers to ask questions about the above-mentioned conventions, he believes that one of the most responsible ways to address this problem is to use the forms of the Biblical Hebrew text that we have at our disposal as our point of departure. In this aspect he maintains a view similar to that of scholars like Richter (1978–1980, 1985), Schweizer (1981, 1986) and Hoftijzer (1981 and 1985). This is the reason why a form-to-function, in contrast to a function-to-form approaches of Andersen (1974)[23] and Longacre (1989),[24] assumed by Schneider appeals to him, in particular in using distributional criteria at a textual level.
— Talstra believes that computer programmes could provide the tools needed for the above-mentioned type of description of Biblical Hebrew,

[21] Note that he uses the term "subordination" to refer to subordination at a textual level, in contrast to subordination at a grammatical level (Niccacci 1994: 127–128).
[22] Talstra (1978: 169–174, 1982: 26–38, 1983, 1987: 95–105, 1991: 180–193 and 1995: 166–180).
[23] In more recent studies of his, Andersen appears to have dropped this stance, cf. Andersen (1994: 99–116).
[24] Cf. den Exter Blokland (1995: 26–107).

in particular if they could be designed in such a way as to recognize as many formal patterns as possible at the level of morphology, syntax and the text. On each level the computer should be utilized to build formal grammars based on formal patterns identified at earlier stages. Each level should build hierarchically on the next one. It should always be possible to manipulate and/or retrieve information of a lower level at a higher level and vice versa.

— Although he tries to design a database that is as theoretically independent as possible, he acknowledges the fact that the higher level of linguistic description the less possible it is to be theoretically independent.

— The reasons why Talstra adopted the assumptions of Weinrich and Schneider make more sense if we take into consideration that Talstra was and is still in the process of experimenting with what type of question his computer programmes should be able to ask, if it wishes to provide a tool for Biblical Hebrew grammarians and exegetes that could make the most of *all* the formal patterns of the Old Testament text, from the level of morphemes to the level of texts. *All* may include different types of formal patterns, not only those of the surface level of the text, but also formalisable semantic and pragmatic distinctions.[25]

— Talstra also maintains the distinction between narrative vs. discourse as a basic point of departure for the investigation of Biblical Hebrew texts. However, for him they are labels of *an explicitly defined set of linguistic markers*. In his use of them, he does not allow them to be used as psychological concepts. Compare in contrast Niccacci's line of reasoning (1994a: 133).

— He supports Andersen's (1974) view (in contrast to Niccacci) that one should always take the position of a clause in the hierarchical cluster of clauses in which it occurs into consideration when one tries to understand the word order of that clause. The same applies when one tries to determine the mood that is signaled by a verb. The fact of the matter is, apart from the hierarchical position of a clause, it may also be necessary to take a number of other variables into account.[26]

---

[25] Cf. Winther-Nielsen (1995) and Winther-Nielsen and Talstra (1995).

[26] Cf. the parameters de Regt (1988) experimented with. Den Exter Blokland (1995) developed (with Talstra as promoter) a list of syntactic parameters for the segmentation of Biblical Hebrew texts.

— It is imperative to distinguish clearly between the level of clauses and the level of the texts in the investigation of linguistic phenomena.

On account of a recent investigation,[27] Talstra claims that neither tense nor aspect is basic to the Biblical Hebrew grammatical system. They are categories of text external reference. They are expressed by texts and can be derived from the categories domain and perspective. *Domain* here is a refinement of Schneider's "speaker orientation" by de Regt (1995: 147–161). *Perspective* refers to the point of reference during the actual communication process.

4.4.5 *Eskhult*

According to Eskhult (1990: 9) the aim of his study is "to shed light on the system of aspectual contrast in Biblical Hebrew, and more particular how aspectual contrasts are used as a device in narrative techniques". For him it is important that when one interprets Biblical Hebrew prose "one is clear about which clauses carry on a narrative, and which depict a background state of affairs. In narrative discourse the skeleton is made up of sequential *wayyiqtol-clauses*, while the *subj-qtl* clause almost exclusively furnishes some background information". He then concentrates on "the *(w^e)subj-qtl* clause as a feature that separates sections of main-line narrative clauses, providing a structuring mechanism for narrative texts" (Dawson 1994: 40).[28]

4.4.6 *Endo*

Endo (1993) investigates the function of verb forms in the Biblical Hebrew narrative using the Joseph story as his corpus. According to him, the distinctions between direct discourse and narrative do not play a significant role in the functional distinction of the verbal forms. In the former "a greater variety of verbal forms . . . and more free-standing verbal forms were available" (1993: 329). The distinction between background and foreground also "seems to be a secondary phenomenon or by-product of the issue of the sequentially and non-sequentially". According to him, the distinction past vs. non-past that corresponds with the traditional aspectual opposition complete vs. incomplete "basically works as a factor in the choice of the free-standing conjugations, except for the stative verb, a verb with a stative

[27] Talstra (forthcoming).

[28] For a critical assessment of Eskhult, cf. Dawson (1994: 40–46). For a review of Dawson (1994) by Eskult, cf. Eskult (forthcoming).

sense, the passive construction, or the performative utterance" (1993: ii). The parameter past vs. non-past, however, is of no use to explain the formal oppositions *qatal* vs. *wayyiqtol* and *yiqtol* and *w^{e}qatal.* The functional opposition *sequential vs. non-sequential* corresponds rather with these oppositions. A characteristic of the sequential forms is that they, in contrast to verbal forms with conjunctions, always look forward to the next clause (1993: 332). For Endo the functional opposition sequential vs. non-sequential is more comprehensive than terms like "temporal or logical succession, consequence or explanation". Furthermore, it is "purely syntactical. It controls the flow of the story as discourse; the non-sequential form stops the flow (i.e. stand still) while the sequential form lets the story flow on". However, each form could play an opposite role to produce special literary effects (1993: ii).

4.4.7 *Joosten*

According to Joosten "it is more prudent, and not less correct methodologically, provisory to limit our research to those parts of the Biblical Hebrew verbal system which remain obscure, or which have not hitherto received much attention" (1992: 1). I will assume that this principle also led to his investigation of the predicatively used participle in Biblical Hebrew (Joosten 1989: 128–159). In the latter paper he argues that the predicatively used participle should be regarded as an integral part of the Biblical Hebrew verbal system. It expresses two aspects of the present tense, viz. the cursive or actual present by means of the sequence *Subject-Participle* and the constative or factual present (i.e. the action that is regarded as a fact contemporary with the moment of speaking) by means of the sequence *Participle-Subject.* Joosten (1992: 1–15) investigates the function of the *weqatal* form and comes to the conclusion that it is best described in terms of modality. Cases where *w^{e}qatal* has an iterative function could be explained as an extension of the modal functions. Although he concedes that "it is only a rapid schema" he regards the views (of Niccacci and Revell)[29] that the Biblical Hebrew verbal system has two systems as a useful frame of reference for "even those scholars who prefer a 'text-linguistic approach'". Regarding the latter, he remarks "I am attracted by the approach of Eskhult . . . for whom

[29] The fact that Revell and Niccacci ascribe to his *w^{e}qatal* and *x-yiqtol* opposition an indicative and not a modal function, constitutes for him no problem. It is "mostly as matter of terminology" (Joosten 1992: 13).

morphosyntax and text-linguistics are not mutually exclusive, but, on the contrary complementary. He sees the text-linguistic function of the different tenses as an actualization of their morphological function" (1992: 14).

5. *To summarize*

1. We know relatively little of Biblical Hebrew narrative syntax due to a very restricted linguistic frame of reference that was used in western circles to describe the grammar of a language.
2. Recent shifts in the study of language resulted in a much broader conception about what constitutes knowledge of a language. In the process, the limitations of our knowledge of Biblical Hebrew has been exposed.
3. Form-to-function approaches in which mainly distributional criteria are used to identify functional categories, dominate studies from a narrative syntactic point of view.
4. Weinrich, particularly his distinctions between narrative vs. discourse and foreground vs. background and his views on perspective, had a major impact on the study of the Biblical Hebrew verbal system.

References

Andersen, F.I., 1974, *The Sentence in Biblical Hebrew* (Janua Linguarum Series Practica 231), The Hague: Mouton.

———, 1994, "Salience, Implicature, Ambiguity and Redundancy", in: Bergen, R.D. (ed.), *Biblical Hebrew and Discourse Linguistics*, Winona Lake (Ind.): Eisenbrauns, 99–116.

Bandstra, B.R., 1992, "Word Order and Emphasis in Biblical Hebrew Narrative: Syntactic Observations on Genesis 22 from a Discourse Perspective", in: Bodine, W.R. (ed.), *Linguistics and Biblical Hebrew*, Winona Lake (Ind.): Eisenbrauns, 109–123.

Bauer, H. & Leander, P., 1922, *Historische Grammatik der hebräische Sprache des Alten Testaments*, Halle: Niemeyer (reprint Hildesheim: George Olms, 1962).

Bergen, R.D. (ed.), 1994, *Biblical Hebrew and Discourse Linguistics*, Winona Lake (Ind.): Eisenbrauns.

Bergsträsser, G., 1929, *Hebräische Grammatik. Mit Benutzung der von E. Kautzsch bearbeiten 28. Auflage von Wilhelm Gesenius' hebräischer Grammatik*, Leipzig: J.C. Hinrichs, (reprint Hildesheim: George Olms, 1962).

Bodine, W.R. (ed.), 1992, *Linguistics and Biblical Hebrew*, Winona Lake (Ind.): Eisenbrauns.

———, 1992a, "The Study of Linguistics and Biblical Hebrew", in: Bodine, W.R. (ed.), *Linguistics and Biblical Hebrew*, Winona Lake: Eisenbrauns, 1–5.

———, 1992b, "How Linguists Study Syntax", in: Bodine, W.R. (ed.), *Linguistics and Biblical Hebrew*, Winona Lake (Ind.): Eisenbrauns, 89–107.

——— (ed.), 1995, *Discourse Analysis of Biblical Literature. What It Is and What It Offers*, Atlanta: Scholars, 1995.

Brockelmann, C., 1956, *Hebräische Syntax*, Neukirchen-Vluyn: Neukirchener.

Buth, R., 1992, 'The Hebrew Verb in Current Discussions', *Journal of Translation and Textlinguistics* 5:91–105.

———, 1994, "Methodological Collision Between Source Criticism and Discourse: The Problem of 'Unmarked Overlay' and the Pluperfect *wayyiqtol*", in: Bergen, R.D. (ed.), *Biblical Hebrew and Discourse Linguistics*, Winona Lake (Ind.): Eisenbrauns, 138–154.

———, 1995, "Functional Grammar, Hebrew and Aramaic: An Integrated, Exegetically Significant Textlinguistic Approach to Syntax", in: Bodine, W.R. (ed.), *Discourse Analysis of Biblical Literature. What It Is and What It Offers*, Atlanta: Scholars, 77–102.

Comrie, B., 1976, *Aspect: An Introduction to the Study of Verbal Aspect and Related Problems* (Cambridge Textbooks in Linguistics), Cambridge: Cambridge University Press.

Dawson, D.A., 1994, *Text-linguistics and Biblical Hebrew* (Journal for the Study of the Old Testament Supplement Series 177), Sheffield: Sheffield Academic Press.

DeCaen, V., 1995, *On the Placement and Interpretation of the Verbs in Standard Biblical Hebrew Prose*, Ph.D. diss., University of Toronto.

———, 1996, "Ewald and Driver on Biblical Hebrew 'Aspect': Anteriority and the Orientalist Framework", *Zeitschrift für Althebraistik* 9:129–151.

Dressler, W. (ed.), 1978, *Textlinguistik*, Darmstadt: Wissenschaftliche Buchgesellschaft.

Endo, Y., 1993, *The Verbal System of Classical Hebrew in the Joseph Story: an Approach from Discourse Analysis*, Ph.D. diss., University of Bristol.

Eskhult, M., 1990, *Studies in Verbal Aspect and Narrative Technique in Biblical Hebrew Prose* (Acta Universitatis Upsaliensis, Studia Semitica Upsaliensia 12), Uppsala: Almqvist & Wiksell.

———, 1996, "The Old Testament and Text Linguistics", manuscript.

Exter Blokland, A.F. den, 1995, *In Search of Text Syntax. Towards a Syntactic Segmentation Model for Biblical Hebrew*, Amsterdam: VU University Press.

Fleisch, H., 1994, "Arabic Linguistics", in: Lepschy, G. (ed.), *History of Linguistics. The Eastern Traditions of Linguistics. Vol. 1*, London: Longman, 164–184.

Gesenius, W., Kautzsch, E. & Cowley, E.A., 1910, *Gesenius' Hebrew Grammar*, second ed., Oxford: Clarendon.

Givón, T. (ed.), 1979, *Discourse and Semantics* (Syntax and Semantics 12), New York: Academic Press.

Hendel, R.S., 1996, "In the Margins of the Hebrew Verbal System: Situation, Tense, Aspect, Mood", *Zeitschrift für Althebraistik* 9:152–181.

Hoftijzer, J., 1974, *Verbale vragen*, Leiden: E.J. Brill.

———, 1981, *A Search for Method: A Study in the Syntactical Use of the H-locale in Classical Hebrew*, Leiden: E.J. Brill.

———, 1995, *The Function and Use of the Imperfect Forms with Nun-paragogicum in Classical Hebrew* (Studia Semitica Neerlandica 21), Assen: Van Gorcum.

Hopper, P.J., 1979, "Aspect and Foregrounding in Discourse", in: Givón, T. (ed.), *Discourse and Semantics* (Syntax and Semantics 12), New York: Academic Press, 213–241.

Jongeling, K., Murre-Van den Berg, H.L. & van Rompay, L. (eds.), 1991, *Studies in Hebrew and Aramaic Syntax: Presented to Professor J. Hoftijzer on the Occasion of his Sixty-Fifth Birthday*, Leiden: E.J. Brill.

Joosten, J., 1989, "The Predicative Participle in Biblical Hebrew", *Zeitschrift für Althebraistik* 2:128–159.

———, 1992, "Biblical Hebrew *w^eqatal* and Syriac *hwa qaṭēl* Expressing Repetition in the Past", *Zeitschrift für Althebraistik* 5:1–14.

Joüon, P., 1923, *Grammaire de l'hebreu biblique*, Roma: Pontificio Istituto Biblico.

Joüon, P. & Muraoka, T., 1991, *A Grammar of Biblical Hebrew*, 2 Vols., Roma: Pontificio Istituto Biblico.
König, F.E., 1897, *Historisch-kritisches Lehrgebäude der hebräischen Sprache*, Leipzig: J.C. Hinrich (reprint Hildesheim: George Olms, 1979).
Leitner, G., 1984, "English Grammatology", *International Review of Applied Linguistics* 23:199–215.
Lepschy, G. (ed.), 1994, *History of Linguistics. The Eastern Traditions of Linguistics. Vol. 1*, London: Longman.
Ljungberg, B.-J., 1995, "Tense, Aspect and Modality in Some Theories of the Biblical Hebrew Verbal System", *Journal of Translation and Textlinguistics* 7:82–96.
Loewe, R., 1994, 'Hebrew Linguistics', in: Lepschy, G. (ed.), *History of Linguistics, The Eastern Traditions of Linguistics*, Vol. 1, London: Longman, 97–163.
Longacre, R.E., 1989, *Joseph: A Story of Divine Providence: A Text Theoretical and Textlinguistic Analysis of Genesis 37 and 39–48*, Winona Lake (Ind.): Eisenbrauns.
———, 1992, "Discourse Perspective on the Hebrew Verb: Affirmation and Restatement", in: Bodine, W.R., *Linguistics and Biblical Hebrew*, Winona Lake (Ind.): Eisenbrauns, 177–190.
———, 1994, "*Weqatal* Forms in Biblical Hebrew Prose: A Discourse-Modular Approach", in: Bergen, R.D. (ed.), *Biblical Hebrew and Discourse Linguistics*, Winona Lake (Ind.): Eisenbrauns, 50–99.
Loprieno, A., 1980, "The Sequential Forms in Late Egyptian and Biblical Hebrew: a Parallel Development of Verbal Systems", *Afroasiatic Linguistics* 7:1–20.
Lyons, J., 1981, *Language and Linguistics. An Introduction*, Cambridge: Cambridge University Press.
McFall, L., 1982, *The Enigma of the Hebrew Verbal System; Solutions from Ewald to the Present Day*, Sheffield: Almond.
Merwe, C.H.J. van der, 1994, "Discourse Linguistics and Biblical Hebrew Grammar", in: Bergen, R.D. (ed.), *Biblical Hebrew and Discourse Linguistics*, Winona Lake (Ind.): Eisenbrauns, 13–49.
Mettinger, T.N.D., 1974, "The Hebrew Verbal System: a Survey of Recent Research", *Annual of the Swedish Theological Society* 9:64–84.
Mey, J.L., 1993, *Pragmatics. An Introduction*, Oxford: Blackwell.
Michel, D., 1960, *Tempora und Satzstellung in den Psalmen*, Bonn: Bouvier.
Muraoka, T., 1969, *Emphasis in Biblical Hebrew*, Ph.D. diss., Hebrew University Jerusalem.
———, 1985, *Emphatic Words and Structures in Biblical Hebrew*, Jerusalem/Leiden: Magnes/E.J. Brill.
Niccacci, A., 1990, *The Syntax of the Verb in Classical Hebrew Prose* (Journal for the Study of the Old Testament Supplement Series 86), Sheffield: Sheffield Academic Press.
———, 1994a, "On the Hebrew Verbal System", in: Bergen, R.D. (ed.), *Biblical Hebrew and Discourse Linguistics*, Winona Lake (Ind.): Eisenbrauns, 117–137.
———, 1994b, "Analysis of Biblical Narrative", in: Bergen, R.D. (ed.), *Biblical Hebrew and Discourse Linguistics*, Winona Lake (Ind.): Eisenbrauns, 175–198.
———, 1995, "Essential Hebrew Syntax", in: Talstra, E. (ed.), *Narrative and Comment. Contributions Presented to Wolfgang Schneider*, Amsterdam: Societas Hebraica Amstelodamensis, 111–125.
Rainey, A.F., 1988, "Further Remarks on the Hebrew Verbal System", *Hebrew Studies* 29:35–42.
Regt, L. de, 1988, *A Parametric Model for Syntactic Studies of a Textual Corpus, Demonstrated on the Hebrew of Deuteronomy 1–30* (Studia Semitica Neerlandica 24), Assen: Van Gorcum.
———, 1995, "Domains and Subdomains in Biblical Hebrew Discourse", in: Talstra, E. (ed.), *Narrative and Comment. Contributions Presented to Wolfgang Schneider*, Amsterdam: Societas Hebraica Amstelodamensis, 147–161.

Revell, E.J., 1989, "The System of the Verb in Standard Biblical Prose", *Hebrew Union College Annual* 60:1–37.

Richter, W., 1978–80, *Grundlagen einer althebräischen Grammatik. A. Grundfragen einer sprachwissenschaftlichen Grammatik. B. Beschreibungsebene: Bd. I. Das Wort, Bd. II. Die Wortfügung (morphosyntax), Bd. III. Der Satz* (Arbeiten zu Text und Sprache im Alten Testament), St. Ottilien: EOS.

———, 1985, *Untersuchungen zur Valenz althebräischer Verben 1*, St. Ottilien: EOS.

Schneider, W., 1982, *Grammatik des Biblischen Hebräisch. Völlig neue Bearbeitung der* "Hebräischen Grammatik für den akademischen Unterricht" *von Oskar Grether*, München: Claudius.

Schweizer, H., 1981, *Metaphorische Grammatik* (Arbeiten zu Text und Sprache im Alten Testament), St. Ottilien: EOS.

———, 1986, *Biblische Texte verstehen*, Stuttgart: Kohlhammer.

Talstra, E., 1978, "Text Grammar and Hebrew Bible 1: Elements of a Theory", *Bibliotheca Orientalis* 35:168–175.

———, 1982, "Text Grammar and Hebrew Bible 2: Syntax and Semantics", *Bibliotheca Orientalis* 39:26–38.

———, 1983, *2 Kön. 3: Etüden zur Textgrammatik*, Amsterdam: VU University Press.

———, 1987, "Towards a Distributional Definition of Clauses in Classical Hebrew: a Computer-assisted Description of Clauses and Clause Types in Deut. 4:3–8", *Ephemerides Theologicae Lovanienes* 63:95–105.

———, 1991, "Biblical Hebrew Clause Types and Clause Hierarchy", in: Jongeling, K. et al. (eds.), *Studies in Hebrew and Aramaic Syntax: Presented to professor J. Hoftijzer on the Occasion of his Sixty-Fifth Birthday*, Leiden: E.J. Brill, 180–193.

———, 1992, "Text Grammar and Biblical Hebrew: The Viewpoint of Wolfgang Schneider", *Journal of Translation and Textlinguistics* 5:269–287.

———. (ed.), 1995, *Narrative and Comment. Contributions Presented to Wolfgang Schneider*, Amsterdam: Societas Hebraica Amstelodamensis.

———, 1995, "Clause Types and Textual Structure: an Experiment in Narrative Syntax", in: Talstra, E. (ed.), *Narrative and Comment. Contributions Presented to Wolfgang Schneider*, Amsterdam, 166–180.

———, forthcoming, "Tense, Aspect and Clause Connections, The Syntax of Joshua 23", *Journal of Northwest Semitic Languages*.

Waltke, B.K. & O'Connor, M., 1990, *An Introduction to Biblical Hebrew Syntax*, Winona Lake (Ind.): Eisenbrauns.

Weinrich, H., 1971, *Tempus: Besprochene und erzählte Welt*, second edition, Stuttgart: Kohlhammer.

———, 1978, "Die Textpartitur als heuristische Methode", in: Dressler, W. (ed.), *Textlinguistik*, Darmstadt: Wissenschaftliche Buchgesellschaft, 391–412.

Winther-Nielsen, N., 1995, *A Functional Discourse Grammar of Joshua. A Computer-assisted Rhetorical Structure Analysis* (Coniectanea Biblica, Old Testament Series 40), Stockholm: Almqvist & Wiksell.

——— & Talstra, E., 1995, *A Computational Display of Joshua. A Computer-assisted Analysis and Textual Interpretation* (Applicatio 13), Amsterdam: VU University Press.

LINGUISTIC MOTIVATION AND BIBLICAL EXEGESIS

Ellen van Wolde
(Tilburg)

Modern exegesis of the Hebrew Bible is both historically and literary orientated, the former concentrating on the historical development of the Biblical texts and the latter on the Biblical text as a literary unity, in which a growing awareness is revealed for the reader's contribution to the interpretation of the text. What then is the significance of linguistic descriptions of the Hebrew verb system, as presented in this book *Narrative Syntax and the Hebrew Bible*, for Biblical exegesis? Of course, the starting point of every exegesis is that the Hebrew language system provides the conditions for the textual communication, and that therefore linguistics is necessary for exegetes to acquire basic insights into the elementary phonological, morphological, syntactic, semantic and pragmatic features of Biblical Hebrew. However, the disadvantages of linguistic studies are easily discovered as well. One of these is the inaccessibility of linguistic literature; another is the lack of clear definitions and criteria, and another, even more important, is the scarcity of explanations of the choices made and of the principles on which these choices are based; these problematic aspects often are reinforced by a cryptic or diagrammatic style.

At the same time most linguistic studies of Biblical Hebrew mainly focus on the analysis of *how* the forms are organized. Only a few deal with the question of motivation and ask *why* a specific form is used in a certain text. The present paper opts for a study of the question: What motivates an author of Biblical Hebrew to choose a certain verbal form or a certain clause arrangement to communicate his message to the reader? This study starts with the concept of markedness and unmarkedness, continues with views of a pragmatically oriented Hebrew narrative syntax and deals mainly with questions of narrative representation and grounding. The intention is to show the consequences of such a linguistic approach for Biblical exegesis and to elucidate the importance of a linguistic study for the literary study of narrative texts in the Hebrew Bible.

Questions on "how" and/or "why"

Features and structures of Biblical Hebrew are generally described in linguistics from three different perspectives, namely either

a. *formally* oriented: language constituents are explained on the basis of their perceptible form, or
b. *distributionally* oriented: language constituents are explained according to their dispersion or distribution, or
c. *functionally* oriented: language constituents are explained in their relations to other constituents.

In the *formal* approach the distinct phonological, morphological or morpho-syntactic form is studied in relation to a distinct invariant meaning: an invariance in form refers to an invariance in meaning. In a less strictly formal analysis one form can relate to more than one function or meaning, in which case criteria should clarify the difference in function. In the *distributional* approach, the difference in phonological, morphological or morpho-syntactic form is studied on the basis of its quantitative occurrence in actual Biblical texts. This so-called bottom up approach starts from the linguistic data as they are found in texts in the Hebrew Bible. The arrangement of language constituents in clauses or textual units is considered to explain the meaning and function of these constituents. This approach postulates the existence of exclusive categories which mark the use of distinct forms, because if the forms do not exclude each other but overlap or interfere, their distribution cannot be elucidated. In *functionally* oriented linguistics, finally, language constituents are analysed on the basis of their function in relationship to other elements. Its presupposition is that a form and its function cannot be described in itself (i.e. as a one-to-one relationship), but only in correlation with other functions in specific contexts.

In most linguistic studies of Biblical Hebrew, language features and structures are accounted for by the analysis of *how* the forms are organized, *how* they are distributed and *how* they relate functionally. Few deal with the question of what motivates the choice of a certain form in a certain text. This question leads to a syntactic inquiry which acknowledges context dependency, to a pragmatically oriented (narrative) text syntax.[1] Pragmatics does not assume, as other non-

[1] Pragmatics covers context-dependent aspects of language structure and principles

pragmatic approaches to linguistics do, that categories are discrete. Non-discreteness is related to the central notion of "context": in pragmatics the context is the crucial mediator.[2]

To clarify the meaning and importance of this motivation-oriented syntactic inquiry, an excursion into the field of semantics might be instructive.

Excursion: "how" and "why" in semantic research

A language, as for example Biblical Hebrew, determines a meaning of words on the basis of conventions. In these conventions the relations between a particular form and a particular content have been defined. The definitions are laid down in a language system, also called paradigm or primary code. This code consists of carefully distinguished rules and elements that constitute the range of possibilities from which selections for utterances can be made. A concrete text or syntagm is the result of a selection procedure and consists of a specific combination of selected elements. Usually this is described by two axes: the paradigm or axis of selection, and the syntagm or axis of combination.

There is, however, no direct transition from a language system or paradigm (e.g. Biblical Hebrew as recorded in a dictionary) into an actual text or syntagm. One might learn from James Barr[3] that an intermediary stage should be acknowledged. In a paradigm every word functions in a field or group of words, a specific semantic field. The basis for the procedure to study this intermediary stage is an analysis of the word meanings as functions of choices within the lexical stock of a given language at a given time. It is the choice, rather than the word itself, which signifies. For example in the text "A man walks in the street", the selection of the word "walk" is motivated by both the language code in which "to walk" is "a movement in a horizontal direction accomplished by putting one foot in front of the other on the ground", and is motivated by the choice out of the semantic

of language usage, see: S.C. Levinson, *Pragmatics* (Cambridge Textbooks in Linguistics), Cambridge: Cambridge University Press, 1983, 9.

[2] T. Givón, *Mind, Code and Context. Essays in Pragmatics*, Hillsdale/London: Erlbaum, 1989, 1.

[3] J. Barr, *The Semantics of Biblical Language*, Oxford: Oxford University Press 1961; J. Barr, "The Image of God in the Book of Genesis—A Study in Terminology", *Bulletin of the John Rylands Library of Manchester* 51 (1968) 11–26, esp. 14–15.

field in which "to walk" differs from "to run", "to linger", "to dawdle" or "to hike". These paradigmatically marked relations in a semantic field or cluster make a motivated choice of a specific word in a particular context possible. There are, therefore, two paradigmatic procedures: the first regarding the conventionally defined relationship between form and meaning, and the second regarding the functioning of a word in a semantic field or coherent lexical stock. Together they form the primary layer of meaning, which create the conditions for a motivated selection in a text.

A selected word enters into relationships with other words to form a context. In such a context additional meanings are given to the already paradigmatically defined linguistic elements. The contextual or syntagmatic relationships create a "secondary" layer of meanings or connotations, which extend the conventionally defined relationships with new information. Thus the textual syntagm (and especially a literary text) is able to create a new textual world. An example is the syntagm of Genesis 2–3 where the two distinct lexemes ערום and עירם, which are paradigmatically defined as "shrewd" (or "knowing") and "naked" respectively, are related to each other in a syntagmatic relationship. In verse 2:25 the form ערומּים is used as the plural form of עירם to describe the nakedness of man and woman. Verse 3:1 immediately follows and here the word ערום describes the shrewdness of the serpent. As such עירם is "naked" (see 3:10,11) and its plural form is עירמּם (see 3:7), while the plural form of ערום is ערומים. In 2:25, however, the plural form ערומּים (which, apart from the geminated *mem*, is identical to the plural form of ערום) is used as a plural of עירם, to make visible a relationship between "naked" and "knowing". The syntagmatic arrangement thus creates a new world of meaning in which "nakedness" and "knowledge" are interrelated. The verses 3:1–6 confirm and extend this relationship.[4] Consequently semantic research explains that the meaning of a word in a Biblical text cannot be restricted to the root or triconsonantal form nor to the lexeme. Meaning is also defined by the relationships with other lexemes in the lexical stock of Biblical Hebrew at a given time, and by the relationships with other lexemes in the particular textual context in which it occurs.

Finally, meaning involves a contextual judgement as well. Without

[4] See: E.J. van Wolde, *Words Become Worlds. Semantic Studies of Genesis 1–11* (Biblical Interpretation Series 6), Leiden: E.J. Brill, 1994, 3–12.

being interpreted, the language elements become a mere potential and cease to be a viable force. The selected and combined elements of meaning are intended to function in communication. In communication the concept of "norm" or "ground" is important. The ground (norm) is the context vis-à-vis which information is salient.[5] It explains why paradigmatically and syntagmatically (thus purely linguistically) defined language elements can mediate between the text and the author's/reader's world of experience, and can function as information in a communicative process. One might say that the language system or paradigm offers the potential or possible meanings, the syntagmatic arrangement presents the contextual meanings, and the inferences by the reader is the effect of meaning. Therefore, meaning is triadic: meaning is dependent on the language system, is context-bound and is the effect of interpretation. Consequently a linguistic analysis has to explain the interaction of these three procedures in order to answer not only the question of *how* words have meaning, but also *what* motivates their linguistic selection, contextual coherence and interpretative effect.

Hebrew syntax and the concept of markedness

Based on the isomorphism hypothesis implying that all levels in a language are organized in a similar manner, the linguistic insights in semantic procedures are equally applicable to syntax. The language system or paradigm defines the syntactic possibilities, the syntagmatic arrangement produces the actual existence of clauses and texts, and the pragmatic procedures guide the transition of syntactic forms into syntactic information. The interaction of these three procedures might explain the motivation of the choice of certain syntactic forms and functions.

The basis of this explanation is the concept of markedness. Markedness is a theoretical concept of qualitative oppositions that enable linguists to analyse the inherently asymmetric relationships by which linguistic elements function.[6] This concept was introduced by Nikolai

---

[5] Cf. T. Givón, *Mind, Code and Context*, 1989, 8.

[6] Cf. E. Andrews, *Markedness Theory. The Union of Asymmetry and Semiosis in Language* (The Roman Jakobson Series in Linguistics and Poetics), Durham and London: Duke University Press, 1990, 1 and 9–29.

Trubetzkoy to explain important features of phonology. He describes the terms "marked" and "unmarked" as a binary opposition in which two phonemes are identical except that one contains a mark which the other lacks (e.g. an "open" vocal vs. a "closed" vocal).[7] Influenced by these ideas Roman Jakobson developed a theory of morphological markedness.[8] He starts from binary oppositions and adds to it the notion of asymmetry, so that the unmarked term is not on a par with the marked term. In phonology a given feature (e.g. voicing) is either present or absent in a particular class of phonemes. Therefore, the oppositions in phonology are privative. In morphology, however, "marked" means the necessary presence of an element, while "unmarked" means the element may or may not be present: it is simply not specified. Therefore, in morphology "unmarked" does not merely imply negation. Jakobson's concept of markedness has been generally accepted in linguistics, especially in morphology and syntax; in this article I elaborate on his view.

Word forms and word-order, clause forms and clause order can be analysed in their mutually exclusive and inclusive relationships on the basis of this Jakobsonian concept of markedness. It postulates a set of distinctive features which can be placed in an asymmetric markedness relationship; in this relationship the linguistic sign marked for a certain feature is making a specific claim for the presence of that feature.[9] For example, Hebrew nominal forms are marked for two features, viz. number and gender: the masculine singular form (the triconsonantal root xxx) is unmarked (Ø), while the other nominal forms are marked. The form xxx-*a* is marked for singular feminine, xxx-*im* for plural masculine and xxx-*ot* for plural feminine, whereas the form xxx-*ayim* is marked for dual, but unmarked for gender.[10] Hebrew verb forms, on the other hand, are marked for

[7] He also distinguished two other phonemic oppositions: the gradual oppositions (e.g. /i/ ~ /e/ ~ /æ/) and the equipollent oppositions, in which each member has a mark that the others lack (e.g. /p/ ~ /t/ ~ /k/). N.S. Trubetzkoy, "Die phonologischen Systeme", *Travaux du Cercle Linguistique de Prague* 4 (1931) 96–116.

[8] R. Jakobson, "Shifters, Verbal Categories and the Russian Verb". In *Selected Writings II*, The Hague: Mouton, 1957/1991, 130–147.

[9] Cf. Y. Tobin, "Process and Result and the Hebrew Infinitive: A Study in Linguistic Isomorphism", in: K. Jongeling et al. (eds.), *Studies in Hebrew and Aramaic Syntax. Presented to Professor J. Hoftijzer on Occasion of his Sixty-Fifth Birthday*, Leiden: Brill, 1991, 194–209; and Y. Tobin, *Invariance, Markedness and Distinctive Feature Analysis. A Contrastive Study of Sign Systems in English and Hebrew* (Current Issues in Linguistic Theory 111), Amsterdam and Philadelphia: John Benjamins, 1994, 41–45.

[10] In other words, the dual form is in an opposition of exclusion to the singular

three features: person, number and gender. So, in contrast with for instance English and Dutch which mark verb forms for person and number, Hebrew marks verb forms for gender as well.

As this article concentrates on narrative syntax, I will not enter at length into the morphology of the Hebrew verb forms, but restrict myself to some preliminary remarks on the concept of markedness in relation to verb forms in order to show how this concept will help us to answer the question of *why* a specific form or clause is used. To start with Jakobson:

> Any verb is concerned with a narrated event. Verbal categories may be subdivided into those which do and those which do not involve the participants of the event: (...) categories implying such a reference to the speech event or its participants are to be termed "shifters", those without such a reference are "non-shifters". Among categories involving the participants of the narrated event, gender and number characterize the participants themselves without reference to the speech event: gender qualifies, and number quantifies the participants. (...) Person characterizes the participants of the narrated event with reference to the participants of the speech event. Thus first person signals the identity of a participant of the narrated event with the performer of the speech event, and the second person, the identity with the actual or potential undergoer of the speech event.[11]

In Biblical Hebrew the verb form *qatal* third person masculine singular is unmarked for "person", "gender" and "number" (Ø). This zero markedness presents this person as a participant of the narrated event which does not participate in the speech event: it is a non-shifter. The first and second person, on the other hand, are shifters and presuppose a speech event. They relate the participants of the narrated event to the participants of the speech events: the first person refers to the addresser and the second person to the addressee. Number and gender are additional markings to the person marking: the verb forms in the third person are partly marked for gender (masculine singular, Ø, marked for gender in feminine singular, *-a*, and unmarked for gender in the plural, *-u*), the verb forms in the second person are in the singular as in the plural marked for gender (*-ta* and *-te, -tem*

form and in an opposition of inclusion to the plural form, because the dual "two" is included in the plural "more than one". See Y. Tobin, *Invariance, Markedness and Distinctive Feature Analysis*, 1994, 48–50.

[11] R. Jakobson, "Shifters, Verbal Categories and the Russian Verb", 1957/1991, 45.

and *-ten*). The first person is, however, not marked for gender, neither in the singular nor in the plural (*-ti* and *-nu*).

It may thus become clear that markedness is not defined absolutely, but relatively. The Hebrew third person masculine singular verb form is the least marked, the first person is more marked (for number, not for gender), and the second person is the most marked verb form (for person, number, gender). This hierarchy of markedness can therefore be described as:[12]

third person → first person → second person.

It explains *why* the third person masculine singular is a kind of silent unmarked presence: all other persons are defined in relationship with it and as such depending on it. The unmarked form of the third person defines the first and second person as marked forms; and because the first person is hierarchically higher than the second person, the last is dependent on the first. This and other hierarchies can explain why a reader is guided more or less by certain relatively defined verb forms: not only the most marked forms influence the reader, but even more so the implicit force of the unmarked features and of the less marked forms. This hierarchy can explain their differences in influence exerted on the reader.

With regard to the *binyanim* or conjugations, the usefulness of the concept of markedness can be even more instructive. In Biblical Hebrew thirteen hundred roots or triconsonantal forms function as carriers of meaning which are arranged according to the seven main *binyanim*: Qal, Nifʿal, Piʿel, Puʿal, Hitpaʿel, Hifʿil and Hofʿal.[13] Since hardly ever all seven *binyanim* occur for a given verb root, and since sometimes the Piʿel forms take over functions from the Hifʿil forms, and since sometimes verb forms overlap, one cannot but conclude that an analysis based on discrete categories is not sufficient as an explanation. A *binyan* does not have a discrete field of functions on its own, distinct and closed within its borders; it does not have a single function or a set of functions which is unique to it alone. This,

[12] See: R. Fradkin, "Typologies of Person Categories in Slavic and Semitic", in: E. Andrews & Y. Tobin (eds.), *Toward a Calculus of Meaning. Studies in Markedness, Distinctive Features and Deixis* (Studies in Functional and Structural Linguistics 43), Amsterdam/Philadelphia: John Benjamins, 1996, 319–345.

[13] See: J. Hoftijzer, "Überlegungen zum System der Stammesmodifikationen im klassischen Hebräisch", *Zeitschrift für Althebraistik* 5 (1992) 117–134. He shows that only four roots occur in all of these seven conjugations, and 75% of all verb roots occur in Qal, 34% in Piʿel, 36% in Hifʿil, 32% in Nifʿal, 14% in Puʿal, 17% in Hitpaʿel and 8% in Hofʿal.

together with the asymmetric distribution of the roots within the *binyanim*, requires a closer examination of the *binyanim* and their exclusively and inclusively defined relationships of markedness and unmarkedness.

It is a generally accepted view that the Qal form is the basic *binyan*: it is the most simple form, unmarked by prefixes or infixes. The other *binyanim* are usually labeled according to the syntactic and semantic functions derived from the Qal: "intensive", "causative", "transitive", "passive" and "reflexive" etc. In a recent study Yishai Tobin criticizes the fact that most scholars, despite the asymmetric distribution of the roots within the *binyanim*, still explain the *binyan* system by exclusive categories.[14] He starts with the acknowledgement that the interaction between a root and a *binyan* serves the communicative function of identifying, conceptualizing and classifying different kinds of actions or states. In this interaction the root presents the general semantic field of action or state and the *binyan* deictically conceptualizes and categorizes the kind of action or state. The categorization in the *binyanim* is thus based on the deictic point of view of the narrator at the "here and now" point of narrating.[15] Tobin intends to show the importance of the (at least) three deictic relationships for the Hebrew *binyan* system: (1) the *objective* vs. *subjective* viewing of actions, states or events: the narrator may be merely presenting the facts or may be appraising the facts, i.e. revealing more of his own personal point of view, impressions or opinions of the scene; (2) the *single* vs. *multiple* perceptions of these actions, states, or events: the action may be identified as a single perception or may need more than one perception to be identified; (3) the *autonomy* vs. *non-autonomy* of the actions or states: the action/state may be identified independently or dependently on other elements.

Further analysis should prove whether Tobin's categorization is feasible or not. Nevertheless the asymmetric distribution of Hebrew roots within the *binyanim* is a fact to be acknowledged. Another, even more important conclusion can be drawn, too. As the *binyanim* are

---

[14] Y. Tobin, "Invariance, Markedness and Distinctive Feature Theory. The Modern Hebrew Verb", in: E. Andrews & Y. Tobin (eds.), *Toward a Calculus of Meaning. Studies in Markedness, Dinstinctive Features and Deixis* (Studies in Functional and Structural Linguistics 43), Amsterdam/Philadelphia: John Benjamins, 1996, 347–379. Despite the title of this article refering to "Modern Hebrew", Tobin explicitly mentions Biblical Hebrew and states in note 10 that "This paper will take a panchronic view of the *binyan* system in Hebrew".

[15] Tobin speaks of "encoder" and "encoding" instead of "narrator" and "narrating" preferred here.

not only part of the language paradigm but of a deictic system as well, they require a relationship with a narrator who selects a certain *binyan* to narrate the actions or states. Thus the conceptualizations of actions or states in the *binyanim* are always related to the spatio-temporal and experiental perceptions of a narrator. This implies that the *binyanim* are not only the application of an already defined paradigmatic system, but are partly determined by their syntagmatic functioning and dependent on the unmarked narrator's position and the deictic relationships between the *binyanim* and the narrator's position. A hierarchy of (un)markedness relationships can thus explain the paradigmatically and syntagmatically defined verb forms.

Apart from the paradigmatic and the syntagmatic aspects, a third factor motivates the author's choice, viz. the intended communicative function of a text. The author anticipates the reader's need to create coherence and the reader's "passion for iconization", and (s)he builds iconicity into his or her textual arrangement. The concept of iconicity in language explains the fact that the systematic relationships of language elements (which do not themselves resemble their referents) reflect the experienced relationships of their referents in reality. Jakobson advances the idea that markedness is an iconic principle of language: a simple form reflects a neutral or unmarked function, a compound or complex form reflects a marked function. In other words, the newer the information, the more marked its expression in language and text will be.[16] This idea of iconicity implies also that the choice of a syntactic form, for example a verbal clause, is partly iconic in character and anticipates the reader's iconizing activity: in verbal clauses the sequence of actions implicitly refers to an analogously experienced sequence in reality. This iconic relationship enables the reader to understand the difference between: "she becomes pregnant and marries" and "she marries and becomes pregnant". Textual order reflects, or is understood as reflecting, the order in the experienced world.[17] Another example of a syntactic relationship which is partly defined by its pragmatic and communicative function, is the category of definiteness. A definite form (a noun) needs a context in which to function. It involves the assumptions the writer makes about what

---

[16] R. Jakobson, "Implications of Language Universals for Linguistics", in: Greenberg, J.H. (ed.), *Universals of Language. Report of a Conference Held at Dobbs Ferry, New York, April 13–15, 1961*, Cambridge (Mass.): MIT Press, 1963[1] (1973[2]), 263–278.

[17] For the use of the concept of iconicity in Biblical studies in general and with respect to Gen. 1–11 in particular, see: E. van Wolde, *Words Become Worlds*, 1994.

the reader knows, is familiar with or can identify. Definite descriptions are essentially about knowledge by one mind of the knowledge of another mind. And consequently, about the ground for one mind making assumptions about what another mind may know.[18] In short, markedness is relatively defined, partly dependent on the context and functioning in interaction with the communicative partners. Mastery of the language code, guidance by the text and its context, and experience of reality enable the reader to enter into dialogue with the text.

Hebrew narrative syntax and a first category of markedness/unmarkedness

The concept of markedness can be used to explain interclausal and textual relationships as well. Biblical Hebrew linguistics only recently started with syntactic research of interclausal relationships in narrative texts.[19] The following sections deal with this syntax of narrative texts or narrative syntax and will concentrate on two questions: (1) What does text linguistics tell us of the motivation of the choice of certain forms in narrative texts in the Hebrew Bible? and (2) Which categories of markedness and unmarkedness function in the communication of narrative texts?

A first category of markedness and unmarkedness relates to narrative embedding and representation. Every narrative text is characterized by a distinction between clauses in which the narrator tells about events or actions, and clauses which represent a character's speech: the former is called *narrator's text* and the latter *character's text* (or direct speech). A character's text is always embedded in a narrator's text. Within a character's text, a character may let himself or herself or another character speak, so that a direct speech may be embedded in a direct speech. A narrative text can thus be arranged in a hierarchical structure of one or more embedded character's texts in a narrator's text.[20] The concept of markedness and unmarkedness explains this

---

[18] See Givón, *Mind, Code, and Context,* 1989, 206.

[19] See the historical survey of C. van der Merwe in this volume.

[20] H. Weinrich (*Tempus. Besprochene und erzählte Welt.* Stuttgart: Kohlhammer, 1964[1], 1985[4]) made a distinction between "besprochener und erzählter Text" as determinative category of markedness in French and German. His study stongly influenced W. Schneider in his *Grammatik des Biblischen Hebräisch* (München: Claudius Verlag, 1974). Schneider formulated the hypothesis that the distinction between "besprechende" and "erzählende Texte" is determinative for Biblical Hebrew verb forms, as it was for French and German. Schneider's hypothesis became E. Talstra's starting

distinctive feature of Biblical Hebrew. The narrator's text is unmarked. When no distinctive features are provided in a text, the narrator is telling from his (or her) perspective. He usually represents the actions of the characters with verb forms in the third person. The reader is guided by the language system to assume that the representation is "neutral". The verb form marking the narrated event is the *wayyiqtol*-form. The embedded character's text is linguistically marked by the verb אמר, so that the reader is explicitly aware of the partial perspective the embedded character's text offers.[21] This is corroborated by the multiple use of first and second persons in the verb forms: they confirm that the information presented is bound to the domain of the character and his or her addressee.

The representation of perspective in a narrator's text can take two forms: a *direct narrator's text* (the narrator telling about the actions of characters) and an *indirect narrator's text*: the narrator does not directly speak from a narrator's point of view but indirectly, through the character's point of view: the character is represented as a thinking, observing, feeling or speaking subject, but the representing is done by the narrator. The representation of perspective in an embedded character's text differs from that of a narrator's text. Here the narrator may let the reader look at actions or events through the words and the mental awareness, perception or feeling of a character. The embedded speaker is responsible for the content, the "I" and the verb tenses no longer refer to the narrator but to the speaking character, who is responsible for the content as well as the form of the clause. This

---

point for computer assisted syntactic analysis ("Text Grammar and Hebrew Bible. I: Elements of a Theory", *Bibliotheca Orientalis* 35 (1978) 168–175; "Text Grammar and Hebrew Bible. II: Syntax and Semantics", *Bibliotheca Orientalis* 39 (1982) 26–38; "Text Grammar and Biblical Hebrew. The Point of View of Wolfgang Schneider", *Journal of Translation and Text Linguistics* 5 (1992) 269–287). Weinrich and Schneider influenced A. Niccacci (*The Syntax of the Verb in Classical Hebrew Prose* (JSOT 86), Sheffield: Sheffield Academic Press, 1990 (original Italian version 1986); *Lettura Sintattica della Prosa Ebraico-Biblica. Principi e applicazioni.* Jerusalem: Franciscan Printing Press, 1991) who translated the distinction "erzählend" and "besprechend" into "narrative" and "discourse". Because the term "discourse" in American linguistics and cognitive linguistics is used in the sense of "text" or "text in communication", it might better be replaced by "character's text" or "direct speech", as Niccacci did in his later publications.

[21] G. Goldenberg, "On Direct Speech and the Hebrew Bible", in: K. Jongeling et al. (eds.) *Studies in Hebrew and Aramaic Syntax. Presented to Professor J. Hoftijzer on Occasion of his Sixty-Fifth Birthday*, Leiden: E.J. Brill, 1991, 79–96, esp. 85–86. A direct speech always requires the verb אמר and cannot be presented by any other *verbum dicendi*, as is evident from the fact that some form of אמר, especially the infinitive לאמר, is required to be added after another verb of saying.

implies that the finite verbs, the possessive pronouns and the locative and temporal adjuncts are conceived from the point of view of the speaking, observing, feeling or thinking character.[22]

Biblical Hebrew offers the possibility to represent speech in a narrative text in different ways, in which the (direct or indirect) narrator's text is continuous or unmarked and the embedded character's text is discrete or marked. Their relationship is not a binary opposition, but an asymmetric one. In the first position the information is grounded, no specific claims are made, thus implying a neutral continuous (everything and everybody including) position, while the direct speech is marked explicitly for its discontinuity, thus implying a specific character-bound position. The asymmetric unmarked-marked relationship may therefore be visualised in the following diagrams:[23]

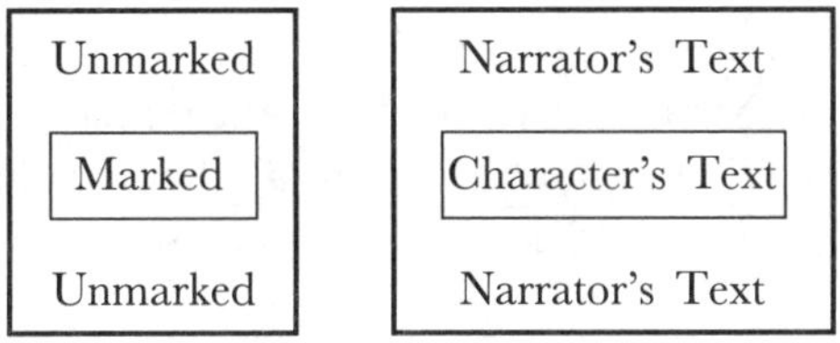

In the Hebrew Bible the narrator's text is presented as an inclusive and continuous category: it is the all-embracing representation in which the character's text is included. From a linguistic point of view one might say that the unmarked member of the opposition, i.e. the narrator's text, is more open, because it makes no specific claim regarding the absence or presence of a distinctive semantic feature. From the same linguistic point of view one might conclude that the marked member of the opposition, i.e. the character's text, which

[22] See: E.J. van Wolde, "Who Guides Whom? Embeddedness and Perspective in Biblical Hebrew and in 1 Kings 3:16–28", *Journal of Biblical Literature* 114 (1995) 623–642.

[23] The asymmetric unmarked-marked relationships in diagrams is represented differently by different authors: Tobin depicts it as two quadrangles in which the larger one encloses the smaller (cf. Tobin, *Invariance, Markedness and Distinctive Feature Analysis*, 1994: 74), Andrews uses two circles in which the larger encloses the smaller and both circles are part of a larger quadrangle (cf. Andrews, *Markedness Theory*, 1990, 10), and Kirsner presents it as a diagram of two circles in which the larger enclosing the smaller one (cf. R. Kirsner, "The Human Factor and the Insufficiency of Invariant Meanings", in: E. Andrews & Y. Tobin (eds.), *Toward a Calculus of Meaning. Studies in Markedness, Distinctive Features and Deixis* (Studies in Functional and Structural Linguistics 43), Amsterdam/Philadelphia: John Benjamins, 1996, 83–107, esp. 94).

claims the presence of a semantic feature, is less flexible and usually more limited because of its greater precision in meaning.[24] A literary and ideology-critical approach, however, may show just the opposite: what is proposed to be neutral and continuous is, actually, linked to one (usually male, white, belonging to the social or religious elite, rich, educated) point of view. Nevertheless the reader is guided by the language system to read this narrator's perspective as a neutral one. This is reinforced by its positive validation and valuation as religious literature. That is to say, in religious literature God is presented as a character, so that God's actions, God's speech and God's presence are part of the narrator's representation. At the same time God is presented by the narrator as being "higher" in hierarchy, as more continuous, as the one who passed the word to the narrator (this is most explicitly stated in the prophetic literature, but it is also implicitly present in narrative texts such as Gen. 1).[25] That is why the reader is still more inclined to believe the narrator's "unmarked" position. This category of unmarkedness and markedness very much determines the reader's comprehension of the narrative text. It is imposed on her or him and in that sense inescapable.

A second category of markedness in text syntax: grounding

Another category of (un)markedness determines a narrative text to an even greater extent, namely the one that defines continuity or coherence and marks interruption or discontinuity. Since the Prague school in the 1930s the relationship between continuity and discontinuity in a text is described as the relationship between "topic" and "comment", the former referring to "the things we talk about" and the latter to "what we say about the topical things". This distinction is later on also referred to as "given" information (already known material) versus "new" information (added to the given material). From the 1970s onward there has been a fair amount of discussion in linguistic literature on how to relate various syntactic phenomena to this topic-comment distinction. The earliest proposals are those of Harald

[24] Cf. Tobin, *Invariance, Markedness and Distinctive Feature Analysis*, 1994, 73.

[25] E.J. van Wolde, "The Text as an Eloquent Guide. Rhetorical, Linguistic and Literary Features in Gen. 1", in: L.J. de Regt, J. de Waard, J.P. Fokkelman (eds.), *Literary Structure and Rhetorical Strategies in the Hebrew Bible*, Assen: Van Gorcum, 1996, 134–151.

Weinrich[26] and of William Labov and J. Waletzky.[27] The former proposal was more or less neglected in general linguistics. The latter approach was very influential and was later extended to studies of what became called "foregrounding" and "backgrounding".[28] Because the study of Paul Hopper (and that of Hopper and Thompson) is seminal in this respect, his approach will be dealt with in the following paragraphs.[29]

In a narrative text Hopper distinguishes the language of the actual story line from the language of supportive material which does not itself narrate the main event. The former he calls "foreground", i.e. the language which relates events belonging to the skeletal structure

---

[26] H. Weinrich (*Tempus*) proposed the distinction "Reliefgebung", i.e. the relationship between "Vordergrund" (foreground) and "Hintergrund" (background). Text-linguistic studies of Biblical Hebrew explicitly make use of this category (for literature see note 21). Weinrich's book has, however, not been influential or accepted in general linguistics, although some of the presented theories on grounding show some similarities. Thus a rather odd situation exists: although Weinrich's book is the cornerstone of Hebrew text-linguistic studies, it is not accepted in general linguistics. At the same time, the text-linguistic studies of Biblical Hebrew neglect recent developments in functional and cognitive linguistics with regard to modern concepts of grounding, saliency, topic continuity etc. (see the literature mentioned in note 29).

[27] W. Labov and J. Waletzky, "Narrative Analysis: Oral Versions of Personal Experience", in: J. Helm (ed.), *Essays on the Verbal and Visual Arts*, Seattle: University of Washington Press, 1967, 12–44; W. Labov, "The Transformation of Experience in Narrative Syntax", in: W. Labov, *Language in the Inner City*, Philadelphia: University of Pennsylvania Press, 1972, 354–396.

[28] The main literature on foregrounding and backgrounding in chronological order: J. Grimes, *The Thread of Discourse*, The Hague: Mouton, 1975 (chapters 4, 5, 6); P.J. Hopper, "Aspect and Foregrounding in Discourse", in: T. Givón (ed.), *Discourse and Syntax* (Syntax and Semantics 12), New York: Academic Press 1979, 213–241; P.J. Hopper and S.A. Thompson, "Transitivity in Grammar and Discourse", *Language* 56 (1980) 251–299; R.E. Longacre, "Vertical Threads of Cohesion in Discourse", in: F. Neubauer (ed.), *Coherence in Natural Language Texts*, Hamburg: Helmut Buske Verlag, 1983; J.-J. Weber, "The Foreground-Background Distinction: A Survey of Its Definitions and Applications", *Language in Literature* 8 (1983) 1–15; H.A. Dry, "The Movement of Narrative Time", *Journal of Literary Semantics* 12 (1983) 19–53; T. Reinhart, "Principles of Gestalt Perception in the Temporal Organizations of Narrative Texts", *Linguistics* 22 (1984) 779–809; C.V. Chvany, "Foregrounding, Saliency, Transitivity", *Essays in Poetics* 10 (1985) 1–23; W. Van Peer, *Stylistics and Psychology: Investigations of Foregrounding*, London: Croom Helm, 1986; S.A. Thompson, "'Subordination' and Narrative Event Structure", in: R.S. Tomlin, *Coherence and Grounding in Discourse* (Typological Studies in Language 11), Amsterdam/Philadelphia: John Benjamins, 1987, 435–454; T. Givón, "Beyond Foreground and Background", in: R.S. Tomlin, *Coherence and Grounding in Discourse* (Typological Studies in Language 11), Amsterdam/Philadelphia: John Benjamins, 1987, 175–188; S. Fleischmann, *Tense and Narrativity. From Medieval Performance to Modern Fiction*, Austin (Texas): University of Texas Press, 1990, 168–214.

[29] P.J. Hopper, "Aspect and Foregrounding in Discourse", 1979; P.J. Hopper and S.A. Thompson, "Transitivity in Grammar and Discourse", 1980.

of the discourse, and the latter he calls "background", i.e. the language of the supportative material. The difference between the clauses in the foreground (the "main line" of events) and the one in the background (the "shunted" events) is to be seen in connection with *sequentiality*. The foreground events succeed one another in the narrative usually in the same order as their succession in the real world (iconicity); the background events are not in sequence to the foreground events, but are simultaneous with them. Because of this feature of *simultaneity*, background events usually amplify or comment on the events of the main narrative. Furthermore, background clauses are not sequenced with respect to one another. Because the sequentiality constraint is lifted, background clauses may be located at any point along the time axis or indeed may not be located on the time axis at all. Consequently, the relationships between background clauses are often quite loose. Nevertheless, the reader is able to understand their connection because of his or her iconizing abilities. Only foreground clauses are, strictly speaking, narrated. Background clauses do not themselves narrate, but instead they support, amplify or comment on the narrative. In a narrative, the author is asserting the occurrence of events. Background, however, does not constitute the assertion of the events in the story line but makes statements which are dependent on the story line event.

Hopper summarizes the characteristics of the foreground clauses as follows. (a) The subject of the verbs is "given" or "topical". This topicality of the subject in the foreground is a natural consequence of the tendency for narratives to be concerned principally with a small number of participants and, hence, to have continuity of topic-subject in the main story-line. (b) The time frame of the foreground clauses is measured and unidirectional. It represents a chronological sequencing, without back-tracking or glances forward. (c) The verb forms tend to be active and punctual. Foreground clauses denote the discrete, measured events of the narrative, and generally refer to events which are dynamic and active. (d) Foregrounding requires fronting of the verb. Because the foreground clauses are the locus of the actions and events, the new part of the narrative clause is focused upon and therefore put in the clause's first position, which is usually the verb form (in VSO languages).

Background clauses, on the other hand, have different characteristics. (a) The subjects of the verbs are relatively new or unexpected, that is, non-topical. Because the information given in the background clauses is new, the subjects are usually indefinite and must be spelt out in full. There is no stability in subject either, but frequent changes of subjects occur. (b) Simultaneity or overlapping of situations is essential for background clauses. The time frame of the narrative framework with sequenced actions is distorted. In the background access to any point on the time scale can be made. Often a "wandering" up and down the temporal-deictic axis occurs. (c) Because of its static nature, the background contains mostly verbs denoting states, processes and descriptions. (d) Background requires fronting of the topic focused upon: this could be a subject focus, an instrument focus or an adverbial focus. In many languages the foreground/background distinction is realized through word-order, specialized verb morphology and sentence particles.

Hopper's (and Hopper and Thompson's) description of foreground and background is followed by many linguists,[30] but criticized as well. In the first place criticism is raised against the terminology. Developed in the beginning as a temporal juncture, the terms and their interpretation suggest that foreground clauses carry the most important material of the story and the background clauses the less important material. The temporal ordering criterion and the criterion indicating importance, however, need to be sharply distinguished. Temporality might be relevant syntactic marking, importance may not be.[31] Another point of criticism concerns Hopper's elaboration of the background. It is simply not true that the subjects in background clauses are always new or unexpected. Often the subjects are known from the previous context and therefore topical. Also the suggestion that the background presupposes simultaneity with regard to the actions of the foreground, is opposed to occurrences of background clauses which refer to previous or future events.

From the mid 1980s onward syntactic studies of foreground and background have become part of a general pragmatic approach. In this functional perspective the foreground-background distinction is reframed in cognitive terms as "ground" and "figure", as "norm" and "counter-norm", or as "grounding" and "saliency".[32] "Grounding" implies that a coherent text is organized in a way that makes information accessible and predictable to a reader. A coherent text tends

---

[30] See literature note 29.
[31] S. Thompson, "'Subordination' and Narrative Event Structure", 1987, 436.
[32] T. Givón, "Beyond Foreground and Background", 1987, 175–188.

to maintain the same referent or topic, the same or contiguous time and location, and sequential action. At the same time new or marked information is focused upon by the procedure of saliency. Therefore the "ground" is the context vis-à-vis which new or salient information is given.[33]

Texture or textual coherence is determined by the way information is grounded in a narrative text. A grounding procedure is composed of two processes. The first one is essentially *anaphoric*, involving grounding of a particular point in the discourse in relation to the preceding text; or, to be more precise, grounding with regard to what the author can assume about shared knowledge with the reader. The second is a *cataphoric* process, involving clues the author gives the reader at a particular point in the text as to how to ground it in relation to the following discourse.[34] The differentiation between anaphoric and cataphoric orientation in a text is known as the grammar of referential coherence. Thus, for example, definite articles are primarily anaphoric devices, while indefinite articles are primarily cataphoric devices, alerting the reader as to what to expect in the subsequent text. One cannot conclude, therefore, that topic always precedes comment. It depends on the context: a more predictable topic, i.e. a topic anaphorically referred to, follows the comment and a less predictable topic, i.e. a topic cataphorically linked to the context, precedes the comment. Anaphoric references, as related to previously given information, very often function as a motivation or explanation of introduced topics (or topic-subjects). In contrast, cataphoric references which are related to material in the following context, have a wider and less predictable scope of reference.

Consequently, textual coherence is marked by means of grounding and saliency. The distinction of foreground and background, viewed as a continuum in which saliency is a matter of degree, shows how different degrees of grounding are expressed through an interaction of the grammatical procedures available in a language. Of these procedures the anaphoric and cataphoric references are very noticeable. Thus the narrative syntax provides the writer with devices to ground the information differently into the reader's existing knowledge.

In conclusion, the motivation of the choice of verb forms and of

---

[33] T. Givón, *Syntax. A Functional-Typological Introduction. Vol. 2*, Amsterdam/Philadelphia: John Benjamins, 1990, 896–899.

[34] Cf. T. Givón, "Beyond Foreground and Background", 1987, 176.

textual coherence, cannot be reduced to the paradigm or language system which offers the conventionalized procedures. It also depends on the syntagmatic context which determines the ground vis-à-vis which salient information is given, on the author who uses context dependent devices of foregrounding and backgrounding, and on the supposed reader's knowledge.

Grounding and coherence in Biblical Hebrew

In Biblical narratives a distinction can be made between the clauses presenting continuity in a text, and interrupting clauses, indicating a change in situation. Their difference can be described as "sequential" versus "non-sequential", or as "foreground clauses" versus "background clauses". The sequential clause creates coherence and presupposes, by default, topic and subject continuity. When no change has occurred, it is inferred that there has been no change in the present grounding. It is only in cases when the verb forms, word-order, or redundantly repeated subject nouns or pronouns occur, that Biblical Hebrew marks the transition to a non-default situation or circumstance.[35]

The sequenced series of verbal clauses are indicated by *wayyiqtol* forms presented by the narrator (thus in a narrator's text). They refer to single, sequential actions or events advancing the plot and present the information as foregrounded material, whereas the word-order VSO puts the new information (expressed in the verb) in a fronted position. The sequentiality marked by the *wayyiqtol*-clauses is iconic in nature, because it reflects (or is understood as reflecting) the order in the experienced world. An interruption in this chain of actions or events is indicated by non-sequential verb forms, of which the *(x-) qatal, w^ex-qatal* and *(x-)qotel* forms are the most frequently used, as well as by a word-order in which the verb is not fronted but the subject, object or adverb. Thus the verb form and the word-order are the devices used in Biblical Hebrew to mark the transition from the foreground (sequentiality) to the background (non-sequentiality).[36]

---

[35] Cf. F.I. Andersen, "Salience, Implicature, Ambiguity, and Redundancy", in: R.D. Bergen (ed.), *Biblical Hebrew and Discourse Linguistics*, Winona Lake (Ind.): Eisenbrauns, 1994, 99–116.

[36] In Biblical Hebrew, word-order is a rather difficult device. Classical grammars of Biblical Hebrew describe the word-order in verbal clauses as VSO, although it is

In the background the scenery is viewed as occurring simultaneously with the main events and the information offered functions either anaphorically, when it presents additional material to previously introduced participants, or cataphorically, when a new subject, object or adverb(ial construction) is topicalized by putting it in a fronted position.[37] This implies that topicalization, fronting of verb or of subject or object, strongly correlates with the context.[38]

If it is not the narrator, but a character who presents the information and this is represented in a direct speech or embedded character's text, the Hebrew verbal clauses show different verb forms. Volitive and *yiqtol* forms in fronted position mark foregrounding in a character's text: the character presents the actions or events as sequential. Whereas the sequential actions in the narrator's text are represented by non-modal forms, in the character's texts they are represented by modal forms (*yiqtol* and volitives) which are contingent on the relationship with the speaking subject and linked to the domain of the character.[39] This series of actions can be interrupted, as is shown by a different

generally recognized that very frequently the reverse order SVO is found. Cf. Gesenius-Kautzsch-Cowley, § 140–144; Joüon-Muraoka, § 153–155: "In the verbal clause the statistically dominant and unmarked word-order is 'verb-subject'. (. . .) But, as in the case of the nominal clause, there is no lack of exceptions". Waltke-O'Connor, § 8.3b: "For verbal clauses the basic Hebrew word-order is *verb* + *subject* (VS)". Other linguistic studies, however, start from the flexible subject position in which the subject is placed either pre-verbally or post-verbally, and conclude that Early Biblical Hebrew is a VO language, in which not the order of verb and subject is stable or conventionalized, but the order of verb and object: the verb always precedes the object. See: A. Fox, "Topic Continuity in Biblical Hebrew", in: T. Givón (ed.), *Topic Continuity in Discourse: Quantified Cross-Language Studies* (Typological Language Studies 3), Amsterdam/Philadelphia: John Benjamins, 1983, 215–254; and T. Givón, *Mind, Code, and Context*, 1989, 228–232.

[37] The terms "anticipatory" and "retrospective" used by W. Schneider, Talstra and Niccacci, suggest too much a temporal aspect. The categories anaphora and cataphora are purely contextually determined.

[38] Word-order is consequently not only a question of emphasis. See: T. Muraoka, *Emphatic Words and Structures in Biblical Hebrew*, Jerusalem/Leiden: Magnes/E.J. Brill, 1985; and cf. B.L. Bandstra, "Word-Order and Emphasis in Biblical Hebrew Narrative: Syntactic Observations on Genesis 22 from a Discourse Perspective", in: W. Bodine (ed.), *Linguistics and Biblical Hebrew*, Winona Lake (Ind.): Eisenbrauns, 1992, 109–124.

[39] Occasionally a *yiqtol* form occurs in a narrator's text; one might infer that such a clause expresses the narrator's discourse to the reader. Cf. W. Schneider, *Grammatik des Biblischen Hebräisch*, 1974, 195: "Der Übergang vom Narrativ zum Imperfekt innerhalb eines erzählenden Kontexts kann anzeigen, daß der Autor aus seiner Sprechhaltung als Erzähler heraustritt und mit seinen Hörern etwas bespricht, eine Anmerkung macht, die sie auch außerhalb der erzählten Welt interessieren soll".

word-order and different verb forms, and this interruption indicates the background in a character's text. The verb forms are the same as those in the background clauses in the narrator's text, of which the most frequently used are the *(x-)qatal*, *w^ex-qatal* and *(x-)qotel.* These view the material as a scenery existing simultaneously with the foreground actions. They refer either backwards (anaphorically) or forwards (cataphorically).

Verbless clauses function identically in narrator's texts and character's texts and always present background or non-sequential information. Verbless clauses consist of two or more elements, which can be relatively more or less definite: the relatively more definite elements represent "given" or "known" information and refer back to earlier presented material. The relatively less definite elements represent "new" information and refer to the following context. One might conclude that verbless clauses with word-order "given-new" function anaphorically; verbless clauses with word-order "new-given" function cataphorically.[40]

A parallellism in the arrangement of information in verbal and verbless clauses might then be discovered. In foreground clauses the verb is fronted, which indicates a strong cataphoric function, as it points at the context to come. The verb is thus part of a chain of sequenced actions. At the same time a foreground clause is characterized by subject continuity and thus an anaphoric relation to the preceding context is suggested. This is why a foreground clause expresses sequentiality and subject or topic continuity, and thus functions cataphorically and anaphorically at the same time. Background clauses, on the other hand, function either cataphorically or anaphorically. When a less definite or unknown element is fronted in background (verbal or verbless) clauses, they introduce a new element which functions cataphorically in consequent events, actions or situations. In verbal or verbless background clauses with word-order "given-new", i.e. clauses with a relatively more definite element in front position, reference is made to a previously presented element: it underlines the topic continuity by providing additional information to already known subjects, objects or actions. This type of background clause

[40] Cf. E.J. van Wolde, "The Verbless Clause and its Communicative Function", in: C. Miller (ed.), *The Verbless Clause in Biblical Hebrew*, Winona Lake: Eisenbrauns, 1998 (in press).

functions anaphorically, as the given elements (previously occurring in the context) are given depth or are elaborated by means of additional information. This can be summarized in the following diagram:

clause type	grounding	word-order	order of info	function
verbal	foreground	verb fronted	new-given	1. sequential 2. cataphoric + anaphoric
	background	verb not fronted	new-given	1. non-sequential 2. cataphoric
			given-new	1. non-sequential 2. anaphoric
verbless	background	no verb	new-given	1. non-sequential 2. cataphoric
			given-new	1. non-sequential 2. anaphoric

In Biblical Hebrew the procedure for grounding is demonstrable in the verb morphology and word-order. Criteria for identifying grounding in a narrative are (1) whether or not a clause serves to advance the plot or move narrative time forward, is sequential or non-sequential; this presupposes an ability on the part of the reader to make iconic relationships, and is thus linked to the reader's knowledge of the world; (2) whether the word-order is either "more definite-less definite" or "less definite-more definite"; this order enables the reader to determine the anaphoric or the cataphoric relationship in the context; and (3) whether the elements presented to the reader are more or less predictable or accessible; zero anaphora and redundant subject repetitions are, among others, very predictable but do not add much new information, while newly introduced subjects or indefinite nouns are less predictable and ask more of the reader's attention and activity. With these criteria one can explain how the reader is able to create coherence, to ground the textual information in his or her own pre-existing knowledge, and to understand and integrate new information in his or her mental representation.

This study shows how relative markedness, relative definiteness and context determine textual grounding and coherence in Biblical Hebrew.

One cannot conclude that the foreground is unmarked and the background is marked: markedness is not a member of a binary opposition, but a continuum of relatively more or less marked elements. One might compare this concept of markedness with the user interface of the operating system WINDOWS for computers. The window environment shows a computer user how to activate certain programmes, files or activities. The user works within one file while using a programme, but he or she might open other programmes, keeping the previous programme sleeping or inactive. The user can also, in one programme, return from time to time to previous levels; (s)he can open two or more windows at the same time and be active in them. Working in a window environment presupposes the presence of a previous environment: various programmes and files are active at the same time, they do not disappear. This may give rise to the question of what level influences a computer user most: is it the basic programme, for example MS-DOS, or is it the active programme that is being used, for example WordPerfect, or is it the file one being worked on? They are all important, but their influences differ on the various levels.

With regard to the grounding procedure similar questions can be asked. Which textual environment influences a reader most in his or her creation of coherence, grounding and evaluation? Is it the basic topic created at the beginning, which functions as comment or background information for the sequential actions to come, or is it the foreground textual sequentiality and topic continuity, or are the non-sequential clauses more influential, those which point either forward or backward? Is markedness more influential than non-markedness, or non-markedness more influential than markedness? Referring to the above diagram, one might conclude that both foreground and background clauses can be very influential in getting the reader to create grounding and saliency, but that the clauses which function cataphorically, i.e. foreground clauses, background verbal clauses with word-order "new-given" and verbless clauses with word-order "new-given", are the most determinative in the grounding of new information. On the other hand, the background clauses with a given or already known element in front position (i.e. word-order "given-new") fulfills an important function as well, because it grounds the new information into the already-stored old information. Cognitively, it furnishes the address or label for the storage locus in the episodic memory. The cataphoric and anaphoric features are, therefore, in their own ways influential in the reader's building of a coherent mental representation of the text, and both should therefore be analysed. An example of such an analysis will be given in the next section.

Some consequences for biblical exegesis

The linguistic study on markedness/unmarkedness and grounding can give a biblical exegete the possibilites to reflect more seriously on the rhetorical procedure used by an author to steer a reader in his or her creation of a textual image or mental representation. It can demonstrate the importance of the grounding procedure and give some knowledge of what motivates the author's choice of textual elements to build up textual coherence. It can explain why topic continuity and the non-sequential information invite the reader to construe a coherent image of the text and why a reader is sometimes strongly influenced by certain background clauses. These consequences of linguistic research for biblical exegesis can be illustrated by an example, viz. Gen. 28:12–13.

In Genesis 28, the story of the Jacob's ladder, Jacob starts to dream:

וַיַּחֲלֹם	12a
וְהִנֵּה סֻלָּם מֻצָּב אַרְצָה	12b
וְרֹאשׁוֹ מַגִּיעַ הַשָּׁמָיְמָה	12c
וְהִנֵּה מַלְאֲכֵי אֱלֹהִים עֹלִים וְיֹרְדִים בּוֹ	12d
וְהִנֵּה יְהוָה נִצָּב עָלָיו	13a
וַיֹּאמַר	13b

In this narrator's text the first and last clause, 12a and 13b, are foregrounded, as is indicated by the *wayyiqtol* forms ויחלם and ויאמר. The verb forms represent the sequence of actions and the subject continuity expressed in the zero anaphora (i.e. the subject is not mentioned). Nevertheless the subject in 12a differs from the one in 13b. This change of subjects is made possible by the background clauses 12b–13a, where no sequential actions are represented. They draw the attention to three types of information, all three marked by the macrosyntactic sign והנה.

The first aspect that is highlighted, is the event unfolding before Jacob's eyes in 12bc. Clause 12b is a *x-qotel* clause, in which the undefinite noun סלם is followed by the *qotel* or passive participle מצב. The word-order "new-given" shows that a new element, "ladder", is presented which had not been mentioned before. Therefore, the clause functions cataphorically. Clause 12c is a *x-qotel* clause of which the first word is relatively more definite: ראשו, and the pronominal suffix shows its relationship to the previous clause. In this clause the word-order is "given-new" and the clause functions therefore anaphorically. That is to say, the information given in this clause elaborates already known material. Both *qotel* or participle clauses present an action as a state.[41] Together they represent one image, constructed by a first clause (12b) which introduces the new subject and refers to the second clause (12c), and by a second clause (12c) which gives additional information on this new subject and thus refers to the first clause (12b). This is Jacob's first vision, as it is evoked before the eyes of the reader.

The second aspect, introduced by the attention marker והנה, sheds light upon another situation. It is described in 12d in a *x-qotel* clause in which an indefinite noun, מלאכי אלהים, is presented as a new subject. The verb phrase consists of two *qotel* forms, which picture the ascending and descending activity of the messengers of God as a state, and is followed by one prepositional phrase בו.[42] On the one hand, the word-order "new-given" indicates that this state is cataphorically linked to the following context. On the other hand, the prepositional clause בו refers back to the ladder of 12bc, and thus links it to the previous aspect of Jacob's dream. Whereas the first image in 12bc shows Jacob's vision of the ladder, the second image in 12d elucidates his vision of the divine messengers going up and down. Both images together give depth to Jacob's dreaming activity, as expressed in 12a by the *wayyiqtol* form ויחלם.

A third piece of information, presented in 13a, is marked again by the attention marker והנה: והנה יהוה נצב עליו. The subject of this action, YHWH, is new in this context and the word-order subject-*qotel* topicalizes this character as a new subject. The *qotel* נצב represents YHWH's action of "standing beside him" as a state. Once introduced, YHWH can be referred to in ויאמר (zero anaphora) in clause 13b. The word-order "new-given" in 13a thus indicates a cataphoric relationship to the

---

[41] Cf. Joüon-Muraoka § 121c.

[42] Remarkably the divine messengers start with the activity of ascending and not with that of descending. By a process of iconization the reader assumes that the sequence of actions described in these two *qotel* forms refer to a similar sequence in the described actions. Thus the readers infer that the divine messengers' starting point is the earth.

following context: this clause preludes YHWH's speech act in the verses 13–15. In contrast to the clauses 12bd, which show a certain closure in the representation of the images (in 12bc by the anaphoric linking of וראשו in 12c, and in 12d by the anaphoric phrase בו), the last clause is not grounded by anaphoric relationships, but only cataphorically related to the following context.

In Gen. 28:12–13a the reader's attention is drawn to three aspects, marked by the attention marker והנה, of which the first two differ from the last. The background-clauses in 12b–d depict the situation Jacob views in his dream as a twofold image, whereas the background-clause in 13a presents a situation which creates the conditions for the speech act of YHWH to come. The narrator has thus chosen in this episode to represent only the action of Jacob's dreaming and of YHWH's speaking (in 12a and 13b respectively) as foreground information or sequenced actions. Jacob's perceptions in 12bcd and the "standing beside Jacob"—activity of YHWH in 13a are not presented as a sequenced action (see the lack of a *wayyiqtol*-form) but as background information. Although the terms "foreground" and "background" are misleading, since the foreground does not present the most important action nor the background the less important material, with the theory of grounding one can explain the procedure by which coherence is built up in the mind of a reader. In this process the background clauses, especially those with word-order "new-given", are most determinative in the grounding of new information, and the foreground clauses are very important in the construction of the skeletal structure of actions. In Gen. 28:12–13a the three background clauses mark three new pieces of information as salient. They explicitly topicalize and focalize the ladder, the divine messengers and YHWH. Because they are represented not as part of a continuous changing flow of actions (which should have been expressed in foreground clauses), they evoke a strong impression on the reader's mind, in order to be firmly established in the episodic memory of the reader.

This text-syntactic approach needs some further narratological remarks. In Gen. 28:12 the perception or mental awareness of the character Jacob is represented in the words of the narrator; it is, therefore, an indirect narrator's text.[43] By representing Jacob's dream as directly as possible (twice והנה), the narrator guides the reader to

[43] See E. Van Wolde, "Who Guides Whom?", 1995.

feel present in this unique situation and to be involved in Jacob's perception of a ladder and divine messengers ascending and descending this ladder. The third use of the focalizer והנה explicitly draws attention to the fact that YHWH is standing beside Jacob. But it is not quite clear whose awareness is presupposed here: is it Jacob's perception which is still presupposed (and an indirect narrator's text), or is it the narrator's awareness (and a direct narrator's text)? The latter seems most plausible because of the strong cataphoric relationship between 13a and 13b. Though the reader is not allowed to perceive what Jacob perceives, the culminating images evoked in the indirect narrator's text and the situation of YHWH taking his stand described in the direct narrator's text, create a positive condition to validate YHWH's direct speech in verses 13 and 14 as truly divine speech. Whereas Jacob is prepared by the dream to listen carefully to YHWH's words, so are we, the readers, prepared by the background clauses to ground the text of verses 13 and 14 and evaluate them as YHWH's words.

Although much attention is paid to the background clauses, it would be wrong to overemphasize the role of these clauses at the expense of the foreground clauses. The chain of *wayyiqtol* forms in foreground clauses is still the main coherence building feature of a text. They define the skeleton of the story. And when summarizing a story, one usually tells this main line of actions. Background clauses interrupt this sequence of actions and subjects; they present new elements and give depth to already known elements and become thus part of the enduring memory of the reader.

Our main question *why* an author uses a specific linguistic form in a certain narrative text, can thus be answered by referring to these rhetorical procedures of grounding and representation. Because the author relies on the reader's confidence in the narrator's representation and counts on the reader's passion for iconization, identification and grounding, this author exercizes his authority by making use of this confidence and these passions in his or her rhetorical procedures. By offering sequential information in foreground clauses and non-sequential information in anaphorically and cataphorically functioning background clauses, the reader's longing for new or salient elements is used, as well as his or her ability of integrating this new knowledge into the pre-existing knowledge. This interaction process may then result in the creation of a coherent mental representation in the mind of the reader.

References

Andersen, F.I., *The Hebrew Verbless Clause in the Pentateuch* (Journal of Biblical Literature Monograph Series XIV), Nashville: Abingdon, 1970.

———, "Salience, Implicature, Ambiguity and Redundancy", in: Bergen, R.D. (ed.), *Biblical Hebrew and Discourse Linguistics*, Winona Lake (Ind.): Eisenbrauns, 1994, 99–116.

Andrews, E., *Markedness Theory. The Union of Asymmetry and Semiosis in Language* (The Roman Jakobson Series in Linguistics and Poetics), Durham and London: Duke University Press, 1990.

Andrews, E. & Tobin, Y. (eds.), *Toward a Calculus of Meaning. Studies in Markedness, Distinctive Features and Deixis* (Studies in Functional and Structural Linguistics 43), Amsterdam/Philadelphia: John Benjamins, 1996.

Bandstra, B.R., "Word Order and Emphasis in Biblical Hebrew Narrative: Syntactic Observations on Genesis 22 from a Discourse Perspective", in: Bodine, W.R. (ed.), *Linguistics and Biblical Hebrew*, Winona Lake (Ind.): Eisenbrauns, 1992, 109–123.

Barr, J., *The Semantics of Biblical Language*, Oxford: Oxford University Press, 1961.

———, "The Image of God in the Book of Genesis—A Study in Terminology", *Bulletin of the John Rylands Library of Manchester* 51 (1968) 11–26.

Chvany, C.V., "Foregrounding, Saliency, Transitivity", *Essays in Poetics* 10 (1985) 1–23.

Dry, H.A., "The Movement of Narrative Time", *Journal of Literary Semantics* 12 (1983) 19–53.

Fleischmann, S., *Tense and Narrativity. From Medieval Performance to Modern Fiction*, Austin (Texas): University of Texas Press, 1990.

Fox, A., "Topic Continuity in Biblical Hebrew", in: Givón, T. (ed.), *Topic Continuity in Discourse: Quantified Cross-Language Studies* (Typological Studies in Language 3), Amsterdam/Philadelphia: John Benjamins, 1983, 215–254.

Fradkin, R., "Typologies of Person Categories in Slavic and Semitic", in: Andrews, E. & Tobin, Y. (eds.), *Toward a Calculus of Meaning. Studies in Markedness, Distinctive Features and Deixis* (Studies in Functional and Structural Linguistics 43), Amsterdam/Philadelphia: John Benjamins, 1996, 319–345.

Gesenius, W., Kautzsch, E. & Cowley, E.A., *Gesenius' Hebrew Grammar*, second ed., Oxford: Clarendon, 1910.

Givón, T. (ed.), *Discourse and Syntax* (Syntax and Semantics 12), New York: Academic Press 1979.

———, "Introduction", in: Givón, T. (ed.), *Topic Continuity in Discourse* (Typological Studies in Language 3), Amsterdam/Philadelphia: John Benjamins, 1983, 1–42.

——— (ed.), *Topic Continuity in Discourse: A Quantitative Cross-Language Study* (Typological Studies in Language 3), Amsterdam/Philadelphia: John Benjamins, 1983.

———, "Beyond Foreground and Background", in: Tomlin, R.S., *Coherence and Grounding in Discourse* (Typological Studies in Language 11), Amsterdam/Philadelphia: John Benjamins, 1987, 175–188.

———, *Mind, Code and Context. Essays in Pragmatics*, Hillsdale (NJ)/London: Erlbaum, 1989.

———, *Syntax. A Functional-typological Introduction*, 2 Vols., Amsterdam/Philadelphia: John Benjamins, 1984–1990.

———, *Functionalism and Grammar*, Amsterdam/Philadelphia: John Benjamins 1995.

Goldenberg, G., "On Direct Speech and the Hebrew Bible", in: Jongeling, K. et al. (eds.), *Studies in Hebrew and Aramaic Syntax. Presented to Professor J. Hoftijzer on the Occasion of his Sixty-Fifth Birthday*, Leiden: E.J. Brill, 1991, 79–96.

Grimes, J., *The Thread of Discourse*, The Hague: Mouton, 1975.

Haiman, J., *Natural Syntax. Iconicity and Erosion*, Cambridge: Cambridge University Press, 1985.

Hoftijzer, J., "Überlegungen zum System der Stammesmodifikationen im klassischen Hebräisch", *Zeitschrift für Althebraistik* 5 (1992) 117–134.
Hopper, P.J., "Aspect and Foregrounding in Discourse", in: Givón, T. (ed.), *Discourse and Semantics* (Syntax and Semantics 12), New York: Academic Press, 1979, 213–241.
——— & Thompson S.A., "Transitivity in Grammar and Discourse", *Language* 56 (1980) 251–299.
Jakobson, R., "Shifters, Verbal Categories and the Russian Verb", in: Jakobson, R., *Selected Writings II*, The Hague: Mouton, 1957/1991, 130–147.
———, "Implications of Language Universals for Linguistics", in: Greenberg, J.H. (ed.), *Universals of Language. Report of a Conference held at Dobbs Ferry, New York, April 13–15, 1961*, Cambridge (Mass.): MIT, 1963[1] (1973[2]), 263–278.
Joüon, P. & Muraoka, T., *A Grammar of Biblical Hebrew*, 2 Vols., Roma: Pontificio Istituto Biblico, 1991.
Kirsner, R., "The Human Factor and the Insufficiency of Invariant Meanings", in: Andrews, E. & Tobin, Y. (eds.), *Toward a Calculus of Meaning. Studies in Markedness, Distinctive Features and Deixis* (Studies in Functional and Structural Linguistics 43), Amsterdam/Philadelphia: John Benjamins, 1996, 83–107.
Labov, W., "The Transformation of Experience in Narrative Syntax", in: Labov, W., *Language in the Inner City*, Philadelphia: University of Pennsylvania Press, 1972, 354–396.
——— & Waletzky, J., "Narrative Analysis: Oral Versions of Personal Experience", in: Helm, J. (ed.), *Essays on the Verbal and Visual Arts*, Seattle: University of Washington Press, 1967, 12–44.
Levinson, S.C., *Pragmatics* (Cambridge Textbooks in Linguistics), Cambridge: Cambridge University Press, 1983.
Longacre, R.E., "Vertical Threads of Cohesion in Discourse", in: Neubauer, F. (ed.), *Coherence in Natural Language Texts*, Hamburg: Helmut Buske, 1983.
Muraoka, T., *Emphatic Words and Structures in Biblical Hebrew*, Jerusalem/Leiden: Magnes/E.J. Brill, 1985.
Niccacci, A., *The Syntax of the Verb in Classical Hebrew Prose* (Journal for the Study of the Old Testament Supplement Series 86), Sheffield: Sheffield Academic Press, 1990.
———, *Lettura sintattica della prosa Ebraico-Biblica. Principi e applicazioni* (Studium Biblicum Franciscanum, Analecta 31), Jerusalem: Franciscan Printing Press, 1991.
Reinhart, T., "Principles of Gestalt Perception in the Temporal Organizations of Narrative Texts", *Linguistics* 22 (1984) 779–809.
Schneider, W., *Grammatik des Biblischen Hebräisch. Völlig neue Bearbeitung der* "Hebräischen Grammatik für den akademischen Unterricht" *von Oskar Grether*, München: Claudius, 1974.
Talstra, E., "Text Grammar and Hebrew Bible 1: Elements of a Theory", *Bibliotheca Orientalis* 35 (1978) 168–175.
———, "Text Grammar and Hebrew Bible 2: Syntax and Semantics", *Bibliotheca Orientalis* 39 (1982) 26–38.
———, "Text Grammar and Biblical Hebrew: The Viewpoint of Wolfgang Schneider", *Journal of Translation and Textlinguistics* 5 (1992) 269–287.
Thompson, S., "'Subordination' and Narrative Event Structure", in: Tomlin, R.S. (ed.), *Coherence and Grounding in Discourse* (Typological Studies in Linguistics 11), Amsterdam/Philadelphia: John Benjamins, 1987, 435–454.
Tobin, Y., "Process and Result and the Hebrew Infinitive: A Study in Linguistic Isomorphism", in: Jongeling, K. et al. (eds.), *Studies in Hebrew and Aramaic Syntax: Presented to Professor J. Hoftijzer on the Occasion of his Sixty-Fifth Birthday*, Leiden: E.J. Brill, 1991, 194–209.
———, *Invariance, Markedness and Distinctive Feature Analysis. A Contrastive Study of Sign*

Systems in English and Hebrew (Current Issues in Linguistic Theory 111), Amsterdam/Philadelphia: John Benjamins, 1994.

———, "Invariance, Markedness and Distinctive Feature Theory. The Modern Hebrew Verb", in: Andrews, E. & Tobin, Y. (eds.), *Toward a Calculus of Meaning. Studies in Markedness, Distinctive Features and Deixis* (Studies in Functional and Structural Linguistics 43), Amsterdam/Philadelphia: John Benjamins, 1996, 347–379.

Tomlin, R.S., *Basic Word Order: Functional Principles*, London: Croom Helm, 1986.

Trubetzkoy, N.S., "Die phonologischen Systeme", *Travaux du Cercle Linguistique de Prague* 4 (1931) 96–116.

Van Peer, W., *Stylistics and Psychology: Investigations of Foregrounding*, London: Croom Helm, 1986.

Waltke, B.K. & O'Connor, M., *An Introduction to Biblical Hebrew Syntax*, Winona Lake (Ind.): Eisenbrauns, 1990.

Weber, J.-J., "The Foreground-Background Distinction: A Survey of Its Definitions and Applications", *Language in Literature* 8 (1983) 1–15.

Weinrich, H., *Tempus: Besprochene und erzählte Welt*, Stuttgart: Kohlhammer, 1964[1], 1985[4].

Wolde, E.J. van, *Words Become Worlds, Semantic Studies of Genesis 1–11* (Biblical Interpretation Series 6), Leiden: E.J. Brill, 1994.

———, "Who Guides Whom? Embeddedness and Perspective in Biblical Hebrew and in 1 Kings 3:16–28", *Journal of Biblical Literature* 114 (1995) 623–642.

———, "The Text as an Eloquent Guide. Rhetorical, Linguistic and Literary Features in Genesis 1", in: de Regt, L.J., de Waard, J., Fokkelman, J. (eds.), *Literary Structure and Rhetorical Strategies in the Hebrew Bible*, Assen: Van Gorcum, 1996, 134–151.

———, "The Verbless Clause and its Communicative Function", in: Miller, C. (ed.), *The Verbless Clause in Biblical Hebrew*, Winona Lake (Ind.): Eisenbrauns, 1998 (in press).

THE INDICATIVE SYSTEM OF THE BIBLICAL HEBREW VERB AND ITS LITERARY EXPLOITATION

Jan Joosten
(Strasbourg)

Introduction

Under the general label of "text linguistics" (or "discourse analysis"), the focus of grammatical research on Biblical Hebrew has, during the last twenty years or so,[1] moved from forms and clauses to the text as the ultimate frame of reference. This change of perspective has permitted an exciting range of experiments, especially in the study of the verbal system, and new insights are being reached all the time.[2] And yet, as I will argue, there is reason for caution as well. Text linguistics is not a panacea; discourse factors alone cannot explain all the features of the Biblical Hebrew verb. New questions will lead to new answers, but not—at least not necessarily—to the solution of old, and famously recalcitrant, problems.

The first thesis of the present paper is that the recent text-linguistic and discourse-oriented approaches to the problem of the Biblical Hebrew verb do not replace earlier analyses in terms of tense and aspect, but are complementary to them. A satisfactory solution to the enigma of the Biblical Hebrew verb will be one that integrates insights of the analysis on the level of the single form with attention to functions on the level of the sentence and of the text. As a general principle this statement will probably be accepted by a majority of scholars embracing the new approaches.[3] What is needed, however,

---

[1] The first published treatment of Biblical Hebrew grammar from a text-linguistic perspective would seem to be that of W. Schneider, *Grammatik des biblischen Hebräisch*, München: Claudius, 1974.

[2] Cf. the bibliographical references in C.H.J. van der Merwe's contributions to the present volume.

[3] The complementarity of morphosyntactic and text-linguistic analysis is central to the work of M. Eskhult, *Studies in Verbal Aspect and Narrative Technique in Biblical Hebrew Prose*, Uppsala, 1990. A. Niccacci, too, has recently supplemented his text-linguistic theory with an analysis in terms of tense and aspect, see A. Niccacci, "On the Hebrew Verbal System", in R.D. Bergen, ed., *Biblical Hebrew and Discourse Linguistics*,

is greater theoretical clarity as to the scope of each approach and the way the two relate to one another. In the first section of this paper, an attempt will be made to attain such clarity by the help of the theory of linguistic levels as formulated by the French linguist, Emile Benveniste.

The second thesis is the following: if the text-linguistic approach is to exist side by side with the more traditional morphosyntactic approach, then research focused on the morphosyntactic function of the verb forms remains legitimate and, indeed, necessary. In the second section of this paper, an analysis of the Biblical Hebrew verbal system in terms of tense and aspect will be proposed. This proposal incorporates some points of view developed in my earlier articles on the predicative participle and on *w^eqatal*.[4] Because of time constraints, the focus will be on the indicative subsystem, leaving the modal subsystem aside for the time being.

In a third and last section, a few reflections will be formulated as to how the indicative verb forms may be seen to function on the higher level of the text. Here the complementarity of the morphosyntactic and the text-linguistic approach will again be emphasized, but now from a more practical point of view.

1. *Benveniste's theory of linguistic levels*

Emile Benveniste was born in 1902. A professor of general linguistics at the Collège de France and a prolific writer of articles, he perpetuated the best European structuralist, Saussurian, tradition.[5] This does not mean that his interest was strictly limited to the sub-clausal level. In 1959, Benveniste published an article entitled "Les relations de temps dans le verbe français",[6] in which he advanced the thesis that French has not one, but two verbal systems: one for "historical" and

---

Winona Lake: Eisenbrauns, 1994, 117–137, in part. 128–130. See also R. Buth, *Word Order in Aramaic from the Perspectives of Functional Grammar and Discourse Analysis*, Ph.D. diss., Los Angeles 1987, 26–27.

[4] J. Joosten, "The Predicative Participle in Biblical Hebrew", *ZAH* 2 (1989) 128–159; idem, "Biblical Hebrew *w^eqāṭal* and Syriac *hwā qāṭel* Expressing Repetition in the Past", *ZAH* 5 (1992) 1–14.

[5] Cf. Benveniste's studies on de Saussure and his linguistic theories, conveniently accessible in E. Benveniste, *Problèmes de linguistique générale 1*, Paris: Gallimard, 1966, 3–17; 18–31; 32–45.

[6] Reprinted in Benveniste, *Problèmes*, 1966, 237–250.

one for discursive texts. Historical texts, typically formulated in the third person, employ the *passé simple, imparfait* and *plus-que-parfait*, while discursive texts, where the three persons may be freely used, have a verbal system consisting of the *présent, futur* and *passé composé.* Readers familiar with Harald Weinrich's *Tempus* will readily recognize here the outline of the theory developed in that work, which was first published in 1964.[7] This may raise some interesting questions with regard to the history of research.[8] The important point, however, is to show that Benveniste was aware of linguistic realities beyond the level of the sentence.

In 1962, at the ninth International Congress of Linguists, Benveniste read a paper entitled "Les niveaux de l'analyse linguistique" (the levels of linguistic analysis).[9] In this study, he enumerates the following levels: at the lowest level we find the "merisms" or traits—such as voiced/unvoiced etc.—which make up the phoneme; then comes the phoneme, then the word (with the morpheme as an intermediate level between phoneme and word), and finally the sentence (with the word-group as an intermediate between the word and the sentence). The relevance of this analysis lies in the fact that linguistic elements do not only entertain relations with elements of the same level—the phoneme [b] being opposed to the phoneme [p], etc.—but also with elements of the lower and the higher levels: words are *composed* of phonemes, while they are *integrated* into sentences, and so on. A central observation of Benveniste's is that while the *form* of a linguistic element is determined by its relation to lower-level elements, its *meaning* is determined by its relation to higher-level elements. The phonemes [l] and [r] differ formally by the phonological traits which make them up (liquid versus vibrant, dental versus velar etc.); but in order to decide that they are meaningfully opposed within a given language system, one needs to have recourse to the higher level of the word, through the principle of minimal pairs for instance. Pairs like [long]—[wrong] establish the phonemic status of the opposition between [l] and [r] in the English language system, while the absence of such pairs from Kinyarwanda, for example, show the two sounds to be

[7] H. Weinrich, *Tempus. Besprochene und erzählte Welt*, Stuttgart: Kohlhammer, 1964[1], 1985[4].

[8] In the third edition of 1977, 224–226, Weinrich refers to Benveniste's article; I have not been able to check whether this reference was already contained in the first edition of *Tempus.*

[9] Reprinted in Benveniste, *Problèmes*, 1966, 119–131.

mere allophones within that language. Let us consider a second example: a word like [samedi] in French. If we break it up into the lower-level elements of which it is composed—the phonemes [s], [a], [m], [d] and [i]—this will lead to a purely formal analysis: the phonemes do not express any part of the meaning of the word; no property of the single phonemes could have led us to predict that their combination would mean "saturday". The meaning of the word [samedi], on the other hand, is defined in relation to units of a higher level. The meaning of the word is its capacity to be integrated into sentences like: *je viendrai samedi, le samedi je ne travaille pas*, etc. The implication of this view is *not* that a word has no meaning in and of itself. [samedi] does have such a meaning: [samedi] is not the same as [vendredi] or as [télévision]; but the meaning of the word is determined in regard to elements of a higher level.

Benveniste's reflections are of capital importance for structuralist linguistic theory. The theory of linguistic levels is an indispensable complement to de Saussure's celebrated axioms: the distinction of the synchronic and the diachronic approach, the sign composed of *signifiant* and *signifié*, the syntagmatic and paradigmatic relations among linguistic signs. For our purposes, however, we need to expand the theory a little bit beyond the bounds imposed upon it by its author. For Benveniste, the highest attainable level is the sentence: the sentence can be decomposed into words, but it cannot be integrated into a unit of a higher level. This seems arbitrary,[10] and also, in view of his reflections on the French verbal system, somewhat inconsistent. I see no obstacle to saying that sentences themselves are integrated into linguistic units of a higher level, which are texts.[11] The dichotomy between form and meaning as defined by Benveniste would certainly apply on this level: the "meaning" of a sentence is defined in function of the texts into which it can be integrated, in the same way as the meaning of the word [samedi] is defined in function of the sentences within which it can occur. Although a sentence like "Can you mow the lawn?" has a fairly definite meaning of and by itself, that meaning can be inflected in different ways depending on the context in which it is uttered. "Can you mow the lawn?" could mean "Please do mow the lawn" when said by a mother to her teenage son, for instance;

[10] See, however, the arguments of Benveniste, *Problèmes*, 129.

[11] "Integrated" does not mean that they are necessarily combined with other sentences (although this is usually the case): just as one phoneme can make up a word—the phoneme [u] is French *où*, "where?" etc.—so one sentence can make up a text.

or it could mean "Are you able to mow the lawn now that you have a bionic arm?" in a conversation between disabled ex-servicemen.[12]

So let us recapitulate the main levels of linguistic analysis, with particular attention to the question of meaning, which is the one that will occupy us further on:

— Phonemes have phonemic meaning, which becomes operative on the level of the word, for instance in order to distinguish between [long] and [wrong].
— Words have lexical meaning—i.e. the type of meaning one can find in a unilingual dictionary—which is meant to function on the level of the sentence.
— Sentences have predicational, or propositional, meaning; they serve to state that something "is". The meaning of the predication is achieved on the level of the text.
— The text itself, finally, has referential meaning;[13] it should be viewed as an element of human communication, and it is on that higher level that it receives its meaning. This, however, leads us out of the domain of linguistics into questions of psychology and sociology, a trail which need not be pursued here.

Because of the dialectic between form and meaning in Benveniste's description, there can be no direct relation between elements of non-contiguous levels: phonemes do not function on the level of the sentence, for instance. In spite of some seeming exceptions—such as the play on sound in poetry, or the characterization of certain texts as vulgar by the use of items of vocabulary—I think that principle is sound. Phonemes have no direct relationship to lexical meaning, nor words to predicational meaning: it is that principle, and it alone, which allows a language like South-American Spanish, with twenty-one phonemes, to generate a hundred thousand words, an infinite amount of sentences, and texts as abundant and multifarious as human experience itself.[14]

---

[12] The "textual" meaning of a sentence here includes what is called illocutionary meaning in Speech Act theory, whereas the "propositional" meaning is the locutionary meaning. The example is taken from E. Closs Traugott and M.L. Pratt, *Linguistics for Students of Literature*, New York: Jovanovich, 1980, 236.

[13] This does not imply that there is a concrete reference to extratextual reality: poetry and imaginative prose are text types without such specific reference.

[14] In other words, the theory of linguistic levels is an expansion of the concept of "double articulation", cf. J. Lyons, *Introduction to Theoretical Linguistics*, Cambridge: CUP, 1968, 54.

The implication for our subject is clear: since verb forms belong to the class of words (or word groups),[15] their primary function is operative on the level of the sentence—and not of the text. It is, therefore, theoretically untenable to ascribe text-linguistic functions to verb forms as such. Text-linguistic functions should be attributed to the elements of which the text is immediately composed—and which represent the contiguous level—namely sentences (or clauses). One might object that verb forms, at least in Biblical Hebrew, are themselves predicational; a word like צמאתי "I'm thirsty" can make up a complete sentence.[16] But there is no escaping the fact that Biblical Hebrew sentences usually involve more than just a verb form; indeed, the variety of sentence structure is provided by a configuration involving the verb form and other constituents: VSO, SVO etc. Sentences, not words, are the building blocks of which texts are made up. It is the meaning of the sentences contained in it that will provide the "form" of the text.

Let us consider one specific example, in anticipation of what will be said further on in section 3 of this paper. In Biblical Hebrew narrative, the opposition between foreground and background—an opposition which will be well-known to most of you—is operative on the level of the text. It is a device providing, through the distinction of what is essential to the storyline and what is not, for easier processing of the discourse.[17] Theoretically, therefore, we may not, if we follow Benveniste, affirm that that opposition is expressed by verb forms as such (*wayyiqtol* versus *qatal*, for instance). Rather the distinction between foreground and background is expressed by different *types of clause*: foreground by clauses with a verb form in first position, background by clauses which have other elements preceding the verb.

Thus a clause like וארם יצאו גדודים "the Aramaeans went out in

[15] Although it shows appreciable complexity, the theory of linguistic levels outlined above is very far from being complete. One of its insufficiencies becomes manifest when we address the question of the function of verb forms. A word—the notion *is* vague—not only has a lexical meaning, it also has a grammatical form, expressive of a function which interacts with the lexical meaning. How the internal complexity of the meaning of a word relates to the inferior and superior levels is left undecided in Benveniste's model. See the discussion in F. Rundgren, *Integrated Morphemics. A Short Outline of a Theory of Morphemics* (Acta Societatis Linguisticae Upsaliensis, Nova Series 3:1) Uppsala: Almqvist & Wiksell, 1976. Rundgren shows awareness of the problem, but his solution is hard to grasp.

[16] Even so, I think we should distinguish between צמאתי as a verb form and צמאתי as a sentence: just as one phoneme can make up a word, one word can make up a sentence (cf. above, note 10).

[17] Cf. Buth, *Word Order*, 1987, 52.

bands" (2 Kgs. 5:2), is characterized as a background clause by its word order (*waw*—subject—verb). What is expressed by the verb form יצאו, however, is left open in this analysis.

2. *The Biblical Hebrew verbal paradigm: the indicative system*

So let us turn now to the question of the function of the Biblical Hebrew verb on the level of the individual forms. Within the paradigm of the Biblical Hebrew verb, what is expressed by the different forms? Before making a specific proposal, a few general remarks—but not too general[18]—are in order.

The traditional quest for the meaning of the Biblical Hebrew verb forms has, for all its fruitfulness, notoriously fallen short of providing a satisfactory solution to the problem. This failure is not, in my opinion, due to some "higher" principle's eluding the perspicacity of researchers.[19] Rather, two fundamental errors have marred almost all treatments of the subject. Firstly, the supposition has been that the central opposition of the verbal system is that between *qatal* and *yiqtol* (or between *qatal/wayyiqtol* versus *yiqtol/w^{e}qatal*).[20] In view of the formation of these forms, *qatal-ta* versus *ti-qtol*, this opposition seems obvious; and historically, it is very likely that the Biblical Hebrew system grew out of a system where the suffix conjugation and the prefix conjugation did make out the main opposition. However, in a synchronic approach this opposition should not play any role whatever, for Biblical Hebrew *yiqtol*—in its regular, long from—is basically a modal form.[21] Biblical Hebrew *yiqtol* is not a form expressing the present-future, nor

---

[18] Prolegomena which could not be made because of time constraints notably include the following: a) Structuralist methodology is taken for granted: language is a system where signification is effected through the opposition of formal signs; for an application of this methodology to problems of verbal functions cf. R. Jakobson, "Zur Struktur des russischen Verbums", in R. Jakobson, *Form und Sinn*, München: Fink, 1974, 55–67; cf. also the works of J. Kuryłowicz and F. Rundgren. b) The *wayyiqtol* and *w^{e}qatal* forms are to be regarded as distinct morphological entities (i.e. distinct from *yiqtol* and *qatal* respectively), occupying well-defined positions within the verbal paradigm.

[19] The phrase is S.R. Driver's, *A Treatise on the Hebrew Tenses* (Oxford 1881^2), VII.

[20] For easy verification cf. L. McFall, *The Enigma of the Hebrew Verbal System* (Sheffield 1982); the more recent period, not covered by McFall, has not brought much change on this point.

[21] This was realized by B. Zuber, *Das Tempussystem des biblischen Hebräisch* (BZAW 164), Berlin: De Gruyter, 1985; nevertheless, he maintains as his central opposition *qatal/wayyiqtol* vs. *yiqtol/w^{e}qatal.*

an expression of non-completed action, nor an expression of cursive aspect. Since this is an important point, it will briefly be argued.

In Biblical Hebrew, *yiqtol* usually expresses that an action will happen in the future, that it may, should or could happen: these are modal uses. The seemingly indicative functions of *yiqtol* can on closer inspection be explained as being modal as well:[22]

a. *yiqtol* expresses the general present, e.g. הדלת תסוב על צירה "the door turns on its hinges" (Prov. 26:14).[23] In such clauses, however, the form does not express that the action is really happening, only that it is liable to happen. The use is therefore consonant with the modal function; other languages, too, may use modal verbal forms to express a similar function. Thus, in English, Prov. 26:14 could adequately be rendered: "a door will turn on its hinges".
b. *yiqtol* may express the real present in questions, e.g. מה תבקש "what are you looking for?" (Gen. 37:15). In my opinion, these cases are the vanishing traces of an historically earlier use of the prefix conjugation,[24] preserved here in a closed syntagm.[25] However, when pressed, one could simply say that even in these examples, the action is not entirely "real": it is questioned.[26]

In light of all this, *yiqtol* should be pulled out of the indicative system and set on one side, together with the other modal verb forms of Biblical Hebrew: the imperative, the jussive, the cohortative, and *w^{e}qatal*.[27] These forms constitute a modal subsystem opposed *en bloc* to the indicative system.[28]

---

[22] The justification for doing so is the massive predominance of the modal use of *yiqtol*. If the functions discussed here (a and b) were much more frequent, we might explain the form as indicative with a modal secondary function, as is done by DeCaen, *Placement*, 1995 (cf. note 29).

[23] Also habitual present, e.g. Num. 12:8.

[24] Cf. Joosten, "Predicative Participle", 1989, 156–157.

[25] Cf., for example, the preservation of the preterite function of the short form of the prefix conjugation in Arabic *lam yaqtul* "he did not kill" (otherwise this preterite function has totally vanished from the language). For Biblical Hebrew we may point to the function of *yiqtol* (long form) expressing past action following the particle אז. For אז preceding *yiqtol* cf. F. Rundgren, "Erneuerung des Verbalaspekts im Semitischen" (Acta Universitatis Upsaliensis, Acta Societatis Linguisticae Upsaliensis, Nova Series 3:1) Uppsala, 1963, 49–108, in part. 88f.

[26] Martin Baasten, in an oral communication, has pointed out to me that questions employing *yiqtol* often tolerate a modal translation: Gen. 37:15 could be rendered "What might you be looking for?"—whereas in Gen. 37:16 (את אחי אנכי מבקש) a modal rendering would be unacceptable ("I might be looking for my brothers").

[27] *W^{e}qatal* is basically modal, cf. J. Joosten, "Biblical Hebrew", 1992, 1–14.

[28] Cf. Zuber, *Tempussystem*, 1985.

The second flaw hampering almost all approaches to the Biblical Hebrew verbal system is that the participle is not given its rightful place.[29] The participle, it is true, is not a conjugated verbal form like *qatal* and *yiqtol*, which contain in one form an expression of the predicate and the subject. The difference, however, between periphrastic אני קוטל and synthetic אקטול is not relevant with regard to the morphosyntactic status of these forms;[30] the difference is not more serious than that between the *passé composé* ("j'ai tué") and the *présent* ("je tue"), both of which are considered to be part of the French verbal paradigm. When combined with an explicit subject, whether pronominal or nominal, the Biblical Hebrew participle is indeed capable of expressing verbal functions. More than that: at least one important verbal function, the expression of the real present,[31] can only be expressed by means of the predicative participle.[32] The predicative participle should therefore be viewed as an integral part of the verbal paradigm. Indeed, it should be considered one of the pillars of the indicative subsystem in Biblical Hebrew.

So, how is the indicative subsystem—comprising the predicative participle, but excluding *yiqtol*, *w^eqatal* and other modal forms—structured? The following proposal is based mainly on the syntax of prose texts from the books of Genesis–2 Kings.

[29] Cf. the axiomatic statement in J. Hoftijzer, "A Preliminary Remark on the Study of the Verbal System in Classical Hebrew", in A.S. Kaye, ed., *Semitic Studies in Honor of Wolf Leslau*, Wiesbaden: Harrassowitz, 1991, 645–651. The neglect of the participle is perpetuated even by some scholars who show awareness of its importance, cf., e.g., M. Eskhult, *Studies*, 1989, 24–25, n. 28. Scholars who do treat the participle as a member of the verbal paradigm are R. Bartelmus, *HYH. Bedeutung und Funktion eines hebräischen* "Allerweltswortes"—*zugleich ein Beitrag zur Frage des hebräischen Tempussystems*, St. Ottilien: EOS, 1982; D. Cohen, *La phrase nominale et l'évolution du système verbal en sémitique*, Louvain: Peeters, 1984, 298–328; V.J.J. DeCaen, *On the Placement and Interpretation of the Verb in Standard Biblical Hebrew Prose*, Ph.D. diss., Toronto 1995.

[30] Cf. in general G. Goldenberg, "Verbal Category and the Hebrew Verb", in M. Bar-Asher (ed.), *Language Studies* 1, Jerusalem: Magnes, 1985, 295–348, in part. 316–318; and with regard to Biblical Hebrew V. De Caen, "Ewald and Driver on Biblical 'Aspect': Anteriority and the Orientalist Framework", *ZAH* 9 (1996), 129–151, in part. 137.

[31] I.e. the representation of an action as really going on at the moment of speaking.

[32] It is often stated that this is Mishnaic Hebrew usage, the first traces of which can be found in Biblical Hebrew in direct speech. Against this: a. the usage is a regular one in Biblical Hebrew (although *yiqtol* is still regular in some functions expressed by the participle in Mishnaic Hebrew); b. the concentration of cases in direct speech is not amazing, for it is only in direct speech that the representation of an action as really going on at the moment of speaking is likely to occur.

The forms we will have to structure are *wayyiqtol, qatal* and the predicative participle.[33] It seems that the most economical hypothesis involves recognizing three successive oppositions.[34]

a. *wayyiqtol* versus *qatal* and participle

Wayyiqtol expresses contemporaneity with a moment in the past, while both *qatal* and the participle take the moment of speaking—the present—as their point of reference. In main clauses, a *wayyiqtol* form usually expresses that an action happened at a moment of the past, whereas both *qatal* and the participle represent actions from the point of view of the present.

b. *qatal* versus participle

Within the sphere of the present, *qatal* expresses anteriority to, while the predicative participle expresses contemporaneity with, the moment of speaking. In main clauses, *qatal* designates an action as having taken place before the moment of speaking, while the participle presents the action as taking place at the moment of speaking.

c. Subject-participle versus participle-subject

Although both sequences involving the participle and its subject express contemporaneity with the moment of speaking, they do not do so in the same way: whereas the sequence subject-participle represents an action as actually going on at the moment of speaking, participle-subject represents the action as a fact.

It is obviously impossible, within the limits of the present paper, to argue each of these oppositions in detail. All that can be done is make some observations and refer to other studies.

a. In and of itself, *wayyiqtol* does not express the same function as *qatal*. This fact is well illustrated by the by now famous examples collected by H.J. Polotsky,[35] e.g.:

---

[33] These are merely the main tense forms: a full description should take account of the periphrastic tenses (*haya qotel* and *wayhi qotel*) and of indicative *wᵉqatal*. There are also some anomalous cases of *yiqtol* referring to past action: Gen. 37:7; Deut. 2:12; Judg. 2:1; 1 Kgs. 7:8; 20:33; 21:6; 2 Kgs. 8:29 = 9:5; etc. For *yiqtol* with אז see above, note 25.

[34] For oppositions a and b, cf. J. Kuryłowicz, "Verbal Aspect in Semitic", *Orientalia* 42 (1973) 114–120.

[35] Cf. H.J. Polotsky, "A Note on the Sequential Verb-Form in Ramesside Egyptian and in Biblical Hebrew", in S. Israelit-Groll (ed.), *Pharaonic Egypt, the Bible and Christianity*, Jerusalem: Magnes, 1985, 157–161. More examples can be found in A. Niccacci, *The Syntax of the Verb in Classical Hebrew Prose* (JSOTS 86), Sheffield: Sheffield Academic Press, 1990, 42–43.

2 Sam. 12:26 **וַיִּלָּחֶם** יוֹאָב בְּרַבַּת בְּנֵי עַמּוֹן **וַיִּלְכֹּד** אֶת־עִיר הַמְּלוּכָה

Now Joab fought against Rabbah of the Ammonites, and took the royal city.

2 Sam. 12:27 וַיֹּאמֶר **נִלְחַמְתִּי** בְרַבָּה גַּם־**לָכַדְתִּי** אֶת־עִיר הַמָּיִם

And (Joab) said: "I have fought against Rabbah; moreover, I have taken the city of waters".

The actions recounted in 2 Sam. 12:26 are characterized as belonging to a more or less distant past not directly connected to the time of the speaker, i.e. the narrator. In the imbedded direct speech in 2 Sam. 12:27, on the other hand, the actions are characterized as relating directly to the time of speaking, i.e. the time of Joab and his King.

It has to be admitted, however, that *qatal* occurs very often in contexts where we would expect a verb form expressing contemporaneity with the past, e.g.:

Gen. 1:5 וַיִּקְרָא אֱלֹהִים לָאוֹר יוֹם וְלַחֹשֶׁךְ **קָרָא** לָיְלָה

God called the light Day, and the darkness he called Night.

Here, as very often, *qatal* is met with in a context firmly characterized as narrative; it would be futile to argue that the second clause is more directly related to the time of the narrator than the first.

Conversely, *wayyiqtol* often occurs in a context where we would expect a verb form expressing relation to the present, e.g.:

Jdg. 18:4 כָּזֹה וְכָזֶה עָשָׂה לִי מִיכָה **וַיִּשְׂכְּרֵנִי** **וָאֱהִי**־לוֹ לְכֹהֵן

Thus and thus has Micah dealt with me, he has hired me and I have become his priest.

This partial promiscuity of *wayyiqtol* and *qatal* can be explained in different ways. Two important factors may be mentioned here: firstly, neither of these verb forms is entirely free with regard to position in the clause: *wayyiqtol* is notoriously incapable of occupying any but the first position in its clause,[36] while *qatal* may have been avoided in first position following copulative *waw*, for fear of confusion with modal

---

[36] The ubiquity of *wayyiqtol* in Biblical Hebrew should not obscure the fact that the form is a syntactic fossile (cf. H. Bauer), the endangered last trace of a more regular use of the short form of the prefix conjugation to express the preterite—a use attested by Ugaritic and by archaic Biblical Hebrew texts like Deuteronomy 32.

w^e^qatal.[37] These constraints certainly contributed to the use of *qatal* as a surrogate for *wayyiqtol* and vice versa. Secondly, and more fundamentally, the functions of *wayyiqtol* and *qatal*, although distinct, are very close: the past is anterior to the present, and what is anterior to the present is, indeed, past. This is not merely a common-sense consideration; linguistically too, the two functions are quite close, as is shown by a) the general propensity of forms expressing anteriority to the present—such as the French *passé composé*, or the Aramaic *qṭīl leh* form—to take over functions of the form expressing contemporaneity with the past;[38] b) the fact that many languages, among them Classical Syriac and Latin, get by with one verb form for expressing both functions.

b. If it be accepted that *qatal* expresses anteriority with regard to the moment of speaking, the opposition between *qatal* expressing anteriority and the predicative participle expressing contemporaneity with the moment of speaking will readily be recognized.[39] In main clauses in direct speech this opposition is observed consistently, e.g.:

1 Sam. 24:15 אַחֲרֵי מִי יָצָא מֶלֶךְ יִשְׂרָאֵל אַחֲרֵי מִי אַתָּה רֹדֵף

After whom *has* the king of Israel *come out*? After whom *do you pursue*?

A possible objection to describing the opposition in these terms is that *qatal* too can express contemporaneity; notably with stative verbs (e.g. קטנתי "I'm small"), with verbs expressing an activity of the inner person (ידעתי "I know") and in performative expressions such as הגדתי "I hereby declare".[40] This subsidiary problem can be solved if we postulate for *qatal* a "post-terminal" meaning:[41] what is represented as anterior to the moment of speaking is not the entire action expressed by the verb, but its significant "term", which, with stative

[37] Cf. F.I. Andersen, "Salience, Implicature, Ambiguity, and Redundancy in Clause-Clause Relationships in Biblical Hebrew", in R.D. Bergen, ed., *Biblical Hebrew and Discourse Linguistics*, Winona Lake: Eisenbrauns, 1994, 99–116, in part. 101.

[38] Cf. G. Goldenberg, "Aramaic Perfects", *IOS* 12 (1992) 113–137, in part. 113–114.

[39] Of course, the participle with expressed subject, just like the English simple present or the French *présent*, may relate actions which belong, objectively, to the past or to the future, but the action is grammatically represented as contemporary with the moment of speaking. For a conspectus of functions of the predicative participle see Joosten, "Predicative Participle", 1989.

[40] Some of these expressions, like הרימתי ידי "I lift up my hand", are not strictly performative. Cf. D.R. Hillers, "Some Performative Utterances in the Bible", in D.P. Wright et al. (eds.), *Pomegranates and Golden Bells, Fs J. Milgrom*, Winona Lake: Eisenbrauns, 1995, 757–766.

[41] Cf. F. Rundgren, *Das althebräische Verbum*, 1961, 56–65.

verbs is the initial one: ידעתי does not mean "I have known (but have now forgotten)", but "I have come to knowledge, I know".[42] Latin perfects like *novi* "I know" and *memini* "I remember" spring to mind as an analogy.[43] The post-terminal function would also explain the performative *qatal* forms, e.g. נתתי "I give": with the utterance, the main component of the action is past.

Both *qatal* and the predicative participle exert a secondary function in circumstantial clauses of the type: *waw*—subject—verb form. In circumstantial clauses, the point of reference of these forms is not the moment of speaking, but the time frame expressed by the main clause. Thus, in narrative, the temporal value of the structure *waw*—subject—*qatal* is that of anteriority with regard to the main verb (usually *wayyiqtol*);[44] a sentence like:

2 Sam. 3:36 וְכָל־הָעָם הִכִּירוּ וַיִּיטַב בְּעֵינֵיהֶם

must be literally translated "and all the people *having taken notice*, were pleased".[45] The temporal value of *waw*—subject—participle, on the other hand, is contemporaneity with the action expressed by the main verb.[46]

c. With regard to the last opposition, that between the sequences subject-participle and participle-subject I will simply refer to my article in the *Zeitschrift für Althebraistik* of 1989, where detailed analysis is offered. The opposition is not central to the system as a whole, nor its demonstration essential to the present argument.

---

[42] This view does not imply that, e.g., קטנתי connotes the meaning "I have become small". The focus is not on the term as such, but on the state which ensues.

[43] Cf. also English examples like: "I've lived in the States for forty years (and I still do)", O. Jespersen, *Essentials of English Grammar*, London: Allen & Unwin, 1933, 245. Compare also French "il l'a mérité" which is more or less synonymous with "il le mérite".

[44] An illustration of the difference in temporal value between *qatal* in the circumstantial clause and *wayyiqtol* in the main clause is the following. Two successive *wayyiqtol* forms can describe the same action, as is illustrated by the formula ויען ויאמר "he answered saying" (occurring some 130 times according to BDB). We don't even once find *והוא ענה ויאמר, however. As it seems, this construction is impossible because it would imply that the answering precedes the saying. In Gen. 19:5 ויקראו אל לוט ויאמרו לו means: "they shouted at Lot saying . . ."—the two verbs refer to the same action; but 2 Kgs. 9:1 ואלישע הנביא קרא לאחד הנבאים ויאמר לו means "And Elisha the prophet, *having summoned* one of the sons of the prophets, said to him . . ."—the shouting precedes the saying.

[45] This has been verified only for cases where the circumstantial clause precedes the main clause.

[46] Cf., e.g., 2 Sam. 6:13; 14:13. The same opposition has been observed in relative clauses: *qatal* generally expresses anteriority with regard to the main clause, the partici-

When it is seen in these terms, the Biblical Hebrew tense system reveals a certain measure of structural similarity to other verbal systems. One could say, very roughly, that the predicative participle, *qatal*, and *wayyiqtol* stand in the same relationship to one another as the Modern German Präsens "ich gehe", Perfekt "ich bin gegangen", and Imperfekt "ich ging", with the important qualification that German has only one verb form for expressing contemporaneity with the present whereas Biblical Hebrew has two (the sequences subject-participle and participle-subject). Let us quickly cast an eye on some other indicative systems. Hellenistic Greek and literary French are structurally similar to Biblical Hebrew as well, as shown by the diagram. However, whereas Biblical Hebrew has just one form expressing contemporaneity with a moment of the past, Greek and French have two: one expressing the cursive, the other the punctual aspect. The comparison indicates that *wayyiqtol* is aspectually neutral: not being opposed to a form expressing cursivity, it does not express punctuality. The appreciable number of cases where *wayyiqtol* is translated by the Greek imperfect in the Septuagint lend empirical support to this point.[47] Latin and Syriac have just one principal form for the expression of anteriority to the moment of speaking and contemporaneity with a moment of the past, a circumstance already alluded to above; both languages, however, maintain a form expressing durative aspect in the past. Modern Hebrew, finally, and other languages, like Classical Ethiopic and Swiss German, make do with only two indicative verb forms: one expressing the present and the other the non-present (i.e. past).[48]

The point of these comparisons is not to show that the Biblical Hebrew verbal system is, after all, quite simple. On no point is there a one to one correspondence between a Biblical Hebrew verb form and any verb form in another language: the similarity is strictly limited to the structural level. The precise organisation of each system remains an object of grammatical analysis. Moreover, grammatical tense—in whichever language—is itself a very complicated phenomenon, deeply rooted in human consciousness; a description of its essence could

ple contemporaneity with regard to the main clause, cf. W. Gross, "Das nicht substantivierte Partizip als Prädikat im Relativsatz hebräischen Prosa", *JNSL* 4 (1975) 23–47.

[47] See, e.g., Gen. 7:18; 19:3,5,9,15; 25:22; 26:21; 27:41; 30:39; Ruth 1:7.

[48] Comparisons of this kind illustrate the importance of a structural approach: verb forms exert functions, not by dint of a kind of tagging—"this means that"—but as members of a system dividing among them all the psychologically relevant meanings.

Diagram 1

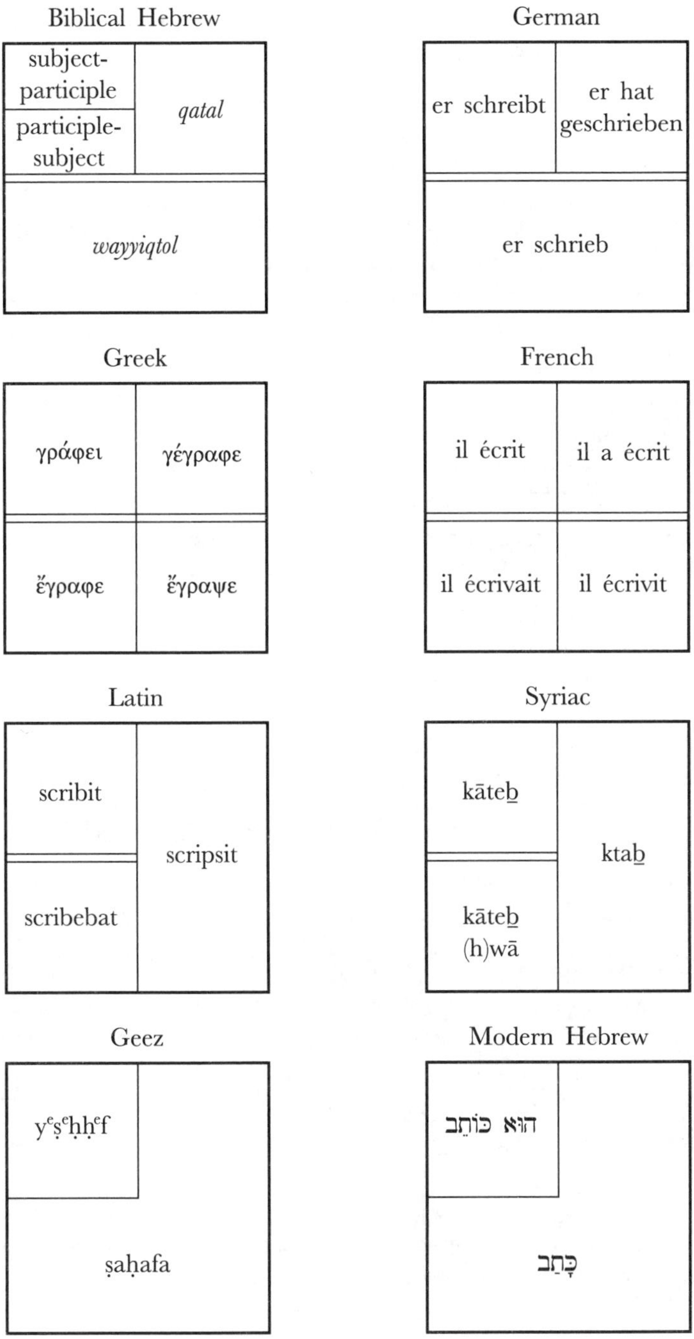
Biblical Hebrew
subject-participle
participle-subject
qatal
wayyiqtol
German
er schreibt
er hat geschrieben
er schrieb
Greek
γράφει
γέγραφε
ἔγραφε
ἔγραψε
French
il écrit
il a écrit
il écrivait
il écrivit
Latin
scribit
scribebat
scripsit
Syriac
kāteb̲
kāteb̲ (h)wā
ktab̲
Geez
y^{e}ṣ^{e}ḥḥ^{e}f
ṣaḥafa
Modern Hebrew
הוּא כּוֹתֵב
כָּתַב

only be obtained by the help of psychology. I do think, however, that it is healthy practice, when studying the Biblical Hebrew verbal system, to keep an eye on other verbal systems and on general linguistic theory concerning what functions they are likely to express.[49]

3. *Text-linguistic functions and the verb forms*

The view of the Biblical Hebrew verb that has been very rapidly sketched in the preceding section is quite amenable to text-linguistic elaboration of the Weinrichian-Niccaccian kind. To mention only one point, *wayyiqtol*'s function of expressing contemporaneity with a moment in the past makes it the natural candidate for leading tense in narrative, while *qatal*'s reference to the moment of speaking eminently qualifies it for use in discursive texts. Nevertheless, it would be false to say that it is only a question of which type of labels to attach to the different forms. There are important advantages in maintaining the distinction between the modal/temporal/aspectual function inherent to the verb form as such, and the text-linguistic function exerted by the form within specific clause types.

To begin with, the distinction of the two levels makes it easier to explain the fact that all the verb forms of Biblical Hebrew are used in more than one text-linguistic function. *Wayyiqtol*, for instance, is used to express the main line of events in narrative; but the form also occurs in digressions from the main line, e.g.:

1 Sam. 28:3 וּשְׁמוּאֵל מֵת **וַיִּסְפְּדוּ**־לוֹ כָּל־יִשְׂרָאֵל **וַיִּקְבְּרֻהוּ** בָרָמָה וּבְעִירוֹ . . .

Now Samuel had died, and all Israel had mourned for him and buried him in Ramah, his own city . . .

And it is used even in discourse, as was seen in Judg. 18:4 quoted above. Niccacci calls this the "continuative" *wayyiqtol* and implies that the clauses in question are to be regarded as subordinate clauses.[50] As a theoretical explanation, however, this is awkward, for it amounts to saying that although *wayyiqtol* inherently expresses a text-linguistic function, it sometimes manages to lose that function entirely and to

---

[49] See now the dissertation of V. DeCaen (above, note 29), where the Biblical Hebrew verbal system is emphatically studied within the framework of language typology and "universal grammar".

[50] Niccacci, *Syntax*, 1990, 176–180.

express something different altogether. I think it is preferable to ascribe to *wayyiqtol* the function of expressing actions contemporary with a moment of the past, and to say that, with that basic temporal function, *wayyiqtol* could be deployed in several text-linguistic functions, one of which is that of leading tense in narrative.

Secondly, the approach here advocated allows for greater precision in the description of the verb forms' functioning in the text. Thus I would quite agree that a clause of the type *waw*—subject—*qatal* in narrative (e.g. in 2 Kgs. 5:2, quoted above) expresses off-the-line, background, material. But there is also a temporal component to a clause of this type: the *qatal* form expresses anteriority with regard to the main clause. Whereas the "background" function is expressed by the clause structure, the nuance of "anteriority" is expressed by the verb form. If *qatal* were replaced with the participle, the background function would remain, but the temporal ordering would change.

Thirdly, and most fundamentally, the approach here proposed will force us, when analysing text-linguistic functions, to pay attention to clause structure. The verb form by itself does not express text-linguistic functions: it is the clause, with the verb form as its nucleus, which expresses these. What is called for is an analysis of Hebrew clause structure from a text-linguistic perspective.[51] The distinction between verb-initial and non verb-initial clauses is a first step in the right direction,[52] but much greater precision is called for: is the element preceding the verb form the subject, or another constituent? What is the function of different particles and conjunctions? And what about post-verbal word order?[53] The prospective fruitfulness of this undertaking may be illustrated by a final example. The sequence subject-participle has the temporal/aspectual function of expressing the cursive present, i.e. it represents actions as actually going on at the moment of speaking. Now this sequence has some important functions in narrative texts. The most conspicuous of these is the one already alluded to above, in circumstantial clauses, e.g.:

1 Sam. 18:10 וַיְהִי מִמָּחֳרָת וַתִּצְלַח רוּחַ אֱלֹהִים רָעָה אֶל־שָׁאוּל
וַיִּתְנַבֵּא בְתוֹךְ־הַבַּיִת וְדָוִד מְנַגֵּן בְּיָדוֹ כְּיוֹם בְּיוֹם

[51] Cf. the treatment of Biblical Aramaic in Buth, *Word Order*, 1987, and the contribution of E. Talstra to the present volume.

[52] This distinction plays an important part in the treatments of Niccacci and Eskhult.

[53] Cf. L. Lode, "Postverbal Word Order in Biblical Hebrew. Structure and Function", *Semitics* 9 (1984) 113–164.

And on the morrow an evil spirit from God rushed upon Saul, and he raved within his house, *while David was playing* the lyre, as he did day by day.

In this type of clause, the predicative participle depicts the circumstances attending the main events of the story: the action is concomitant, and it is backgrounded.[54]

The sequence subject-participle also has another function in narrative texts, however, namely that of the "historic present". In this use, the narrator presents an event from his story as if it were actually happening "now", in his own present time.[55] The historic present is especially likely to occur at important moments of the story, e.g.:

Judg. 11:34 וַיָּבֹא יִפְתָּח הַמִּצְפָּה אֶל־בֵּיתוֹ וְהִנֵּה **בִתּוֹ יֹצֵאת** לִקְרָאתוֹ בְּתֻפִּים וּבִמְחֹלוֹת

Then Jephthah came to his home at Mizpah; and behold, *his daughter is coming out to meet him* with timbrels and with dances. . . .

Here the action expressed by the participle is not really concomitant; more importantly, it is not backgrounded. On the contrary, it represents one of the most dramatic events in the whole story of Jephthah.

Now the temporal/aspectual value of the predicative participle in either construction—concomitance in the first, historic present in the second—can, I believe, be readily derived from its main function of expressing the actual present. However, the various text-linguistic functions—background in the first conctruction, highlighted foreground in the second—do not relate directly to the verbal form. They are, rather, to be connected to the different clause structures represented:[56] *waw*—subject—participle for the circumstantial clause, *waw*—הנה—subject—participle for the historic present.[57] The text-linguistic functions are not inherent to the verb form, but to the clause structure within which the verb form is incorporated.

[54] In some cases, the circumstantial clause communicates information absolutely central to the narrative, e.g. 2 Sam. 11:1; Jonah 1:5 (an example I owe to E. Eynikel); cf. the contribution of E. van Wolde to this volume. In these cases, there is a contrast between what is expressed grammatically and what is meant, a contrast that may be exploited for reasons of irony, for instance (cf. M. Sternberg).

[55] Cf. Joosten, "Predicative Participle", 1989, 142–144.

[56] The difference does not lie in the mere particle הנה, for the temporal value of the sequence subject-particple, too, changes. Rather, the particle is the formal mark differentiating the two structures.

[57] A full description would also take into account the syntactic environment in which each structure is likely to appear.

4. *Conclusions*

Having come to the end of my paper, I am fully conscious that the views put forth here raise as many problems as they pretend to solve, or maybe more. A detailed analysis of the verbal system, even one limited to the level of the individual forms, could not be offered within the time at my disposal; probably, only a book could do full justice to the subject at hand. Let me try briefly to recapitulate some points which I do hope I have been able to put across. Firstly, the theory of linguistic levels, developed from Saussurian linguistics, provides a framework within which the morphosyntactic and the text-linguistic approaches can be assigned their rightful places: they are not rivals, but complementary theories dealing with distinct levels of linguistic analysis. Whereas morphosyntax properly studies the function of individual forms—viewed, of course, as a system—the task of text-linguistics is to define the function of clauses within the larger edifice of the text; admittedly, within these clauses, the verb will usually constitute the main, and sometimes the only, element.

Secondly, existing morphosyntactic analyses of the Biblical Hebrew verb, based as they are on the opposition *qatal* versus *yiqtol* (or on *qatal* and *wayyiqtol* versus *yiqtol* and *w^{e}qatal*), are not satisfactory. Central questions remain to be debated, at least some of which will not be solved on the level of discourse analysis. The present enthusiasm for the text-linguistic approach, in as far as it neglects morphosyntactic research, has all the characteristics of a *fuite en avant*. A satisfying treatment of the Biblical Hebrew verb will be one that combines accurate analysis of the function of the individual forms with attention to the different ways these functions are exploited on the level of the text.

Thirdly, the combination of the morphosyntactic and the text-linguistic approaches is not a cumbersome and over-complicated enterprise: on the contrary, the analysis of the verb forms in terms of tense and aspect naturally links up with discourse functions such as narration versus discussion. Moreover, the added theoretical complexity accommodates differentiated analysis of what is after all—who would deny it?—a complex reality.

References

Andersen, F.I., "Salience, Implicature, Ambiguity and Redundancy", in: Bergen, R.D. (ed.), *Biblical Hebrew and Discourse Linguistics*, Winona Lake (Ind.): Eisenbrauns, 1994, 99–116.

Bartelmus, R., *HYH. Bedeutung und Funktion eines hebräischen* "Allerweltswortes"—*zugleich ein Beitrag zur Frage des hebräischen Tempussystems* (Arbeiten zu Text und Sprache im Alten Testament 17), St. Ottilien: EOS, 1982.

Benveniste, E., *Problèmes de linguistique générale*, Paris: Gallimard, 1966.

Blass, F., Debrunner, A. & Rehkopf, F., *Grammatik des neutestamentlichen Griechisch*, Göttingen: Vandenhoeck & Ruprecht, 1990.

Buth, R., *Word Order in Aramaic from the Perspectives of Functional Grammar and Discourse Analysis*, Ph.D. diss., Los Angeles, 1987.

Closs Traugott, E. & Pratt, M.L., *Linguistics for Students of Literature*, New York: Jovanovich, 1980.

Cohen, D., *La phrase nominale et l'évolution du système verbal en sémitique. Etudes de syntaxe historique*, Leuven: Peeters, 1984.

DeCaen, V., *On the Placement and Interpretation of the Verbs in Standard Biblical Hebrew Prose*, Ph.D. diss., University of Toronto, 1995.

———, "Ewald and Driver on Biblical Hebrew 'Aspect': Anteriority and the Orientalist Framework", *Zeitschrift für Althebraistik* 9 (1996) 129–151.

Driver, S.R., *A Treatise on the Use of the Tenses in Hebrew and some Other Syntactical Questions*, Oxford: Clarendon, 1892[3] (reprint 1969).

Eskhult, M., *Studies in Verbal Aspect and Narrative Technique in Biblical Hebrew Prose* (Acta Universitatis Upsaliensis, Studia Semitica Upsaliensia 12), Uppsala: Almqvist & Wiksell, 1990.

Goldenberg, G., "Verbal Category and the Hebrew Verb". In: Bar-Asher, M. (ed.), *Language Studies*, Jerusalem: Magnes, 1985, 295–348.

———, "Aramaic Perfects", in: *Israel Oriental Studies* 12 (1992) 113–137.

Gross, W., "Das nicht substantivierte Partizip als Prädikat im Relativsatz hebräischen Prosa", *Journal of Northwest Semitic Languages* 4 (1975) 23–47.

Hillers, D.R., "Some Performative Utterances in the Bible", in: Wright, D.P. et al. (eds.) *Pomegranates and Golden Bells, Fs J. Milgrom*, Winona Lake (Ind.): Eisenbrauns, 1995, 757–766.

Hoftijzer, J., "A Preliminary Remark on the Study of the Verbal System in Classical Hebrew", in: Kaye, A.S., *Semitic Studies in Honour of Wolf Leslau*, Wiesbaden: Harrassowitz, 1991, 645–651.

Jakobson, R., "Zur Struktur des Russischen Verbums", in: Jakobson, R., *Form und Sinn. Sprachwissenschaftliche Betrachtungen*, München: Fink, 1974, 55–67.

Jespersen, O., *Essentials of English Grammar*, London: Allen & Unwin, 1933.

Joosten, J., "The Predicative Participle in Biblical Hebrew", *Zeitschrift für Althebraistik* 2 (1989) 128–159.

———, "Biblical Hebrew *wᵉqāṭal* and Syriac *hwā qāṭel* Expressing Repetition in the Past", *Zeitschrift für Althebraistik* 5 (1992) 1–14.

Kuryłowicz, J., "Verbal Aspect in Semitic", *Orientalia* 42 (1973) 114–120.

Lode, L., "Postverbal Word Order in Biblical Hebrew. Structure and Function", *Semitics* 9 (1984) 113–164.

Longacre, R.E., "*weqatal* Forms in Biblical Hebrew Prose: A Discourse-modular Approach", in: Bergen, R.D. (ed.), *Biblical Hebrew and Discourse Linguistics*, Winona Lake (Ind.): Eisenbrauns, 1994, 50–99.

Lyons, J., *Introduction to Theoretical Linguistics*, Cambridge: Cambridge University Press, 1968.

MacKay, K.L., "Repeated Action, the Potential and Reality in Ancient Greek", *Antichthon* 15 (1981) 36–46.

McFall, L., *The Enigma of the Hebrew Verbal System; Solutions from Ewald to the Present Day*, Sheffield: Almond, 1982.
Niccacci, A., "A Neglected Point of Hebrew Syntax: Yiqtol and Position in the Sentence", *Liber Annuus* 37 (1987) 7–19.
———, *The Syntax of the Verb in Classical Hebrew Prose* (Journal for the Study of the Old Testament, Supplement Series 86), Sheffield: Sheffield Academic Press, 1990.
———, "On the Hebrew Verbal System", in: Bergen, R.D. (ed.), *Biblical Hebrew and Discourse Linguistics*, Winona Lake (Ind.): Eisenbrauns, 1994, 117–137.
Polotsky, H.J., "The Coptic Conjugation System", *Orientalia* 29 (1960) 392–422.
———, "A Note on the Sequential Verb-form in Ramesside Egyptian and in Biblical Hebrew", in: Israelit-Groll, S. (ed.), *Pharaonic Egypt, the Bible and Christianity*, Jerusalem: Magnes, 1985, 157–161.
Revell, E.J., "The System of the Verb in Standard Biblical Prose", *Hebrew Union College Annual* 60 (1989) 1–37.
Rundgren, F., *Das althebräische Verbum*, Uppsala: Almqvist & Wiksell, 1961.
———, *Erneuerung des Verbalaspekts im Semitischen: funktionell-diachronische Studien zur semitischen Verblehre* (Acta Societatis Linguisticae Upsaliensis, Nova Series 1:3), Uppsala: Almqvist & Wiksell, 1963.
———, *Integrated Morphemics. A Short Outline of a Theory of Morphemics* (Acta Societatis Linguisticae Upsaliensis, Nova Series 3:1), Uppsala: Almqvist & Wiksell, 1976.
Schneider, W., *Grammatik des Biblischen Hebräisch. Völlig neue Bearbeitung der* "Hebräischen Grammatik für den akademischen Unterricht" *von Oskar Grether*, München: Claudius, 1974.
Weinrich, H., *Tempus: Besprochene und erzählte Welt*, Stuttgart: Kohlhammer, 1964[1], 1985[4].
Zuber, B., *Das Tempussystem des biblischen Hebräisch* (Beiheft zur Zeitschrift für die alttestamentliche Wissenschaft 164), Berlin: De Gruyter, 1986.

WORKSHOP: MEANING AND USE OF THE TENSES IN 1 SAMUEL 1

Jan Joosten
(Strasbourg)

1. *The verb forms in 1 Samuel 1: an overview*

In order to show—very roughly—how the theory outlined in my paper could be applied to Hebrew texts, a brief overview will be given of the use of the tenses in 1 Samuel 1. In doing this it will be necessary to distinguish the narrative proper from the embedded direct discourse, not because narrative and discourse use different verb forms, but because they exploit them in different ways. As I will argue below, such difference in usage does not contradict basic identity of meaning in the verb forms.

1.1 *The use of verb forms in the narrative*

Within the narrative, we again need to separate the exposition—the setting of the scene, so to say—from the narration of the sequence of events.

1.1.1 *The exposition (v. 1–7)*

The relatively long exposition in verses 1–7 serves to acquaint us with Elqanah and his family and, less emphatically, with Eli and his sons, and to describe what used to happen among Elqanah's family whenever they went up to Shiloh for the annual sacrifice.

On the grammatical level the exposition is characterized by nominal clauses on the one hand, by a mix of *w^e^qatal* and *yiqtol* on the other hand. As very often in narrative, *w^e^qatal* and *yiqtol* here express habitual action:[1]

[1] As will be explained below, I consider the frequentative function of these verb forms a regular extension of their basic, modal, function.

v. 3 ועלה . . . and that man would go up from his city every year . . .
v. 4 ונתן . . . and he would give portions to Peninnah . . .
v. 5 יתן . . . but to Hannah he would give a special (?) portion . . .
v. 6 וכעסתה . . . and her rival would provoke her . . .
v. 7 יעשה . . . and thus it would go every year . . .
תכעסנה . . . every time she would provoke her . . .
תאכל . . . and she would not eat . . .

In this passage, *yiqtol* and *w^eqatal* have the same, or very nearly the same, function. The selection of either form depends strictly on the word order: if any element is to be placed before the verb, *yiqtol* is used, otherwise the clause begins with *w^eqatal*. The element preceding the verb may be a particle (כן, לא), or a constituent to which a certain emphasis is to be imparted (חנה in v. 5, because of the opposition: Peninnah-Hannah).

Apart from the frequentative pair, we encounter several other verb forms. Thus there are three cases of *qatal* (v. 5, 5, 6), expressing an antecedent fact: YHWH had closed the womb of Hannah; or an antecedent state: Elqanah loved Hannah. Finally we find two cases of *wayyiqtol*, one in v. 2, where ויהי continues a series of nominal clauses, and one in v. 7 where the form continues the description of what used to happen every year: Peninnah would provoke, and Hannah would cry. The best explanation of the *wayyiqtol* form in v. 7 is to say that although it is not marked for frequentativity—it merely expresses that the action occurred in the past—it does relate an action that took place habitually; its frequentative meaning derives entirely from the context.

The *wayyiqtol* forms in v. 4 stand on a different level. The expression ויהי היום indicates that what is related here is not something that happened every year, but a single event happening "one day". I therefore take v. 4a as the beginning of the narrative, a kind of "false start": having begun to recount what happened on the precise day when Hannah prayed for a child, the narrator is then reminded, as it were, that he hasn't yet provided all the necessary background—and launches into another series of frequentatives. If this analysis is acceptable, then we should probably suppose that the "false start" is a calculated step in the narrative strategy of the author: he introduces a break in the long exposition, in order not to loose the attention of his audience.

1.1.2 *The action (v. 8–28)*

The main line of events is expressed by a series of *wayyiqtol* forms, as is usual Biblical Hebrew narrative. In addition, several other verb forms are used.

Thus we find *qatal*, both in its main function of expressing anteriority (here anteriority to the time frame of the narrative):

v. 24 גמלתו (she took him up with her) when she had weaned him . . .

and in its function of surrogate for *wayyiqtol*, i.e. expressing contemporaneity with the time-frame of the narrative:

v. 22a עלתה . . . but Hannah did not go up . . .

In clauses like the one in v. 22a, the use of *qatal* is due to the word order. The opposition between Hannah and the rest of the family led to emphasis on Hannah and hence to the order subject-verb (on top of this the verb is negated). Since *wayyiqtol* cannot occupy any other than the first position in the clause, *qatal* is selected as a stand-in. The temporal/aspectual meaning of *wayyiqtol* and of *qatal* in this specific use is, unless I err, identical.[2]

The case of indicative *w^{e}qatal* in v. 12 poses a problem: והיה here seems to be more or less synonymous with ויהי. The traditional solution to this problem seems to me to be the preferable one: indicative *w^{e}qatal* should simply be analysed as *waw* + indicative *qatal*. The solution is not elegant, because it postulates a case of grammatical "homonymy"—two forms which are superficially identical but express different meanings—but it is linguistically feasible.[3]

Next there are two cases of *yiqtol*. The occurrence in v. 13 must be interpreted as a modal form: וקולה לא ישמע "but her voice *could not be heard*". This accords with the analysis of *yiqtol* proposed in my paper. In v. 10, however, the interpretation of the form is more problematic:

v. 10b וַתִּתְפַּלֵּל עַל־יְהוָה וּבָכֹה תִבְכֶּה

---

[2] Whether *qatal* in v. 12, 22b expresses anteriority or contemporaneity I do not know. A decision on that point would require careful analysis of the syntactic environment and comparison with similar cases. However, for the purposes of the theory it is only required that *qatal* express either of these functions, which seems to be a reasonable proposition.

[3] Cf. F.I. Andersen, "Salience, Implicature, Ambiguity, and Redundancy in Clause-Clause Relationships in Biblical Hebrew", in R.D. Bergen (ed.), *Biblical Hebrew and Discourse Linguistics*, Winona Lake: Eisenbraums, 1994, 99–116, in part. 100–102. For a similar case of grammatical homonymy, in Coptic, cf. H.J. Polotsky, "The Coptic Conjugation System", *Orientalia* 29 (1960) 392–422, on 398.

Three interpretations could be thought of: a) The easiest way is to take the *yiqtol* as a frequentative "she used to cry"; in this case the form could be due to a kind of overflow from the exposition. However, since we are, in v. 10, well into the narrative proper I consider this explanation unlikely. b) We could take the *yiqtol* as an expression of the imperfective aspect: "she prayed to YHWH while she was crying". Although it is contextually feasible, I reject this interpretation because it is contrary to the general use of *yiqtol*. c) A solution in keeping both with the context and with the modal function of *yiqtol* is to interpret the form as a prospective: "she was about to cry".[4] The prospective use of *yiqtol* in narrative is fairly usual in relative clauses.[5] A case syntactically somewhat similar to ours is 2 Sam. 15:37:

וַיָּבֹא חוּשַׁי רֵעֶה דָוִד הָעִיר וְאַבְשָׁלֹם **יָבֹא** יְרוּשָׁלָֽם

> So Hushai, David's friend, came into the city, just as Absalom *was about to enter* Jerusalem.[6]

The parallels for the prospective interpretation are, admittedly, rather few (due, I would say, to the limits of the corpus of Biblical Hebrew).

The sequence subject-participle occurs in two distinct functions. In v. 9 and 12 it is found in circumstantial clauses, where it expresses backgrounded actions contemporary with the time frame of the narrative.

> v. 9 ועלי הכהן ישב . . . (Hannah rose) while Eli, the priest, was sitting beside the doorpost . . .

> v. 12 ועלי שמר . . . (Hannah prayed) while Eli watched her mouth . . .

The circumstantial clause should be analysed as a type of subordinate clause. It brings the function of the sequence subject-participle (i.e. the expression of an action as ongoing at the moment of speaking) into the time frame of the main clause.

The participles in v. 13aαβ fall in a different class:

> v. 13 וְחַנָּה הִיא מְדַבֶּרֶת עַל־לִבָּהּ רַק שְׂפָתֶיהָ נָּעוֹת . . .

[4] The tautological infinitive is no obstacle to this interpretation if we submit that it expresses contrast rather than emphasis—as, e.g., in 2 Sam. 24:24 קנו אקנה "I will *buy* it from you (not receive it as a gift)"—cf. GKC § 113p. In this case we could consider a translation like "she prayed to YHWH but crying she was about to cry"; or somewhat more freely: "she prayed to YHWH but her tears almost wouldn't let her".

[5] See, e.g., Judg. 17:8; 1 Kgs. 7:7, 8; 2 Kgs. 3:27; 13:14; Ps. 78:6.

[6] See also Num. 7:9; Jer. 52:7 (but cf. Jer. 39:4); and maybe Ex. 8:20; Isa. 6:4.

The personal pronoun set between the subject and the participle in the first clause shows that this is not a circumstantial clause (which would have been expressed as ותנה מדברת or והיא מדברת). In an earlier article I proposed to view it as a historic present: "And Hannah, she is speaking in her heart, only her lips are moving, but her voice cannot be heard".[7] This interpretation takes account of the dramatic importance of these clauses within the sequence of events recounted in v. 9–18. Moreover, a contextual justification may be found in v. 12: after having stated that Eli watches Hannah's mouth, the story then glides into the present tense describing, as it were, the events as they were perceived by Eli.[8]

1.2 *The use of verb forms in direct speech*

There is no "leading tense" for Biblical Hebrew direct discourse as there is for Biblical Hebrew narrative. Of course, in any given speech a specific verb form may dominate. The speeches in 1 Samuel 1 are all rather short, so that the domination of one or other verb form does not mean much.

In one passage, *yiqtol* is used to express the real present, in questions:

v. 8 לָמֶה תִבְכִּי וְלָמֶה לֹא תֹאכְלִי וְלָמֶה יֵרַע לְבָבֵךְ

why are you crying, and why do you not eat, and why are you sad?

Cases like these present a problem if one wants to analyse *yiqtol* (the long form of the prefix conjugation) as a modal form. The key to a solution for this problem may be found in the fact that *yiqtol* expresses the real present in questions only.[9] Perhaps one could say that questions are inherently modal or, to the least, susceptible of a modal interpretation; one could translate v. 8—without doing too much violence to Elqanah's intended meaning or to the English language—as "why should you be crying . . .?"[10] From a different point of view, one could

[7] Cf. J. Joosten, "The Predicative Participle in Biblical Hebrew", *ZAH* 2 (1989) 128–159, in part. 144.

[8] On the visual character of historic present in Biblical Hebrew, cf. Joosten, "Predicative Participle", 1989, 142–144.

[9] See, e.g., Gen. 16:18; 32:18; Ex. 3:3; Josh. 9:8; Judg. 17:9; 19:17; 1 Sam. 11:5; 2 Sam. 1:3; 19:30; Isa. 3:15; Jona 1:8; Job 2:2. Some exceptions may be found in poetry: Num. 23:9; Ps. 29:8–9.

[10] In the question in v. 14 the *yiqtol* form certainly is modal: "How long *will* you be drunk?"

say that this use of *yiqtol* perpetuates an historically earlier, indicative function of the prefix conjugation (long form). It has often been observed that set phrases, or fixed types of expressions—among which questions introduced by למה, מה etc. could possibly be reckoned—may in certain cases preserve archaic forms or meanings long after they have disappeared from the language in general.

The other cases of *yiqtol* in direct discourse in 1 Samuel 1 clearly are modal. Just as the frequentative *yiqtol* in v. 3–7, modal *yiqtol* functions side by side with *w^eqatal*.

v. 11 אִם־רָאֹה תִרְאֶה... וּזְכַרְתַּנִי וְלֹא־תִשְׁכַּח... וְנָתַתָּה... וּנְתַתִּיו...
וּמוֹרָה לֹא־יַעֲלֶה

> If you look (*yiqtol*) on my affliction, and remember (*w^eqatal*) me and do not forget (*yiqtol*) me, and give (*w^eqatal*) me a son, then I will give (*w^eqatal*) him to YHWH and no razor shall touch (*yiqtol*) his head.

Both in the protasis and the apodosis of this conditional sentence *yiqtol* and *w^eqatal* intermingle.

v. 22 עַד יִגָּמֵל... וַהֲבִאֹתִיו... וְנִרְאָה... וְיָשַׁב...

> until he be weaned, and I will bring him up, and he will appear before YHWH and remain there for ever.

Again, the principle of selection is simply one of position in the clause. Where the verb form occupies the first place in the clause, *w^eqatal* occurs, if any other element precedes the verb form, we find *yiqtol* (cf. above in 1.1.1). No semantic distinction seems to be expressed by the variation between these two verb forms.

Semantically, the modal pair *x-yiqtol/w^eqatal* is opposed to a series of verb forms making up a second "tier" within the modal subsystem of the Biblical Hebrew verb: the cohortative (not attested in 1 Samuel 1), the *imperative*, the *jussive* and אל + *jussive*. These occur in v. 14b, 16a, 17abα(?), 18a, 23. Even where the jussive is not formally differentiated from normal *yiqtol*, it can often be identified by the position it occupies in the clause: unlike *yiqtol* (long form), the jussive can, and usually does, occur in first position.[11] Thus in v. 18 תמצא שפחתך חן בעיניך we may interpret the verb form as jussive because it heads the clause: "may your maid-servant find grace in your eyes".

[11] Cf. A. Niccacci, "A Neglected Point of Hebrew Syntax: Yiqtol and Position in the Sentence", *Liber Annuus* 37 (1987) 7–19.

The precise functional difference between *x-yiqtol* and *wᵉqatal* on the one hand and the jussive and consorts on the other hand is difficult to determine. In an earlier publication I have tentatively proposed to define the function of the first tier as "extrinsic modality" (the action is viewed as not being subject to human control) and that of the second tier as "intrinsic modality" (the action is viewed as in some way subject to human control).[12] Concretely, something of the difference may be apprehended by a comparison between Hannah's speech in v. 22 ("I will bring him up etc.") and Elqanah's speech in v. 23 (". . . may YHWH establish his word . . .").

Qatal is used to express anteriority with regard to the moment of speaking in v. 15, 16, 17, 20, 27a, 27b.[13] In two passages such a *qatal* form is followed by a *wayyiqtol* form expressing the same, or very nearly the same, meaning:

v. 15 אִשָּׁה קְשַׁת־רוּחַ אָנֹכִי וְיַיִן וְשֵׁכָר לֹא שָׁתִיתִי וָאֶשְׁפֹּךְ אֶת־נַפְשִׁי לִפְנֵי יְהוָה

I am an obstinate (?) woman, and I have drunk neither wine nor strong drink, but I have poured out my soul before YHWH.

v. 27 אֶל־הַנַּעַר הַזֶּה הִתְפַּלָּלְתִּי וַיִּתֵּן יְהוָה לִי אֶת־שְׁאֵלָתִי

For this child I prayed, and YHWH has granted me my petition.

Since Biblical Hebrew allows the use of indicative *wᵉqatal* in similar syntactic situations (e.g. 1 Sam. 10:2 והנה נטש אביך את דברי האתנות ודאג לכם "and now your father has ceased to care about the asses and worries about you"), we may ask what nuance could be expressed here by *wayyiqtol*.

In v. 28 we find *qatal* in a performative expression:

v. 28 וְגַם אָנֹכִי הִשְׁאִלְתִּהוּ לַיהוָה and I in turn lend him to YHWH

The "lending" of Samuel to YHWH is effected through the enunciation of this phrase. In this type of expression, Biblical Hebrew usually employs *qatal*.

1 Samuel 1 contains no examples of the sequence subject-participle expressing the real present. This lack is due, it seems, to the simple fact that no expression of the real present was needed in this text (except in questions, where *yiqtol* could be used, see above).

---

[12] Cf. J. Joosten, "Biblical Hebrew *wᵉqāṭal* and Syriac *hwā qāṭel* Expressing Repetition in the Past", *ZAH* 5 (1992) 1–14, in part. 13.

[13] In v. 28, היה seems to be the result of a scribal accident (cf. BHS).

2. *Morphosyntax and text linguistics*

The overview of the use of the tenses in 1 Samuel 1 given above in section 1 serves to show that the theory outlined in my paper can fruitfully be applied to a Biblical Hebrew text. The second section will attempt to demonstrate that the theory is more powerful than an approach from text linguistics alone.

2.1 *Thesis*

A verb form as such—meaning: a verb form as one element in a verbal paradigm—expresses an abstract function which should be described in terms of tense, aspect and modality. With this basic, "morphological" function, the verb form can be deployed in several "text-linguistic" or discourse functions.

These discourse functions are not to be played down: they are real, and they should be described in a grammatical treatment of Biblical Hebrew. From the point of view of the individual verb forms, however, discourse functions are secondary, contextual applications of a more basic temporal, aspectual or modal function.

Discourse functions are not inherent to the verb form, but to the clauses within which the verb form is incorporated.

2.2 *Illustrations from 1 Samuel 1*

From a text-linguistic perspective, the Hebrew verb forms are characterized by a certain degree of polysemy. Every verb form has several contextual uses.

2.2.1 ויהי

What I mean can be illustrated from the occurrences of ויהי in our chapter. The form occurs in verses 1, 2, 4, 20. In v. 1, it introduces the narrative unit—a very frequent usage in Biblical Hebrew. In v. 4 and in v. 20 it functions on the level of the main line of action: in v. 4 it introduces the events that happened on the specific day when Elqanah brought his sacrifice (even though the narration of those specific events is then suspended for another 3 and a half verses), in v. 20 it introduces the resolution of the first half of the narrative: the birth of a son to Hannah. The usage in v. 4 and 20 could possibly be brought together with that in v. 1 in one and the same category, although one would have to allow for different nuances.

The occurrence in v. 2, however, definitely falls into a different category:

> וְלוֹ שְׁתֵּי נָשִׁים שֵׁם אַחַת חַנָּה וְשֵׁם הַשֵּׁנִית פְּנִנָּה וַיְהִי לִפְנִנָּה יְלָדִים וּלְחַנָּה אֵין יְלָדִים
>
> He had two wives, the name of the one was Hannah, and the name of the other Peninnah. And (ויהי) Peninnah had children, but Hannah had no children.

Here ויהי is used, not in the narration of the events, but in the exposition of the circumstances. To be sure, within this context, the form does play an important part: "He had two wives . . . their names where such and such . . . and—pay attention—the one had children, the other didn't have children". The last remark is what will set the narrative in motion. Nevertheless, the verb form remains strictly on the level of the exposition: it neither expresses nor introduces an event belonging to the main line of action. Moreover, whereas ויהי on the level of the main line of events (v. 4, 20) expresses rather lower salience—i.e. it serves to introduce another event—ויהי on the level of the exposition (v. 2) seems to express higher salience.

2.2.2 wayyiqtol

What is true for ויהי is more or less true for *wayyiqtol* in general. The form has an important function in the expression of the main line of events (v. 8ff), but it also functions within the exposition. In v. 7, ותבכה continues the description of what used to happen every year.[14] Only the context can tell that *wayyiqtol* signals the beginning of the main line of action in v. 4 and 8, but continues the exposition in v. 7. The two usages are quite distinct, however: it would make a real difference for the understanding of the text if we would take the main line of action to set in with v. 7b ותבכה.

This "contextual polysemy", which is as characteristic of *wayyiqtol* as of the other verb forms, can be described by text linguistics; indeed: it can be adequately described by text linguistics only. What text linguistics cannot do, however, is to bring about an understanding of the phenomenon and to provide a satisfactory explanation of it. In order to understand why *wayyiqtol* can express the functions discussed above (and several others), but cannot express the real present,[15] for

---

[14] This is a regular function of *wayyiqtol*, cf., e.g., Judg. 6:4–5.

[15] The one possible example, 2 Sam. 19:2, should be explained otherwise. The

instance, one needs to turn to morphosyntax. The basic meaning of *wayyiqtol*, namely the expression of actions as belonging to a moment of the past, may lead to its being used to express the main line of events, or to continue an exposition of circumstances; it is incompatible, however, with the expression of the real present.

The contextual polysemy of verb forms may be compared to the contextual polysemy of words (in any language).[16] In 1 Sam. 1:15, the Hebrew word אשה means "woman", but in v. 2 it means "wife". In cases like these, and the examples could be multiplied without end, we should not, I think, say that the word in question has two meanings ("woman" and "wife"): it has one basic meaning, which can be inflected in different ways according to the context within which it occurs. A verbal category such as *wayyiqtol* functions, *mutatis mutandis*, in the same way: it has a basic meaning in and of itself, which meaning may be inflected in different ways according to the context within which the form occurs.

2.2.3 w^eqatal

The inflection of the basic—temporal/aspectual/modal—function of the verb form can be demonstrated for all the different forms of Biblical Hebrew. The most striking instance is that of *w^eqatal*. 1 Samuel 1 provides some interesting examples. In direct speech, *w^eqatal* usually[17] expresses actions which have not been performed yet, and which are subjected to obligation, potentiality, prediction, commitment etc. (see above, section 1.2). On the other hand, in past tense contexts, and most notably in narrative, *w^eqatal* usually[18] expresses repeated action (see above, section 1.1.1).

In an earlier publication, I have argued that the frequentative function of *w^eqatal* is a regular extension of its modal function. The basic function of this verb form is the expression of actions as "not real": i.e. as neither really occurring, nor really having occurred. From this

---

most attractive proposal is that of E.J. Revell, "The System of the Verb in Standard Biblical Prose", *HUCA* 60 (1989) 1–37, in part. 9: "(ויתאבל) . . . could, in fact, begin the following narrative. (19:2) 'Joab was told "The King is weeping"—and he (the king) mourned. . . .'"

[16] This idea was suggested to me by Jack Collins of St. Louis, Missouri, in a letter.

[17] Not always: the form may have a frequentative function in direct speech: 1 Sam. 17:34f.; Am. 4:7.

[18] But cf. 2 Sam. 17:17 and Am. 7:4, where *w^eqatal* seems to express the prospective in a past tense context. Cf. above at notes 5 and 6.

basic function, *w^eqatal* could be exploited to express obligation, prediction etc., but also, in past-tense contexts, actions that were liable to happen, that *would happen*. Of course, Elqanah really did go up every year, but what is expressed by ועלה (v. 3) is merely that one might expect him to do so. The logic of this explanation may seem strange; but it remains a fact that various languages use modal verb forms to express repeated action in the past: English ("he would go up every year . . ."); Greek: the iterative use of the optative in subordinate clauses,[19] the iterative use of ἄν with aorist (or imperfect) indicative in main clauses;[20] Latin: the iterative use of the subjunctive of the imperfect or pluperfect in subordinate clauses;[21] Syriac: the use of the modal form *hwā qāṭel* to express repetition in the past;[22] and other languages.[23]

On the level of text linguistics the remarkable polysemy of *w^eqatal* can be observed; explaining the phenomenon is possible only by the help of morphosyntax.

---

[19] E.g. Xenophon, *Anabasis*, I. 5, 2: καὶ οἱ μὲν ὄνοι, ἐπεί τις διώκοι, προδραμόντες ἕστασαν "Now those asses, when someone would pursue them they ran away and stood still". In Hellenistic Greek the iterative in subordinate clauses is instead expressed by ἄν with the aorist or imperfect indicative, cf. F. Blass, A. Debrunner, F. Rehkopf, *Grammatik des neutestamentlichen Griechisch* (Göttingen 1990[17]), § 367. As is stated here, n. 1, "Das klass. Iterativpräteritum mit ἄν im *Hauptsatz* ist nur zufällig ähnlich und fehlt im NT wie überhaupt in der einfachen Koine". This "accidental" similarity between the classical and the Hellenistic syntax shows that modal forms have a potential for expressing iterativity in a past tense context.

[20] E.g. Aristophanes, *Frogs* 911ff: πρώτιστα μὲν γὰρ ἕνα τιν' ἂν καθῖσεν ἐγκαλύψας, 'Αχιλλέα τιν' ἢ Νιόβην . . . (914) . . . ὁ δὲ χορός γ' ἤρειδεν ὁρμαθοὺς ἂν μελῶν ἐφεξῆς τέτταρας ξυνεχῶς ἄν· οἱ δ' ἐσίγων "first he would set a veiled figure on the stage, an Achilles or a Niobe, . . . and the chorus would (meanwhile) be reeling off a whole string of odes—four of them without a break; but the characters remained silent". Quoted in K.L. MacKay, "Repeated Action, the Potential and Reality in Ancient Greek", *Antichthon* 15 (1981) 36–46, in part. 41.

[21] E.g. Livy 1,32,13: Id ubi fetialis dixisset, hastam in fines eorum emittebat "Having said those words (which were said at every declaration of war), the fetial threw a spear on their territory".

[22] Cf. Joosten, "Biblical Hebrew", 1992, 9–12.

[23] As can be gathered from Longacre's discussion of a phenomenon in Camsa (S. America), cf. R.E. Longacre, "Weqatal Forms in Biblical Hebrew Prose. A Discourse-modular Approach", in R.L. Bergen, ed., *Biblical Hebrew and Discourse Linguistics*, Winona Lake: Eisenbrauns, 1994, 50–98, in part 56–57.

3. *Conclusion*

Applying a theory of the Biblical Hebrew verbal system to a given text—and 1 Samuel 1 offers a particularly rich variety of verbal usages—is in a sense a humbling experience, for it makes one realise that verb forms in context express more than any theory could possibly account for. To my mind, this should not lead us to abandon theory or limit our efforts to *ad hoc* explanations of given usages. A theory is needed: one flexible enough to encompass all the facts in a tentative fashion, and simple enough to preserve some explanatory power. The theory proposed in my paper and developed somewhat in the present application was formulated with this double exigency—flexibility and simplicity—in mind.

A HIERARCHY OF CLAUSES IN BIBLICAL HEBREW NARRATIVE*

Eep Talstra
(Amsterdam)

1. *Syntactic structure: linguistic system or literary strategy?*

It is no secret that textual analysis in Biblical Studies recently has started to shift its focus from the analysis of words and sentences to the analysis of texts as linguistic compositions.[1] Both from the perspective of biblical interpretation and of linguistic research one can welcome this development. But it is also no secret that a linguistic concentration on "text" raises precisely those questions that are on the agenda of this conference: To what extent is it possible to produce a *grammatical* description of the linguistic mechanisms (the grammatical entities, their features and their relations) that are used in classical Hebrew to establish textual structures? More precisely: how special, how unique is each individual textual composition? To what extent can the linguistic structure of a text be analysed in general terms and categories that are part of the Hebrew language as a system?

Exegetical traditions tend to focus on the unique text rather than on general linguistic features. Older exegetical work expresses this tendency by a special interest in understanding the authors of a text: What did the author want to say with this particular text? More recent exegetical work expresses the same tendency by concentrating on the stylistics of a particular text or text type. What is the rhetorical power of this particular text? Usually exegetes do not pay much attention to the balance which might exist between what an author

* My thanks are due to Dr. Janet W. Dyk and to Tim Walton, for questions and comments and for correcting the English text of my paper.

[1] See, W.R. Bodine, "Introduction. Discourse Analysis of Biblical Literature: What It Is and What It Offers", in: *Discourse Analysis of Biblical Literature. What It Is and What It Offers* (SBL, Semeia Studies), Atlanta: Scholars Press, 1995, 1–20; C.H.J. van der Merwe, "Discourse Linguistics and Biblical Hebrew Grammar", in: Bergen, Robert D. (ed.), *Biblical Hebrew and Discourse Linguistics*, Winona Lake (Ind.): Eisenbrauns, 1994, 13–49; J. Lyons, *Linguistic Semantics. An Introduction*, Cambridge: Cambridge University Press, 1995, 258ff.

or a redactor may choose for the structure of a text and what the language system itself allows or forces him to do. How much of a text is system, how much is strategy?[2]

From my point of view, the task of Bible translation is the best starting point for further research in the area of syntax and text. Translators usually cannot spend too much time discussing the delicate balance between rhetorical and grammatical analysis. The effect is that translators concentrate primarily on lexical meaning and semantics. A discussion on Bible translation usually revolves around style and meaning, instead of around syntax.[3] Either one decides to produce a translation that in its syntax imitates the source language, the Hebrew original,[4] or one decides that the translation should represent a certain stylistic freedom, required by the grammatical and idiomatic features of the target language. This seems to me to be traditional practice: syntax is a matter of constructing clauses or sentences and if one were to say something about the construction of a text, it would be the domain of stylistic and rhetorical analysis. In terms of text grammar, this means that one restricts oneself to a limited set of linguistic parameters. On clause and sentence level, only verb forms and conjunctions are registered, in order to make decisions on coordination and subordination. On text level one hardly registers any syntactic regularity, except for pronominal back reference. The identification of paragraphs, episodes, etc., are regarded a matter of content, theme and coherence.

If the word "text grammar" is to mean anything at all, one has to address the question: to what extent is it possible to produce a grammatical description of the mechanisms that establish textual structures in Biblical Hebrew? Are there, therefore, more observations of the language system possible at text-level, than the information offered by verbal tenses and conjunctions?

---

[2] Cf. the recent volume edited by L.J. de Regt, J. de Waard, J.P. Fokkelman (eds.), *Literary Structure and Rhetorical Strategies in the Hebrew Bible*, Assen/Winona Lake (Ind.): Van Gorcum/Eisenbrauns, 1996.

[3] In my experience even current models of "discourse analysis" exhibit more interest in rhetorics and models of human communication than in observations of grammar and syntax. However, recently one can observe that the various lines of research are beginning to get in touch: Bodine's recently edited volume on Discourse Analysis (see note 1) has an interesting separate section on Grammar with contributions by Miller and Gropp.

[4] For reasons of introduction or exegetical debate it may still be wise to begin this way.

1.1 *An example*

To begin with a relatively simple example, Ex. 2:9–10 is a text with *wayyiqtol*-forms only. If, as in traditional, syntactic studies, one restricts oneself to observations of the verb forms and the conjunctions used, the discussion of text syntax and translation remains a dialogue on stylistic freedom. Translators feel they have to make a choice. One can either be reluctant to deviate from the syntax of the source language, therefore, choose to reproduce in the syntax of the target language an imitation of the serie of *wayyiqtols* by: "and she did", "and he did", "and she did", or one can decide that an ancient text translated into a modern, western language, requires more stylistic variation and for that reason replace the so-called *parataxis* of the source language by *hypotaxis*[5] in the target language, e.g., "When he did A, she did B" (see the two examples listed below). To demonstrate this I compare the text of Ex. 2: 9–10 in the RSV and the NEB.[6] Their texts can be seen as representives of the differing choices translators may make in the debate on syntax and stylistic freedom.

Clause hierarchy implied by RSV[7]

	Text	*Vrs*	*Ln*
So the woman took . . .	[<Su> האשה] [<Pr> תקח] [<Cj> ו] [<Ob> הילד]	09	42
and nursed him.	[<PO> תניקהו] [<Cj> ו] .	09	43
And the child grew,	[<Su> הילד] [<Pr> ינדל] [<Cj> ו]	10	44
and she brought him . . .	[<Co> לבת פרעה] [<PO> תבאהו] [<Cj> ו]	10	45
and he became her son;	[<sC> לה] [<Pr> יהי] [<Cj> ו] [<Co> לבן]	10	46
and she named him . . .	[<Ob> שמו] [<Pr> תקרא] [<Cj> ו] [<Ob> משה]	10	47
for she said,	[<Pr> תאמר] [<Cj> ו] .	10	48
Because I drew him . . .	[<Co> מן המים] [<Cj> כי] . . [<PO> משיתהו]	10	49

[5] For the terminology see, for example, R. Meyer, *Hebraische Grammatik III. Satzlehre* (Sammlung Göschen, Band 5765), Berlin: De Gruyter, 1972³, 81f., 90f.; R. Bartelmus, *Einführung in das Biblische Hebräisch. Mit einem Anhang Biblisches Aramäisch*, Zürich: Theologischer Verlag, 1994, 144, formulates better: one should study Hebrew syntax as a system of its own and leave the categories of "parataxis" and "hypotaxis" alone, since these in fact are only valid for Indo-European languages.

[6] The symbols used are: <Cj> = Conjunction <Po> = Predicate Object <Pr> = Predicate <Co> = Complement <Su> = Subject <Sc> = Supplementary Complement <Ob> = Object

[7] *The Holy Bible. Revised Standard Version*, New York, Glasgow, Toronto, 1952/1971.

Clause Hierarchy implied by NEB[8]

	Text	*Vrs*	*Ln*
So the woman took . . .	[<Su> האשה] [<Pr> תקח] [<Cj> ו] [<Ob> הילד]	09	42
and suckled him	[<PO> תניקהו] [<Cj> ו] . .	09	43
When . . . was old enough	[<Su> הילד] [<Pr> יגדל] [<Cj> ו] ↓.	10	44
she brought him . . .	[<Co> לבת פרעה] [<PO> תבאהו] [<Cj> ו]	10	45
who adopted him	[<Co> לבן] [<sC> לה] [<Pr> יהי] [<Cj> ו] .	10	46
and called him M . . .	[<Ob> שמו] [<Pr> תקרא] [<Cj> ו] . [<Ob> משה]	10	47
"*Because*", she said,	[<Pr> תאמר] [<Cj> ו] ↓. . .	10	48
I drew him out . . .	[<PO> משיתהו] [<Co> מן המים] [<Cj> כי] . .	10	49

Both translations can for the larger part be explained as an expression of a specific textual structure which the translators assumed to be in the text:

RSV: Some variation in the translation seems to be based on the requirements of the target language (see the translation of the *wayyiqtol* in line 42: "So" and of the *wayyiqtol* in line 49: "for"). Other *wayyiqtols* are translated by: "and he/she did". Paragraph structuring, signalled by the use of capitals, is apparently based on the introduction of new explicit subjects in lines 42 and 44. Other changes of subject are not marked. As a result, verse 9 is a paragraph about the "woman" and verse 10 is a paragraph about the "child".

NEB: Similar to the RSV, the *wayyiqtol* in line 42 is translated "So"; in contrast to the RSV the subordination of the *wayyiqtol* in line 44 is rendered: "When. . . ." The *wayyiqtol* in line 46 is translated as an attributive construction: "who . . ."; the כי of line 49 is put before the *wayyiqtol* of line 48. Only the two cases of *wayyiqtol* that continue the subject of the preceding clause (lines 43 and 47) are translated by "and did".

As a result, verse 9 and 10a are a paragraph about the "woman", verse 10b is a paragraph about "Pharao's daughter".

Are the differences found between these two translations just a matter of choice made between the syntax of the source language and the syntax of the target language? Is the RSV, thus, actually doing better in terms of reflecting Hebrew syntax? Is the NEB to be preferred only in terms of English syntax? Or could it also be possible

---

[8] *The New English Bible*, Oxford/Cambridge, 1961, 1971.

to argue in favour of the NEB text on the basis of the syntax of the Hebrew narrative?

The point I want to make in this contribution, is that the syntax of Hebrew narratives allows for the observation of more linguistic details, if one is ready to look for text-level patterns.[9] With this larger set of parameters, the question may be asked whether analysing textual structure is mainly a matter of stylistic skills and exegetical insights. If grammar is restricted to clause-level observations (verbal tenses and conjunctions) and if text-level analysis is taken to be only a matter of content (theme and *coherence*)[10] then the RSV version of this text is the better one. If, however, it is also possible to do grammatical analysis at text level, so that it would be able to identify syntactic signs that mark the *cohesion* and the internal hierarchy of this text, it would mean that the NEB rendering is a better representation of the text's syntactic structure, even though some features of the NEB translation clearly are adaptations to English style.

To illustrate the procedure, I present a preliminary list of "parameters" that I registered as contributors to the hierarchy and the cohesion of the sample text.

1. grammatical clause types: *wayyiqtol* (Subj); *wayyiqtol* (0) and the specific sequences observed of two clauses of these types, e.g.: *wayyiqtol* (Subj) → *wayyiqtol* (Subj); *wayyiqtol* (Subj) → *wayyiqtol* (0);
2. morphological correspondences between clause constituents in two clauses;
3. lexical correspondences between clause constituents of two clauses;
4. syntactic marking of paragraphs (*wayyiqtol*-x [x = subject, see below § 3]);
5. sets of actors in the text (indicated by verbs, proper names, nouns or pronouns).

These parameters are used in computerised procedures being developed for text-level syntactic analysis. The idea is that, when reading

[9] This is, of course, the very starting point of all text linguistics in Hebrew studies, cf. the introductory remarks on "coordination" by F.I. Andersen, *The Sentence in Biblical Hebrew*, (Janua Linguarum, Series Practica, 231), The Hague: Mouton, 1974, 61. The next step, is to experiment with parameters and procedures to establish the grammatical structure of concrete texts, rather than first producing, as Andersen did, a grammar defining the various types of clause connections assumed (<Apposition>, <Coordination>). However, the reader will understand that in experimenting with the data, for labels and categories I also make use of the work of the pioneers in this area, such as Andersen.

[10] J. Lyons, *Linguistic Semantics*, 1995, 263f.

a text clause by clause, the parameters registered can be used as arguments for clause hierarchy. Thus, the syntactic structure of a text will be built up as a result of this reading process.

The complexity of the procedure of identification lies in the fact that linguistic signs of various types are contributing to a text's structure.

For an explanation of the procedure for establishing syntactic structure, I again restrict the description to the example of Ex. 2:9–10. First, I will list what parameters are used as an argument for clause connections (a), second, I will present some details of the computer-assisted "reading" process used for establishing the syntactic structure (b), third, the resulting hierarchy of clauses (c). In the fourth place I will present the resulting paragraphs and actors, with a translation (d).

a. Parameters registered

connect lines:	*arguments*	*effect*
42	after direct speech section: *wayyiqtol* + new NP <Su>	new §
43 ← 42	= verbal tense; = pers.num.gen.; no NP <Su>; sfx ← NP <Ob>	dep.cl.; same §
44 ← 42	= verbal tense; new NP <Su>; NP <Su> ← NP <Ob>; = lex. ילד	par.cl.; new, dep. §
45 ← 42	= verbal tense; = pers.num.gen.; no NP <Su>; sfx ← NP <Ob>	dep.cl.; same §; prev. § emb.
46 ← 45	= verbal tense; VP <Pr> ← sfx <Ob>; PP <sC> ← PP <Co>	dep.cl.; new, embedded §
47 ← 46	= verbal tense; VP <Pr> ← PP <sC>; NPsfx <Ob> ← VP <Pr>	dep.cl.; new, embedded §
48 ← 47	= verbal tense; = pers.num.gen.	par. clause; same §
49 ← 48	*x-qatal* ← *wayyiqtol* (אמר); pers. 1sg ← pers.3sgfem.	direct speech section

Arguments and symbols used

PP <Co>	: *Prepositional Phrase (Complement)*	*x ← y*	: *x connects back to y*
		pers.num.gen.	: *person number gender (verb)*
PP <sC>	: *Prepositional Phrase (supplementary Complement)*	*NP <Ob>*	: *Noun Phrase (Object)*
		par.	: *parallel*
VP <Pr>	: *Verbal Phrase (Predicate)*	*§*	: *paragraph*
NP <Su>	: *Noun Phrase (Subject)*	=	: *of equal value*
lex.	: *lexeme*	*sfx.*	: *pronominal suffix*
dep.	: *dependent*		

b. Procedure: "reading" the clause hierarchy

From the arguments mentioned in section a., a textual hierarchy is constructed line by line. A line contains one clause or, in cases of embedding, a partial clause. For each clause a preceding clause is sought to which it can be matched best according to the parameters listed. If the clause to be posited in the hierarchy is not formally syntactically parallel, it will be presented with one identation added (see b. 1). If further clauses connect back to the same one, this will result in additional indentations (see b. 2 and b. 3).

b. 1

	Text	*§Nr*	*Verse*	*Ln*
	[<Ob> הילד] [<Su> האשה] [<Pr> תקח] [<Cj> ו]	§x	Ex. 2:09	42
43 ← 42	[<PO> תניקהו] [<Cj> ו] .	x	Ex. 2:09	43

b. 2

	Text	*§Nr*	*Verse*	*Ln*
	[<Ob> הילד] [<Su> האשה] [<Pr> תקח] [<Cj> ו]	§x	Ex. 2:09	42
	[<PO> תניקהו] [<Cj> ו] . .	x	Ex. 2:09	43
44 ← 42	[<Su> הילד] [<Pr> יגדל] [<Cj> ו] .	§x.1	Ex. 2:10	44

b. 3

	Text	*§Nr*	*Verse*	*Ln*
	[<Ob> הילד] [<Su> האשה] [<Pr> תקח] [<Cj> ו]	§x	Ex. 2:09	42
	[<PO> תניקהו] [<Cj> ו] . . .	x	Ex. 2:09	43
	[<Su> הילד] [<Pr> יגדל] [<Cj> ו] . .	§x.1	Ex. 2:10	44
45 ← 42	[<PO> תבאהו] [<Cj> ו] .	x	Ex. 2:10	45
	[<Co> לבת פרעה]			

One warning is appropriate here. One should not read these examples or the full textual schema's presented below as simple results of fully automated procedures. The actual version of the programme used for (re)constructing textual hierarchy proposes clause connections and paragraph divisions based on registrations and arguments as listed above. The user must evaluate and correct a number of these proposals. For example, the entire text of Ex. 2, to be presented below, consists of 119 lines (clauses), which implies: 118 possible clause connections. Of the machine-made proposals 82 were acceptable, 36 needed reconsideration. Clearly the text-grammatical research reported here will remain experimental for a long time to come. Moreover, I assume that difficulties in identifying all actors in a text and the complications of semantic or pragmatic analysis will make it virtually impossible for a computer programme ever to produce completely correct textual structures. The advantage of these procedures, however, lies in the possibilities of testing and experimenting with a larger corpus and of reaching a higher degree of consistency than is possible with other methods.

c. Clause hierarchy proposed

Text	*§Nr*	*Verse*	*Ln*
[<Ob> הילד] [<Su> האשה] [<Pr> תקח] [<Cj> ו]	§x	Ex. 2:09	42
[<PO> תניקהו] [<Cj> ו] . . .	x	Ex. 2:09	43
[<Su> הילד] [<Pr> יגדל] [<Cj> ו] . .	§x.1	Ex. 2:10	44
[<Co> לבת פרעה] [<PO> תבאהו] [<Cj> ו] .	x	Ex. 2:10	45
[<Co> לבן] [<sC> לה] [<Pr> יהי] [<Cj> ו] . .	§x.1	Ex. 2:10	46
[<Ob> שמו] [<Pr> תקרא] [<Cj> ו] . . [<Ob> משה]	§x.2	Ex. 2:10	47
[<Pr> תאמר] [<Cj> ו] . .	§x.2	Ex. 2:10	48
[<PO> משיתהו] [<Co> מן המים] [<Cj> כי] . . .	Q	Ex. 2:10	49

d. Resulting paragraphs and listing of actors

Ln	*Type*	*actor 1*	*actor 2*	*actor 3*	*lex. rep.*	*§*	*function/translation*
		"woman"	"child"	"Pharao's daughter"			
42	*way-x*	<Su> האשה	<Ob> הילד	. . .	.	§x	The woman took the child.
43	*way-0*	<Su> ↑	<Ob> sfx. הו-	. . .	.	=	and nursed it.
44	*way-x*	.	<Su> הילד	. . .	הילד	§x.1	When the child grew up
45	*way-0*	<Su> ↑	<Ob> sfx. הו-	<Co> לבת פרצה	.	§x	she brought him to . . .
46	*way-0*	.	<Su> ↑	<sC> +sfx. לה	.	§x.1	He became her son.
47	*way-0*	.	<Ob> sfx. שמו	<Su> –	.	§x.2	She named him . . .
48	*way-0*	.	.	<Su> –	.	=	and said:
49	*x-qatal*	.	<Ob> sfx. הו-	<Su> –	.	Q	"It's because I drew him . . ."

1.2 *The first results*

a. *Text-level linguistic parameters*
The example was intended to demonstrate that it is rewarding to try to register more linguistic parameters in a text than classical grammars used to do. The parameters listed do contribute to textual structure, the problem, of course, being that they are effective only in a great variety of combinations. Both grammatical and lexical parameters play their part. Therefore Weinrich[11] was right in his suggestion that one should try to find a method for reading a text as a musical score, i.e., reading combinations of several kinds of signs.

b. *Form to function*[12]
The study of narrative syntax as presented here assumes that research can begin in a descriptive way. One should start with observations of regularities in syntactic form, before categorising the linguistic data in terms of fully elaborated definitions of their textual functions. A taxonomy of simple and complex forms helps find the arguments necessary for establishing the grammatical structure of a narrative text. Better insight into text syntax will also contribute to the ongoing debate on verb forms: do they express discourse functions and/or aspect and tense?[13] In this way the study of narrative syntax will also result in more solid grounds on which to base a translation.

1.3 *The next task: testing*

After the trial run on this first example of a short text, the parameters and procedures for clause hierarchy need to be tested on larger texts. In the next sections I will present the results of this test, namely,

[11] H. Weinrich, "Die Textpartitur als heuristische Methode", in: W. Dressler (ed.), *Textlinguistik*, Darmstadt: Wissenschaftliche Buchgesellschaft, 1978, 391–412.

[12] For the term, see the introduction by van der Merwe, mentioned in note 1.

[13] See J. Joosten, "Tekstlinguistiek en het Bijbels-Hebreeuwse werkwoord: een kritische uiteenzetting", *Nederlands Theologisch Tijdschrift* 49 (1995) 265–272; cf. 271 on verb forms; 271 on clause types. He is certainly right in his emphasis that more than just the verbs contribute to the analysis of textual structure, because, in my view, this is what text grammar is or should be pursuing. I do not agree with his statement that since verb forms cannot have just one discourse function in a text, one needs to start from temporal and aspectual functions of the verbs. In my view the point is that the various functions of clauses and their verbs can not be derived from a grammatical paradigm. These functions are due to the phenomenon of recursion: the repeated construction of paragraphs and subparagraphs at various text levels.

the clause hierarchies found and the syntactic patterns used as arguments for them. The texts analysed consist of two chapters: Exodus 2 and 2 Kings 1.

Experimentation with the process of registering linguistic parameters and establishing clause hierarchies revealed that the arguments to be used represent two levels of information. One level regards the morpho-syntactic and lexical patterns one can register formally in the clauses of a text. The other level is of a higher abstraction, involving the division of a text into paragraphs and the calculation of the sets of actors in these paragraphs.

Though the actual computer procedures used combine both levels of information in making proposals for clause connections, I will, for the sake of clarity, present the further testing in two steps:

First, linguistic patterns and clause connections (§ 2).

Second, patterns of actants and the identification of paragraphs (§ 3).

2. *Linguistic patterns and clause connections*

To elaborate the parameters mentioned above in section 1.1, a full list of the grammatical and lexical patterns used to define clause connections in the sample texts Exodus 2 and 2 Kings 1 is given. The examples are taken from a broader selection: Exodus 2; 19; 24 and 2 Kings 1. For comparison or to illustrate certain complications, occasional reference is made to a text of a completely different type: Deuteronomy 6.

The reading of a text is regarded here as a process by which, among many other things, also these patterns of clause connections are recognised and applied by the human reader. Of course, the use of computer programming can only be an imitation of the process of recognition of the patterns listed. At the same time the recognition of these patterns is a necessary step in the analysis before semantic or pragmatic information can be applied. From this it may be clear that the contribution of computer programming to the textual analysis presented here is both crucial and limited.

2.1 *Patterns*

In this section I only list the linguistic patterns that have been applied to calculate the hierarchy of clauses in the sample texts. The way in which they are used has been described in section 1.2. The results of this analysis (including the analysis of paragraphs introduced in § 3) are presented with the textual schemas added to this contribution.

I. *phrase-level clause atoms*

1. Attributive clauses. Asyndetic clauses with a participle connect to the immediate preceding clause (Ex. 2:11); אשׁר-clauses connect to the immediate preceding clause (2 Kgs. 1:2);
2. Infinitive clauses connect to the immediate preceding clause (Ex. 2:3,5,15,16; 19:1; 2 Kgs. 1:3).

   Additional remark. From the analysis of other text types it becomes clear that it is insufficient to instruct a computer only according to the two patterns mentioned. More patterns exist, for example:

   — when the clause preceding the infinitive has אשׁר, direct connection is not always possible (Ex. 24:12; cf. Deut. 6:1 with Deut. 6:18)

   — when the אשׁר-clause is not attributive to a NP in the preceding clause, but is a complement to the preceding predicate (cf. Deut. 6:1 with 6:3 לעשׂות . . . אשׁר ייטב)

II. *clause types*

1. Connecting clause types. Sets of frequent connections, e.g.:
   way-x ← *way-x* (Ex. 2:2 ← 2:1; Ex. 2:5 ← 2:2); *way-0* ← *way-x* (Ex. 2:1,2);
   way-0 ← *way-0* (Ex. 2:3); *way-0* ← nominal clause (Ex. 2:16);
   way-x ← *w^{e}x-qatal* (Ex. 19:2f.,18);
   way-0 ← *w^e-לא-qatal* (Ex. 2:3); *way-x-w^e participle* (Ex. 2:5);
2. In actual practice the connection of clauses by reference to their grammatical types depends on two basic decisions:

   a. Connecting two clauses of analogous construction is preferable to other connections (cf. the examples mentioned: *way-x* ← *way-x* (Ex. 2:2 ← 2:1; Ex. 2:5 ← 2:2). Both clauses of each pair have NPdet). This regards:

   — both clauses that do and that do not begin with a conjunction;

   — clauses introducing new actants (NPdet, NP <subj>);

   — clauses that repeat lexical features (words, groups of words);

   b. Connecting a clause to a preceding clause that has a conjunction ו (Ex. 19:24 (line 107 → 105, not to 106), or אשׁר (Ex. 20:21), or infinitive construct (Ex. 19:21 and 23) is to be avoided unless one of the following is true:

— both clauses have an identical clause-opening type (i.e., from the conjunction to the verb (or nominal predicate) the clauses exhibit the same order of words/phrases [Ex. 20:4]);
— the two clauses exhibit clear lexical patterns (see below, IV,1);
— the ו is the only difference in clause-opening type.

3. Start of direct speech sections (e.g., *way-x* ← ה + *yiqtol*; Ex. 2:7).
4. Connecting parts of clauses that are separated due to embedding (Ex. 19:8).
5. Macro-syntactic signs, e.g., ועתה in direct speech section, skipping *wayyiqtols*.

III. *word-level and phrase-level information*
1. morfological correspondences:
identical person-number-gender of the verb; identical person-number-gender of suffix and verb or of suffix and noun phrase (Ex. 2:4 ← 2:3 and Ex. 2:7 ← 2:6: אחתו ← ילד; Ex. 2:16 ותבאנה ← שבע בנות; 2 Kgs. 1:3);
2. identical verb forms (Ex. 2:18 ← 2:16 (3 fem.pl.); 2 Kgs. 1:2)

IV. *lexical patterns*
1. syntactic constructions based on lexical patterns:
כי + ראה (Ex. 2:2)
מה + ידע (Ex. 2:4)
עוד (Hif.) → פן (Ex. 19:21)
לא + *yiqtol* → פן (Ex. 19:24)
In general: ה → אם; לא כן → כי אם
2. Lexical parallels contribute to or confirm the clause connections established with the help of syntactic data.
(Ex. 2:23 ← 2:11 ויהי + ...בימים; 2 Kgs. 1:4 ← 1:2 מלאכים)

V. *Paragraph marking by special clause types*
wayyiqtol-x and *wᵉx-qatal*; x = subject.
wayyiqtol with time reference (Ex. 2:11; 2:23)

2.2 *Conclusions on clause hierarchy*

The set of syntactic parameters listed here, is a preliminary one, since it only registers features of clauses. Its use allows for some preliminary conclusions. The closing statements of section 1 can be confirmed and elaborated:

— Syntactic parameters for clause connections are effective in combinations, not individually;
— The patterns listed are not static definitions of collections of clause combinations. They are to be applied in a process of reading. This not only means that they are applied in combinations, but also that they are applied recursively. A clear example is the repeated embedding of direct speech sections, as in 2 Kgs. 1:3f.,6f., or the transition from an address in direct speech to narrative speech within the same direct speech section, as in 2 Kgs. 1:6 and 7. In the next section I will state that similarly, in a narrative text, paragraphs can be embedded into paragraphs.

3. *Patterns of actants and the identification of paragraphs in narrative texts*

The process of syntactic analysis explained thus far has the capacity of producing a clause hierarchy of the sample texts; however, we have not yet attained a full text-grammatical analysis of these texts. Further experiment with the patterns mentioned in § 2 demonstrated that more text-level syntactic information is needed: we must identify the sets of actors in the text and the changes of subjects in order to remove a number of difficulties that remain after constructing the clause hierarchy of a text.

3.1 *Examples*

Compare the following segments of the text of 2 Kings 1 and the (partial) clause hierarchy made by applying the patterns mentioned in § 2. One can observe that the shorter direct speech sections in most cases are being presented correctly, e.g.:

verse 6:

[<Pr> לכו]	33	imp.	2 plM	2 Kgs. 1:06
[<Co> אל המלך] [<Pr> שובו]	34	imp.	2 plM	2 Kgs. 1:06
[<Ob> אתכם] [<Pr> שלח] [<Re> אשר] . .	35	*x-qatal*	3 sgM	2 Kgs. 1:06
[<Co> אליו] [<Pr> דברתם] [<Cj> ו] .	36	w^{e}*qatal*	2 plM	2 Kgs. 1:06
[<Su> יהוה] [<Pr> אמר] [<Mo> כה] . .	37	*0-qatal*	3 sgM	2 Kgs. 1:06

The larger narrative structures, however, still lack consistency. The sample text below reveals that this shortcoming is due to the fact that clauses with subject phrases introducing new paragraphs are not always connected properly in the schema. A more serious problem is the fact that in many cases the introduction of a new subject in narrative clauses is not explicitly marked by a determinated NP in the text. The result is a textual "structure" that is still but a simple *sequence* of paragraphs. For example, the *wᵉx-qatal* clause in line 11 and the *wayyiqtol-x* clause in line 25 are correctly connected, due to their respective clause types and the repetition of the constituent אליה. But the two *wayyiqtol-x* clauses in line 25 and line 26 should not have been connected: the suffix in אליו does not refer back to the prophet אליה (which a programme working with formal patterns is unable to detect!). The phrase המלאכים in line 26, however, does refer back to line 6 (which a programme can detect). So the programme should have connected lines 6 and 26 which as a result would have made the text of lines 11 to 25 a kind of embedded section.

A similar complication can be seen in lines 56 to 63: the subject of the *wayyiqtol* clauses is changing a number of times, without always being marked by an explicit NP in the text. I am not certain whether a programme working with formal patterns ever would be able to detect this. But clearly, the clause level parameters (pronouns, verb forms, etc.) used in § 2 are insufficient to reach a final decision on syntactic structure. One needs to keep track of the actors involved in a number of clauses. The machine will be of assistance here to some level. If it always registers where a particular actor is (re)introduced, it would at least be able to calculate what set of actors is "on stage" when "reading" the next clause. So, for instance, line 56 (verse 9) introduces two new actors into the narrative (in אליו and שׂר). For that reason the "candidates" for the subject of the next line, ויעל in line 57 (verse 9), come from a different set of actors then the "candidates" for the subject of וישׁלח in line 56. Undoubtedly there is a limit to further grammatical calculations in this area, but it is not clear exactly where. In any case these experiments are helpful in defining the set of linguistic markers and syntactic patterns that are indicative of texual hierarchy in terms of clauses and paragraphs.

"Primitive" clause hierarchy produced from clause-level patterns (§ 2)

	Ln	*ClType*	*§ marker*	*Text*
[<Su> מואב] [<Pr> יפשע] [<Cj> ו] [<Co> בישׂראל]	1	*way-x*	3 sgM	2 Kgs. 1:01
		....		
[<Su> אחזיה] [<Pr> יפל] [<Cj> ו] [<Aj> ... בעד ה]	3	*way-x*	3 sgM	2 Kgs. 1:02
		....		
[<Ob> מלאכים] [<Pr> ישלח] [<Cj> ו]	6	*way-0*	3 sgM	2 Kgs. 1:02
		....		
[<Pr> דבר] [<Su> מלאך יהוה] [<Cj> ו] [... אל אליה]	11	*w*^{e}*x-qatal*	3 sgM	2 Kgs. 1:03
		....		
[<Su> אליה] [<Pr> ילך] [<Cj> ו]	25	*way-x*	3 sgM	2 Kgs. 1:04
[<Su> המלאכים] [<Pr> ישובו] [<Cj> ו] [<Co> אליו]	26	*way-x*	3 plM	2 Kgs. 1:05
[<Co> אליהם] [<Pr> יאמר] [<Cj> ו]	27	*way-0*	3 sgM	2 Kgs. 1:05
		....		
[<Co> אלהם] [<Pr> ידבר] [<Cj> ו]	46	*way-0*	3 sgM	2 Kgs. 1:07
		....		
[<Co> אליו] [<Pr> יאמרו] [<Cj> ו]	51	*way-0*	3 plM	2 Kgs. 1:08
		....		
[<Pr> יאמר] [<Cj> ו]	54	*way-0*	3 sgM	2 Kgs. 1:08
[<Su>הוא] [<PC> אליה/התשבי]	55			2 Kgs. 1:08
[... שׂר] [<Co> אליו] [<Pr> ישלח] [<Cj> ו]	56	*way-0*	3 sgM	2 Kgs. 1:09
[<Co> אליו] [<Pr> יעל] [<Cj> ו]	57	*way-0*	3 sgM	2 Kgs. 1:09
		....		
[<Su> אליה] [<Pr> יענה] [<Cj> ו]	63	*way-x*	3 sgM	2 Kgs. 1:10

3.2 *In search of an operational definition of "paragraph"*

We consider now, how one can expand the procedures for clause hierarchy to include the identification of paragraphs and sets of actors. The distinguishing of paragraphs in a text is especially needed for the identification of "participants". For that reason it is impossible to work from a definition of "paragraph" that is based on the coherence of the set of "participants" found, since that is the goal rather than the starting point of the paragraph definition wanted. Researchers of functional grammar and discourse analysis present some definitions of what a paragraph is. Unfortunately these definitions are either somewhat vague, using words like "often" or "usually",[14] or they are

[14] Andersen, *The Sentence*, 1974, 64: "In classical Hebrew narrative prose the onset of a new paragraph is often marked by using an explicit noun subject to refer to the

actually conclusions based on content,[15] rather than on a description of linguistic features. Therefore, the definitions of paragraph found in discourse linguistics cannot be used directly in more formal procedures of text grammar, for they would allow for too many ambiguities in the analysis. Existing definitions can be used fruitfully, however, in testing the first results of a more formal grammatical analysis. So the next task is to pursue the line of formal, distributional research as far as possible[16] and to see whether some proposals in terms of pattern of actants can be dealt with by a programme. The research, therefore, concentrates on finding an "operational definition",[17] by attempting, first of all, to establish the set of linguistic markers to which a computer programme can respond in proposing the beginning of new paragraphs in the text. Up to this point in the research, two of the most important discoveries appear to be:

a. the presence or the absence of directly observable markers in the texts;
b. the phenomenon of recursion in the applications of markers.

a. *Markers*

The challenge is to work with both *direct markers* present in the text, such as an explicit noun subject in a clause, and *indirect markers* such

---

prime participant, without interrupting the sequence of WP clauses" (WP means: *wayyiqtol*, cf. 15).

[15] Lowery, 258: proposes to define the paragraph "as that group of clauses which have the same major participants".

[16] E. Talstra, "Clause Types and Textual Structure. An experiment in narrative syntax", in: E. Talstra (ed.), *Narrative and Comment. Contributions to Discourse Grammar of Biblical Hebrew, presented to Wolfgang Schneider*, Amsterdam Societes Hebraica Amstelodamenis, 1995, 166–180.

[17] K.E. Lowery, "The Theoretical Foundations of Hebrew Discourse Grammar", in: *Discourse Analysis of Biblical Literature: What It Is and What It Offers* (SBL, Semeia Studies), Atlanta: Scholars Press, 1995, 103–130, cf. 119.

My intention is to take up further discussion with grammatical research of a more functional type at a later stage. First, the experiments with a computer-assisted, distributional type of research have to be continued to the point where they will have contributed fully to the construction of a data base of the syntactically analyzed text of the Hebrew Bible. However, as my paper also demonstrates, not unlike other methods, the distributional approach exhibits a number of restrictions too. In other studies therefore, dialogue with functional approaches to text syntax has started. I refer to the chapter dedicated to Longacre's work in the dissertation by F. den Exter Blokland, *In Search of Text Syntax: Toward a Syntactic Text-Segmentation Model for Biblical Hebrew Narrative* (Applicatio 14, Amsterdam VU University Press, 1995) and to my cooperation project with Nicolai Winther-Nielsen concerning the syntax of the book of Joshua: N. Winther-Nielsen, E. Talstra, *A Computational Display of Joshua. A Computer-Assisted Analysis and Textual Interpretation* (Applicatio 13), Amsterdam: VU University Press, 1995.

as a shift in the set of actors. The fact of a shift in the set of actors can be detected on the basis of observations of forms. However, choosing which one of them might be the new subject in a clause cannot always be determined unequivocally on the basis of the forms observed. More research is needed to discover what additional regularities might be observable, or where the process of reading a text has to rely on a reader's semantic or pragmatic knowledge.

b. *Hierarchy and recursion*

A further challenge is the fact that paragraph markers can be used *recursively* with the effect that paragraphs in a text do not appear sequentially, but can be embedded in higher level paragraphs. A case of embedding results in "gapping", i.e. splitting the higher level paragraph into two or more segments.

Gapping in a paragraph of a narrative text is due to two factors:

— embedding of a narrative paragraph into another narrative paragraph;
— embedding of a direct speech section in the narrative.

From the perspective of the narrative text the direct speech section may not be a clear case of paragraph embedding since it can be analysed as a direct object to a verb of speaking. From the perspective of sequentiality (i.e. analyzing a text line by line, as a computer programme does), however, there is a real gap in the higher level paragraph. (See in the textual schema presented below, for example, the text section Ex. 2:15–19, where line 90 (verse 18) and line 95 (verse 19) continue the paragraph #4.4.1., after interruption by some embedded paragraphs or direct speech sections.)

My claim is that the contribution made by clause types and verb forms to the syntactic structure of a text is determined only preliminarily by their position in a grammatical paradigm. Ultimately it depends on the position they take in the textual hierarchy of clauses and paragraphs. Here I rely on Wolfgang Schneider's[18] implementation of Harald Weinrich's theory of tenses. What clause types and verbal tenses contribute to a text on their own accord is quite abstract. To the reader of a text, they set a small number of switches only. They decide upon "communication type" (narrative or discursive), "relief" (main line or secondary line of the communication) and "perspective" (information preceding or following the actual communication).

[18] W. Schneider, *Grammatik des Biblischen Hebräisch*, München: Claudius, 1982[5].

The actual sequence of clause types, their position in the textual hierarchy and their verb forms determine in what segment of text the setting of these switches is valid and to what situation or time a particular segment of text might refer.

As in section 2.1, I list only the patterns used to identify paragraphs and the clause hierarchy of the sample texts Exodus 2 and 2 Kings 1. The process of the application of such patterns has been shown in section 1.1. The resulting main paragraph structure and the main actors are listed in section 3.4. The full texts are presented in the textual schemas below.

3.3 *Paragraph markers in narrative texts*

I. *Clause-level markers*
1. the clause type:
   wayyiqtol-x or
   w^{e}x-qatal
   where the x is a NPdet marking the subject;
2. the clause type *wayyiqtol-0*, i.e. a *wayyiqtol* clause introducing change of subject not marked by a NPdet, but marked:
   — either by a shift in person-number-gender of the verb (Ex. 19:14,17),
   — or by a shift in the pattern of actors: Object or complement of the previous clause becomes subject of the actual clause (2 Kgs. 1:9,11,17).
3. ויהי + reference of time or place (Ex. 2:11,23);
4. ויהי + כ + infinitive construct + NPdet (subject in the infinitive clause or in the following *wayyiqtol* clause);
5. casus pendens, with a new NPdet or the renominalisation of an actor (2 Kgs. 1:18).

II. *Markers of paragraphs of equal text level*
1. The paragraphs are opened by identical clause types (both start with *wayyiqtol-x*, or with *w^{e}x-qatal*); x (subject) refers to a new actor Ex. 2:2,5).
2. the set of actants (subject + object or complement) equals the set of actants in the preceding paragraph. The roles may change, e.g.: subject → complement and the reverse (Ex. 2:7,8,10).

III. *Markers of paragraph embedding*

1. *wayyiqtol-x*: the subject (x) is new or is identical to a constituent in the clause(s) of the preceding paragraph (object or complement) (Ex. 2:4,7,10);
2. *wᵉx-qatal*: the clause types are different; the subject (x) is new or is identical to a constituent in the clause(s) of the preceding paragraph (object or complement) (2 Kgs. 1:3; Ex. 19:3);
3. *wayyiqtol-0*: the subject is lexically or grammatically identical (person, number, gender) to an actor (object or complement) in the clause(s) of the preceding paragraph (Ex. 2:10,18; 2 Kgs. 1:9,11,17).

IV. *Markers of paragraph-internal cohesion*

1. continuation of verbal tense in the main (non-dependent) clauses;
2. continuation of person-number-gender of the verb;
4. lexical repetition of subject, object or complement;
3. pronominal reference to verb, subject, object or complement.

3.4 *Exodus 2 and 2 Kings 1: resulting paragraph structures*

	§	marking: clause types and actors
Exodus 2		
verse 1	§ 1	*wayyiqtol-x* (Levite)
verse 2	§ 2	*wayyiqtol-x* (Woman; the child)
verse 4	§ 2.1	*wayyiqtol-x* (His sister: pron.ref.)
verse 5	§ 3	*wayyiqtol-x* (Pharao's daughter; the child)
verse 7	§ 3.1	*wayyiqtol-x* (His sister: pron.ref.)
verse 8	§ 3.2	*wayyiqtol-x* (Pharao's daughter; her: pron.ref.)
verse 8	§ 3.3.	*wayyiqtol-x* (the girl; the mother)
verse 9	§ 3.3.1	*wayyiqtol-x* (Pharao's daughter; her: pron.ref.)
verse 9	§ 3.3.2	*wayyiqtol-x* (woman; the child; to Pharao's daughter)
verse 10	§ 3.3.2.1	*wayyiqtol-0* (son; her: pron.ref.)
verse 11	§ 4	*wayyiqtol-x* (ויהי + time)
. . . .		
verse 23	§ 5	*wayyiqtol-x* (ויהי + time)
		A compact set of §§ is concluding the text:
verse 23	§ 5.1	*wayyiqtol-x* (מלך מצרים)
verse 23	§ 5.2	*wayyiqtol-x* (בני ישראל)
verse 23	§ 5.2.1	*wayyiqtol-x* (their cry for help: pron.ref.)
verse 23	§ 5.2.2	*wayyiqtol-x* (אלהים; their crying: pron.ref.)
verse 23	§ 5.2.3	*wayyiqtol-x* (אלהים: lex.rep.)
verse 23	§ 5.2.4	*wayyiqtol-x* (אלהים)
verse 23	§ 5.2.5	*wayyiqtol-x* (אלהים)

Cont.

	§	marking: clause types and actors	
2 Kings 1			
verse 1	§ 1	*wayyiqtol-x*	(Moab; Israel)
verse 2	§ 2	*wayyiqtol-x*	(*Ahaziah*)
		wayyiqtol-0	(וישׁלח He sent מלאכים)
verse 3	§ 2.1	*w*ᵉ*x-Qatal*	(embedded paragraph) (While the מאלך יהוה had spoken to Elijah)
verse 4	§ 2.1.1	*wayyiqtol-x*	(and Elija had gone)
verse 5	§ 2.1	*wayyiqtol-x*	(subparagraph) (מלאכים return to "him")
verse 9	§ 2	*wayyiqtol-0*	(וישׁלח he sent to him)
verse 9	§ 2.1	*wayyiqtol-0*	→ *wayyiqtol-x* (שׂר + Elijah)
verse 11	§ 2	*wayyiqtol-0*	→ *wayyiqtol-0* (וישׁב + וישׁלח he sent to him)
verse 11	§ 2.1	*wayyiqtol-0*	→ *wayyiqtol-x* (שׂר + Elijah)
verse 13	§ 2	*wayyiqtol-0*	→ *wayyiqtol-0* (וישׁב + וישׁלח he sent to him)
verse 13	§ 2.1	*wayyiqtol-0*	→ *wayyiqtol-x* (שׂר + Elijah)
verse 13	§ 2.1.1	*wayyiqtol-x*	→ *wayyiqtol-0* (שׂר)
verse 15	§ 2.1.2	*wayyiqtol-x*	→ (מאלך יהוה spoke to Elijah)
verse 17	§ 2.1.211	*wayyiqtol-0*	→ (He died; cf. preceding dir. speech section)
verse 18	§ 2.1	cas. pendens	(*Ahaziah*)

4. *Concluding statements*

An analysis of textual structure in terms of general linguistic regularities should proceed to an additional analysis in terms of rhetorical strategies that may be characteristic of a particular text.

A text is organised hierarchically. This is true not only of clauses, but also of sentences and even of paragraphs. Ambiguities observed in the use of clause types (*w*ᵉ*x-qatal*) and verb forms (tense, aspect) can be explained in terms of their position in the textual hierarchy.

Linguistic parameters marking "relations" and "structure" are effective in combinations, not individually. The patterns of these combinations are applied in a process and they can be applied recursively, establishing structures and embedded structures.

Discourse analysis could be more effective if it would concentrate first on the linguistic markers used in a specific language before comparing texts on the basis of universal types of human cognition and communication.

A precise analysis of Hebrew text syntax indicates that Hebrew narrative texts exhibit less "parataxis" than suggested by classical grammars, which argue too much only on the basis of clause level observations, i.e.: verbal tenses and conjunctions.

With respect to text-level questions and translations, classical Hebrew syntax works too much as a "system of permitted possibilities" from which a translator may choose, rather than as a grammar explaining syntactic phenomena in the texts in a systematic way.

Exodus 2 and 2 Kings 1. A text-syntactic analysis

Presentation

Textual Hierarchy	*T12*	*Ln*	*§*	*Ttype*	*DCl*	*rel*	*MCl*	*VPNG*	*Txt.ref.*
——————]	0.#	1	1	N	*way-x*	<<	——	3 sgM	Ex. 02:01
—————] .	1..	2	1	N	*way-0*	<<	*way-x*	3 sgM	Ex. 02:01
——————]	0.#	3	2	N	*way-x*	<<	*way-x*	3 sgF	Ex. 02:02

The categories indicated

T Tabulation of the line, indicative of the relation of a clause to its "mother" clause.

1 Clause type definition 1 (= distributional subtype):
- c: casus pendens
- l: ellipsis
- m: macro-syntactic sign
- d: defective clause (due to embedding)

2 Clause type definition 2 (= textual position):
- q: quotation: first clause of direct speech section
- e: embedded clause (in combination with defective clauses)
- #: first clause of a (sub)paragraph

The categories T, 1 and 2 are proposed by a computer programme and can be corrected by the user. The other categories are derived by calculation.

Ln Line Number

§ Paragraph Number (Paragraphs and subparagraphs)

Ttype Text type
- N: narrative text (starting from wayyiqtol)
- Q: discursive text (direct speech, starting from "q")
- D: discursive text (starting from yiqtol in narrative text)

DCl "Daughter" Clause (= grammatical subtype)

Some examples:
- NmCl: nominal clause, with <PC>
- WayX: Wayyiqtol + NP <Su>
- Way0: Wayyiqtol-NP <Su>
- WQtl: W-Qatal
- WXQt: W-X(NP)-Qatal
- WPQt: W-PP-Qatal
- WLQt: W-לא-Qatal
- 0Qtl: asyn. Qatal
- XQtl: . . . Qatal

MCl “Mother” Clause (grammatical subtype; as with “Daughter” Clause)
rel relates to (“Daughter” clause, relates back to “Mother” Clause)
VPNG verbal predicate of the “Daughter” Clause: Person, Number, Gender

The main parsing labels used

<Pr>	Predicate
<PO>	Predicate + Object (vb.fin. + sfx.)
<Su>	Subject Specifier
<Co>	Complement
<Ti>	Time Reference
<PC>	predicative Complement (adj., nom., ptc.)
<Ob>	Object Complement
<Aj>	Adjunct
<Lo>	Locative Reference

Textual Hierarchy of Exodus 2	T12	Ln	§	Ttype	DCl	rel	MCl	VPNG	Txt. ref
[<Aj> מבית לוי] [<Su> איש] [<Pr> ילך] [<Cj> ו]	0.#	1	1	N	Wayq	<<	——	3sgM	Ex. 02:01
[<Ob> את בת לוי] [<Pr> יקח] [<Cj> ו] .	1..	2	1	N	Way0	<<	WayX	3sgM	Ex. 02:01
[<Su> האשה] [<Pr> תהר] [<Cj> ו]	0.#	3	2	N	WayX	<<	WayX	3sgF	Ex. 02:02
[<Ob> בן] [<Pr> תלד] [<Cj> ו] .	1..	4	2	N	Way0	<<	WayX	3sgF	Ex. 02:02
[<Ob> אתו] [<Pr> תרא] [<Cj> ו] .	1..	5	2	N	Way0	<<	Way0	3sgF	Ex. 02:02
[<Su> הוא] [<PC> טוב] [<Cj> כי] . .	2..	6	2	N	AjCl	<<	Way0	-sg-	Ex. 02:02
[<Ti> שלשה ירחים] [<PO> תצפנהו] [<Cj> ו] .	1..	7	2	N	Way0	<<	Way0	3sgF	Ex. 02:02
[<Mo> עוד] [<Pr> יכלה] [<Ng> לא] [<Cj> ו] . .	2..	8	2	N	WLQt	<<	Way0	3sgF	Ex. 02:03
[<PO> הצפינו] . . .	3..	9	2	N	infc.	<<	WLQt	——	Ex. 02:03
[<Ob> תבת גמא] [<Aj> לו] [<Pr> תקח] [<Cj> ו] .	1..	10	2	N	Way0	<<	Way0	3sgF	Ex. 02:03
[<Co> בזפת] [<Cj> ו] [<Co> בחמר] [<PO> תחמרה] [<Cj> ו] .	1..	11	2	N	Way0	<<	Way0	3sgF	Ex. 02:03
[<Ob> את הילד] [<Co> בה] [<Pr> תשם] [<Cj> ו] .	1..	12	2	N	Way0	<<	Way0	3sgF	Ex. 02:03
[<Lo> על שפת היאר] [<Co> בסוף] [<Pr> תשם] [<Cj> ו] .	1..	13	2	N	Way0	<<	Way0	3sgF	Ex. 02:03
[<Lo> מרחק] [<Su> אחתו] [<Pr> תתצב] [<Cj> ו] . .	2.#	14	21	N	WayX	<<	Way0	3sgF	Ex. 02:04
[<Pr> לדעה] . . .	3..	15	21	N	infc.	<<	WayX	——	Ex. 02:04
[<Co> לו] [<Pr> יעשה] [<Su> מה]	4..	16	21	ND	0yqt	<<	infc.	3sgM	Ex. 02:04
[<Su> בת פרעה] [<Pr> תרד] [<Cj> ו]	0.#	17	3	N	WayX	<<	WayX	3sgF	Ex. 02:05
[<Pr> לרחץ]	4.e	18	3	N	infc.	<<	Way0	——	Ex. 02:05
[<Co> על היאר] . . .	3d.	19	3	N	Defc	<<	Way0	3sgF	Ex. 02:05
[<Lo> על יד היאר] [<PC> הלכת] [<Su> נערתיה] [<Cj> ו] . .	2..	20	3	N	ptc.	<<	Way0	-plF	Ex. 02:05
[<Lo> בתוך הסוף] [<Ob> את התבה] [<Pr> תרא] [<Cj> ו] .	1..	21	3	N	Way0	<<	Way0	3sgF	Ex. 02:05
[<Ob> את אמתה] [<Pr> תשלח] [<Cj> ו] .	1..	22	3	N	Way0	<<	Way0	3sgF	Ex. 02:05
[<PO> תקחה] [<Cj> ו] .	1..	23	3	N	Way0	<<	Way0	3sgF	Ex. 02:05
[<Pr> תפתח] [<Cj> ו] .	1..	24	3	N	Way0	<<	Way0	3sgF	Ex. 02:06
[<Ob> את הילד] [<PO> תראהו] [<Cj> ו] .	1..	25	3	N	Way0	<<	Way0	3sgF	Ex. 02:06
[<PC> נער בכה] [<Ij> הנה] [<Cj> ו]	4..	26	3	N	NmCl	<<	Way0	——	Ex. 02:06
[<Co> עליו] [<Pr> תחמל] [<Cj> ו] . . .	3..	27	3	N	Way0	<<	Way0	3sgF	Ex. 02:06
[<Pr> תאמר] [<Cj> ו] . . .	3..	28	3	N	Way0	<<	Way0	3sgF	Ex. 02:06
[<Su> זה] [<PC> מילדי העברים]	4.q	29	30	NQ	NmCl	<<	Way0	——	Ex. 02:06

[<Co> אל בת פרעה] [<Su> אחתו] [<Pr> תאמר] [<Cj> ו]	2.#	30	31	N	WayX	<<	Way0	3sgF	Ex. 02:07
[<Pr> אלך] [<Qu> ה]	4.q	31	310	NQ	0yqt	<<	WayX	1sg-	Ex. 02:07
[<Ob> אשה / מינקת] [<Co> לך] [<Pr> קראתי] [<Cj> ו]	5..	32	310	NQ	WQtl	<<	0yqt	1sg-	Ex. 02:07
[<Ob> את הילד] [<Aj> לך] [<Pr> תינק] [<Cj> ו]	6..	33	310	NQ	Wey0	<<	WQtl	3sgF	Ex. 02:07
[<Su> בת פרעה] [<Co> לה] [<Pr> תאמר] [<Cj> ו]	2.#	34	32	N	WayX	<<	WayX	3sgF	Ex. 02:08
[<Pr> לכי]	4.q	35	320	NQ	imp.	<<	WayX	2sgF	Ex. 02:08
[<Su> העלמה] [<Pr> תלך] [<Cj> ו]	2.#	36	33	N	WayX	<<	WayX	3sgF	Ex. 02:08
[<Ob> את אם הילד] [<Pr> תקרא] [<Cj> ו]	3..	37	33	N	Way0	<<	WayX	3sgF	Ex. 02:08
[<Su> בת פרעה] [<Co> לה] [<Pr> תאמר] [<Cj> ו]	4.#	38	331	N	WayX	<<	Way0	3sgF	Ex. 02:09
[<Ob> את הילד הזה] [<Pr> היליכי]	6.q	39	3310	NQ	imp.	<<	Way0	2sgF	Ex. 02:09
[<Aj> לי] [<PO> הינקהו] [<Cj> ו]	8..	40	3310	NQ	imp.	<<	imp.	2sgF	Ex. 02:09
[<Ob> את שכרך] [<Pr> אתן] [<Su> אני] [<Cj> ו]	7..	41	3310	NQ	WXyq	<<	imp.	1sg-	Ex. 02:09
[<Ob> הילד] [<Su> האשה] [<Pr> תקח] [<Cj> ו]	4.#	42	332	N	WayX	<<	WayX	3sgF	Ex. 02:09
[<PO> תניקהו] [<Cj> ו]	7..	43	332	N	Way0	<<	WayX	3sgF	Ex. 02:09
[<Su> הילד] [<Pr> ינדל] [<Cj> ו]	6.#	44	3321	N	WayX	<<	Way0	3sgM	Ex. 02:10
[<Co> לבת פרעה] [<PO> תבאהו] [<Cj> ו]	5..	45	332	N	Way0	<<	WayX	3sgF	Ex. 02:10
[<Co> לבן] [<Bn> לה] [<Pr> יהי] [<Cj> ו]	6.#	46	3321	N	Way0	<<	Way0	3sgM	Ex. 02:10
[<Ob> משה] [<Ob> שמו] [<Pr> תקרא] [<Cj> ו]	6.#	47	3322	N	Way0	<<	Way0	3sgF	Ex. 02:10
[<Pr> תאמר] [<Cj> ו]	6..	48	3322	N	Way0	<<	Way0	3sgF	Ex. 02:10
[<PO> משיתהו] [<Co> מן המים] [<Cj> כי]	8.q	49	33220	NQ	XQtl	<<	Way0	1sg-	Ex. 02:10
[<Ti> בימים ההם] [<Pr> יהי] [<Cj> ו]	0.#	50	4	N	Way0	<<	Way0	3sgM	Ex. 02:11
[<Su> משה] [<Pr> ינדל] [<Cj> ו]	1.#	51	41	N	WayX	<<	Way0	3sgM	Ex. 02:11
[<Co> אל אחיו] [<Pr> יצא] [<Cj> ו]	2..	52	41	N	Way0	<<	WayX	3sgM	Ex. 02:11
[<Co> בסבלתם] [<Pr> ירא] [<Cj> ו]	3..	53	41	N	Way0	<<	Way0	3sgM	Ex. 02:11
[<Ob> איש מצרי] [<Pr> ירא] [<Cj> ו]	3..	54	41	N	Way0	<<	Way0	3sgM	Ex. 02:11
[<Aj> מאחיו] [<Ob> איש עברי] [<PC> מכה]	4..	55	41	N	ptc.	<<	Way0	-sgM	Ex. 02:11
[<Mo> כה וכה] [<Pr> יפן] [<Cj> ו]	3..	56	41	N	Way0	<<	Way0	3sgM	Ex. 02:12

Textual Hierarchy of Exodus 2	T12	Ln	§	Type	DCl	rel	MCl	VPNG	Txt. ref
[<Pr> ירא] [<Cj> ו]	3.#	571	41	N	Way0	<<	Way0	3sgM	Ex. 02:12
[<PC> אין איש] [<Cj> כי]	4..	58	41	N	NmCl	<<	Way0	——	Ex. 02:12
[<Ob> את המצרי] [<Pr> יך] [<Cj> ו]	3..	59	41	N	Way0	<<	Way0	3sgM	Ex. 02:12
[<Lo> בחול] [<PO> יטמנהו] [<Cj> ו]	3..	60	41	N	Way0	<<	Way0	3sgM	Ex. 02:12
[<Ti> ביום השני] [<Pr> יצא] [<Cj> ו]	2.#	61	42	N	Way0	<<	Way0	3sgM	Ex. 02:13
[<Ij> הנה] [<Cj> ו]	3..	62	42	N	NmCl	<<	Way0	——	Ex. 02:13
[<PC> נצים] [<Su> שני אנשים עברים]	4..	63	42	N	NmCl	<<	NmCl	——	Ex. 02:13
[<Co> לרשע] [<Pr> יאמר] [<Cj> ו]	2..	64	42	N	Way0	<<	Way0	3sgM	Ex. 02:13
[<Ob> רעך] [<Pr> תכה] [<Qu> למה]	4.q	65	420	NQ	0yqt	<<	Way0	2sgM	Ex. 02:13
[<Pr> יאמר] [<Cj> ו]	3.#	66	421	N	Way0	<<	Way0	3sgM	Ex. 02:14
[<Aj> עלינו] [<Co> לאיש / שר ושפט] [<PO> שמך] [<Su> מי]	5.q	67	4210	NQ	0Qtl	<<	Way0	3sgM	Ex. 02:14
[<PO> להרגני] [<Qu> ה]	6..	68	4210	NQ	infc.	<<	0Qtl	——	Ex. 02:14
[<Pr> אמר] [<Su> אתה]	8..	69	4210	NQ	ptc.	<<	infc.	-sgM	Ex. 02:14
[<Ob> את המצרי] [<Pr> הרגת] [<Re> כאשר]	7..	70	4210	NQ	XQtl	<<	infc.	2sgM	Ex. 02:14
[<Su> משה] [<Pr> יירא] [<Cj> ו]	1.#	71	42	N	WayX	<<	WayX	3sgM	Ex. 02:14
[<Pr> יאמר] [<Cj> ו]	2..	72	42	N	Way0	<<	WayX	3sgM	Ex. 02:14
[<Su> הדבר] [<Pr> נודע] [<Ij> אכן]	4.q	73	420	NQ	0Qtl	<<	Way0	3sgM	Ex. 02:14
[<Ob> את הדבר הזה] [<Su> פרעה] [<Pr> ישמע] [<Cj> ו]	1.#	74	43	N	WayX	<<	WayX	3sgM	Ex. 02:15
[<Pr> יבקש] [<Cj> ו]	2..	75	43	N	Way0	<<	WayX	3sgM	Ex. 02:15
[<Ob> את משה] [<Pr> להרג]	3..	76	43	N	infc.	<<	Way0	——	Ex. 02:15
[<Co> מפני פרעה] [<Su> משה] [<Pr> יברח] [<Cj> ו]	1.#	77	44	N	WayX	<<	WayX	3sgM	Ex. 02:15
[<Co> בארץ מדין] [<Pr> ישב] [<Cj> ו]	2..	78	44	N	Way0	<<	WayX	3sgM	Ex. 02:15
[<Co> על הבאר] [<Pr> ישב] [<Cj> ו]	4..	79	44	N	Way0	<<	Way0	3sgM	Ex. 02:15
[<Su> שבע בנות] [<PC> לכהן מדין] [<Cj> ו]	3.#	80	441	N	NmCl	<<	Way0	——	Ex. 02:16
[<Pr> תבאנה] [<Cj> ו]	4..	81	441	N	Way0	<<	NmCl	3plF	Ex. 02:16
[<Pr> תדלנה] [<Cj> ו]	4..	82	441	N	Way0	<<	Way0	3plF	Ex. 02:16

[<Ob> את הרהטים] [<Pr> תמלאנה] [<Cj> ו]	4. .	83	441	N	Way0	<<	Way0	3plF	Ex. 02:16
[<Ob> צאן אביהן] [<Pr> להשקות]	6. .	84	441	N	infc.	<<	Way0	———	Ex. 02:16
[<Su> הרעים] [<Pr> יבאו] [<Cj> ו]	5.#	85	4411	N	WayX	<<	Way0	3plM	Ex. 02:17
[<PO> ינרשום] [<Cj> ו]	6. .	86	4411	N	Way0	<<	WayX	3plM	Ex. 02:17
[<Su> משה] [<Pr> יקם] [<Cj> ו]	5.#	87	4412	N	WayX	<<	WayX	3sgM	Ex. 02:17
[<Pr> יושען] [<Cj> ו]	6. .	88	4412	N	Way0	<<	WayX	3sgM	Ex. 02:17
[<Ob> את צאנם] [<Pr> ישק] [<Cj> ו]	6. .	89	4412	N	Way0	<<	Way0	3sgM	Ex. 02:17
[<Co> אל רעואל / אביהן] [<Pr> תבאנה] [<Cj> ו]	4. .	90	441	N	Way0	<<	Way0	3plF	Ex. 02:18
[<Pr> יאמר] [<Cj> ו]	5.#	91	4411	N	Way0	<<	Way0	3sgM	Ex. 02:18
[<Pr> מהרתן] [<Qu> מדוע]	7.q	92	44110	NQ	0Qtl	<<	Way0	2plF	Ex. 02:18
[<Pr> בא]	9.e	93	44110	NQ	infc.	<<	0Qtl	———	Ex. 02:18
[<Ti> היום]	8d.	94	44110	NQ	Defc	<<	0Qtl	2plF	Ex. 02:18
[<Pr> תאמרן] [<Cj> ו]	4. .	95	441	N	Way0	<<	Way0	3plF	Ex. 02:19
[<Co> מיד הרעים] [<PO> הצילנו] [<Su> איש מצרי]	6.q	96	4410	NQ	XQtl	<<	Way0	3sgM	Ex. 02:19
[<Co> לנו] [<Pr> דלה] [<Mo> דלה] [<Cj> ונם]	7. .	97	4410	NQ	XQtl	<<	XQtl	3sgM	Ex. 02:19
[<Ob> את הצאן] [<Pr> ישק] [<Cj> ו]	8. .	98	4410	NQN	Way0	<<	XQtl	3sgM	Ex. 02:19
[<Co> אל בנתיו] [<Pr> יאמר] [<Cj> ו]	4.#	99	442	N	Way0	<<	Way0	3sgM	Ex. 02:20
[<Qu> איו] [<Cj> ו]	6.q	100	4420	NQ	NmCl	<<	Way0	———	Ex. 02:20
[<Pr> את האיש] [<Pr> עזבתן] [<Qu> למה זה]	8. .	101	4420	NQ	0Qtl	<<	NmCl	2plF	Ex. 02:20
[<Co> לו] [<Pr> קראן]	7. .	102	4420	NQ	imp.	<<	NmCl	2plF	Ex. 02:20
[<Ob> לחם] [<Pr> יאכל] [<Cj> ו]	8. .	103	4420	NQ	Wey0	<<	imp.	3sgM	Ex. 02:20
[<Su> משה] [<Pr> יואל] [<Cj> ו]	1.#	104	45	N	WayX	<<	WayX	3sgM	Ex. 02:21
[<Ob> את האיש] [<Pr> לשבת]	3. .	105	45	N	infc.	<<	WayX	———	Ex. 02:21
[<Co> למשה] [<Ob> את צפרה / בתו] [<Pr> יתן] [<Cj> ו]	2.#	106	451	N	Way0	<<	WayX	3sgM	Ex. 02:21
[<Ob> בן] [<Pr> תלד] [<Cj> ו]	3.#	107	4511	N	Way0	<<	Way0	3sgF	Ex. 02:22
[<Ob> נרשם] [<Ob> את שמו] [<Pr> יקרא] [<Cj> ו]	4.#	108	45111	N	Way0	<<	Way0	3sgM	Ex. 02:22
[<Pr> אמר] [<Cj> כי]	5. .	109	45111	N	XQtl	<<	Way0	3sgM	Ex. 02:22

Textual Hierarchy of Exodus 2	T12	Ln	§	Ttype	DCl	rel	MCl	VPNG	Txt. ref
[<Lo> בארץ נכריה] [<Pr> הייתי] [<PC> נר]	7.q	110	451110	NQ	XQtl	<<	XQtl	1sg-	Ex. 02:22
[<Ti> בימים הרבים ההם] [<Pr> יהי] [<Cj> ו]	0.#	111	5	N	Way0	<<	Way0	3sgM	Ex. 02:23
. [<Su> מלך מצרים] [<Pr> ימת] [<Cj> ו]	1.#	112	51	N	WayX	<<	Way0	3sgM	Ex. 02:23
. [<Aj> מן העבדה] [<Su> בני ישראל] [<Pr> יאנחו] [<Cj> ו]	1.#	113	52	N	WayX	<<	WayX	3plM	Ex. 02:23
. . . [<Pr> יזעקו] [<Cj> ו]	3. .	114	52	N	Way0	<<	WayX	3plM	Ex. 02:23
. . [<Co> אל האלהים] [<Su> שועתם] [<Pr> תעל] [<Cj> ו]	2.#	115	521	N	WayX	<<	WayX	3sgF	Ex. 02:23
[<Aj> מן העבדה]									
. . [<Ob> את נאקתם] [<Su> אלהים] [<Pr> ישמע] [<Cj> ו]	2.#	116	522	N	WayX	<<	WayX	3sgM	Ex. 02:24
. . [<Aj> את בריתו] [<Su> אלהים] [<Pr> יזכר] [<Cj> ו]	2.#	117	523	N	WayX	<<	WayX	3sgM	Ex. 02:24
XYJ T> mHRB> T>}]									
. . [<Ob> את בני ישראל] [<Su> אלהים] [<Pr> ירא] [<Cj> ו]	2.#	118	524	N	WayX	<<	WayX	3sgM	Ex. 02:25
. . [<Su> אלהים] [<Pr> ידע] [<Cj> ו]	3.#	119	525	N	WayX	<<	WayX	3sgM	Ex. 02:25

Textual Hierarchy of 2 Kings 1	T12	Ln	§	Type	DCl	rel	MCl	VPNG	Txt. ref
[<Co> בישראל] [<Su> מואב] [<Pr> יפשע] [<Cj> ו]	0.#	1	1	N	WayX	<<	——	3sgM	2 Kgs. 1:01
[<Su> אחאב] [<Pr> אחרי מות] .	1..	2	1	N	infc.	<<	WayX	——	2 Kgs. 1:01
[<Lo> בעליתו] [<Aj> בעד השבכה] [<Su> אחזיה] [<Pr> יפל] [<Cj> ו]	0.#	3	2	N	WayX	<<	WayX	3sgM	2 Kgs. 1:02
[<PC> בשמרון] [<Re> אשר] . . .	3..	4	2	N	NmCl	<<	WayX	——	2 Kgs. 1:02
[<Pr> יחל] [<Cj> ו] . .	2..	5	2	N	Way0	<<	WayX	3sgM	2 Kgs. 1:02
[<Ob> מלאכים] [<Pr> ישלח] [<Cj> ו] . .	2..	6	2	N	Way0	<<	Way0	3sgM	2 Kgs. 1:02
[<Co> אלהם] [<Pr> יאמר] [<Cj> ו]	5..	7	2	N	Way0	<<	Way0	3sgM	2 Kgs. 1:02
[<Pr> לכו]	6.q	8	20	NQ	imp.	<<	Way0	2plM	2 Kgs. 1:02
[<Co> בבעל זבוב / אלהי עקרון] [<Pr> דרשו]	6..	9	20	NQ	imp.	<<	imp.	2plM	2 Kgs. 1:02
[<Co> מחלי זה] [<Pr> אחיה] [<Cj> אם]	7..	10	20	NQ	Xyqt	<<	imp.	1sg-	2 Kgs. 1:02
[<Pr> דבר] [<Su> מלאך יהוה] [<Cj> ו]	4.#	11	21	N	WXQt	<<	Way0	3sgM	2 Kgs. 1:03
[<Co> אל אליה/התשבי]									
[<Pr> קום]	6.q	12	210	NQ	imp.	<<	WXQt	2sgM	2 Kgs. 1:03
[<Pr> עלה]	6..	13	210	NQ	imp.	<<	imp.	2sgM	2 Kgs. 1:03
[<Ob> מלאכי מלך שמרון] [<Pr> לקראת]	8..	14	210	NQ	infc.	<<	imp.	——	2 Kgs. 1:03
[<Co> אלהם] [<Pr> דבר] [<Cj> ו]	7..	15	210	NQ	imp.	<<	imp.	2sgM	2 Kgs. 1:03
[<PC> מבלי אין אלהים] [<Qu> ה]	8.q	16	2100	NQQ	NmCl	<<	imp.	——	2 Kgs. 1:03
[<Aj> בישראל]									
[<Pr> הלכים] [<Su> אתם]	10..	17	2100	NQQ	ptc.	<<	NmCl	-plM	2 Kgs. 1:03
[<Co> . . בבעל זבוב/א] [<Pr> לדרש]	11..	18	2100	NQQ	infc.	<<	ptc.	——	2 Kgs. 1:03
[<Cj> ולכן]	9m.	19	2100	NQQ	MSyn	<<	NmCl	——	2 Kgs. 1:04
[<Su> יהוה] [<Pr> אמר] [<Mo> כה]	10..	20	2100	NQQ	0Qtl	<<	MSyn	3sgM	2 Kgs. 1:04
[<Fr> המטה]	11cq	21	21000	NQQQ	CPen	<<	0Qtl	——	2 Kgs. 1:04
[. . שם] [<Pr> עלית] [<Re> אשר]	13..	22	21000	NQQQ	XQtl	<<	CPen	2sgM	2 Kgs. 1:04
[<Co> ממנה] [<Pr> תרד] [<Ng> לא]	12..	23	21000	NQQQ	Xyqt	<<	CPen	2sgM	2 Kgs. 1:04
[<Mo> מות] [<Cj> כי]	13..	24	21000	NQQQ	Xyqt	<<	Xyqt	2sgM	2 Kgs. 1:04
[<Pr> תמות]									

Textual Hierarchy of 2 Kings 1	T12	Ln	§	Ttype	DCl	rel	MCl	VPNG	Txt. ref
[<Su> אליה] [<Pr> ילך] [<Cj> ו]	5.#	25	211	N	WayX	<<	WXQt	3sgM	2 Kgs. 1:04
[<Co> אליו] [<Su> המלאכים] [<Pr> ישובו] [<Cj> ו]	3.#	26	21	N	WayX	<<	Way0	3plM	2 Kgs. 1:05
[<Co> אליהם] [<Pr> יאמר] [<Cj> ו]	4..	27	21	N	Way0	<<	WayX	3sgM	2 Kgs. 1:05
[<Pr> שבתם] [<Mo> זה] [<Qu> מה]	6.q	28	210	NQ	0Qtl	<<	Way0	2plM	2 Kgs. 1:05
[<Co> אליו] [<Pr> יאמרו] [<Cj> ו]	4..	29	21	N	Way0	<<	Way0	3plM	2 Kgs. 1:06
[<Pr> עלה] [<Su> איש]	5.q	30	210	NQ	XQtl	<<	Way0	3sgM	2 Kgs. 1:06
[<PO> לקראתנו]	7..	31	210	NQ	infc.	<<	XQtl	——	2 Kgs. 1:06
[<Co> אלינו] [<Pr> יאמר] [<Cj> ו]	6..	32	210	NQN	Way0	<<	XQtl	3sgM	2 Kgs. 1:06
[<Pr> לכו]	7.q	33	2100	NQNQ	imp.	<<	Way0	2plM	2 Kgs. 1:06
[<Co> אל המלך] [<Pr> שובו]	7..	34	2100	NQNQ	imp.	<<	imp.	2plM	2 Kgs. 1:06
[<Ob> אתכם] [<Pr> שלח] [<Re> אשר]	9..	35	2100	NQNQ	XQtl	<<	imp.	3sgM	2 Kgs. 1:06
[<Co> אליו] [<Pr> דברתם] [<Cj> ו]	8..	36	2100	NQNQ	WQt	<<	imp.	2plM	2 Kgs. 1:06
[<Su> יהוה] [<Pr> אמר] [<Mo> כה]	9.q	37	21000	NQNQQ	0Qtl	<<	WQtl	3sgM	2 Kgs. 1:06
[<PC>מבלי אין אלהים] [<Qu> ה] [<Lo> .. ב]	10.q	38	210000	NQNQQQ	NmCl	<<	0Qtl	——	2 Kgs. 1:06
[<Pr> שלח] [<Su> אתה]	12..	39	210000	NQNQQQ	ptc.	<<	NmCl	-sgM	2 Kgs. 1:06
[<Co> .. בבעל ז] [<Pr> לדרש]	13..	40	210000	NQNQQQ	infc.	<<	ptc.	——	2 Kgs. 1:06
[<Cj> לכן]	11m.	41	210000	NQNQQQ	MSyn	<<	NmCl	——	2 Kgs. 1:06
[<Fr> המטה]	12c.	42	210000	NQNQQQ	CPen	<<	MSyn	——	2 Kgs. 1:06
[<Pr> עלית] [<Re> אשר]	14..	43	210000	NQNQQQ	XQtl	<<	CPen	2sgM	2 Kgs. 1:06
[.. מ] [<Pr> תרד] [<Ng> לא]	13..	44	210000	NQNQQQ	Xyqt	<<	CPen	2sgM	2 Kgs. 1:06
ת] [<Mo> מות] [<Cj> כי]	14..	45	210000	NQNQQQ	Xyqt	<<	Xyqt	2sgM	2 Kgs. 1:06
[<Co> אלהם] [<Pr> ידבר] [<Cj> ו]	4..	46	21	N	Way0	<<	Way0	3sgM	2 Kgs. 1:07

[מה <Qu>] [משפט האיש <Su>]	5.q	47	210	NQ	NmCl	<<	Way0	——	2 Kgs. 1:07
[אשר <Re>] [עלה <Pr>]	6..	48	210	NQ	XQtl	<<	NmCl	3sgM	2 Kgs. 1:07
[לקראתכם <PO>]	8..	49	210	NQ	infc.	<<	XQtl	——	2 Kgs. 1:07
[ו <Cj>] [ידבר <Pr>] [אליכם <Co>] [את הדברים .. <Ob>]	7..	50	210	NQN	Way0	<<	XQtl	3sgM	2 Kgs. 1:07
[ו <Cj>] [יאמרו <Pr>] [אליו <Co>]	4..	51	21	N	Way0	<<	Way0	3plM	2 Kgs. 1:08
[איש בעל שער <PC>]	5.q	52	210	NQ	NmCl	<<	Way0	——	2 Kgs. 1:08
[ו <Cj>] [אזור עור <Su>] [אזור <Pr>] [במתניו <Co>]	6..	53	210	NQ	ptcP.	<<	NmCl	-sgM	2 Kgs. 1:08
[ו <Cj>] [יאמר <Pr>]	4..	54	21	N	Way0	<<	Way0	3sgM	2 Kgs. 1:08
[אליה / התשבי <PC>] [הוא <Su>]	5.q	55	210	NQ	NmCl	<<	Way0	——	2 Kgs. 1:08
[ו <Cj>] [ישלח <Pr>] [אליו <Co>] [שר חמשים <Ob>] [ו <Cj>] [חמשיו <Ob>]	2..	56	2	N	Way0	<<	Way0	3sgM	2 Kgs. 1:09
[ו <Cj>] [יעל <Pr>] [אליו <Co>]	3.#	57	21	N	Way0	<<	Way0	3sgM	2 Kgs. 1:09
[ו <Cj>] [הנה <Ij>] [ישב <Pr>] [על ראש ההר <Co>]	4..	58	21	N̂	ptc.	<<	Way0	-sgM	2 Kgs. 1:09
[ו <Cj>] [ידבר <Pr>] [אליו <Co>]	3..	59	21	N	Way0	<<	Way0	3sgM	2 Kgs. 1:09
[איש האלהים <Vo>]	5vq	60	210	NQ	Voct	<<	Way0	——	2 Kgs. 1:09
[המלך <Su>] [דבר <Pr>]	6..	61	210	NQ	XQtl	<<	Voct	3sgM	2 Kgs. 1:09
[רדה <Pr>]	7.q	62	2100	NQQ	imp.	<<	XQtl	2sgM	2 Kgs. 1:09
[ו <Cj>] [יענה <Pr>] [אליהו <Su>]	4.#	63	211	N	WayX	<<	Way0	3sgM	2 Kgs. 1:10
[ו <Cj>] [ידבר <Pr>] [אל שר החמשים <Co>]	5..	64	211	N	Way0	<<	WayX	3sgM	2 Kgs. 1:10
[ואם <Cj>] [איש אלהים <PC>] [אני <Su>]	6.q	65	2110	NQ	NmCl	<<	Way0	——	2 Kgs. 1:10
[תרד <Pr>] [אש <Su>] [מן השמים <Co>]	7..	66	2110	NQ	0yqt	<<	NmCl	3sgF	2 Kgs. 1:10
[ו <Cj>] [תאכל <Pr>] [אתך ו את חמשיך <Ob>]	8..	67	2110	NQ	Wey0	<<	0yqt	3sgF	2 Kgs. 1:10
[ו <Cj>] [תרד <Pr>] [אש <Su>] [מן השמים <Co>]	4.#	68	212	N	Way0	<<	WayX	3sgF	2 Kgs. 1:10

Textual Hierarchy of 2 Kings 1	T12	Ln	§	Ttype	DCl	rel	MCl	VPNG	Txt. ref
[<Cj>ו] [<Ob> אתו] [<Pr> תאכל] [<Cj> ו]	5..	69	212	N	Way0	<<	Way0	3sgF	2 Kgs. 1:10
[<Ob> את חמשיו]									
[<Pr> ישב] [<Cj> ו]	2..	70	2	N	Way0	<<	Way0	3sgM	2 Kgs. 1:11
[<Ob> שר חמשים אחר ו חמשיו] [<Co> אליו] [<Pr> ישלח] [<Cj> ו]	2..	71	2	N	Way0	<<	Way0	3sgM	2 Kgs. 1:11
[<Pr> יען] [<Cj> ו]	3.#	72	21	N	Way0	<<	Way0	3sgM	2 Kgs. 1:11
[<Co> אליו] [<Pr> ידבר] [<Cj> ו]	4..	73	21	N	Way0	<<	Way0	3sgM	2 Kgs. 1:11
[<Vo> איש האלהים]	6vq	74	210	NQ	Voct	<<	Way0	——	2 Kgs. 1:11
[<Su> המלך] [<Pr> אמר] [<Mo> כה]	7..	75	210	NQ	0Qtl	<<	Voct	3sgM	2 Kgs. 1:11
[<Pr> רדה] [<Mo> מהרה]	8.q	76	2100	NQQ	imp.	<<	0Qtl	2sgM	2 Kgs. 1:11
[<Su> אליה] [<Pr> יען] [<Cj> ו]	5.#	77	211	N	WayX	<<	Way0	3sgM	2 Kgs. 1:12
[<Co> אליהם] [<Pr> ידבר] [<Cj> ו]	6..	78	211	N	Way0	<<	WayX	3sgM	2 Kgs. 1:12
[<Su> אני] [<PC> איש האלהים] [<Cj> אם]	7.q	79	2110	NQ	NmCl	<<	Way0	——	2 Kgs. 1:12
[<Co> מן השמים] [<Su> אש] [<Pr> תרד]	8..	80	2110	NQ	0yqt	<<	NmCl	3sgF	2 Kgs. 1:12
[<Ob> אתך ו את חמשיך] [<Pr> תאכל] [<Cj> ו]	9..	81	2110	NQ	Wey0	<<	0yqt	3sgF	2 Kgs. 1:12
[<Co> מן השמים] [<Su> אש אלהים] [<Pr> תרד] [<Cj> ו]	5.#	82	212	N	Way0	<<	WayX	3sgF	2 Kgs. 1:12
[<Ob> את חמשיו] [<Cj> ו] [<Ob> אתו] [<Pr> תאכל] [<Cj> ו]	6..	83	212	N	Way0	<<	Way0	3sgF	2 Kgs. 1:12
[<Pr> ישב] [<Cj> ו]	2..	84	2	N	Way0	<<	Way0	3sgM	2 Kgs. 1:13
[<Ob> חמשיו] [<Cj> ו] [<Ob> שר חמשים שלשים] [<Pr> ישלח] [<Cj> ו]	2..	85	2	N	Way0	<<	Way0	3sgM	2 Kgs. 1:13
[<Pr> יעל] [<Cj> ו]	3.#	86	21	N	Way0	<<	Way0	3sgM	2 Kgs. 1:13
[<Su> שר החמשים השלישי] [<Pr> יבא] [<Cj> ו]	4.#	87	211	N	WayX	<<	Way0	3sgM	2 Kgs. 1:13
[<Aj> לנגד אליהו] [<Co> על ברכיו] [<Pr> יכרע] [<Cj> ו]	5..	88	211	N	Way0	<<	WayX	3sgM	2 Kgs. 1:13
[<Co> אליו] [<Pr> יתחנן] [<Cj> ו]	6..	89	211	N	Way0	<<	Way0	3sgM	2 Kgs. 1:13
[<Co> אליו] [<Pr> ידבר] [<Cj> ו]	6..	90	211	N	Way0	<<	Way0	3sgM	2 Kgs. 1:13
[<Vo> איש האלהים]	7vq	91	2110	NQ	Voct	<<	Way0	——	2 Kgs. 1:13
.. [<Su> נפשי ו נפש עבדיך] [<Ij> נא] [<Pr> תיקר]	8..	92	2110	NQ	0yqt	<<	Voct	3sgF	2 Kgs. 1:13
.. [מן] [<Su> אש] [<Pr> ירדה] [<Ij> הנה]	10..	93	2110	NQ	0Qtl	<<	0yqt	3sgF	2 Kgs. 1:14

[ו <Cj>] [תאכל <Pr>] [את שני שר ..	11..	94	2110	NQN	Way0	<<	0Qtl	3sgF	2 Kgs. 1:14
[ו <Cj>] [עתה <Mo>]	9m.	95	2110	NQ	MSyn	<<	0yqt	——	2 Kgs. 1:14
[תיקר <Pr>] [נפשי <Su>] [בעיניך <Co>]	10..	96	2110	NQ	0yqt	<<	MSyn	3sgF	2 Kgs. 1:14
[ו <Cj>] [ידבר <Pr>] [מלאך יהוה <Su>] [אל אליהו <Co>]	4.#	97	212	N	WayX	<<	WayX	3sgM	2 Kgs. 1:15
[רד <Pr>] [אותו <Aj>]	6.q	98	2120	NQ	imp.	<<	WayX	2sgM	2 Kgs. 1:15
[אל <Ng>] [תירא <Pr>] [מפניו <Co>]	7..	99	2120	NQ	Xyqt	<<	imp.	2sgM	2 Kgs. 1:15
[ו <Cj>] [יקם <Pr>]	5.#	100	2121	N	Way0	<<	WayX	3sgM	2 Kgs. 1:15
[ו <Cj>] [ירד <Pr>] [אותו <Aj>] [אל המלך <Co>]	5..	101	2121	N	Way0	<<	Way0	3sgM	2 Kgs. 1:15
[ו <Cj>] [ידבר <Pr>] [אליו <Co>]	5..	102	2121	N	Way0	<<	Way0	3sgM	2 Kgs. 1:16
[כה <Mo>] [אמר <Pr>] [יהוה <Su>]	7.q	103	21210	NQ	0Qtl	<<	Way0	3sgM	2 Kgs. 1:16
[יען אשר <Cj>] [שלחת <Pr>] [מלאכים <Ob>]	8.q	104	212100	NQQ	XQtl	<<	0Qtl	2sgM	2 Kgs. 1:16
[לדרש <Pr>] [בבעל זבוב .. <Co>]	11..	105	212100	NQQ	infc.	<<	XQtl	——	2 Kgs. 1:16
[ה <Qu>] [מבלי אין אלהים <PC>] [ב ..	10..	106	212100	NQQ	NmCl	<<	XQtl	——	2 Kgs. 1:16
[לדרש <Pr>] [בדברו <Co>]	11..	107	212100	NQQ	infc.	<<	NmCl	——	2 Kgs. 1:16
[לכן <Cj>]	9m.	108	212100	NQQ	MSyn	<<	XQtl	——	2 Kgs. 1:16
[המטה <Fr>]	10c.	109	212100	NQQ	CPen	<<	MSyn	——	2 Kgs. 1:16
[אשר <Re>] [עלית <Pr>] [ש ..	12..	110	212100	NQQ	XQtl	<<	CPen	2sgM	2 Kgs. 1:16
[לא <Ng>] [תרד <Pr>] [מ ..	11..	111	212100	NQQ	Xyqt	<<	CPen	2sgM	2 Kgs. 1:16
[כי <Cj>] [מות <Mo>] [ת ..	12..	112	212100	NQQ	Xyqt	<<	Xyqt	2sgM	2 Kgs. 1:16
[ו <Cj>] [ימת <Pr>] [כדבר יהוה <Aj>]	6.#	113	21211	N	Way0	<<	Way0	3sgM	2 Kgs. 1:17
[אשר <Re>] [דבר <Pr>] [אליהו <Su>]	8..	114	21211	N	XQtl	<<	Way0	3sgM	2 Kgs. 1:17
[ו <Cj>] [ימלך <Pr>] [יהורם <Su>] [תחתיו <Co>] [ב ..	7.#	115	212111	N	WayX	<<	Way0	3sgM	2 Kgs. 1:17
[כי <Cj>] [לא <Ng>] [היה <Pr>] [לו<Bn>] [בן <Su>]	8..	116	212111	N	XQtl	<<	WayX	3sgM	2 Kgs. 1:17
[ו <Cj>] [יתר דברי אחזיהו <Fr>]	1c#	117	21	N	CPen	<<	WayX	——	2 Kgs. 1:18
[אשר <Re>] [עשה <Pr>]	3..	118	21	N	XQtl	<<	CPen	3sgM	2 Kgs. 1:18
[ה <Qu>] [לוא <Ng>] [המה <Su>] [כתובים <Pr>] [על ספר דברי הימים <Co>] ..	2..	119	21	N	ptcP.	<<	CPen	-plM	2 Kgs. 1:18

References

Andersen, F.I., *The Sentence in Biblical Hebrew* (Janua Linguarum, Series Practica 231), The Hague: Mouton, 1974.

Bartelmus, R., *Einführung in das Biblische Hebräisch. Mit einem Anhang Biblisches Aramäisch*, Zürich: Theologischer Verlag, 1994.

Beyerlin, W., *Herkunft und Geschichte der ältesten Sinaitraditionen*, Tübingen: Mohr, 1961.

Bodine, W.R. (ed.), *Discourse Analysis of Biblical Literature. What It Is and What It Offers*, Atlanta: Scholars, 1995.

Buber, M., *Die fünf Bücher der Weisung. Verdeutscht von Martin Buber gemeinsam mit Franz Rosenzweig*, Heidelberg: Schneider, 1981[10].

Childs, B.S., *Exodus. A Commentary* (Old Testament Library), London: SCM, 1974.

Exter Blokland, A.F. den, *In Search of Text Syntax. Towards a Syntactic Segmentation Model for Biblical Hebrew*, Amsterdam: VU University Press, 1995.

Houtman, C., *Exodus*, Vols. 1–2, Kampen: Kok, 1989.

Joosten, J., "Tekstlinguïstiek en het Bijbels-Hebreeuwse werkwoord: een kritische uiteenzetting", *Nederlands Theologisch Tijdschrift* 49 (1995), 265–272.

Lowery, K.E., "The Theoretical Foundations of Hebrew Discourse Grammar", in: Bodine, W.R. (ed.), *Discourse Analysis of Biblical Literature. What It Is and What It Offers*, Atlanta: Scholars, 1995, 213–253.

Lyons, J., *Linguistic Semantics. An Introduction*, Cambridge: Cambridge University Press, 1995.

Merwe, C.H.J. van der, "Discourse Linguistics and Biblical Hebrew Grammar", in: Bergen, R.D. (ed.), *Biblical Hebrew and Discourse Linguistics*, Winona Lake (Ind.): Eisenbrauns, 1994, 13–49.

Meyer, R., *Hebraische Grammatik III. Satzlehre* (Sammlung Göschen, Band 5765), Berlin: De Gruyter, 1972[3].

Noth, M., *Das 2. Buch Mose. Exodus*, Göttingen: Vandenhoeck & Ruprecht, 1978.

Regt, L. de, Waard, J. de, Fokkelman, J.P. (eds.), *Literary Structure and Rhetorical Strategies in the Hebrew Bible*, Assen/Winona Lake: Van Gorcum/Eisenbrauns, 1996.

Schneider, W., *Grammatik des Biblischen Hebräisch. Völlig neue Bearbeitung der* "Hebräischen Grammatik für den akademischen Unterricht" *von Oskar Grether*, München: Claudius, 1974 (1982[5]).

Talstra, E., "Text Grammar and Biblical Hebrew: The Viewpoint of Wolfgang Schneider", *Journal of Translation and Textlinguistics* 5 (1992), 269–287.

———, "Clause Types and Textual Structure: an Experiment in Narrative Syntax", in: Talstra, E. (ed.), *Narrative and Comment. Contributions Presented to Wolfgang Schneider*, Amsterdam: Societas Hebraica Amstelodamensis, 1995, 166–180.

Weinrich, H., "Die Textpartitur als heuristische Methode", in: Dressler, W. (ed.), *Textlinguistik*, Darmstadt: Wissenschaftliche Buchgesellschaft, 1978, 391–412.

Winther-Nielsen, N. & Talstra, E., *A Computational Display of Joshua. A Computer-Assisted Analysis and Textual Interpretation* (Applicatio 13), Amsterdam: VU University Press, 1995.

WORKSHOP: CLAUSE TYPES, TEXTUAL HIERARCHY, TRANSLATION IN EXODUS 19, 20 AND 24

Eep Talstra
(Amsterdam)

1. *Task*

The workshop concentrating on Exodus 19, 20 and 24 intended, first, to test the effectiveness of the patterns listed in my introductory paper as markers of clause connections and of hierarchical text segmentation. Second, the workshop was to test whether one could derive more insight into the function of clause types and verb forms once a textual hierarchy of the clauses had been constructed. Those participating in the workshop received a full syntactic schema of Exodus 19, 20 and 24 to work with. In this report I will restrict myself to the main points discussed.

In preparation two tasks had to be performed, according to the intentions outlined above:

— To apply the patterns defined for hierarchical clause connections. What text linguistic registrations are possible to help establish a textual structure of the chapters to be discussed? Is it possible to construct a textual hierarchy using a minimum of assumptions about the particular functions of individual verb forms and clauses in Biblical Hebrew?
— To consider the discourse functions of the textual hierarchy found. If its grammatical structure is based mainly on linguistic arguments, what does this imply for the dialogue with exegetical and grammatical observations about inconsistencies or tensions in the text?

In the presentation, however, I prefer to start from another angle, i.e., a number of choices made in translations and some exegetical remarks. This procedure is similar to that proposed in my introductory paper. It helps to detect at what points in the text differences of opinion exist as to the grammatical interpretation of clause types and verb forms.

2.1 *Some translations*

	Clause Type	*Buber*[1]	*RSV*[2]	*Childs*[3]
19,1	*PP + L + Inf.*	nach der Ausfahrt	had gone	after had gone forth
19,1	*qatal-x*	kamen sie	they came	they entered
19,2	*wayyiqtol*	Sie zogen	And when they set out	Having set out from
19,2	*wayyiqtol*	und kamen	and came into	they entered
19,2	*wayyiqtol*	und sie lagerten	they encamped;	and camped
19,2	*wayyiqtol-x*	Dort lagerte I.	and there Isr. encamped.	There Israel camped
19,3	w^e*x-qatal*	Mosche stieg auf	And Moses went up	while Moses went up
19,3	*wayyiqtol-x*	da rief ER ihm	and the Lord called	Then the Lord called
19,8	*wayyiqtol-x*	Mosche erstattete	And Moses reported	Moses reported to
19,9	*wayyiqtol-x*	Mosche meldete Ihm	Then Moses told	Moses reported to
19,17	*wayyiqtol-x*	Mosche führte	Then Moses brought	Moses led the people out
19,18	w^e*x-qatal*	rauchte all	was wrapped in	now was enveloped in
19,18	*qatal-x*	darob daß herabfuhr	because . . . descended	for had come down
19,19	ויהי + *ptc.*	Der Schall erstarkte	And as grew louder	As the sound grew
19,19	*x-yiqtol*	—Mosche redete	Moses spoke	Moses was speaking
19,19	w^e*x-yiqtol*	Gott antwortete—	and God answered	and God was answering
19,20	*wayyiqtol-x*	herab fuhr ER	And came down	And . . . came down
20,22	*wayyiqtol-x*	ER sprach	And the Lord said	The Lord said
20,25	*x-qatal*	hast geschwungen	if you wield upon	if you use your chisel
20,25	*wayyiqtol*	hast du preisgegeben	you profane it	you profane it
24,1	w^e*p-qatal*	hatte gesprochen	And he said to	Then to Moses he said

2.2 *Questions of syntax and exegesis*

Looking into these (and other) translations leads to some observations of how the syntax of Hebrew narratives is represented.

---

[1] *Die fünf Bücher der Weisung. Verdeutscht von Martin Buber gemeinsam mit Franz Rosenzweig*, Heidelberg, 1981[10], 203ff.

[2] *The Holy Bible. Revised Standard Version*, New York, Glasgow, Toronto, 1952/1971.

[3] B.S. Childs, *Exodus. A Commentary* (Old Testament Library), London: SCM, 1974, 342, 442, 497.

First, one can observe a general tendency to smooth the text in terms of the tenses used in the translation. For the majority of verb forms in narrative texts the examples listed use a translation in the past tense (for *qatal*, *wayyiqtol* and even *yiqtol*). A similar, though less consistent, tendency is to translate the verb forms of direct speech texts in present or future tense (*yiqtol*, *qatal*, and even *wayyiqtol* [20:25]). Only if the narrative style within a direct speech section is clear (19:4, *wayyiqtol* after an introduction with *qatal*) is the past tense used.

	Narrative	*direct speech*
qatal:	past 19:1,18	present 20:25
wayyiqtol:	past 19:1,2, etc.	present 20:25
*w*ᵉ*x-qatal*:	past 19:3,18 24,1;	. . .
yiqtol:	past 19:19	future/modal (passim); present (some: 19:23)

This evidence alone suggests that literary evaluations have a strong impact on questions of grammar and translation in classical Hebrew.

Second obervation. Once on this track, translators tend to take one further step and to use the flexibility adopted in the interpretation of verb forms and clauses to smooth the texts in terms of their narrative plot as well. For example, the new revision of the Dutch "Willibrord" translation[4] renders the *wayyiqtol-x* clause in Ex. 19:20 וירד יהוה with a causal clause, using a verb in pluperfect: "Want de HEER was neergedaald op de Sinai" (*For* the Lord *had descended* on mount Sinai). No doubt this choice was made to make the text fit with the previous statement of the same event in verse 18 (where *qatal* is used), saying that "the Lord had descended". As a rendering of the *wayyiqtol* of verse 20, however, it is incorrect. Such practices raise a number of questions that are of importance for the study of narrative syntax. Do we know so little about Hebrew clauses and tenses that "anything goes"? Why should a translation smooth a text by adapting it to literary wishes concerning a correct sequential time frame? Should one feel free to "help" the reader with this approach, since literary criticism has long since analysed Exodus 19 and 20 as very composite,[5] so that no proposal of textual coherence might be expected there anyway?

---

[4] *De Bijbel uit de grondtekst vertaald. Willibrordvertaling*, 's-Hertogenbosch: Katholieke Bijbelstichting, 1995.

[5] M. Noth, *Das 2. Buch Mose. Exodus* (ATD 5), Göttingen, 1978, 123ff. W. Beyerlin, *Herkunft und Geschichte der ältesten Sinaitraditionen*, Tübingen, 1961, 10ff.

The reason for discussing these texts and some translations is not that I would propose a rigid consistency in the translation of verb forms, in terms of: let one Hebrew form match one Dutch, one English or one form in any other language. On the contrary, the various positions verb forms can take in clause patterns and the various positions clauses can take in syntactic constructions, already demonstrate that the goal of a one-to-one translation only could be achieved by neglecting grammatical context. Therefore, the argument is not against the option of, for example, a pluperfect translation for a *wayyiqtol*-clause as such, it is against the confusing mixture of literary and grammatical arguments. The challenge is to discover whether it would be possible to base an interpretation of verbs and clauses on a syntactically constructed textual hierarchy, rather than on an interpretation that sometimes results in smoothing the text according to particular desires concerning its literary form.

Further examples, *Chapter 19*

— A discussion similar to that of verse 20 is possible about the translation of the *wayyiqtols* in verse 2, which report about situations that antedate the story at Horeb, Ex. 17:1 and 18:5.[6] Should one, for that non-linguistic reason, interpret the verb forms used as pluperfects? Or do we have linguistic reasons to do so?

— What is the effect of the sequence of the clauses types: *wayyiqtol* → *w^ex-qatal* in verses 3 and 18? The translations hardly indicate that they have noticed any syntactic change here.

— Verses 16–20. What is the textual position of the scene of the third day? What is the signification of the ויהי-clauses in combination with the lexical repetition of קול, שופר and חזק (verses 16 and 18f.)? What is the effect of a *yiqtol* in a narrative text (verse 19)? In relation to this, I repeat the question already mentioned: what is the grammatical interpretation of the two statements about JHWH's descent (ירד) on mount Sinai (verse 18 *qatal*; verse 20 *wayyiqtol*)?

Chapter 20

— Verse 25. What is the status of *qatal* and *wayyiqtol* in a discursive text (direct speech)?

Chapter 24

— Verse 1. What is the effect of introducing this chapter with *w^ePP-qatal*?

[6] Cf. Noth, *op. cit.*, 125.

As stated above, interpreting verbal forms and clauses in such cases usually seems to be the result of a mixture of grammatical and exegetical argumentation. The question is whether we must leave things that way, since with long transmitted and repeatedly reworked ancient texts it appears to be our best option, or whether it is possible, prior to exegetical considerations, to establish a linguistic system in the use of clause types, their verb forms and the construction of texts, in a more independent descriptive way, not asking primarily, what an author or redactor may have had in mind, but asking how the syntactic construction of the final text might affect the reader. In line with the method explained in the introductory paper, I try to avoid starting from an elaborated theory about all possible functions that verb forms may have on their own. First information about the capacity of various linguistic forms to mark textual cohesion must be gathered: in what sequences do clause types and verb forms contribute to textual structure? Of course, this method does not imply that the observations are "free from interpretation", the deliberate choice to start from observations based on form, sequence and frequency, may enhance the opportunity of proceeding with an inductive method as long as possible. Concentrating on a variety of text-level markers—morphological correspondences of verb forms, pronominal references, lexical repetition, clause types, presence or absence of explicitly marked subjects—should lead to a proposal of clause connections in an hierarchical structure of a particular text. Such textual hierarchies are expected to help decide what the effect of verb forms and clause types is in a particular context. The conclusions from particular contexts will lead into more systematic grammatical description.

3. *Hierarchy*

The considerations of the previous paragraph emphasize that establishing a syntactic structure of a text does not in itself imply the solution of any redactional, exegetical or translation question. Rather, it is a reader-oriented process, that, provided the grammatical assumptions of linguistic markers and clause connections on which it is founded are correct, results in a syntactic structure, i.e., the framework of signals that help the reader navigate through the text. This also produces a framework within which questions can be asked about textual consistency and possible redactional activity in its production. The examples presented here result from the application of the patterns of clause connections and paragraph marking, mentioned in the introductory paper. The textual schemas are restricted to those segments of text that have been particularly addressed in the workshop.

3.1 *Exodus 19:1–5,7,8,9*[7]

[<Ti> בחדש השלישי]	1	Defc<<——	3pl-	01
[<Su> בני ישראל] [<Pr> לצאת] . . [<Co> . . מארץ מ]	2	infc<<Defc	——	01
[<Co> מדבר סיני] [<Pr> באו] [<Ti> ביום הזה] .	3	*xqtl*<<Defc	3pl-	01
[<Co> מרפידים] [<Pr> יסעו] [<Cj> ו] . . .	4	*way*0<<*xqtl*	3plM	02
[<Co> מדבר סיני] [<Pr> יבאו] [<Cj> ו] . . .	5	*way*0<<*way*0	3plM	02
[<Lo> במדבר] [<Pr> יחנו] [<Cj> ו] . . .	6	*way*0<<*way*0	3plM	02
[<Lo> שם] [<Pr> יחן] [<Cj> ו] . . . . [<Su> ישראל]	7	*wayx*<<*xqtl*	3sgM	02
[<Pr> עלה] [<Su> משה] [<Cj> ו] . . . [<Co> . . אל]	8	*wxqt*<<*wayx*	3sgM	03
[<Co> אליו] [<Pr> יקרא] [<Cj> ו] . . . . . . [<Su> יהוה]	9	*wayx*<<*wxqt*	3sgM	03
[<Pr> לאמר]	10	infc<<*wayx*	——	03
[<Pr> תאמר] [<Mo> כה] [לבית . .	11	0*yqt*<<infc	2sgM	03
[<Pr> תגיד] [<Cj> ו] . . . [לבני	12	*wey*0<<0*yqt*	2sgM	03
[<Su> אתם] [<Pr> ראיתם]	13	*xqtl*<<0*yqt*	2plM	04
[<Re> אשר] . . <Pr> צשיתי]	14	*xqtl*<<*xqtl*	1sg-	04
ואשא . . אתכם	15	*way*0<<*xqtl*	1sg-	04
ואבא . . אתכם	16	*way*0<<*way*0	1sg-	04
[<Cj> ו] . [<Mo> עתה]	17	MSyn<<*xqtl*	——	05
[<Su> משה] [<Pr> יבא] [<Cj> ו]	25	*wayx*<<*wayx*	3sgM	07
[<Su> משה] [<Pr> ישב] [<Cj> ו] . . . . . . [. . את ד]	34	*wayx*<<*wayx*	3sgM	08
[<Su> משה] [<Pr> יגד] [<Cj> ו] . . . . . . [. . את ד]	40	*wayx*<<*wayx*	3sgM	09

[7] Note: The textual schemas have been simplified in order to fit the format of this document: labels referring to text types (N: Narrative, Q: Direct speech); labels referring to paragraphs, and labels that refer to the level of indentation of clauses, have been omitted. For an impression of textual schemas with full formation, see the appendices added to the introductory article, above.

3.1.1 *Linguistic patterns (lines 1–17; 25; 34)*

Only for this first segment of text will the patterns used as arguments to construct its syntactic schema be listed. The numbers of the patterns listed refer to the introductory paper, § 2 and 3.

verse	*connection*	*arguments*
1	line 2 → 1:	§ 2.I,2 (infinitive clause)
	line 3 → 1:	§ 2.II,4 (complete a "defective" clause after embedding)
2	line 4 → 3:	§ 2.II,1 III,1
	line 5 → 4:	§ 2.II,1 III,2
	line 6 → 5:	§ 2.II,1 III,2
	line 7 → 1:	§ 2.II,1 and § 3.I,1 III,1
3	line 8 → 7:	§ 2.II,1 and § 3.I,1 III,2
	line 9 → 8:	§ 2.II,1 and § 3.I,1 III,1
	line 10 → 9:	§ 2.I,2
	line 11 → 10:	§ 2.II,3 (start-of-direct-speech pattern)
	line 12 → 11:	§ 2.II,1 III,1
4	line 13 → 11:	§ 2.II,3 (start-of-direct-speech pattern)
	line 14 → 13:	§ 2.IV,1
	line 15 → 14:	§ 2.II,1 III,1
	line 16 → 15:	§ 2.II,1 III,2
5	line 17 → 13:	§ 2.II,5 (Macrosyntactic sign, after *wayyiqtols* in direct speech)
7	line 25 → 9:	§ 2.II,1 III,1 + 2 § 3.III,1
8	line 34 → 9:	§ 2.II,1 III,1 § 3.II,2

3.2 *Exodus 19:16–21*

[<Ti> ביום השלישי] [<Pr> יהי] [<Cj> ו] .	67	*way*0<<*xqtl*	3sgM	16
[<Su> הבקר] [<Pr> בהית] . . .	68	infc<<*way*0	——	16
[<Pr> יהי] [<Cj> ו] . .	69	MSyn<<*way*0	3sgM	16
[<Su> קלת וברקים וענן כבד] . . .	70	NmCl<<MSyn	——	16
[<PC> על ההר]				
[<Su> קל שפר חזק מאד] [<Cj> ו]	71	Ellp<<NmCl	——	16
[<Pr> יחרד] [<Cj> ו]	72	*wayx*<<NmCl	3sgM	16
[<Su> כל העם]				
[<PC> במחנה] [<Re> אשר]	73	NmCl<<*wayx*	——	16
[<Su> משה] [<Pr> יוצא] [<Cj> ו]	74	*wayx*<<*wayx*	3sgM	17
[<Ob> את העם]				
[<Pr> לקראת]	75	infc<<*wayx*	——	17
[<Co> האלהים]				
[<Co> מן המחנה]	76	Defc<<*wayx*	3sgM	17
[<Pr> יתיצבו] [<Cj> ו]	77	*way*0<<*wayx*	3plM	17
[<Lo> בתחתית ההר]				
[<Su> הר סיני] [<Cj> ו]	78	*wxqt*<<*way*0	3sgM	18
. . [<Pr> עשן]				
[<Re> מפני אשר]	79	0*qtl*<<*wxqt*	3sgM	18
. . [<Pr> ירד]				
[<Pr> יעל] [<Cj>ו]	80	*wayx*<<*wxqt*	3sgM	18
. . [<Su> עשנו]				

[<Pr> יחרד] [<Cj> ו] . . . . [<Su> כל ההר]	81	*wayx*<<*wayx*	3sgM	18
[<Pr> יהי] [<Cj> ו] . .	82	MSyn<<MSyn	3sgM	19
[<PC> הולך] [<Su> קול השופר]	83	NmCl<<MSyn	-sgM	19
[<PC> חזק מאד] [<Cj> ו]	84	Ellp<<NmCl	-sg-	19
[<Pr> ידבר] [<Su> משה]	85	*xyqt*<<NmCl	3sgM	19
[<Su> האלהים] [<Cj> ו] . . . . . . .ב] [<PO> יעננו]	86	*wxyq*<<*xyqt*	3sgM	19
[<Su> יהוה] [<Pr> ירד] [<Cj> ו] . ..על הר סיני] [אל]	87	*wayx*<<MSyn	3sgM	20

3.3 *Exodus 20:22–26; 24:1*

[<Co> אל משה] [<Su> יהוה] [<Pr> יאמר] [<Cj> ו]	61	*wayx*<<*wxqt*	3sgM	22
[<Ob> מזבח אבנים] [<Cj> ואם] . . . . ל] [<Pr> תעשה]	73	*wPyq*<<*xyqt*	2sgM	25
[<Co> אתהן] [<Pr> תבנה] [<Ng> לא] . . . . . . ג]	74	*xyqt*<<*wPyq*	2sgM	25
[<Pr> הנפת] [<Ob> חרבך] [<Cj> כי] . . . . . עליה]	75	*xqtl*<<*wPyq*	2sgM	25
[<PO> תחללה] [<Cj> ו]	76	*way0*<<*xqtl*	2sgM	25
[<Pr> אמר] [<Co> אל משה] [<Cj> ו] . .	1	*wPqt*<<—	3sgM	01

3.4 *Results*

The primary results of these procedures are the textual hierarchies and the paragraph divisions proposed. They are of importance, since they enable further grammatical and textual analysis. Particular clause-type sequences and questions of syntax and translation of a particular text can now be addressed, not by referring to general grammatical rules about the use of verb forms, but by comparison with sets of textual data, i.e. with patterns of clause type sequences found in the textual hierarchies.

3.4.1

Patterns of clause-type sequences that could be registered in the textual hierarchies constructed are (partly) summarised in the table below:

In narrative sections:
wayyiqtol dominates in these sections (cf. 19:2–3)
— *wayyiqtol* (NP-subj; new §)
— *wayyiqtol* (no NP-subj) continuing *qatal*

— *w*^{e}*x-qatal* continuing *wayyiqtol*; new §
less frequent:
— *yiqtol* in a narrative text (19:19)

In discursive or direct speech sections:
yiqtol and *q*^{e}*tol* dominate in these sections (cf. 19:12–13)
— *yiqtol* continued by *w*^{e}*qatal*: main statement (19:5)
— *q*^{e}*tol* continued by *w*^{e}*qatal*: main statement (19:9)
— *yiqtol* continued by *w*^{e}*yiqtol*: main statement (19:3)
less frequent:
— *wayyiqṭol* continuing a *qatal* in direct speech text (19:4; 20:25)

With the help of these data (and, in the end, of similar data based on the full text of the book of Exodus, or on the entire Hebrew Bible), one can discuss existing grammatical theories of the functions of clause types and verb forms. In my research the crucial part of this discussion is the concentration on text grammar rather than on the paradigms of more or less isolated verb forms. Since this workshop concentrates on the application of the procedures for textual analysis outlined in the introductory paper, for more theoretical considerations I refer to earlier publications[8] and limit myself to some general remarks.

The primary principle is that verb forms and clause types derive from their position in grammatical paradigms but a limited capacity of grammatical marking. Only patterns of clause type sequences in actual texts determine their full grammatical function.

In Wolfgang Schneider's implementation of Harald Weinrich's theory of tenses, this implies that to the reader of a text, verb forms by themselves actually only set a small number of switches. They decide upon "communication type" (narrative or discursive), "relief" (main line or secondary line of the communication) and "perspective" (information preceding or following the actual communication). The actual sequence of clause types, their position in the textual hierarchy and their verb forms determine in what segment of text a particular setting of these switches is valid. This may help to find an

[8] E. Talstra, "Text Grammar and Biblical Hebrew: the viewpoint of Wolfgang Schneider", in: *Journal of Translation and Textlinguistics* 5 (1992) 269–297; E. Talstra, "Clause Types and Textual Structure. An experiment in narrative syntax" in: E. Talstra (ed.), *Narrative and Comment. Contributions to Discourse Grammar of Biblical Hebrew, presented to Wolfgang Schneider*, Amsterdam, 1995, 166–180.

answer to a number of the grammatical questions and translation problems raised.

3.4.2

The syntactic hierarchy of a text, combined with the information about clause type sequences, is used to formulate answers to the grammatical questions listed before.

19:1–2

In the opening verse of this chapter one finds a *qatal* (באו) + NP (explicit subject) introducing a number of *wayyiqtols* (–NP). This differs from the cases where a *wayyiqtol* is combined with a NP (explicit subject), as in verses 2b, 3, 7, etc. This implies that the *wayyiqtols*, as Schneider and others propose, indeed can be seen as "switches", marking the main line of the narrative, but—it is important to add this explicitly—being effective only within the limits of each scene or paragraph that is identified in the textual hierarchy. In this way, one can argue that the sequence *qatal* (+NP), *wayyiqtol* (–NP) in verse 1f. functions as a setting for the narrative that starts with ויחן שם ישׂראל in verse 2b. ". . . Israel had arrived in the Sinai desert. They had left Refidim. . . ." As stated before, it is true that the reader is informed by other texts that the *wayyiqtols* of verse 1f. refer to situations that antedate the story at Horeb;[9] however, it is not this non-linguistic knowledge, but the clause sequence (*qatal* [+NP], *wayyiqtol* [–NP]) that produces the syntactic marking that allows for a pluperfect interpretation. It is for that same reason that the pluperfect interpretation of the *wayyiqtol* וירד in verse 20 has to be rejected (see below). In general, if a text is too easily understood as mimicking real world chronology and consequently this view is applied to syntax, one creates linguistic and, in the end, also textual confusion. It would be better to find out first how a text creates a picture of the world of its own by the syntactic and lexical markers it uses.

19:3,18

The two cases of a the clause type sequence: *wayyiqtol* → *wᵉx-qatal* in chapter 19 have an identical function: they introduce a change of scene,[10] usually a new paragraph that can be continued by a number of subparagraphs. The difference between the two cases, however, lies in their respective hierarchical position in the narrative. The *wᵉx-qatal* in verse 3 opens a complex scene including a number of subparagraphs, i.e., dia-

---

[9] Cf. Noth, *op. cit.*, 125: "Nachholung".

[10] Cf. my article in *Narrative and Comment*, note 8.

logues between God, Moses and Israel. It continues through verse 15. The same construction in verse 18 opens just a short scene, itself a subparagraph in the scene of the third day (verse 16ff.), where the smoking and trembling of mount Sinai is depicted as it was experienced by the people (verses 16f.). Grammatically both cases of this clause sequence perform the same: a change of the scene, which is corroborated by the fact that in both cases *w^{e}x-qatal* in its turn can be continued by *wayyiqtol* clauses where the subject of the *w^{e}x-qatal* clauses returns as one of the actants (verse 3 Moses, verse 18: mountain). Again, this implies that a *wayyiqtol* may be interpreted as referring to the main storyline, but here again, this only applies to the new scene.

19:16–19

Verse 16 starts with ויהי + time reference, marking a new paragraph, but before the narrative continues with acts and dialogues, another ויהי introduces a subparagraph, marked at the beginning and at the end by a ויהי + nominal clause or participle clause. This indicates that a picture is being introduced, rather than narrative. The narrative of the dialogues of God and Moses with respect to the people is resumed at verse 20. The special syntactic position of verses 16–19 also has to be combined with the use of *yiqtol* in verse 19. Generally speaking this is a case of a *yiqtol* in narrative text. According to Schneider's grammar, those cases mark a kind of direct address by the author to the audience or readership. The information is being highlighted: what is told here is of importance to you, now; take special notice. Classical Hebrew Grammars explain such cases in terms of "actio" or "aspect": this *yiqtol* is indicating "iterativeness". In my view this may well be accurate as a second, context-dependent effect, but it seems to me that Schneider's explanation in terms of some kind of "actualising presentation" has a much broader applicability. What would be the use of "repetition" in Ex. 19:19? Rather, as exegetes usually state (more or less contradicting grammatical statements about repetition they may have made first), the emphasis in this passage is about the exclusive position of Moses, as announced in Ex. 19:9.[11] The *yiqtols* actually demonstrate the special role of Moses between God and Israel.

19:18,20

ירד *qatal* and *wayyiqtol*. In my view one should not simply state "that God's descent is told twice",[12] as if syntactic form is of no consequence

[11] Cf. Childs, *op. cit.*, 343: "frequentative sense", 350: "to legitimate him in the eyes of Israel".

[12] Cf. Beyerlin, *op. cit.*, 12.

for higher-level literary research. First, the clause types are distinct and, moreover, they belong to paragraphs with a different status in the text. The *qatal* in verse 18 is part of the special scene in verses 16–19, the pictorial text, just mentioned above. With the *wayyiqtol* in verse 20 the main storyline proceeds.[13] A second observation possible in verse 20 is that we find another type of syntactic marking: two *wayyiqtols* with a repetition of the same NPdet, which implies a sequence of two parallel paragraphs: "JHWH descended upon the mountain. Then JHWH called Moses up to . . ."

20:25

This case is the reverse of the construction of Ex. 19:19: an unexpected *wayyiqtol* in a direct speech context of *yiqtols*. It is important to notice that a *qatal* precedes. So, the question is: what is the status of *qatal* continued by *wayyiqtol* in a discursive text (direct speech)? There is no ground to interprete this text, as translations often do, as if it contained merely another *yiqtol* clause. In the direct speech context this clause type sequence does mark something else. This saying is not about "possible" or "future" state of affairs (as two times *yiqtol* would mean), but it is about a "possible narrative", i.e. a story one would have to narrate, once a particular state of affairs would be present: in case (כי) A has happened (*qatal*), B will have become the result (*wayyiqtol*). In modern languages, the text can be translated that way: "Once you have used your chisel upon it, you have profaned it".

24:1

What is marked by *wᵉPP-qatal* in the introduction of the chapter? This clause is to be connected to the introduction of God's direct speech to Moses, starting in 20:22. Grammatically that direct speech section does not stop until the end of chapter 23. These are all the words which Moses has to address to the Israelites. After that the narrator's text returns to the situation where that direct speech started: after the words to be passed on to the people, come the words meant for Moses himself. Whatever in terms of redaction the position of chapters 21–23 may be, syntactically speaking one has to express in translation the back reference to 20:22 that is constructed here.

The intention of this workshop may be clear. The study of syntax and grammar is to provide a good instrument to help in reading the text as a complete composition, not to remove claims of a composite

[13] C. Houtman, *Exodus* (COT), Kampen, 1989, speaks of "Wiederaufnahme" in this case, 410.

redactional history, though one may become more cautious in formulating such.

One last example: an application of the same approach to lexical material. To literary critics Ex. 19:8 and 9 establish a classical example of a duplicate text.[14] Childs,[15] though not agreeing with the critical view, translates these lines identically: "Moses reported the people's words to the Lord", even when the Hebrew uses two different verbal expressions שׁוב(H) + דבר (8) and נגד(H) + דבר (9). From a semantic point of view the two expressions are not identical (see the translation by Buber, mentioned in the first section of this paper). The first one is more common in dialogues: "answer" or "report someone's answer" (1 Sam. 17:30; 2 Sam. 24:13; 1 Kgs. 12:9; 2 Kgs. 22:20); the second one is less common, but emphasises the information as new or unexpected: "inform someone" (Ex. 4:28; 1 Kgs. 10:3). For that reason it is important to express the linguistic differences first before one analyses the texts as signals of redactional work. One could argue that repeating the statement about the people's reaction from verse 8 and verse 9 fits the actual context of chapter 19, since the chapter strongly emphasises that the people should be careful and keep distance. The focus is on their being ready and holy, even more so than Moses himself expects, one could say (verse 23). One gets the impression that any attempt on Moses' part to give the people any other role has to fail. Their words do not yet count, until they have heard JHWH speak in the next chapter. The acknowledgement of their reaction: "We will do" appears to be postponed from chapter 19 to chapter 24:3 and 7 as a reaction to the words being heard and written down by Moses.

3.5 *Grammar and translation. A proposal*

	Cl. Type	*§ mark*	*Proposal*
19:1	Time ref.		In the third month
19:1	PP + L + Inf. }	§	after leaving
19:1	*qatal-x*		Israel had arrived in the Sinai desert.
19:2	*wayyiqtol*		They had left Refidim,
19:2	*wayyiqtol*		had entered the Sinai desert
19:2	*wayyiqtol*		and made camp in the desert.

[14] Cf. Noth, *op. cit.*, 127: "nicht recht passender Zusatz".

[15] *Op. cit.*, 341, cf. 349.

Cont.

	Cl.Type	*§ mark*	*Proposal*
19:2	*wayyiqtol-x*	§	While Israel camped there opposite the mountain
19:3	*w-x-Qatal*	§	Moses had climbed up to God
19:3	*wayyiqtol-x*	§	Then JHWH called to him
19:8	*wayyiqtol-x*	§	Moses returned the words of the people to JHWH
19:9	*wayyiqtol-x*	§	Moses reported the words of the people to JHWH
19:16	ויהי + time	§	On the third day,
19:16	ויהי		it happened
19:16	NCl		Sounds and lightnings
19:16	*wayyiqtol-x*	§	All of the people trembled
19:17	*wayyiqtol-x*	§	Moses led the people
19:18	*w-x-qatal*	§	while mount Sinai had become all smoke
19:18	*qatal-x*		because JHWH had descended
19:19	ויהי + ptc		And then,
19:19	ptc.Cl		while the voice of the sjofar is getting stronger
19:19	*x-yiqtol*		Moses speaks
19:19	*w-x-yiqtol*		and God answers him in a voice.
19:20	*wayyiqtol-x*	§	JHWH descended on the top of the mountain.
19:20	*wayyiqtol-x*	§	Then JHWH called Moses up to the top of the mountain
20:22	*wayyiqtol-x*	§	JHWH said to Moses
20:25	*x-qatal*		Once you have used your chisel upon it
20:25	*wayyiqtol*		you have profaned it
24:1	*w-PP-qatal*	§	And to Moses he has said

A CRITICAL ANALYSIS OF NARRATIVE SYNTACTIC APPROACHES, WITH SPECIAL ATTENTION TO THEIR RELATIONSHIP TO DISCOURSE ANALYSIS[1]

Christo H.J. van der Merwe
(Stellenbosch)

1. *Introduction*

Biblical Hebrew narrative syntax is the application of insights from a field of study that is still finding its feet. If one considers that there is as yet no agreement among grammarians concerning what a twentieth century sentence syntax should look like,[2] it is not surprising that it is fairly easy to pick holes in the brave attempts to put this new approach to use for the better understanding the language of the Old Testament. For this reason, to criticize is not the primary aim of this paper. It is rather an attempt to position narrative syntax in a field of study that "is widely recognized as one of the most vast, but also one of the least defined, areas in linguistics" (Schiffrin 1994: 5). This may, on the one hand, caution some scholars who over-enthusiastically accept new theories and/or solutions to age old problems or confirm to others the validly of the course taken by them. On the other hand, an attempt to determine the inherent limitations of narrative syntax may reveal an entire range of possibilities for investigating in the field of discourse analysis/text linguistics.

I intend to accomplish the above-mentioned aim as follows:

1. Determine, as far as possible the referents of the terms, narrative syntax, text grammar and text linguistics by the presented approaches, as well as the theoretical frame of reference and assumptions each term may imply.
2. Briefly map out the developments and current state of affairs of what is considered in general linguistics as text linguistics.
3. Describe the attempt of Longacre to address problems of the

[1] Discourse analysis is considered here as a synonym of "text linguistics".
[2] Cf. Bodine (1992: 102–107).

Biblical Hebrew verbal system from the point of view of so-called discourse grammar.

4. Identify in the light of developments in and insights gained by approaches to discourse (1) some of the questionable developments of the presented approaches, and (2) some of the promising developments in the field of study as far as Biblical Hebrew is concerned.

2. *Narrative syntax, text grammar, text linguistics or discourse grammar?*

Narrative syntax is a label seldom used by linguists or grammarians. The organizers of this conference understand it as an approach to the study of Biblical Hebrew that investigates grammatical phenomena, not merely within the scope of sentences, but also within larger text units. In the material I scanned,[3] I found it to be used only once, viz. by Talstra (1995: 166). In the first paragraph of the latter publication Talstra, nevertheless, talks of the "textgrammatical function of..." (1995: 166). It thus seems as if Talstra considers *text grammar* and *narrative syntax* as synonymous. In his earlier works he mainly used the term text grammar (1978, 1982, 1983), most probably inspired by Weinrich. Although Weinrich is considered to be the scholar who made the German term *text linguistik* current (De Beaugrande 1985: 44), Weinrich recently uses the term *text grammar* to depict his description of "die Phänomene der Sprache von Texten her" (1993: 17).[4]

Niccacci (1995: 111) employs the term "text linguistics". He defines it as "a method of analyzing all the elements of a sentence in the framework of the text". Niccacci, however, does not use the term narrative syntax, but remarks elsewhere (1994a: 118): "syntax identifies the relationship among sentences and paragraphs in the framework of a text. Discourse analysis brings to fore macrosyntactic, semantic and pragmatic devices used by the author to convey his message in a forcible way". How these remarks of Niccacci should be understood in the light of his definition of text linguistics is not clear at all. Endo (1993), who uses the terms discourse analysis and discourse grammar

---

[3] Cf. also Lowery (1995: 213–253) for "A classified discourse analysis bibliography".

[4] Whether Talstra would be prepared to go along with the relatively extreme functionalist type of position at the level of the sentence that Weinrich maintains in his *Textgrammatik der deutschen Sprache* (1993), is doubtful.

as synonyms, claims that the term text linguistics is used by German linguists for discourse grammar (1993: 20). He explicitly labels Weinrich's approach as "text linguistics" (1993: 23). Joosten (1992: 14) uses the term "text linguistics" too, but only briefly in a footnote in which he associates himself with the views of Eskhult (1990). Eskhult himself does not use the term. I would therefore not dare to deduce anything from Joosten's brief remark.

What can one then deduce from Biblical Hebrew scholars' use of terms to refer to the study of linguistic phenomena in terms of a higher level than that of the sentence?

— Firstly, there is a tendency to use the term text linguistics in a non-technical fashion.
— Secondly, there is a tendency not to be consistent and unambiguous, cf. Talstra's use of the terms narrative syntax and text grammar, Niccacci's use of the terms syntax, discourse analysis and text linguistics. Furthermore, the term *narrative* syntax may be ambiguous in a context where a distinction is made between the domains (speaker orientation) *narrative* and *discourse.*
— Thirdly, the terms text grammar, narrative syntax and discourse grammar imply an approach that assumes that (1) texts or narratives have a grammar or syntax along the same lines as sentences and (2) that interpreting texts or narratives involves only an analysis of encoded linguistic signs (assuming a code model of communication). In other words, the terminology used by Talstra and the content given to their terms by Niccacci and Endo reflect a structuralist frame of reference (with its assumed code model of communication) in which distributional criteria are assumed to render one or other system at the level of the text.

One may, on the one hand, criticize some of the above-mentioned scholars of imprecision as far as their terminology is concerned, in particular Niccacci and Endo. On the other hand, it must be kept in mind that they are venturing in a new field of study that is still in the process of finding its feet, also as far as terminology is concerned. This will be more evident in the light of our discussion of developments and the current state of affairs in the field of study I will be referring to as text linguistics.

3. *Developments and the current state of affairs in the field of text linguistics*

It is, of course, impossible to provide a representative outline of developments in this vast field of study here.[5] This outline is merely an attempt to obtain a critical perspective on the work of Longacre to be discussed below, as well as works treated in my first paper.

In Europe the most common term used for approaches to the description of language that involves texts as their object of research is indeed "text linguistics".[6] In America it is referred to as "discourse analysis".[7] However, this does not mean that trends in this vast area of linguistics in America and Europe have been similar. On the contrary, in America, under the influence of scholars like Bloomfield and Chomsky, the trend has always been more formalistic than in Europe. The sentence has been regarded as the largest unit of grammatical description and it has been maintained that its structure should be described without taking recourse to its meaning. Harris (1952), the first linguist to refer to the concept "discourse analysis" (according to Schiffrin 1994: 24), even claimed that discourse, "the next level in a hierarchy of morphemes, clauses and sentences", should be investigated without recourse to its meaning (Schiffrin 1994: 24). Although Harris's approach has recently been modified by himself and others, "what is critical to structural views of discourse is that discourse is comprised of *units*" (Schiffrin 1994: 24). It is against this background that the tagmemic approach of Pike must be understood.

Tagmemics (as initiated by Pike 1967), however, diverted radically from main stream North American linguistics of the second half of this century in two ways:[8] Firstly, it is not mentalistic but an attempt to understand language in the general context of human behavior; secondly, it does not regard syntax and semantics as two autonomous modules of the human language capacity, but argues that the form of a linguistic unit can never be divorced from its meaning. Eight

---

[5] For more representative outlines, cf. De Beaugrande and Dressler (1981: 15–31), De Beaugrande (1985: 41–70) and Verschueren, Östman and Blommaert (1995: 2–19).

[6] Cf. De Beaugrande and Dressler (1981: 15).

[7] Cf. also Bodine (1995: 4 footnote 12) and Lowery (1995: 107).

[8] De Beaugrande (1985: 43) remarks: "In American linguistics, Pike's tagmemics remained isolated for some years while the majority followed the heritage of Harris. However, discourse itself disappeared when Chomsky (1957) put Harris' (1952) notion of transformation to a new use".

hierarchically structural levels are distinguished by Longacre (1983),[9] viz. morpheme, stem, word, phrase, clause, sentence, paragraph and discourse. At each level construction types (or syntagmemes), e.g. clause types, sentence types, paragraph types and discourse types are distinguished. These on their part consist of tagmemes. The discourse type (or syntagmeme) *narrative discourse* would be composed of the following tagmemes: title, aperture, stage, episode, peak and closure. The clause type (or syntagmeme) *transitive clause* would comprise the tagmemes, subject, object and transitive predicate. Each tagmeme is both a function and a set. The *function* refers to "the peculiar . . . role of one formally distinguishable part of a construction in relation to other parts of the same construction",[10] in a transitive clause the subject, object and transitive predicate are considered to be functions because each plays a particular role at the level of the clause. At the discourse level, the tagmemes title, aperture, stage, episode, peak and closure are considered to be functions because they play the same type of role at that level. *Set* is the second half of the concept tagmeme and "refers to the various ways or forms by means of which a particular function can be expressed",[11] e.g. a subject can be a noun, a noun phrase or a construction with an embedded relative clause. At the discourse level, a set would be all the constructions that could fill the slot of title, aperture, stage, episode, peak and closure respectively. Function and set are combined in this way in the tagmeme, "because tagmemics wants to pay attention both to functions and to the forms in which they manifest themselves, rather than to one of either to the neglect of the other".[12] From our discussion below it will be evident that Pike and Longacre were in some regards more in line with trends in Europe than in America.

As far as the tendency in Europe is concerned, De Beaugrande (1985: 43) remarks: "While American linguistics was preoccupied with isolated, invented sentences, researchers in other countries saw no obstacle to the investigation of real discourse. Such studies had been advocated by the major founders of European language research", e.g. Mathesius in Prague, Firth in London and Hjemslev in Copenhagen. According to De Beaugrande (1985: 44) two of the major

---

[9] According to Gary A. Long (personal conversation) a revision of Longacre (1983) is to be published soon.

[10] Longacre (1965) as cited in Den Exter Blokland (1995: 28).

[11] Den Exter Blokland (1995: 28).

[12] Den Exter Blokland (1995: 29).

forces in Germany were Hartmann and Weinrich. Although text linguistics did not gain wide recognition before the 1970s, the views put forward in the above-mentioned circles were amenable to the analysis of larger contexts. The reason being amongst others:

— the trend to assume functional distinctions to operate at all levels of linguistic description (hence the label "functional" approaches),
— the trend to emphasize the social dimensions of language, e.g. by Firth who insisted that language needs to be studied as the means used by people to function in society,
— and the trend to take into account that language could be used for different purposes, e.g. to render a description, to render a self expression or to establish and maintain social roles and relations.

In the 1970s a variety of approaches arose to study texts. Initially the main idea was to supplement sentence syntax with a macrosyntax (Gülich 1970) or text syntax (Dressler 1970). In some circles texts were considered to be sequences of sentences that could be described with the same methods and in terms of the same type of categories as sentences. According to Heinemann and Viehweger (1991: 26), these type of approaches saw "Texte als transphrastische Ganzheiten". They classify the "Satzverknüpfungshypothese" of Isenberg (1974), "Texte als Pronominalisierungsketten" of Harweg (1968), the approach of Weinrich (1971) in which "das Problem der Kommunikationssteuerung met Hilfe grammatischer Mittel", viz. "Artikeln und Tempusmorphemen", constitutes its main point of departure and the functional sentence perspective of the Prague school as developed by Daneš (1976) as representatives of this type of approach. The main problem with these approaches is according to Heinemann and Viehweger (1991: 26) that they assume texts to be complete and static units and that the surface structure of texts "zureichenden Reflex von Textbedeutung and Textfunktion darstellen". In other words, they do not leave room for the systematic consideration of the pragmatic information that is not encoded in texts. The same type of inadequacies are inherent of "semantisch orientierten Textbeschreibungsansätzen" in which not the surface level features of the texts are the point the departure but the semantic deep structures they reflect (Heinemann and Viehweger 1991: 49). They classify under this heading the "Isotopieansatz" of Greimas (1966), the initial textual deep structure approaches of van Dijk (1972) and Petöfi (1972), the later developments of van Dijk (1977 and 1978), as well as the "Text-Thema" approach of Brinker (1973) and Kallmeyer and Meyer-Hermann (1980).

In America a number of similar linguistically orientated approaches were developed. The most prominent are Mann and Thompson's Rhetorical Structure Theory (1988)[13] and the work of Hopper (1979). The latter is well-known for his claims that the foreground and background information in a narrative could be traced by means of grammatical forms. According to Lowery (1995: 115) the "definite synthesis of the grammatical approach by a discourse linguist to date must be Longacre's *The grammar of discourse*".

Although in some of the above-mentioned *linguistically* orientated approaches the function of texts in society is assigned an important role, pragmatic considerations in most cases play a peripheral role. Attempts to address this problem, on the one hand, range from adding a pragmatic component to sentence grammar (Dik 1978 and 1989), "adding social context to methods and concepts borrowed from linguistic analyses" (variation analysis of Labov),[14] to the attempts by Halliday "to establish a network of systems of a relationships which will account for all the semantically relevant choices in a language as a whole" (Berns 1990: 12).[15] Important to note is that most of these approaches operate in terms of the code model of communication. In other words, mainly information that is signaled by means of the linguistic code of the text is systematically analyzed.

On the other hand, approaches were developed in which texts are viewed as part of a communication *process* in which not only participants, a particular context and a particular mode of communication, but also the entire conceptual world of each participant inside and outside the text, are involved. Two of the main trends to be distinguished are: (1) attempts to determine, apart from the information conveyed by means of the linguistic and any other overt communication signals, which and how contextual factors should be incorporated systematically when reading a text (e.g. Schmidt 1980) and (2) attempts that treat texts as a mode of human communication in which communication takes place according to general principles of communication (e.g. Grice's principle of cooperative principle,[16] Sperber and Wilson's

[13] According to Mann, Matthiessen and Thompson (1992: 46–47), "RST provides a general way to describe the relations among organizational elements in a text, whether or not those relations are grammatically or lexically signaled".

[14] Cf. Schiffrin (1994: 291).

[15] According to Berns (1990: 14) Halliday's recent publications are "concerned with semiotics, particularly with a semiotics that brings together European functionalism, cultural analysis, social theory, and his theory of language as social system".

[16] Cf. Schiffrin (1994: 190–227).

relevance principle[17]). A basic notion, however, is that during communication not only the encoding and decoding of the linguistic codes are involved, but also inferences continually made by each participant in the communication process, each in terms of his/her own conceptual world. Although the assumption of Grice and Sperber and Wilson that the entire mankind communicates according to the same principles could be questioned, their attention to the process of communication, highlighted once again the complexity of human communication, as well as, the inadequacies of the code model of communication which underlie many structuralist attempts to describe language use.

To conclude this section; it is evident that the field of study *text linguistics* or *discourse analysis* is indeed still finding its feet. The following tensions in the field illustrate this further:

— On the one hand, a clear picture is starting to emerge as to what constitutes the domain of text linguistics,[18] viz. in the words of Heinemann and Viehweger (1991: 17): "Die textlinguistik kann nicht als Superwissenschaft verstanden werden, wohl auch nicht als Textwissenschaft" (i.e. the study of texts in general). "Vielmehr muss sich die Textlinguistik auf die Erforschung von Textstrukturen und Textformulieren beschränken, jeweil in ihrer Einbettung in kommunikative, allgemeine soziologische und psychologische Zusammenhänge". On the other hand, how exactly this field should be deliminated from communication science and psycho-linguistics and how some of the categories and methods of these disciplines should be treated in text linguistics are still not clear.

— On the one hand, it is argued that (1) a sentence-syntax driven approach towards interpreting texts is not tenable,[19] (2) using only distributional criteria in terms of the code model of communication

[17] Cf. Sperber and Wilson (1995).

[18] Text is defined as "die Gesamtmenge der in einer kommunikativer Interaktion auftretenden sprachlichen kommunikativen Signale". Cf. Heinemann and Viehweger (1991: 16).

[19] Couper-Kuhlen (1989: 13) remarks: "syntactic structure cannot be relied on blindly in determining the foreground". This view has been echoed by other linguists from various perspectives (e.g. Schleppegrel 1991: 323–337 and Bakker 1991: 233). The following remark of Bakker is of particular relevance here: ". . . instead of determining whether a subclause is backgrounded, we have to investigate in what sense it is backgrounded with respect to its main clause. Only when we have determined what a subclause actually "does" in its context can we gauge the value of the subclauses with respect to the notions "sequentiality" and "foregrounding, or, for that purpose what it means for a subclause to lie within, or outside the narrative assertion".

has its limitations for understanding the use of language[20] and (3) a text linguistic approach should transcend the methods and categories of describing sentence grammar. On the other hand, the exact relationship between text linguistics and sentence grammar is not clear. The follow questions must still be answered: (1) How should linguistic phenomena at the "lower" levels of description be investigated in the light of the textual level? (2) How will it be determined whether and which grammatical elements have relevance at a textual level? At this stage it appears that recognizing the existence of three autonomous modules, viz. syntax, phonology and the lexicon enjoys in general more support (also in terms of empirical evidence) than postulating a fourth pragmatic module[21] or including a pragmatic level at sentence level.[22]

— On the one hand, the need of distinguishing between text types as modes of communication that function under specific conditions is recognized; on the other hand, which text types and criteria needed to distinguish them are not clear.[23]

I have suggested above that the tagmemic approach was more in line with what was happening in Europe than in America. However, den Exter Blokland recently (1995: 26) drew attention to the fact that "Discourse grammar in tagmemics turns out to be essentially a grammar of semantics, whereas text-grammar is usually associated with the description of the syntactical structure of the linguistic utterance itself". Furthermore, Longacre is currently prepared to make much bolder claims than most of the his European counterparts. His current use of the term "text linguistics" in an American publication may be an attempt to convey this notion (1989 and 1994). Before trying to

---

Some linguists have even abandoned the notions foreground and background. Van Kuppevelt (1995: 809–833) talks of main structures and side structures.

[20] Couper-Kuhlen (1987: 25) concludes in her study of English temporal clauses: "discourse cannot be treated as a string of sentences organized at some local level only, nor can temporal interpretation in texts be reduced to a reiterative application of syntax-driven semantic rules". Blass's (1993: 109) answer to the question in the title of her article, "Are there logical relations in a text?" reads: "My conclusion is that if discourse analysis is to be sensitive to all the factors involved in communication and comprehension, then it is clearly wrong to pay attention only to what is linguistically encoded. Rather it is necessary to pay serious attention to contextual factors and inferential processes".

[21] Cf. Mey (1993: 42–47) and Sinclair (1995: 509–539).

[22] Cf. Dik (1978 and 1989).

[23] However, cf. Longacre (1989) and Werlich (1983).

evaluate both Longacre and the approaches referred to in my previous paper, we need to elaborate briefly on some of Longacre's views.

4. *Longacre*

Some basic assumptions of Longacre's discourse grammar (which he later refers to as a text linguistic approach)[24] are the following:

1. "Any morphosyntactic form in a text represents the author's choice whether conscious or automatic; we may not know the why's of all such choices, but we may speculate on them as implementations of different discourse strategies" (Longacre and Hwang 1994: 337). It is most probably against this background that Longacre (1983: xv) argues that there is an entire range of problems that could only be solved by discourse grammar: "Among these problems have been deixis and the use of articles. Pronominalization, and other anaphoric ways of referring to a participant; better understanding of tense, aspect, mode, and voice in verbs; use of optional temporal and spatial expressions; the function of extraposition; left dislocation, and others such features; subject selection, object selection, and other focus phenomena; the functions and thrust of conjunctions and other sequence signals; and the function of mystery particles which occur in connected contexts in some language, which the native speaker knows where to use and where not to use, but which defy translation".

2. "In the grammar of language, there are hierarchical levels from morpheme to stem, word, phrase, clause, sentence, paragraph, and discourse" (Longacre and Hwang 1994: 336).

3. At each level a number of *syntagmemes* or *discourse types* that consist of *tagmemes* are distinguishable (cf. my explanation in section 3), e.g. at the level of discourse four discourse types are distinguished in terms of the parameters "agent and temporal succession", viz. *narrative*

---

[24] Cf. the title of Dawson (1994), *Text-linguistics and Biblical Hebrew*. It tries to illustrate the advantages of the approach of Longacre for the better understanding of Biblical Hebrew. However, the type of criteria Dawson uses in this regard can by no means be described as purely linguistic (or even in my understanding of the concept, scientific), e.g. he states (1994: 209): "It is claimed (1) that the Hebrew language can be described elegantly and helpfully at the level of 'text', and (2) that this cannot be accomplished if the researcher's theoretical starting point does not allow for the possibility of a variety of text-types, or if the write-up does not explain itself so that linguistically astute, but non-linguistically trained, hebraists can both trace the procedures and comprehend the results".

(+agent, +succession), *procedural* (–agent, +temporal succession), *hortatory* (+agent, –succession) and *expository* (–agent, –temporal succession). More recently he also distinguishes a fifth discourse type, viz. *instructional discourse* (Longacre 1995: 23). However, it does not seem to be distinguished in terms of the same parameters as the other four types.

4. Each discourse type has its own grammatical rules, e.g.

— There is a different word order in the clauses that encode their mainline information, as in Biblical Hebrew, where the order VSO (verb, subject, object) prevails in narrative, but SVO in exposition.

— On account of the verbs forms used, Longacre does not distinguish only between storyline (or main line) and background information. The verb forms can refer to different types of backgrounds, which are hierarchically ranked. In a narrative the *wayyiqtol* would signal the storyline, the *perfect* and noun + *perfect* background actions, הנה + participle, participle or noun + participle background activities, the perfect of היה a setting, etc.[25]

5. The narrative discourse type consists of the following tagmemes, viz. title, aperture, stage, episode, peak, a peak' (in which the peak is resolved) and closure. Each tagmeme has a set of constructions that are associated with it, e.g. the peak and peak' has the following type of surface structure characteristics: "(1) rhetorical underlining by means of repetition and paraphrase, (2) heightened vividness by a tense shift or by person shift, . . . (7) 'slowing the camera down' by treating structures that are not usually on the event line as if they were".[26]

— It is in terms of this frame of reference that Longacre (1994: 71–72) explains the most problematic *w^e^qatal* form in Judg. 3:23 as marking climatic/pivotal events.[27]

וַיֵּצֵא אֵהוּד הַמִּסְדְּרוֹנָה וַיִּסְגֹּר דַּלְתוֹת הָעֲלִיָּה בַּעֲדוֹ וְנָעָל׃	Then Ehud went out into the vestibule, and closed the doors of the roof chamber upon him, *and locked* them (Judg. 3:23)

6. "Comprehension of a story results from multiple processing, including top-down (use of the schema) and bottom-up (use of content and cues provided by the text" (Hwang 1984: 136).

---

[25] Cf. Dawson for a more complete picture of the verb-ranking of the different discourse types (1994: 115–116). Cf. Longacre for the verb-ranking scheme of instructional discourse (1995: 47).

[26] Citation from a summary of these features by den Exter Blokland (1995: 38).

[27] Cf. also Buth (1994: 141) who regards the *x-qatal* form in Judg. 6:21 as signaling a "dramatic pause".

It is impossible to do full justice to Longacre here. His approach is based on observations of a variety of languages and is still scrutinized by him on a regular basis in the light of new findings. His claim concerning the entire range of problems that could be solved only by discourse grammar (cf. my quotation from Longacre 1983: xv above) and his attempt to provide a theoretical frame of reference in this regard contributed without doubt to a new look at old problems, as well as an interest in constructions that hitherto had not been investigated systematically. In comparison with the approaches of Niccacci, Muraoka and Joosten one may argue that he has a much more sophisticated frame of reference. However, whether his approach would be able to meet all the expectations it creates, is questionable. I base this reservation concerning his approach, amongst other, on the following:

1. His own notional framework often tends to override the formal aspects of his data, which in terms of his own theory should play an equal role. Den Exter Blokland (1995: 89) recently determined that "in spite of the incorporation of syntactical features, exploring the workings of the Hebrew text syntax does not seem Longacre's primary concern. Rather his concern is in bringing to the text a kind of universal syntax of semantics, a formalization of textual interpretation . . . to which syntactical features appears to be systematically subordinated".

2. Although a simultaneous top-down and bottom up approach towards the comprehension of a Biblical Hebrew narrative cannot be faulted, the fact that Longacre does not provide any criteria in this regard, resulted in a state of affairs in which "a given passage will usually accommodate a variety of analytical options". Such an indeterminate model "can be made to fit various readings of the same text, making the fit rather meaningless", e.g. in Jer. 38:28b he assigns to והיה a cataphoric function that is exactly the opposite of the anaphoric functions elsewhere, e.g. Jer. 3:9; 37:11 and 40:3. Ironically, Stipp (1991: 544) indicates through conclusive arguments that these problematic cases of והיה in the book of Jeremiah are due to the transmission of the text and should be understood as ויהי.

3. Some of his suggestions throw a shadow over the level of Biblical Hebrew knowledge that underlies his analysis at the lower levels of description, e.g. in his analysis of 1 Sam. 17:47–48 he claims that והיה functions like the narrative counterpart of ועתה in hortatory discourse: "In both we are saying that the preliminaries are over and the substantive saying or action will follow". This is not the case at

all. ועתה as a rule introduces a logical consequence of a foregoing state of affairs, introduced by a verb with a directive function, e.g. an imperative.

5. *Caution, confirmation and new horizons*

The aim of this investigation has been to position narrative syntax in the field of discourse analysis/text linguistics because I hypothesize that it may caution some scholars who over-enthusiastically accept or develop new theories and/or solutions to age-old problems, it may confirm to others the validly of the course taken by others or it may open up an entire range of new possibilities to investigate.

In section 2 I argued that terms like text grammar, narrative syntax and discourse grammar, as well as the content given to the term text linguistics by Niccacci, imply an approach to the study of texts that used to a large extent the same methods and types of categories as those of sentence grammar. Furthermore, they all are mainly concerned with what is *encoded* in their object of study, viz. the text. Despite the fact that he more recently uses the term "text linguistics", it is evident from our outline of developments in the field of text linguistics in general that Longacre's approach, which according to den Exter Blokland's findings could be described as dominantly text semantic, shares the same type of assumptions concerning his object of research.

What can we then gather from our outline of current developments in the field of text linguistics?

1. The growing awareness of the complexity of human communication and that trying to understand a text involves much more than decoding a linguistic code, caution us towards the following:

— the holistic type of text semantic type of approach of Longacre and

— claims like "it is my conviction that the verb forms in a narrative constitute the main clue to the author's perspective in presenting information" (Niccacci 1994b: 175).[28]

— Talstra's dedication to distributional criteria is understandable as far as his analysis of Biblical Hebrew linguistic data is concerned.

[28] Talstra (1995: 174) also provides convincing arguments why Niccacci should "allow for more embeddings in a story than only a 'main story line' and 'background' information".

One may even ask: Is there a more responsible way to embark upon at this stage? However, the limitations of such approaches that concentrate only on the encoded information should always be kept in mind.[29]

2. The uncertainties concerning the exact relationship between sentence syntax and text linguistics, as well as the tendency to regard syntax as an autonomous module of the mind, raise amongst others the question whether some solutions from a text linguistic point of view in Biblical Hebrew are not premature. This may be because Biblical Hebrew scholars have not yet addressed some sentence syntactic phenomena adequately or with the appropriate theoretical frame of reference,[30] e.g.:

— DeCaen (1995) argues that the problem of the Biblical Hebrew verbal system is by no ways unique. There are many other languages in which aspect and tense are signaled by the same forms and in which the position of the verb in the sentence may help to determine the mood of the verbal form. DeCaen then uses recent developments in generative linguistics to explain these phenomena.

— Muraoka (1985) resorts to a psychological definition of the concept "emphasis" to explain some cases of what he regards as the marked word order in Biblical Hebrew. The unmarked Biblical Hebrew word order for him is VSO. In my earlier paper I indicated that also Niccacci maintains that the VSO order in Biblical Hebrew is the unmarked one and that at the sentence level the marked element may be emphasized.[31] However, emphasis is not involved in every compound noun clause (i.e. x-verb clause). In some cases the compound noun clause may "on the broader level of the text" have "the function of making the sentence as a whole dependent on another" verbal sentence. However, in some cases this marked structure may

[29] Cf. Hardmeier's (1990: 72–73) justified criticism of Schweizer's *Metaphorische Grammatik*. This similar type of criticism has recently been launched by Disse (1996) against Schweizer (1981).

[30] It may even be possible that Biblical Hebrew text linguists are not well acquainted with existing Biblical Hebrew publications, e.g. Longacre's interpretation of ועתה referred to above.

[31] Although Niccacci tries to define the term "emphasis", the type of definition he comes up with was abandoned by general linguists some years ago already, cf. van der Merwe (1989: 118–132). Both Gross (1996) and Disse (1996) use instead, like van der Merwe, the well-defined semantic-pragmatic concept focus. Gross (1996) illustrates how in terms of his definition of the concept, focused items could be distinguished from non-focused one, both in preverbal and postverbal positions. On this issue, cf. also Bandstra (1992: 109–123) and Buth (1995: 77–102).

have both an emphasizing and subordinating function (1994: 126). In my earlier paper I also posed the following questions in this regard: How should one recognize those cases that have both an emphasizing and subordinating function and how should a non-emphasized marked structure be described at the sentence level? Recently scholars like Gross (1996) and DeCaen (1995), who have quite different theoretic points of view, argued that the SVO order could be the unmarked order in Biblical Hebrew. The crucial question is now, if Gross and DeCaen are right, how would this perspective on Biblical Hebrew word order affect one of the pillars of Niccacci's theory?
— Biblical Hebrew has a variety of temporal constructions, many of which have apparently the same meaning, e.g.

וַתְּכַל לְהַשְׁקֹתוֹ וַתֹּאמֶר	And she finished giving him a drink, *and (then) she said*[32] (Gen. 24:19).
וַיְהִי כְּכַלּוֹת מֹשֶׁה לִכְתֹּב וַיְצַו מֹשֶׁה אֶת־הַלְוִיִּם	*When Moses had finished writing* . . ., Moses commanded the Levites (Deut. 31:24).
וַיְהִי כַּאֲשֶׁר כִּלּוּ הַגְּמַלִּים לִשְׁתּוֹת וַיִּקַּח הָאִישׁ נֶזֶם זָהָב	*When the camels had done drinking*, the man took a gold ring (Gen. 24:22).
וַיֵּלֶךְ יְהוָה כַּאֲשֶׁר כִּלָּה לְדַבֵּר אֶל־אַבְרָהָם וְאַבְרָהָם שָׁב לִמְקֹמוֹ׃	And the Lord went his way, *when he had finished speaking to Abraham*; and Abraham returned to his place (Gen. 18:33).

Wheatley-Irving (1993) could identify no semantic differences among these type of sentences. Groppe (1995: 183), however, found that "the function of these constructions can only be more adequately described within a model of syntax that goes above and beyond the 'sentence'". He made this conclusion in the light of findings of an investigation of the functional differences between כְּ + infinitive and בּ + infinitive in a Biblical Hebrew narrative text. Van der Merwe (forthcoming a) in an independent investigation came to conclusions similar to that of Groppe concerning the differences between כְּ + infinitive and בּ + infinitive. However, he found on account of Jenni's two seminal studies of these prepositions (1992 and 1994) that the main difference between the two constructions are also related to the semantic difference between the prepositions כְּ and בּ. Furthermore,

[32] The translation is that of Joüon-Muraoka § 166b. The RSV, and most other English translations, prefer the following translation: *When she had finished giving him a drink*, she said.

van der Merwe (forthcoming b) found that the position of Biblical Hebrew temporal constructions in a sentence are related to the fact whether they refer to a *temporal position, duration* or *frequency*,[33] in other words, semantic considerations.

3. Developments in narrative syntax that are confirmed by our outline of development in text linguistics in general are:
— Although for different reasons, the reluctance of Talstra and Niccacci to distinguish like Longacre at this stage a range of discourse types.
— The attempts of Talstra towards developing an electronic instrument with which different hypothesized Biblical Hebrew notional frames of reference can be verified.[34] It may be used to verify (1) a particular theory concerning the semantic relationships between Biblical Hebrew clauses (cf. Winther-Nielsen 1995 and Winther-Nielsen and Talstra 1995 scrutinizing Mann and Thompson's Rhetorical Structural Theory) or (2) the contribution of theories towards the syntactic text segmentation of Biblical Hebrew (cf. den Exter Blokland's 1995 scrutinization of Longacre's tagmemic model and Gülich and Raible's "Überlegungen zu einer makrostrukturellen Textanalyse").

4. Although Niccacci understands text linguistics as "a method of analyzing all the elements of a sentence in the framework of the text" and Longacre lists a number of linguistic phenomena, e.g. participant referents, mystery particles upon which new light could be shed by his discourse grammar, few real solutions have yet been offered in this regard. Most attention has been paid, in particular by Niccacci, to the role of verb forms. The emerging view that text linguistics is a field of study that concentrates on "die Erforschung von Textstrukturen und Textformulieren . . . jeweil in ihrer Einbettung in kommunikative, allgemeine soziologische und psychologische Zusammenhänge" to my opinion indeed opens new horizons as far as the social and psychological dimensions of Biblical Hebrew are concerned. I restrict myself to two areas in this regard:

— Firstly, the sociolinguistic conventions that underlie Biblical Hebrew communication, e.g.

[33] Van der Merwe (forthcoming b) illustrates the value of taking the *temporal perspective* (referred to by English grammarians as reference time in contrast to the event time) of an utterance into consideration for explaining the difference between syntactically different temporal constructions.

[34] Hardmeier (1990: 72) remarks "Eine Textgrammatik des Althebräischen musste die traditionelle semasiologische Fragestellung komplementär durch eine onomasiologische Betrachtungsweise ergänzen".

In Biblical Hebrew references to participants in narratives in some cases appear to be *overspecified* while in other cases they appear to be *underspecified* for speakers of modern Indo-European languages, e.g.

23 וַיֹּאמֶר אֲלֵהֶם גִּדְעוֹן לֹא־אֶמְשֹׁל אֲנִי בָּכֶם . . . יְהוָה יִמְשֹׁל בָּכֶם׃ 24 וַיֹּאמֶר אֲלֵהֶם גִּדְעוֹן אֶשְׁאֲלָה . . .	23 *Gideon said to them*, "I will not rule over you, . . . the LORD will rule over you". 24 *And Gideon said to them*, "Let me make a request . . . (Judg. 8:23)
וַתֹּאמֶר רוּת הַמּוֹאֲבִיָּה אֶל־נָעֳמִי	And Ruth *the Moabitess* said to Naomi (Ruth 2:2)
וַתִּקַּח מִפִּרְיוֹ וַתֹּאכַל וַתִּתֵּן גַּם־לְאִישָׁהּ עִמָּהּ וַיֹּאכַל	She took of its fruit and ate; and she also gave (*some* = ellipses in Biblical Hebrew text) to her husband, and he ate (Gen. 3:6).

Biblical Hebrew scholars did recognize the phenomena. As far as the cases of underspecification are concerned, Irsigler (1984: 58–61) uses the notion "Satzbund" to describe the clustering of sentences by means of an ellipsed constituent. He, however, does not assign any functional value to them. Longacre (1989: 30, 145) and Andersen (1994: 107) made isolated suggestions on the function of the overspecification of referents. However, it is de Regt (1991–92) that represents one of the first systematic investigations of this phenomenon.[35] Recently den Exter Blokland (1995: 149–152 and 169–179) illustrated how the nature of references to participants in a narrative could play a role in the segmentation of Biblical Hebrew narratives. Revell, however, describes and analyses the phenomenon from a different angle, viz. "the way individual characters are referred to and addressed in biblical narratives" (1996: 1). He summarizes his findings as follows: "It has considerable significance as a way in which the speaker or narrator conveys his feelings about the matters presented, and attempts to influence the addressee or the reader" (1996: 361). It is evident that a range of explanations are offered to explain the apparently same type of phenomenon. De Regt is certainly correct by arguing that different parameters may be involved,[36] a claim that is confirmed by the work of den Exter Blokland. An investigation along these lines

---

[35] For a summary, of Longacre, Andersen and de Regt, cf. van der Merwe (1994: 34–36).

[36] De Regt recently gave me a copy of an unpublished article called "Rules and

could in my opinion, certainly shed new light on this problem, in particular if a range of sociolinguistic parameters are also considered and more attention is paid to similar phenomena in the literature of neighbouring cultures.

— Secondly, the role of some particles in establishing and/or displaying relationships between the conceptual worlds of participants in a communication process.[37]

Some Biblical Hebrew particles were traditionally seldom adequately treated or treated at all in Biblical Hebrew grammars and/or lexica. They were normally assigned a mere sentence semantic function, the semantic value "emphasis", or were simply ignored.[38] In Deut. 4:1 ועתה signals that 4:1ff should be heeded in the light of what was said in Deuteronomy 1–3. In Is. 5:7 כי introduces the motivation of what was said in 5:1–6. The NIV's translations of these discourse markers are typical in their interpretation of ועתה and כי, viz. very little of their anchoring functions in the communication context or co-text are reflected.

וְעַתָּה יִשְׂרָאֵל שְׁמַע . . .	Hear now, O Israel, . . . (Deut. 4:1).
כִּי כֶרֶם יְהוָה צְבָאוֹת בֵּית יִשְׂרָאֵל וְאִישׁ יְהוּדָה נְטַע שַׁעֲשׁוּעָיו	The vineyard of the LORD Almighty is the house of Israel, and the men of Judah are the garden of his delight (Is. 5:7).

Schneider (1982) and Richter (1980) were some of the first Biblical Hebrew grammarians who introduced the notions "Makrosyntaktische Zeichen" and "superordinate conjunction, modal word, text-deictic" in their respective grammars in order to accommodate these lexical items in a Biblical Hebrew grammar. Bandstra (1982) and Muraoka (1985) too did pioneering work in scrutinizing the so-called emphatic words. Van der Merwe (1992: 181–199 and 1993: 27–44) provides a new perspective on the function of some Biblical Hebrew particles. He does it in the light of the application of Blakemore (1987) of a mentalistic theory of communication developed by Sperber and Wilson

conventions of participant reference in Biblical Hebrew and Aramaic". Where it will be published is still uncertain.

[37] Cf. Schiffrin (1987) and Foolen (1993) for developments in the study of particles. Blakemore (1987) pays attention to the "relevance" of some particles in a communication process.

[38] Cf. van der Merwe (1993: 27–44).

(1986 and 1995), referred to as *Relevance Theory*,[39] to the interpretation of these type of particles. The novelty of this perspective is the notion that some particles should be understood not as establishing or displaying relationships between clauses, sentences or even cluster of sentences encoded in a text, but also between information contained in the conceptual worlds of a speaker, an audience or an implied reader.[40]

6. *Concluding statement*

The type of Biblical Hebrew text linguistics that I have in mind does not imply the study of an abstract system similar to that of sentences. As a study of the structures and formulae displayed in specific communication processes it involves both the conceptual and social world of all the participants in- and outside the text of the Old Testament. When you embark upon this approach to Biblical Hebrew you cannot escape the fact that you are in the domain of the study of language *use*. In other words, you are studying human communication and human communication is as complex as human beings can be. Important though is that we realize that we are still in the initial phases of a new paradigm of language study.

References

Althaus, H.P., Henne, H. & Wiegang, E. (eds.), 1980, *Lexicon der germanistischen Linguistik*, Tübingen: Niemeyer.

Andersen, F.I., 1994, "Salience, Implicature, Ambiguity and Redundancy", in: Bergen, R.D. (ed.), *Biblical Hebrew and Discourse Linguistics*, Winona Lake (Ind.): Eisenbrauns, 99–116.

Bakker, E.J., 1991, "Foregrounding and Indirect Discourse: Temporal Subclauses in a Herodotean Short Story", *Journal of Pragmatics* 16: 225–247.

Bandstra, B.R., 1982, *The Syntax of the Particle ky in Biblical Hebrew and Ugaritic*, Ph.D. diss., Yale University.

[39] Quite independent of the work of van der Merwe, insights of *Relevance Theory* were recently made use of for the description of הִנֵּה. Cf. Follingstad (1995: 1–24) and van der Merwe (1994: 38). For a suggestion of using Relevance Theory towards a better understanding of the use of so-called "unmarked overlay" in a Biblical Hebrew narrative, cf. Buth (1994: 151).

[40] In van der Merwe, Naudé and Kroeze (1996) the pragmatic use of some of these types of lexemes (e.g. כי, ועתה, גם, אך, רק, הנה) is for the first time systematically described in a Biblical Hebrew reference grammar.

———, 1992, "Word Order and Emphasis in Biblical Hebrew Narrative: Syntactic Observations on Genesis 22 from a Discourse Perspective", in: Bodine, W.R. (ed.), *Linguistics and Biblical Hebrew*, Winona Lake (Ind.): Eisenbrauns, 109–123.

Bergen, R.D. (ed.), 1994, *Biblical Hebrew and Discourse Linguistics*, Winona Lake (Ind.): Eisenbrauns.

Berns, M., 1990, *Contexts of Competence. Social and Cultural Considerations in Communicative Language Teaching*, New York: Plenum.

Blakemore, D., 1987, *Semantic Constraints on Relevance*, Oxford: Basil Blackwell.

Blass, R., 1993, "Are There Logical Relations in a Text?", *Lingua* 90:91–110.

Bodine, W.R. (ed.), 1992, *Linguistics and Biblical Hebrew*, Winona Lake (Ind.): Eisenbrauns.

———, 1992, "How Linguists Study Syntax", in: Bodine, W.R. (ed.), *Linguistics and Biblical Hebrew*, Winona Lake (Ind.): Eisenbrauns, 89–107.

——— (ed.), 1995, *Discourse Analysis of Biblical Literature. What It Is and What It Offers*, Atlanta: Scholars, 1995.

Brinker, K., 1973, "Zum Textbegriff in der heutigen Linguistik", in: Sitta, H. & Brinker, K. (eds.), *Studien zur Texttheorie und zur deutschen Grammatik*, Düsseldorf: Schwann, 9–41.

Buth, R., 1994, "Methodological Collision Between Source Criticism and Discourse: The Problem of 'Unmarked Overlay' and the Pluperfect *wayyiqtol*", in: Bergen, R.D. (ed.), *Biblical Hebrew and Discourse Linguistics*, Winona Lake (Ind.): Eisenbrauns, 138–154.

———, 1995, "Functional Grammar, Hebrew and Aramaic: An Integrated, Exegetically Significant Textlinguistic Approach to Syntax", in: Bodine, W.R. (ed.), *Discourse Analysis of Biblical Literature. What It Is and What It Offers*, Atlanta: Scholars, 77–102.

Chomsky, N., 1957, *Syntactic Structures*, The Hague: Mouton.

Couper-Kuhlen, E., 1987, "Temporal Relations and Reference Time in Narrative Discourse", in: Schopf, A. (ed.), *Essays on Tensing in English. Time, Text and Modality*, Vol. 1, Tübingen: Niemeyer, 7–25.

———, 1989, "Foregrounding and Temporal Relations in Narrative Discourse", in: Schopf, A. (ed.), *Essays on Tensing in English. Time, Text and Modality*, Vol. 2, Tübingen: Niemeyer, 7–29.

Daneš, F., 1976, "Zur semantische und thematischen Struktur des Kommunikats", in: Daneš, F. & Viehweger, D. (eds.), *Probleme der Textgrammatik*, Berlin: Akademieverlag, 29–40.

——— & Viehweger, D. (eds.), 1976, *Probleme der Textgrammatik*, Berlin: Akademieverlag.

Dawson, D.A., 1994, *Text-linguistics and Biblical Hebrew* (Journal for the Study of the Old Testament, Supplement Series 177), Sheffield: Sheffield Academic Press.

De Beaugrande, R. & Dressler, W., 1981, *Einführung in die Textlinguistik*, Tübingen: Niemeyer.

———, 1985, "Text Linguistics and Discourse Studies", in: Dijk, T.A. van (ed.), *Handbook of Discourse Analysis*, Vol. 1: Disciplines of Discourse, London: Academic Press, 41–70.

DeCaen, V., 1995, *On the Placement and Interpretation of the Verbs in Standard Biblical Hebrew Prose*, Ph.D. diss., University of Toronto.

Dijk, T.A. van, 1972, *Some Aspects of Text Grammars*, The Hague: Mouton.

———, 1977, *Text and Context*, London: Longman, 1977.

———, 1978, *Facts: The Organization of Proposition in Discourse Comprehension*, Amsterdam: University of Amsterdam Institute for General Literature Studies.

——— (ed.), 1985, *Handbook of Discourse Analysis*, Vol. 1: Disciplines of Discourse, London: Academic Press.

———, Ihwe, J., Petöfi, J. & Rieser, H. (eds.), 1972, *Zur Bestimmung Narrativer Strukturen auf der Grundlage von Textgrammatiken*, Hamburg: Buske.

——— & Petöfi, J. (eds.), 1977, *Research in Texttheory/Untersuchungen in Texttheorie: Grammars and Descriptions*, Berlin: De Gruyter.
Dik, S.C., 1978, *Functional Grammar*, Amsterdam: North Holland.
———, 1980, *Studies in Functional Grammar*, London: Academic Press.
———, 1989, *The Theory of Functional Grammar*, Dordrecht: Foris.
Disse, A., 1996, *Informationsstruktur im Biblischen Hebräisch. Sprachwissenschaftliche Grundlagen und Exegetische Konsequenzen einer Korpus Untersuchung zu den Büchern Deuteronomium, Richter und 2 Könige*, Ph.D. diss., Universität Tübingen.
Dressler, W., 1970, "Textsyntax", *Lingua e Stile* 5:191–213.
——— (ed.), 1978, *Textlinguistik*, Darmstadt: Wissenschaftliche Buchgesellschaft.
Endo, Y., 1993, *The Verbal System of Classical Hebrew in the Joseph Story: An Approach from Discourse Analysis*, Ph.D. diss., University of Bristol.
Eskhult, M., 1990, *Studies in Verbal Aspect and Narrative Technique in Biblical Hebrew Prose* (Acta Universitatis Upsaliensis, Studia Semitica Upsaliensia 12), Uppsala: Almqvist & Wiksell.
Exter Blokland, A.F. den, 1995, *In Search of Text Syntax. Towards a Syntactic Segmentation Model for Biblical Hebrew*, Amsterdam: VU University Press.
Fokkelman, J.P., 1993, *Narrative Art and Poetry in the Books of Samuel. Vol. IV. Vow and Desire.* (Studia Semitica Neerlandica), Assen: Van Gorcum.
Follingstad, C.M., 1995, "*Hinneh* and Focus Function with Application to Tyap", *Journal of Translation and Textlinguistics* 7:1–24.
Foolen, A., 1993, *De betekenis van Partikels. Een dokumentatie van de stand van het onderzoek met bijzondere aandacht voor* "maar", Nijmegen: Ad Foolen.
Givón, T. (ed.), 1979, *Discourse and Semantics* (Syntax and Semantics 12), New York: Academic Press.
Greimas, A.J., 1966, *Sémantique Structurale*, Paris: Larousse.
Grice, H.P., 1975, "Logic and Conversation", in: Cole, P. & Morgan, J.L. (eds.), *Syntax and Semantics 3: Speech Acts*, London: Academic Press, 41–58.
Groppe, D., 1995, "Progress and Cohesion in Biblical Hebrew Narrative: the Function of *ke/be* + the Infinitive Construct", in: Bodine, W.R. (ed.), *Discourse Analysis of Biblical Literature. What It Is and What It Offers*, Atlanta: Scholars, 183–192.
Gross, W., Irsigler, H. & Seidl, T. (eds.), 1991, *Text, Methode und Grammatik: Wolfgang Richter zum 65. Geburtstag*, St. Ottilien: EOS.
———, 1996, *Die Satzteilfolge im Verbalsatz alttestamentlicher Prosa*, Tübingen: J.C.B. Mohr.
Gülich, E., 1970, *Makrosyntax der Gleiderungssignale im gesprochenen Französisch*, München: Fink.
——— & Raible, W., 1977, "Überlegungen zu einer makrostrukturellen Textanalyse: J. Thurber, 'The Lover and His Lass'", in: Dijk, T.A. van & Petöfi, J. (eds.), *Research in Texttheory/Untersuchungen in Texttheorie: Grammars and Descriptions*, Berlin: De Gruyter.
Hardmeier, C., 1990, *Prophetie im Streit vor dem Untergang Judas. Erzählkommunikative Studien zur Enstehungssituation der Jesaja- und Jeremiaerzählungen in II Reg 18–20 und Jer 37–40* (Beiheft zur Zeitschrift für die alttestamentliche Wissenschaft 187), Berlin: De Gruyter.
Harris, Z., 1952, "Discourse Analysis", *Language* 28:1–30.
Harweg, R., 1968, *Pronomina und Textkonstitution*, München: Fink.
Heinemann, W. & Viehweger, D., 1991, *Textlinguistik. Eine Einführung*, Tübingen: Niemeyer.
Hopper, P.J., 1979, "Aspect and Foregrounding in Discourse", in: Givón, T. (ed.), *Discourse and Semantics* (Syntax and Semantics 12), New York: Academic Press, 213–241.
Hwang, S.J.J., 1984, "A Cognitive Basis for Discourse Grammar", *Southwest Journal of Linguistics* 7:133–156.
Irsigler, H., 1984, *Ps. 73—Monolog eines Weisen* (Arbeiten zu Text und Sprache im Alten Testament 20), St. Ottilien: EOS.

Isenberg, H., 1974, *Texttheorie und Gegenstand der Grammatik*, Berlin: Akademie.
Jenni, E., 1992, *Die Hebräischen Präpositionen. Band 1: Die Präposition beth*, Stuttgart: Kohlhammer.
———, 1994, *Die Hebräischen Präpositionen. Band 2: Die Präposition caph*, Stuttgart: Kohlhammer.
Joosten, J., 1989, "The Predicative Participle in Biblical Hebrew", *Zeitschrift für Althebraistik* 2:128–159.
———, 1992, "Biblical Hebrew *wᵉqatal* and Syriac *hwa qat ēl* Expressing Repetition in the Past", *Zeitschrift für Althebraistik* 5:1–14.
Joüon, P. & Muraoka, T., 1991, *A Grammar of Biblical Hebrew*, 2 Vols., Roma: Pontificio Istituto Biblico.
Kallmeyer, W. & Meyer-Hermann, R., 1980, "Textlinguistik", in: Althaus, H.P., Henne, H. & Wiegang, E. (eds.), *Lexikon der germanistischen Linguistik*, Tübingen: Niemeyer, 242–258.
Kuppevelt, J. van, 1995, "Main Structure and Side Structure in Discourse", *Linguistics* 33:809–833.
Longacre, R.E., "Some Fundamental Insights of Tagmemics", *Language* 41 (1965) 65–76.
———, 1983, *The Grammar of Discourse*, New York: Plenum.
———, 1989, *Joseph: A Story of Divine Providence: A Text Theoretical and Textlinguistic Analysis of Genesis 37 and 39–48*, Winona Lake (Ind.): Eisenbrauns.
———, 1994, "*Weqatal* Forms in Biblical Hebrew Prose: A Discourse-Modular Approach", in: Bergen, R.D. (ed.), *Biblical Hebrew and Discourse Linguistics*, Winona Lake (Ind.): Eisenbrauns, 50–99.
———, 1995, "Building for the Worship of God: Exodus 25:1–30:10", in: Bodine, W.R. (ed.), *Discourse Analysis of Biblical Literature. What It Is and What It Offers*, Atlanta: Scholars, 21–49.
——— & Hwang, S.J.J., 1994, "A Textlinguistic Approach to the Biblical Hebrew Narrative of Jonah", in: Bergen, R.D. (ed.), *Biblical Hebrew and Discourse Linguistics*, Winona Lake (Ind.): Eisenbrauns, 336–358.
Lowery, K.E., 1995, "The Theoretical Foundations of Hebrew Discourse Grammar", in: Bodine, W.R. (ed.), *Discourse Analysis of Biblical Literature. What It Is and What It Offers*, Atlanta: Scholars, 213–253.
Mann, W.C. & Thompson, S.A., 1988, "Rhetorical Structure Theory: Towards a Functional Theory of Text Organization", *Text* 8:243–281.
——— & Thompson, S.A. (eds.), 1992, *Discourse Description: Diverse Linguistic Analysis of a Fund-raising Text*, Amsterdam: John Benjamins.
———, Matthiessen, M.I.M. & Thompson, S.A., 1992, "Rhetorical Structure Theory and Text Analysis", in: Mann, W.C. & Thompson, S.A. (eds.), *Discourse Description: Diverse Linguistic Analysis of a Fund-raising Text*, Amsterdam: John Benjamins, 39–78.
Merwe, C.H.J. van der, 1989, "The Vague Term 'Emphasis'", *Journal for Semitics* 1:118–132.
———, 1992, "Pragmatics of the Translation Value of *gam*", *Journal for Semitics* 4:181–199.
———, 1993, "Particles and the Interpretation of Old Testament Texts", *Journal for the Study of the Old Testament* 60:27–44.
———, 1994, "Discourse Linguistics and Biblical Hebrew Grammar", in: Bergen, R.D. (ed.), *Biblical Hebrew and Discourse Linguistics*, Winona Lake (Ind.): Eisenbrauns, 13–49.
———, forthcoming a, "Reconsidering Biblical Hebrew Temporal Expressions", *Zeitschrift für Althebraistik*.
———, forthcoming b, "The Concept 'Reference Time' and Biblical Hebrew Temporal Expressions", *Biblica* (submitted for publication).

———, Naudé, J.A., & Kroeze, J., 1996, "A Biblical Hebrew Reference Grammar for Students", University of Stellenbosch, manuscript.
Mey, J.L., 1993, *Pragmatics. An Introduction*, Oxford: Blackwell.
Miller, C.L., 1996, *The Representation of Speech in Biblical Hebrew Narrative. A Linguistic Analysis*, Atlanta: Scholars Press.
Muraoka, T., 1985, *Emphatic Words and Structures in Biblical Hebrew*, Jerusalem/Leiden: Magnes/E.J. Brill.
Niccacci, A., 1990, *The Syntax of the Verb in Classical Hebrew Prose* (Journal for the Study of the Old Testament, Supplement Series 86), Sheffield: Sheffield Academic Press.
———, 1994a, "On the Hebrew Verbal System", in: Bergen, R.D. (ed.), *Biblical Hebrew and Discourse Linguistics*, Winona Lake (Ind.): Eisenbrauns, 117–137.
———, 1994b, "Analysis of Biblical Narrative", in: Bergen, R.D. (ed.), *Biblical Hebrew and Discourse Linguistics*, Winona Lake (Ind.): Eisenbrauns, 175–198.
———, 1995, "Essential Hebrew Syntax", in: Talstra, E. (ed.), *Narrative and Comment. Contributions Presented to Wolfgang Schneider*, Amsterdam: Societas Hebraica Amstelodamensis, 111–125.
Petöfi, J., 1972, "Eine Textgrammatik mit einer nicht-linear festgelegten Basis", in: Dijk, T.A. van, *Some Aspects of Text Grammars*, The Hague: Mouton, 77–129.
Pike, K.L., 1967, *Language and Its Relation to a Unified Theory of the Structure of Human Behaviour*, The Hague: Mouton.
Regt, L. de, 1991–92, "Devices of Participant Reference in Some Biblical Hebrew Texts: Their Importance in Translation", *Jaarbericht* "Ex Oriente Lux" 32, 150–171.
———, 1996, "Rules and Conventions of Participant Reference in Biblical Hebrew and Aramaic", manuscript.
Revell, E.J., 1996, *The Designation of the Individual. Expressive Usage in Biblical Narrative*, Kampen: Kok Pharos.
Richter, W., 1978–80, *Grundlagen einer althebräischen Grammatik. A. Grundfragen einer sprachwissenschaftlichen Grammatik. B. Beschreibungsebene: Bd. I. Das Wort, Bd. II. Die Wortfügung (morphosyntax), Bd. III. Der Satz* (Arbeiten zu Text und Sprache im Alten Testament), St. Ottilien: EOS.
———, 1991, *Biblia Hebraica Transcripta. 1 und 2 Samuel* (Arbeiten zu Text und Sprache im Alten Testament), St. Ottilien: EOS.
Schiffrin, D., 1987, *Discourse Markers*, Cambridge: Cambridge University Press.
———, 1994, *Approaches to Discourse*, Oxford: Blackwell.
Schleppegrel, M.J., 1991, "Paratactic Because", *Journal of Pragmatics* 16:323–337.
Schmidt, S.J., 1980, *Grundriß der empirischen Literaturwissenschaft. Teilband 1*, Braunschweig: Vieweg.
Schneider, W., 1982, *Grammatik des Biblischen Hebräisch. Völlig neue Bearbeitung der* "Hebräischen Grammatik für den akademischen Unterricht" *von Oskar Grether*, fifth ed., München: Claudius.
Schopf, A., 1987–1989, *Essays on Tensing in English. Time, Text and modality*, 2 Vols., Tübingen, Niemeyer.
Schweizer, H., 1981, *Metaphorische Grammatik* (Arbeiten zu Text und Sprache im Alten Testament), St. Ottilien: EOS.
———, 1986, *Biblische Texte verstehen*, Stuttgart: Kohlhammer.
Sinclair, M., 1995, "Fitting Pragmatics into the Mind. Some Issues in Mentalist Pragmatics", *Journal of Pragmatics* 23:509–539.
Sitta, H. & Brinker, K. (eds.), 1973, *Studien zur Texttheorie und zur deutschen Grammatik*, Düsseldorf: Schwann.
Sperber, D. & Wilson, D., 1986 (1995²), *Relevance, Communication and Cognition*, Cambridge (Mass.): Harvard University Press.
Stipp, H.J., 1991, "*Wehaya* für nichtiterative Vergangenheit? Zu syntaktischen Modernisierungen im masoretischen Jeremiabuch", in: Gross, W., Irsigler, H. &

Seidl, T. (eds.), *Text, Methode und Grammatik: Wolfgang Richter zum 65.Geburtstag*, St. Ottilien: EOS, 521–547.

Talstra, E., 1978, "Text Grammar and Hebrew Bible 1: Elements of a Theory", *Bibliotheca Orientalis* 35:168–175.

———, 1982, "Text Grammar and Hebrew Bible 2: Syntax and Semantics", *Bibliotheca Orientalis* 39:26–38.

———, 1983, *2 Kön. 3: Etüden zur Textgrammatik*, Amsterdam: VU University Press.

——— (ed.), 1995, *Narrative and Comment. Contributions Presented to Wolfgang Schneider*, Amsterdam: Societas Hebraica Amstelodamensis.

———, 1995, "Clause Types and Textual Structure: an Experiment in Narrative Syntax", in: Talstra, E. (ed.), *Narrative and Comment. Contributions Presented to Wolfgang Schneider*, Amsterdam, 166–180.

Verschueren, J., Östman, J.-O. & Blommaert, J. (eds.), 1995, *Handbook of Pragmatics, Manual*, Amsterdam: John Benjamins.

Weinrich, H., 1971, *Tempus: Besprochene und erzählte Welt*, second ed., Stuttgart: Kohlhammer.

———, 1978, "Die Textpartitur als heuristische Methode", in: Dressler, W. (ed.), *Textlinguistik*, Darmstadt: Wissenschaftliche Buchgesellschaft, 391–412.

———, 1993, *Textgrammatik der deutschen Sprache*, Mannheim: Duden.

Werlich, E., 1983, *A Text Grammar of English*, Heidelberg: Quelle & Meyer.

Wheatley-Irving, L., 1993, "Semantics of Biblical Hebrew Temporal Subordinate Clauses in 1 Samuel and 1 Kings: When You Say 'When'?" Paper Read at Seminar "Biblical Hebrew and Discourse Linguistics", Dallas, Texas, June 1993.

Winther-Nielsen, N., 1995, *A Functional Discourse Grammar of Joshua. A Computer-Assisted Rhetorical Structure Analysis* (Coniectanea Biblica. Old Testament Series 40), Stockholm: Almqvist & Wiksell.

——— & Talstra, E., 1995, *A Computational Display of Joshua. A Computer-Assisted Analysis and Textual Interpretation* (Applicatio 13), Amsterdam: VU University Press.

WORKSHOP: TEXT LINGUISTICS AND THE STRUCTURE OF 1 SAMUEL 1

Christo H.J. van der Merwe
(Stellenbosch)

1. *Purpose of workshop*

The primary aim of this workshop is to introduce participants to a possible way of approaching a text from a text linguistic point of view. To accomplish this aim I envisage the following:

— Illustrate how a possible structure of 1 Samuel 1 could be determined by using existing sources, but also how often it is difficult to decide where one paragraph or sub-paragraph ends and the next begins.
— Illustrate how a close observation of a small selection of surface-level phenomena may help in refining the above-mentioned structure. Here again the value and/or inadequacies of existing sources will be demonstrated, as well as that of usefulness of compiling examples by means of an electronic concordance programme like *Bible Works*.

2. *Procedure*

The following is no recipe, but tries to provide a practical guideline for analyzing a Biblical Hebrew text from a text linguistic point of view.

— Commence with dividing 1 Samuel 1 into sentences. Fokkelman (1993: 648–649) and Richter (1991: 2–11) are helpful in this regard. Electronic programmes like *LOGOS 2, Bible Works 3* or *Bible Windows 4* can be used to manipulate the Hebrew text.
— Make a distinction between narrative and discourse.
— Make a first attempt to identify the relationships between sentences.
— Make a first attempt to identify larger groupings.

3. *Structure of 1 Samuel 1*

I came up with the following preliminary structure of 1 Samuel 1:

1 וַיְהִי אִישׁ אֶחָד מִן־הָרָמָתַיִם צוֹפִים מֵהַר אֶפְרָיִם
וּשְׁמוֹ אֶלְקָנָה בֶּן־יְרֹחָם בֶּן־אֱלִיהוּא בֶּן־תֹּחוּ בֶן־צוּף אֶפְרָתִי׃
2 וְלוֹ שְׁתֵּי נָשִׁים
. . . . שֵׁם אַחַת חַנָּה
. . . . וְשֵׁם הַשֵּׁנִית פְּנִנָּה
וַיְהִי לִפְנִנָּה יְלָדִים
וּלְחַנָּה אֵין יְלָדִים׃
3 וְעָלָה הָאִישׁ הַהוּא מֵעִירוֹ מִיָּמִים יָמִימָה לְהִשְׁתַּחֲוֹת וְלִזְבֹּחַ לַיהוָה
צְבָאוֹת בְּשִׁלֹה
. . . . שָׁם שְׁנֵי בְנֵי־עֵלִי חָפְנִי וּפִנְחָס כֹּהֲנִים לַיהוָה׃

4 וַיְהִי הַיּוֹם
וַיִּזְבַּח אֶלְקָנָה
וְנָתַן לִפְנִנָּה אִשְׁתּוֹ וּלְכָל־בָּנֶיהָ וּבְנוֹתֶיהָ מָנוֹת׃
5 וּלְחַנָּה יִתֵּן מָנָה אַחַת אַפָּיִם
. . . . כִּי אֶת־חַנָּה אָהֵב
וַיהוָה סָגַר רַחְמָהּ׃
6 וְכִעֲסַתָּה צָרָתָהּ גַּם־כַּעַס בַּעֲבוּר הַרְּעִמָהּ
. . . . כִּי־סָגַר יְהוָה בְּעַד רַחְמָהּ׃
7 וְכֵן יַעֲשֶׂה שָׁנָה בְשָׁנָה
מִדֵּי עֲלֹתָהּ בְּבֵית יְהוָה כֵּן תַּכְעִסֶנָּה
וַתִּבְכֶּה
וְלֹא תֹאכַל׃
8 וַיֹּאמֶר לָהּ אֶלְקָנָה אִישָׁהּ
. . . . חַנָּה . . . לָמֶה תִבְכִּי
. . . . וְלָמֶה לֹא תֹאכְלִי
. . . . וְלָמֶה יֵרַע לְבָבֵךְ
. . . . הֲלוֹא אָנֹכִי טוֹב לָךְ מֵעֲשָׂרָה בָּנִים׃

9 וַתָּקָם חַנָּה אַחֲרֵי אָכְלָה בְשִׁלֹה וְאַחֲרֵי שָׁתֹה
. . . וְעֵלִי הַכֹּהֵן יֹשֵׁב עַל־הַכִּסֵּא עַל־מְזוּזַת הֵיכַל יְהוָה׃
10 . . . . וְהִיא מָרַת נָפֶשׁ
וַתִּתְפַּלֵּל עַל־יְהוָה
וּבָכֹה תִבְכֶּה׃
11 וַתִּדֹּר נֶדֶר
וַתֹּאמַר
. . . יְהוָה צְבָאוֹת . . אִם־רָאֹה תִרְאֶה בָּעֳנִי אֲמָתֶךָ
. . . . וּזְכַרְתַּנִי
. . . . וְלֹא־תִשְׁכַּח אֶת־אֲמָתֶךָ
. . . . וְנָתַתָּה לַאֲמָתְךָ זֶרַע אֲנָשִׁים

. . . . וּנְתַתִּיו לַיהוָה כָּל־יְמֵי חַיָּיו
. . . . וּמוֹרָה לֹא־יַעֲלֶה עַל־רֹאשׁוֹ׃

12 וְהָיָה
כִּי הִרְבְּתָה לְהִתְפַּלֵּל לִפְנֵי יְהוָה
וְעֵלִי שֹׁמֵר אֶת־פִּיהָ׃
13 וְחַנָּה . . . . הִיא מְדַבֶּרֶת עַל־לִבָּהּ
. . . . רַק שְׂפָתֶיהָ נָּעוֹת
. . . . וְקוֹלָהּ לֹא יִשָּׁמֵעַ
וַיַּחְשְׁבֶהָ עֵלִי לְשִׁכֹּרָה׃
14 וַיֹּאמֶר אֵלֶיהָ עֵלִי
. . . . עַד־מָתַי תִּשְׁתַּכָּרִין
. . . . הָסִירִי אֶת־יֵינֵךְ מֵעָלָיִךְ׃
15 וַתַּעַן חַנָּה
וַתֹּאמֶר
. . . . לֹא אֲדֹנִי
. . . . אִשָּׁה קְשַׁת־רוּחַ אָנֹכִי
. . . . וְיַיִן וְשֵׁכָר לֹא שָׁתִיתִי
. . . . וָאֶשְׁפֹּךְ אֶת־נַפְשִׁי לִפְנֵי יְהוָה׃
16 . . . . אַל־תִּתֵּן אֶת־אֲמָתְךָ לִפְנֵי בַּת־בְּלִיָּעַל
. . . . כִּי־מֵרֹב שִׂיחִי וְכַעְסִי דִּבַּרְתִּי עַד־הֵנָּה׃
17 וַיַּעַן עֵלִי
וַיֹּאמֶר
. . . . לְכִי לְשָׁלוֹם
. . . . וֵאלֹהֵי יִשְׂרָאֵל יִתֵּן אֶת־שֵׁלָתֵךְ אֲשֶׁר שָׁאַלְתְּ מֵעִמּוֹ׃
18 וַתֹּאמֶר
. . . . תִּמְצָא שִׁפְחָתְךָ חֵן בְּעֵינֶיךָ
וַתֵּלֶךְ הָאִשָּׁה לְדַרְכָּהּ
וַתֹּאכַל
וּפָנֶיהָ לֹא־הָיוּ־לָהּ עוֹד׃

19 וַיַּשְׁכִּמוּ בַבֹּקֶר
וַיִּשְׁתַּחֲווּ לִפְנֵי יְהוָה
וַיָּשֻׁבוּ
וַיָּבֹאוּ אֶל־בֵּיתָם הָרָמָתָה
וַיֵּדַע אֶלְקָנָה אֶת־חַנָּה אִשְׁתּוֹ
וַיִּזְכְּרֶהָ יְהוָה׃
20 וַיְהִי לִתְקֻפוֹת הַיָּמִים
וַתַּהַר חַנָּה
וַתֵּלֶד בֵּן
וַתִּקְרָא אֶת־שְׁמוֹ שְׁמוּאֵל
. . . כִּי מֵיְהוָה שְׁאִלְתִּיו׃

21 וַיַּעַל הָאִישׁ אֶלְקָנָה וְכָל־בֵּיתוֹ לִזְבֹּחַ לַיהוָה אֶת־זֶבַח הַיָּמִים וְאֶת־נִדְרוֹ׃

22 וְחַנָּה לֹא עָלָתָה
. . . . כִּֽי־אָמְרָה לְאִישָׁהּ
. . . . עַד יִגָּמֵל הַנַּעַר
. . . . וַהֲבִאֹתִיו
. . . . וְנִרְאָה אֶת־פְּנֵי יְהוָה
. . . . וְיָשַׁב שָׁם עַד־עוֹלָם׃
23 וַיֹּאמֶר לָהּ אֶלְקָנָה אִישָׁהּ
. . . . עֲשִׂי הַטּוֹב בְּעֵינַיִךְ
. . . . שְׁבִי עַד־גָּמְלֵךְ אֹתוֹ
. . . . אַךְ יָקֵם יְהוָה אֶת־דְּבָרוֹ
וַתֵּשֶׁב הָאִשָּׁה
וַתֵּינֶק אֶת־בְּנָהּ עַד־גָמְלָהּ אֹתוֹ׃

24 וַתַּעֲלֵהוּ עִמָּהּ כַּאֲשֶׁר גְּמָלַתּוּ בְּפָרִים שְׁלֹשָׁה וְאֵיפָה אַחַת קֶמַח וְנֵבֶל יַיִן
וַתְּבִאֵהוּ בֵית־יְהוָה שִׁלוֹ
. . . וְהַנַּעַר נָעַר׃
25 וַיִּשְׁחֲטוּ אֶת־הַפָּר
וַיָּבִאוּ אֶת־הַנַּעַר אֶל־עֵלִי׃
26 וַתֹּאמֶר
. . . . בִּי אֲדֹנִי חֵי נַפְשְׁךָ אֲדֹנִי אֲנִי הָאִשָּׁה הַנִּצֶּבֶת עִמְּכָה בָּזֶה לְהִתְפַּלֵּל
אֶל־יְהוָה׃
27 . . . . . אֶל־הַנַּעַר הַזֶּה הִתְפַּלָּלְתִּי
. . . . . וַיִּתֵּן יְהוָה לִי אֶת־שְׁאֵלָתִי אֲשֶׁר שָׁאַלְתִּי מֵעִמּוֹ׃
28 . . . . . וְגַם אָנֹכִי הִשְׁאִלְתִּהוּ לַיהוָה כָּל־הַיָּמִים אֲשֶׁר הָיָה
. . . . . הוּא שָׁאוּל לַיהוָה

29 וַיִּשְׁתַּחוּ שָׁם לַיהוָה׃ פ

Problematic in determining the structure of 1 Samuel 1 are, for example, the following:

— Does a new paragraph indeed commence in v. 9?
— Are v. 1–3 indeed one paragraph? Should sub-paragraphs be identified among them?
— Does ויהי indeed introduce a paragraph or sub-paragraph in v. 20?
— Why are multiple speech frames used in v. 11, 15 and 17, but not in 8, 14, 18, 23 and 26?

4. *Discussion*

I suggest that the following type of questions might be helpful determining the structure of 1 Samuel 1.

— What is the function of ויהי?
— What is the function of והיה?
— Why would the subject be lexicalized in verse x, but not in verse y?
— Why would the narrator use multiple speech frames in x but not in y?

The problem that then emerged is: Where does one find solutions to these type of questions? I suggest that one could turn to a Biblical Hebrew reference grammar, a commentary, or launch concordant searches for constructions that are similar to the one(s) at hand. For the purpose of the workshop I decided on the first and third options. I therefore provide (1) sections from a *Biblical Hebrew Reference Grammar for Students* (= *BHR*)[1] that I (in cooperation with two colleagues) recently wrote and (2) concordant examples that I have compiled by means of *Bible Works*. Participants were requested to discuss the abovementioned questions in the light of *BHR* and the examples supplied:

1. *What is the function of* וַיְהִי?

1 Sam. 1:1

> According to *BHR* § 44.5.1(i) ויהי may introduce a new paragraph. However, this usually happens when ויהי is followed by a temporal expression. It is obvious that at least a new paragraph is introduced in 1 Sam. 1:1. The question that is not answered by the grammar is: Why is ויהי used here, but not in Job 1:1? Comparing 1 Sam. 1:1 with Judg. 13:2; 17:1; 17:7 and 1 Sam. 9:1 it appears that in most of these cases the participant that is introduced by means of ויהי is not prominent in the rest of the subsequent narrative. An exception is Judg. 17:1, where, like in Job 1:1, the participant that is introduced, is one of the main actors in the subsequent narrative.

Examples 1

Job 1:1	אִישׁ הָיָה בְאֶרֶץ־עוּץ אִיּוֹב שְׁמוֹ וְהָיָה הָאִישׁ הַהוּא תָּם וְיָשָׁר וִירֵא אֱלֹהִים וְסָר מֵרָע׃
Judg. 13:2	וַיְהִי אִישׁ אֶחָד מִצָּרְעָה מִמִּשְׁפַּחַת הַדָּנִי וּשְׁמוֹ מָנוֹחַ

[1] Van der Merwe, Naudé, and Kroeze (1996).

Judg. 17:1	וַיְהִי־אִישׁ מֵהַר־אֶפְרָיִם וּשְׁמוֹ מִיכָיְהוּ׃
Judg. 17:7	וַיְהִי־נַעַר מִבֵּית לֶחֶם יְהוּדָה מִמִּשְׁפַּחַת יְהוּדָה וְהוּא לֵוִי וְהוּא גָר־שָׁם׃
1 Sam. 9:1	וַיְהִי־אִישׁ [מִבִּנְיָמִין] וּשְׁמוֹ קִישׁ בֶּן־אֲבִיאֵל בֶּן־צְרוֹר בֶּן־בְּכוֹרַת בֶּן־אֲפִיחַ בֶּן־אִישׁ יְמִינִי גִּבּוֹר חָיִל׃

1 Sam. 1:2

According to *BHR* § 44.5.2 ויהי may incorporate a state of affairs (described with nominal sentences) into the mainstream of a story. This is a way of preventing this state of affairs from being regarded as incidental background information. In 1 Sam. 1:2 background information is indeed involved. However, it is embedded in a paragraph (v. 1–3) that contains only background information. Again the grammar provides only a partial solution.

If one compares 2 Sam. 4:2, 2 Kgs. 10:1, Josh. 17:8 and Num. 32:1 with 1 Sam. 1:2 it is clear that the author was not compelled to use ויהי. Like in Gen. 26:14 and 1 Kgs. 11:3 he obviously had a reason for doing so. One may argue on account of the content of the narratives that are involved that ויהי "marks" the reference to a state of affairs that plays in pivotal role in the plot of the scene, episode or narrative it is part of.

Examples 2

2 Sam. 4:2	וּשְׁנֵי אֲנָשִׁים שָׂרֵי־גְדוּדִים הָיוּ בֶן־שָׁאוּל שֵׁם הָאֶחָד בַּעֲנָה וְשֵׁם הַשֵּׁנִי רֵכָב
2 Kgs. 10:1	וּלְאַחְאָב שִׁבְעִים בָּנִים בְּשֹׁמְרוֹן
Josh. 17:8	לִמְנַשֶּׁה הָיְתָה אֶרֶץ תַּפּוּחַ וְתַפּוּחַ אֶל־גְּבוּל מְנַשֶּׁה לִבְנֵי אֶפְרָיִם׃
Num. 32:1	וּמִקְנֶה רַב הָיָה לִבְנֵי רְאוּבֵן וְלִבְנֵי־גָד עָצוּם מְאֹד
1 Kgs. 11:3	וַיְהִי־לוֹ נָשִׁים שָׂרוֹת שְׁבַע מֵאוֹת וּפִלַגְשִׁים שְׁלֹשׁ מֵאוֹת וַיַּטּוּ נָשָׁיו אֶת־לִבּוֹ
Gen. 26:14	וַיִּגְדַּל הָאִישׁ וַיֵּלֶךְ הָלוֹךְ וְגָדֵל עַד כִּי־גָדַל מְאֹד׃ וַיְהִי־לוֹ מִקְנֵה־צֹאן וּמִקְנֵה בָקָר וַעֲבֻדָּה רַבָּה וַיְקַנְאוּ אֹתוֹ פְּלִשְׁתִּים

1 Sam. 1:4

According to *BHR* § 44.5.1(i) ויהי may introduce a new paragraph. This usually happens when, like in 1 Sam. 1:4, ויהי is followed by a temporal expression. It is again obvious that a new paragraph is introduced. However, the problem is: How should the temporal expression be interpreted and where does the paragraph that it governs terminate?

When comparing the use the construction ויהי היום in 1 Sam. 14:1, 2 Kgs. 4:8 and Job 2:1,[2] with its use in 1 Sam. 1:4, it is evident that 1 Sam. 1:4 differs from the rest. In the latter case the events referred to are iterative actions in the past, referred to first by means of a *wayyiqtol* form of the verb (ויזבח), and then by means of a *weqatal* form (ונתן). Although I did not purport to solve the problem of interpreting 1 Sam. 1:4–8, the way in which *wayyiqtol* forms are used in 2 Sam. 15:2 hints that the *wayyiqtol* forms in 1:4 could also be interpreted as referring to iterative actions. This would imply that one might regard 1 Sam. 1:4–8 as one paragraph.

Examples 3

1 Sam. 14:1 — וַיְהִי הַיּוֹם וַיֹּאמֶר יוֹנָתָן בֶּן־שָׁאוּל אֶל־הַנַּעַר

2 Kgs. 4:8 — וַיְהִי הַיּוֹם וַיַּעֲבֹר אֱלִישָׁע אֶל־שׁוּנֵם

Job 2:1 — וַיְהִי הַיּוֹם וַיָּבֹאוּ בְּנֵי הָאֱלֹהִים לְהִתְיַצֵּב עַל־יְהוָה

2 Sam. 15:2 — וְהִשְׁכִּים אַבְשָׁלוֹם וְעָמַד עַל־יַד דֶּרֶךְ הַשָּׁעַר
וַיְהִי כָּל־הָאִישׁ אֲשֶׁר־יִהְיֶה־לּוֹ־רִיב לָבוֹא אֶל־הַמֶּלֶךְ לַמִּשְׁפָּט
וַיִּקְרָא אַבְשָׁלוֹם אֵלָיו וַיֹּאמֶר אֵי־מִזֶּה עִיר אַתָּה
וַיֹּאמֶר מֵאַחַד שִׁבְטֵי־יִשְׂרָאֵל עַבְדֶּךָ

1 Sam. 1:20

According to *BHR* § 44.5.1(i) ויהי may introduce a new paragraph. This usually happens when, like in 1 Sam. 1:20, ויהי is followed by a temporal expression. The question is: Is a new (sub-)paragraph indeed introduced in v. 20?

Considering 1 Sam. 5:10; 9:26 and 24:17, it is apparent that ויהי plus temporal expression does not necessarily signal the introduction of a new paragraph. Although one may argue that a new sub-paragraph is introduced in 1 Sam. 1:20, these examples illustrate the fact that one cannot rely only on surface level criteria for this type of decision.

Examples 4

1 Sam. 5:10 — וַיְשַׁלְּחוּ אֶת־אֲרוֹן הָאֱלֹהִים עֶקְרוֹן
וַיְהִי כְּבוֹא אֲרוֹן הָאֱלֹהִים עֶקְרוֹן וַיִּזְעֲקוּ

1 Sam. 9:26 — וַיַּשְׁכִּמוּ וַיְהִי כַּעֲלוֹת הַשַּׁחַר וַיִּקְרָא שְׁמוּאֵל אֶל־שָׁאוּל

---

[2] Cf. also 2 Kgs. 4:11,18 and Job 1:6,13.

1 Sam. 24:17

. . . וְיִשְׁפְּטֵנִי מִיָּדֶךָ
וַיְהִי כְּכַלּוֹת דָּוִד לְדַבֵּר אֶת־הַדְּבָרִים הָאֵלֶּה אֶל־שָׁאוּל
וַיֹּאמֶר שָׁאוּל הֲקֹלְךָ זֶה בְּנִי דָוִד

2. *What is the function of* והיה?

1 Sam. 1:12

It is obvious that והיה introduces a new paragraph. Furthermore, the construction והיה כי־ is not uncommon in the Old Testament (38×) and 1 Sam. (4×). Problematic is the fact that והיה כי־ as a rule occurs in discourse and involves incomplete events, cf. e.g. Gen. 12:12. One would rather expect in 1 Sam. 1:12 ויהי כי (like in Gen. 26:8). The latter construction normally occurs in narratives (17×). Significant is that none of them occurs in 1 Samuel. Instead, one encounters the similar unusual use of והיה כי־ elsewhere in 1 Samuel, viz. 17:48. It is therefore most probable that the use of והיה כי־ in 1 Sam. 1:12 instead of ויהי כי is not semantically or text-linguistically motivated.[3]

Examples 5

1 Sam. 17:48

וְהָיָה כִּי־קָם הַפְּלִשְׁתִּי וַיֵּלֶךְ וַיִּקְרַב לִקְרַאת דָּוִד
וַיְמַהֵר דָּוִד וַיָּרָץ הַמַּעֲרָכָה לִקְרַאת הַפְּלִשְׁתִּי

Gen. 12:12

הָיָה כִּי־יִרְאוּ אֹתָךְ הַמִּצְרִים
וְאָמְרוּ אִשְׁתּוֹ זֹאת וְהָרְגוּ אֹתִי

Gen. 26:8

וַיְהִי כִּי אָרְכוּ־לוֹ שָׁם הַיָּמִים
וַיַּשְׁקֵף אֲבִימֶלֶךְ מֶלֶךְ פְּלִשְׁתִּים בְּעַד הַחַלּוֹן וַיַּרְא

3. *Why would the subject be lexicalized in verse x, but not in verse y? Is the phenomenon in anyway related to the introduction of a paragraph or sub-paragraph?*

If one considers cases with lexicalized subjects that are not topicalized[4] in v. 8, 9, 13, 14, 15, 17, 18, 19, 21, 23, it appears that only in v. 9 and 21 new paragraphs are unambiguously involved. Debatable are v. 8, 19 and 23. In cases where the subjects are not lexicalized, e.g. 7, 10, 11, 19, 20, 24, 25, 26, 27 and 28, only in the case of v. 19 it is unambiguous (due to the change in time signaled by the temporal expression) that a new paragraph is introduced.

---

[3] Cf. Stipp (1991: 544).

[4] A subject in Biblical Hebrew is topicalized when it precedes the verb, e.g. 1 Sam. 1:5a.

Highlighted in the above-mentioned search for paragraph boundaries is the lack of a suitable definition for the concepts *paragraph and sub-paragraph.* Furthermore, it not clear whether the paragraph is an arbitrary linguistic structure, or reflect any real world distinctions.

4. *Why would the narrator use multiple speech frames in x but not in y?*

If one compares those cases where multiple speech frames are used, viz. v. 11, 15 and 17 with those cases where they are not used, viz. v. 8, 14, 18, 22, 23, 26, it appears that Miller (1996: 405) is correct when she remarks that multiple-verb frames "are usually used in dialogic situations and often index the most salient utterance in a conversation".

BASIC FACTS AND THEORY OF THE BIBLICAL HEBREW VERB SYSTEM IN PROSE

Alviero Niccacci
(Jerusalem)

The speakers have been requested by the organizer to pay explicit attention in their presentation to the following points:

1. Function of the verb form in narrative text; function in the clause and in larger textual units; hierarchy of clauses;
2. Function of the verbless clause and verbal clauses in Biblical Hebrew;
3. Position of the verb form in a clause;
4. Time and aspect of the verb form;
5. Relationship between syntax and semantics or text-interpretation.

I will try to discuss the first four points in this presentation. The fifth point shall be dealt with in my other paper in this volume, "Narrative Syntax of Exodus 19–24".

First of all, a word should be said on methodology. Let us begin with the biblical text. In Gen. 3:11, 13 and 14 we read a series of God's speeches to the man, to the woman and to the serpent, respectively. They are all *wayyiqtol* forms: *wayyōʾmer* (3:11), *wayyōʾmer yhwh ʾĕlōhîm lāʾiššâ* (3:13), and *wayyōʾmer yhwh ʾĕlōhîm ʾel-hannāḥāš* (3:14). By contrast, in another series of speeches the verb forms used are different in two cases: *wayyōʾmer yhwh ʾĕlōhîm ʾel-hannāḥāš* (3:14), *ʾel-hāʾiššâ ʾāmar* (3:16), and *ûlᵉʾādām ʾāmar* (3:17). Thus, we find two types of sentence: one with a finite verb (*wayyiqtol*) in the first place and the rest after it (V-x), and the other with a non-verbal "x" element in the first place and a finite verb in the second (x-V).[1] Why this difference?[2]

---

[1] "X" comprises every non-verbal element of the sentence except *waw, wᵉlōʾ* and *wᵉʾal* that are an integral part of the verb forms—the so-called "inversive" verb forms and the negative constructions, respectively. See also note 22 below.

[2] C. den Hertog, "Die invertierten Verbalsätze im hebräischen Josuabuch. Eine Fallstudie zu einem vernachlässigten Kapitel der hebräischen Syntax", in: C. Mayer – K. Müller – G. Schmalenberg (eds.), *Nach den Anfängen fragen. Herrn Prof.Dr.theol. Gerhard Dautzenberg zum 60. Geburtstag am 30. Januar 1994*, Giessen: Justus-Liebig Universität 1994, 227–291, complains (with some exaggeration) that the phenomenon of what

To answer this question I looked for specific syntactic settings capable of showing the function of the grammatical construction x-V. Note this sequence: firstly, one identifies a certain grammatical construction; secondly, one tries to understand its function in the text; thirdly, one chooses the corresponding verb form or construction in the language of translation to render it.

A further step is to look for other grammatical constructions—if any—capable of accomplishing the same function. For the principle of paradigmatic substitution, the constructions capable of accomplishing the same function are syntactically equivalent and interchangeable; however, being grammatically different, they signal a variance in aspect.

In the analysis one has to proceed from the level of grammar (i.e. different types of sentences) to the level of syntax (i.e. relations among different types of sentence) and to the level of the text (i.e. role of the different sentences in shaping a text: its beginning, body and end).[3] This means that one should not begin with semantics or interpretation but with morphology and function. Semantics is important but subservient to morphology and function (or syntax).[4]

Coming back to our problem, many scholars agree that a grammatical element different from the finite verb sometimes takes the first place in the sentence for the sake of emphasis (or stress, or focus).[5] The question is, first, whether or not in this case (x-V) we have the same type of sentence as when the verb is in the first place (V-x); second, how are we to explain the fact that in many cases the grammatical element in the first place does not seem to carry any emphasis; and, third, whether or not any regularity, or even a system, is discernible in the distribution and function of first-place and second-place verb forms.[6]

---

he calls "inverted verbal sentences" (i.e. *x-qatal* and *x-yiqtol*) is not treated by grammarians.

[3] I explained the reason for this "bottom-up" methodology in "On the Hebrew Verbal System", in: R.D. Bergen (ed.), *Biblical Hebrew and Discourse Linguistics*, Winona Lake (Ind.): Eisenbrauns, 1994, 117–137, esp. 117–118.

[4] See my *Syntax of the Verb in Classical Hebrew Prose*, Sheffield: Sheffield Academic Press, 1990, §§ 128ff.

[5] Discussion (and confusion) on this point is going on. I use "emphasis" or "stress" to indicate what is traditionally called "predicate", or the "new element" of the sentence; see my "Marked Syntactical Structures in Biblical Greek in Comparison with Biblical Hebrew", *Liber Annuus* 43 (1993) 9–69, §§ 5–6.

[6] Y. Endo, *The Verbal System of Classical Hebrew in the Joseph Story. An Approach from Discourse Analysis*, Assen: Van Gorcum, 1996, fails to base his study on a sound

Grammarians seem not to take too seriously the fact that this is *the* problem of Biblical Hebrew syntax. They venture to draw a list of text types, markers of clause hierarchy, and compositional devices of all kinds without having ascertained beforehand what is a sentence.

Let us review the evidence and then draw a theory. Indeed, Biblical Hebrew syntax cannot be learned from textbooks but from the Bible itself examined with a text-linguistic approach. For this purpose, I have followed the lead of W. Schneider in applying the text-linguistic methodology of H. Weinrich to Biblical Hebrew.[7] Because I have presented more than once my description of the Biblical Hebrew verb system, I will try this time to review the fundamental facts that constitute the basis of my theory.

It is preferable to begin with a few good examples rather than with a whole corpus. A few good examples teach us more than a large corpus, especially if this is a congeries of not well sorted passages. From good examples one formulates a working hypothesis, which is then tested, corrected, refined on the basis of a larger corpus, and when it is sufficiently confirmed it becomes a theory. Indeed, one needs a good working hypothesis in order to marshal a large corpus.[8]

1. *Emphatic constructions with second-place verb forms*

There are two syntactic settings particularly suitable to show that in a sentence with the finite verb in the second place, the element

grammatical description of the sentence; therefore, his results are questionable. He relies on semantics in his classification of "tenses" (declarative, interrogative etc.) and in his distinction of "sequentiality/non-sequentiality" despite his claim that this distinction "should strictly be described as a syntactic function, not as a semantic function" (p. 296). As noted above, semantics is important but must be subservient to grammar and syntax. Similarly, R.S. Hendel, "In the Margins of the Hebrew Verbal System: Situation, Tense, Aspect, Mood", *ZAH* 9 (1996) 129–181, embarks in a high-level analysis without first defining the sentence and the function(s) of the various verb forms, and is, therefore, forced to rely on semantics. Had he started with a good syntactic basis, he would have seen that the functions he (rightly) points out in his paper are not "in the margins of the Hebrew verbal system" but are well accounted for in it.

[7] W. Schneider, *Grammatik des biblischen Hebräisch*, München: Claudius, 1974; fifth ed. 1982; H. Weinrich, *Tempus. Besprochene und erzählte Welt*, fourth ed., Stuttgart: Kohlhammer, 1985.

[8] This need is patent, e.g., in W. Groß, "Die Position des Subjekts im hebräischen Verbalsatz, untersucht an den asyndetischen ersten Redesätze in Gen., Ex. 1–19, Jos., 2 Kön.", *ZAH* 6 (1993) 170–187; and "Zur syntaktischen Struktur des Vorfelds im hebräischen Verbalsatz", *ZAH* 7 (1994) 203–214.

occupying the first place receives a special emphasis as a consequence of its very position. The settings are, first, "personal pronoun—finite verb," and, second, "interrogative pronoun—finite verb".

1.1 *Personal pronoun—finite verb* (x-qatal, *or* x-yiqtol)[9]

(**1**) Judg. 6:8 (*x-qatal* in direct speech in d)[10]

(a) The Lord sent a prophet to the Israelites	וַיִּשְׁלַח יְהוָה אִישׁ נָבִיא אֶל־בְּנֵי יִשְׂרָאֵל
(b) and he said to them,	וַיֹּאמֶר לָהֶם
(c) "Thus says the Lord:	כֹּה־אָמַר יְהוָה אֱלֹהֵי יִשְׂרָאֵל
(d) 'It is I that made you come up from Egypt'".	אָנֹכִי הֶעֱלֵיתִי אֶתְכֶם מִמִּצְרַיִם

1.2 *Interrogative pronoun/adverb—finite verb* (x-qatal, *or* x-yiqtol)[11]

(**2**) Judg. 1:1–2 (question with *x-yiqtol* in c; reply with *x-yiqtol* in e)

(a) And after the death of Joshua	וַיְהִי אַחֲרֵי מוֹת יְהוֹשֻׁעַ
(b) the Israelites inquired of the Lord, saying,	וַיִּשְׁאֲלוּ בְּנֵי יִשְׂרָאֵל בַּיהוָה לֵאמֹר
(c) "Who shall go up for us first against the Canaanites,	מִי יַעֲלֶה־לָּנוּ אֶל־הַכְּנַעֲנִי בַּתְּחִלָּה
to fight against them?"	לְהִלָּחֶם בּוֹ
(d) The Lord said,	וַיֹּאמֶר יְהוָה
(e) "It is Judah that shall go up . . ."	יְהוּדָה יַעֲלֶה

(**3**) Judg. 20:18 (question with *x-yiqtol* in e; reply without verb in g)

(a) They arose,	וַיָּקֻמוּ
(b) went up to Bethel,	וַיַּעֲלוּ בֵית־אֵל
(c) and inquired of God.	וַיִּשְׁאֲלוּ בֵאלֹהִים
(d) The Israelites said,	וַיֹּאמְרוּ בְּנֵי יִשְׂרָאֵל
(e) "Who us shall go up for us first to battle against the Benjaminites?"	מִי יַעֲלֶה־לָּנוּ בַתְּחִלָּה לַמִּלְחָמָה עִם־בְּנֵי בִנְיָמִן

[9] Compare (**22**) below, which shows a similar construction with a participle and article in (e) and *'ăšer* + *qatal* (f) instead of the finite verb. Other examples are 2 Sam. 24:17; 1 Chr. 21:17; 2 Kgs. 18:22; Josh. 24:17; see *Syntax* § 6; "Marked Syntactical Structures" §§ 1–2; 6.1–3.

[10] I use the RSV, modified when needed. I normally quote one example for each case. Each sentence is numbered (a, b, c, etc.) for convenience.

[11] Cf. Ex. 33:16; *Syntax* § 6; "Marked Syntactical Structures" § 6.3.

(f) The Lord said, — וַיֹּאמֶר יְהוָה
(g) "Judah, first". — יְהוּדָה בַתְּחִלָּה

(**4**) Judg. 6:29 (question with *x-qatal* in b; reply with *x-qatal* in f)

(a) They said to one another, — וַיֹּאמְרוּ אִישׁ אֶל־רֵעֵהוּ
(b) "Who has done this thing?" — מִי עָשָׂה הַדָּבָר הַזֶּה
(c) They made search, — וַיִּדְרְשׁוּ
(d) inquired, — וַיְבַקְשׁוּ
(e) and said, — וַיֹּאמְרוּ
(f) "It is Gideon the son of Joash that has done this thing". — גִּדְעוֹן בֶּן־יוֹאָשׁ עָשָׂה הַדָּבָר הַזֶּה

(**5**) Judg. 15:6 (question with *x-qatal* in b; reply without verb in d)

(a) Then the Philistines said, — וַיֹּאמְרוּ פְלִשְׁתִּים
(b) "Who has done this?" — מִי עָשָׂה זֹאת
(c) And they said, — וַיֹּאמְרוּ
(d) "It is Samson, the son-in-law of the Timnite . . ." — שִׁמְשׁוֹן חֲתַן הַתִּמְנִי

These sentences, with an "x" non-verbal element in the first place and the finite verb in the second, are marked. Their characteristic is that the verb is not the main element, or the "new" information, or the predicate, but the "given" information, or the subject, and as such it can be dispensed with (**3g; 5d**).[12]

Note that the predicate occupies the first place of the sentence and the subject the second. Indeed, this is a feature of Biblical Hebrew and of the Semitic languages in general. Characteristic of the marked sentences is that the predicate is not what is expected to fulfill this function, i.e. the verb, but what normally is the subject (i.e. a pronoun, or a noun), or even an adverb and a prepositional phrase (**9b–c**). On the contrary, in the unmarked sentences the roles are as expected, i.e. the verb is the predicate while the noun and the pronoun are the subject, or the object, or the complement, e.g. in the sentences with *wayyiqtol* (**1–5**).

These marked types of sentence (*x-qatal*, or *x-yiqtol*) are the Biblical Hebrew equivalent of the cleft sentence in English, the "phrase coupée" in French and of the "frase scissa" in Italian.

[12] See my discussion in "Marked Syntactical Structures", § 3.

2. Wayyiqtol *versus* Qatal

Four syntactic settings help us understand the difference between first-place, narrative *wayyiqtol* and second-place *qatal*, i.e. *x-qatal* or *wᵉx-qatal*:[13]

1. antecedent information
2. circumstance
3. contrast
4. oral report.

2.1 *Antecedent information*[14]

(**6**) 1 Sam. 25:1 (narrative *wayyiqtol* in a)

(a) Samuel died	וַיָּמָת שְׁמוּאֵל
(b) and all Israel assembled	וַיִּקָּבְצוּ כָל־יִשְׂרָאֵל
(c) and mourned for him,	וַיִּסְפְּדוּ־לוֹ
(d) and buried him in his house at Ramah.	וַיִּקְבְּרֻהוּ בְּבֵיתוֹ בָּרָמָה

versus 1 Sam. 28:3 (*wᵉx-qatal* for antecedent information in e)

(e) Now Samuel had died,	וּשְׁמוּאֵל מֵת
(f) and all Israel had mourned for him	וַיִּסְפְּדוּ־לוֹ כָּל־יִשְׂרָאֵל
(g) and had buried him in Ramah, his own city.	וַיִּקְבְּרֻהוּ בָרָמָה וּבְעִירוֹ
(h) Now Saul had put the mediums and the wizards out of the land.	וְשָׁאוּל הֵסִיר הָאֹבוֹת וְאֶת־הַיִּדְּעֹנִים מֵהָאָרֶץ

The information concerning Samuel's death is given with narrative *wayyiqtol* in (a) and is then recalled, or resumed, with *wᵉx-qatal* as a beginning of a new story, or of an episode of the same story in (e). Thus 28:3 is not a repetition, or a doublet, but a literary resumption (*Wiederaufnahme*) of 25:1.[15]

In 28:3 the resumptive *wᵉx-qatal* is followed by two *wayyiqtol* (f–g), which are not narrative but continuation forms. As such, they do

---

[13] The presence or absence of *waw* makes no difference: see my "Essential Hebrew Syntax", in: E. Talstra (ed.), *Narrative and Comment. Contributions presented to Wolfgang Schneider*, Amsterdam: Societas Hebraica Amstelodamensis, 1995, 111–125, note 35.

[14] Cf. Gen. 37:28 vs. 39: 1; 1 Sam. 19:12 vs. 19:18; 2 Sam. 13:34 vs. 13:38; Gen. 1:1–2; 2:5–6; see *Syntax* §§ 15–16; 18–19; "Marked Syntactical Structures" § 7.2.

[15] See *Syntax*, 201, note 33. M. Anbar, "La 'reprise'", *VT* 38 (1988) 385–398, examines a series of biblical and also Akkadian cases of resumptive repetition. He also discusses what he calls "reprises secondaires" of later redactors as distinct from "reprises originales" without even mentioning the verb forms used.

not have a time value of their own but take on that of the preceding verb (therefore, I translated "*had* mourned—*had* buried"). The two continuation *wayyiqtol* forms contrast the corresponding, purely narrative forms found in 25:1 (c–d). Narrative *wayyiqtol* begins the main line of narrative and also continues it appearing in a chain of selfsame forms; instead, continuation *wayyiqtol* is found after a verb form different from narrative *wayyiqtol* and even after a non-verbal clause.[16]

In the case of Samuel's death, and in other few similar cases, the same information is conveyed twice in a different linguistic level—respectively in the main line, or foreground, as a historical news communicated to the reader for the first time, and as a "recovered information", i.e. an information already known to the reader that is resumed as "antecedent information" in order to start a new story.[17] However, antecedent information is also found when no historical news has been given earlier in the text. (**6h**) is one such case because nowhere we read that Saul had eradicated the mediums and the wizards from the land.

Antecedent information, or *antefactum*, is a technique attested in many literatures of opening a story with information providing the setting, date, or similar. The antecedent information is recognizable by the fact that it is given in the secondary line of communication at the beginning of a story. The narrative proper begins afterwards with the main-line verb form, i.e. *wayyiqtol* in Biblical Hebrew.[18]

2.2 *Circumstance (or comparison)*[19]

(**7**) Ex. 19:2b–3a (*wayyiqtol* → *w*^{e}*x-qatal*)

(a) Thus, Israel encamped there, before the mountain, — וַיִּחַן־שָׁם יִשְׂרָאֵל נֶגֶד הָהָר

(b) while Moses went up toward God. — וּמֹשֶׁה עָלָה אֶל־הָאֱלֹהִים

[16] As documented in *Syntax* § 146:2.

[17] In H. Weinrich's terms; see *Syntax* § 2; *Lettura sintattica della prosa ebraico-biblica. Principi e applicazioni*, Jerusalem: Franciscan Printing Press, 1991, § 1.

[18] E.g. both Gen. 1:1–2 and 2:5–6 provide "antecedent information", and 1:3 and 2:7 start the respective main-line narrative. See (**14**) below and consult *Syntax* § 19; *Lettura* § 6.1; "Analysis of Biblical Narrative", in: R.D. Bergen (ed.), *Biblical Hebrew and Discourse Linguistics*, 175–198, esp. pp. 182–187.

[19] Cf. Ex. 9:23,33; 10:13; see *Syntax* §§ 41ff.; "Marked Syntactical Structures" § 7.1; "Finite Verb in the Second Position of the Sentence. Coherence of the Hebrew Verbal System", *ZAW* 108 (1996) 434–440, esp. pp. 435–436 (**6**).

(**8**) Gen. 4:2–5 (*wayyiqtol* → *w^e^x-qatal* in a–b, d–e, f–g)

(a) Abel was a keeper of sheep,	וַיְהִי־הֶבֶל רֹעֵה צֹאן
(b) while Cain was a tiller of the ground.	וְקַיִן הָיָה עֹבֵד אֲדָמָה
(c) Moreover, after some time,	וַיְהִי מִקֵּץ יָמִים
(d) Cain brought of the fruit of the land as an offering to the Lord,	וַיָּבֵא קַיִן מִפְּרִי הָאֲדָמָה מִנְחָה לַיהוָה
(e) while Abel, too, brought of the firstlings of his flock and of their fat products.	וְהֶבֶל הֵבִיא גַם־הוּא מִבְּכֹרוֹת צֹאנוֹ וּמֵחֶלְבֵהֶן
(f) And the Lord looked with favor at Abel and his offering,	וַיִּשַׁע יְהוָה אֶל־הֶבֶל וְאֶל־מִנְחָתוֹ
(g) while to Cain and his offering he did not look with favor.	וְאֶל־קַיִן וְאֶל־מִנְחָתוֹ לֹא שָׁעָה

2.3 *Contrast (or specification)*[20]

(**9**) Job 32:2–3 (*wayyiqtol* → (*w^e^*)*x-qatal* in a–c)

(a) Then the anger of Elihu, son of Berachel the Buzite, of the family of Ram, flared up;	וַיִּחַר אַף אֱלִיהוּא בֶן־בַּרַכְאֵל הַבּוּזִי מִמִּשְׁפַּחַת רָם
(b) it is against Job that his anger flared up because he declared himself right before God;	בְּאִיּוֹב חָרָה אַפּוֹ עַל־צַדְּקוֹ נַפְשׁוֹ מֵאֱלֹהִים
(c) and it is against his three friends that his anger flared up	וּבִשְׁלֹשֶׁת רֵעָיו חָרָה אַפּוֹ
(d) because they had not found any answer	עַל אֲשֶׁר לֹא־מָצְאוּ מַעֲנֶה
(e) and still had declared Job guilty.	וַיַּרְשִׁיעוּ אֶת־אִיּוֹב

Contrast is a special case of circumstance, the difference being that the "x" element preceding the finite verb carries the emphasis of the sentence, i.e. is the predicate. In (**9**) we have, therefore, two cleft sentences (b–c; see § 1 above) contrasting a plain sentence with a *wayyiqtol* of the same verb (a). The *wayyiqtol* in (e) is a continuation form (see **6f–g** above). Semantically, the contrast serves to specify or underline a detail of the main information given with *wayyiqtol* (a).

[20] Cf. Gen. 1:27; 41:12b; Ex. 7:6; 12:28,50; 2 Kgs. 18:10; *Syntax* § 48; see "On the Hebrew Verbal System" §§ 5–6.

2.4 *Oral report*[21]

(**10**) 2 Sam. 12:26–27 (narrative *wayyiqtol* in a–b vs. direct-speech *qatal* in e–f)

(a) Joab fought against Rabbah of the Ammonites,	וַיִּלָּחֶם יוֹאָב בְּרַבַּת בְּנֵי עַמּוֹן
(b) and took the royal city.	וַיִּלְכֹּד אֶת־עִיר הַמְּלוּכָה
(c) Then Joab sent messengers to David,	וַיִּשְׁלַח יוֹאָב מַלְאָכִים אֶל־דָּוִד
(d) and said,	וַיֹּאמֶר
(e) "I have fought against Rabbah	נִלְחַמְתִּי בְרַבָּה
(f) and also have taken the city of waters".	גַּם־לָכַדְתִּי אֶת־עִיר הַמָּיִם

The opposition between the historical news with *wayyiqtol* (a–b) and the oral report with *qatal* (e–f) concerning the same event is striking. As the analysis of the evidence shows, qatal can be first-place or second-place verb form (i.e. *qatal*, or *x-qatal*) with no difference, because in both cases it contrasts narrative *wayyiqtol* and therefore conveys main-line information.

3. *Theory on first-place versus second-place verb forms*

From the previous analysis follows that the x-V type of sentence is not a stylistic variant of the V-x type but a different type with distinctively different functions. In narrative texts an opposition exists between first-place *wayyiqtol* and second-place *qatal* (i.e. *x-qatal* or *w^{e}x-qatal* with no difference).[22] The syntactic settings illustrated above fall into three categories (I–III):

---

[21] Cf. 1 Kgs. 16:9–10 vs. 16:16; Gen. 40:2 vs. 41:10; 40:5 vs. 40:8; Ruth 3:15 vs. 3:17; 4:13 vs. 4:17; see my "Syntactic Analysis of Ruth", *Liber Annuus* 45 (1995) 69–106, p. 103; *Syntax* §§ 22–23. See also my book review of D.A. Dawson, *Text-Linguistics and Biblical Hebrew*, Sheffield: Sheffield Academic Press, 1994, *Liber Annuus* 45 (1995) 543–580, esp. § 4a.

[22] *Waw* may have different semantic values (see recently H.-P. Müller, "Nicht-junktiver Gebrauch von *w-* im Althebräischen", *ZAH* 7 [1994] 141–174) as well as pragmatic values but syntactically it has no role. If one does not take into account the role of the position of the finite verb to express syntactic coordination and subordination (§ 9.5 below), all the burden falls on "poor *waw*", which is actually unable to carry it. The consequence is a long list of semantic designations such as "*waw* explicativum", "concomitantiae", "relativum", etc. Therefore, Müller's considerations in the paper just quoted on the "discreteness" ("Abstufbarkeit, Diskretheit") and "fuzzy logic" ("unscharfe Logik") of Biblical Hebrew may be partly misplaced. Biblical

I—Emphasis on "x"	II—No emphasis on "x"	III—No emphasis on "x"
§ 1.1. x (= PP)—V (D) § 1.2. x (= IP)—V (D) § 2.3. x-V (contrast; N)	§ 2.1. x-V (ant. inf.) (N) § 2.2. x-V (circumst.) (N)	§ 2.4. Oral report (D)

D = direct speech; IP = interrogative pronoun; N = historical narrative; PP = personal pronoun; V = finite verb; x = a non-verbal element

Categories I and II consist of secondary-line constructions in narrative texts. In category I the "x" element is stressed and is the predicate while the verb is the subject; conversely, in category II the "x" element is not stressed and is not the predicate.[23] In category II the verb is the (grammatical) predicate but the sentence as a whole is made (syntactically) dependent.[24]

The "x" element is not stressed in category III as in category II. The difference is that in oral report *(x-)qatal* indicates the main line of communication and is independent.

Wayyiqtol is the narrative verb form *par excellence* because it is the only one indicating the main line of communication. *Qatal*, on the contrary, indicates a secondary line of communication in historical narrative, i.e. background (circumstance, or contrast) to a preceding *wayyiqtol* (§§ 2.2; 2.3), or antecedent information to a following *wayyiqtol* (§ 2.1). This *wayyiqtol* marks the beginning of the main line of narrative.

First-place verb form constitutes a plain, unmarked sentence where the verb is the predicate, as expected. On the contrary, second-place verb form constitutes a marked sentence where the verb is demoted to the role of subject, or "given" information (§ 1), or the sentence as a whole is demoted to the status of syntactic dependence. The latter is the case with the constructions of antecedent information (§ 2.1), on the one side, and of circumstance and of contrast (§§ 2.2–2.3), on the other. In both cases, the *x-qatal* construction is dependent on *wayyiqtol*; however, the exact relationship is reversed: "*w^{e}x-qatal* → *wayyiqtol*" for "antecedent information → beginning of the main line of narrative" (§ 2.1), and "*wayyiqtol* → *w^{e}x-qatal*" for "foreground → background information" (§§ 2.2; 2.3).

Hebrew is a much more sophisticated and much less naive language than thought by many scholars.

[23] See "Marked Syntactical Structures" § 7.

[24] On the difference between grammatical and syntactic subject and predicate see § 8 below.

Wayyiqtol and related *x-qatal* construction make up an indivisible syntactic unit. The *x-qatal* sentence is syntactically dependent on the *wayyiqtol* sentence although the *x-qatal* sentence is not governed by a subordinating conjunction such as *kî, ʾăšer, ʾim*, etc.

An important consequence from the point of view of narrative syntax is that the tense shift "*wᵉx-qatal* → *wayyiqtol*" for "antecedent information → beginning of the main line of narrative" (§ 2.1) breaks the line of communication and marks the beginning of a new text, or of a new episode of the same text, while the reversed tense shift "*wayyiqtol* → *wᵉx-qatal*" for "foreground → background information" (§§ 2.2; 2.3) does not break the line of communication but only serves to convey a comment and produces a pause in the narrative.

Coming back to Genesis 3 from where we started, the speeches of v. 11, 13 and 14—all the three introduced with *wayyiqtol*—are presented as discrete, coordinate items, all on the same linguistic main level and successive one to the other: "He said . . . *Then* the Lord God said to the woman . . . *And then* the Lord God said to the serpent". On the contrary, in v. 14, 16 and 17 the three speeches—the first introduced with *wayyiqtol*, the other two with (*wᵉ*)*x-qatal*—are presented as related items, in the sense that the second and the third are related to the first as background to foreground: "And then the Lord God said to the serpent . . . *while* to the woman he said . . . *and* to Adam he said".[25]

This is a small example of how syntax assists interpretation. We need to realize that by means of the syntactic devices of Biblical

---

[25] A sequence of narrative *wayyiqtol* (also called "narrative chain") chiefly denotes succession of one information or action after the other, but also logical conclusion without temporal succession, and even literary resumption; see *Syntax* § 140, and p. 201, note 33. The main point is that *wayyiqtol* indicates the main line of narrative; all the rest is semantic specification. On his part, Endo, *The Verbal System*, 1996, discusses at length the various semantic nuances of *wayyiqtol* ranging from temporal succession to consequential and antithetical link, to simultaneous action, "complex link", etc. (§ 7.3). He concludes: "Thus the function of waYYIQTOL as the sequential form should be understood not at the semantic level, but at the syntactic level: the waYYIQTOL seems to have an unstable nature which always lets the story flow on" (281). Because of this assumption, Endo finds it difficult to explain the *wayyiqtol* introducing a dialogue (which "apparently stands alone and does not form a sequence", 264) and the one found at the end of a narrative. On the basis of semantic evaluation only, with no syntactic argument, he also claims that in some cases *wayyiqtol* is used for "off-the line material", i.e. as "pseudo-independent form", "temporal clause", etc. (§ 7.3.2). According to him, *wayᵉhî* or *wᵉhāyâ* followed by a temporal clause is "a kind of 'cleft sentence' (i.e. a thematically partitioned construction)" (176; *sic!*). In other words, in the reign of semantics everyone is a king.

Hebrew the biblical authors presented their information in a structured form. Our interpretation must be based on them, not on our modern understanding or taste.[26]

This correspondence between position of the finite verb in the sentence (first or second), on the one side, and line of communication (main or secondary), on the other, is extremely important. Position of the finite verb in the sentence and line of communication are the two pillars of the Biblical Hebrew verb system.[27]

Accordingly, a sentence with a finite verb form in the first place, and indicating the main line of communication, is verbal, while a sentence with a finite verb form in the second place, and indicating the secondary line of communication (antecedent: § 2.1, or background information: §§ 2.2; 2–3) is nominal. A verbal sentence is an unmarked, plain construction with word-order "V (finite verb)—x (non-verbal element)"; it informs on an event in general terms. On the contrary, a nominal sentence is a marked construction with word-order "x-V"; it informs on details of an event—who, what, where, when, how.[28]

In sum, *wayyiqtol* is the main-line verb form in Biblical Hebrew narrative while *qatal* is a secondary-line verb form. In this sense, *qatal* is not a narrative form; it is used for comment of different kinds (antecedent information: § 2.1, circumstance: § 2.2, or contrast: § 2.3). This contradicts the accepted view that *wayyiqtol* is a continuation form *per se*, in the sense that a narrative is said to begin with *qatal* and then to go on with a chain of *wayyiqtol*. This is true grammatically but syntactically *qatal* conveys information of a secondary line (antecedent or background); in other words, *qatal* and *wayyiqtol* are not coordinated but the first is subordinated to the latter in Biblical Hebrew narrative.[29]

This applies to historical narrative, not to oral narrative. In the latter, *qatal* is found at the beginning of a report (§ 2.4) and of an oral narrative (§ 5 below); it corresponds to narrative *wayyiqtol* in historical narrative and conveys main-line information.[30] It constitutes, therefore, a verbal sentence even when it appears as second-place *qatal* (*x-qatal*). Conversely, in oral narrative *wayyiqtol* is found as continuation form, not at the very beginning.

---

[26] See on this point "Narrative Syntax of Exodus 19–24" in this volume.
[27] See most recently: "Finite Verb".
[28] Also see § 8 below.
[29] *Syntax* § 17.
[30] See "narrative discourse" in *Syntax* §§ 74–77.

4. *Other second-place-verb constructions*

Both antecedent (§ 2.1) and background information (§§ 2.2; 2.3), which represent the secondary line of communication, are conveyed by the following constructions besides *x-qatal*:

1. *x-yiqtol*
2. *w^{e}qatal*
3. non-verbal clause.

For background information see (**11b–g**) with *w^{e}qatal*, (**12d–e**) with *x-yiqtol*, and (**13b**) with non-verbal clause; for antecedent information, see (**14**) with *x-yiqtol* (a–b.e; with *ṭerem* in a–b) and *w^{e}qatal* (f).[31]

(**11**) 1 Sam. 16:22–23[32] (*wayyiqtol* → *w^{e}qatal*)

(a) Saul sent (someone) to Jesse saying (. . .).	וַיִּשְׁלַח שָׁאוּל אֶל־יִשַׁי לֵאמֹר (. . .)
(b) Now, when a spirit from God came on Saul,	וְהָיָה בִּהְיוֹת רוּחַ־אֱלֹהִים אֶל־שָׁאוּל
(c) David used to take the lyre	וְלָקַח דָּוִד אֶת־הַכִּנּוֹר
(d) and play by his hand,	וְנִגֵּן בְּיָדוֹ
(e) and so Saul was relieved,	וְרָוַח לְשָׁאוּל
(f) he was well	וְטוֹב לוֹ
(g) and the bad spirit used to depart from upon him.[33]	וְסָרָה מֵעָלָיו רוּחַ הָרָעָה

(**12**) Ex. 18:25–26 (*wayyiqtol* → *w^{e}qatal*/(*w^e*)*x-yiqtol*)

(a) Moses chose men of valor from all Israel	וַיִּבְחַר מֹשֶׁה אַנְשֵׁי־חַיִל מִכָּל־יִשְׂרָאֵל

---

[31] Consult *Syntax* §§ 18–19 for antecedent information; §§ 43.46–47 for background; and "Essential Hebrew" §§ 1.1–1.3.

[32] On this text compare R.D. Bergen, "Evil Spirits and Eccentric Grammar: A Study of the Relationship between Text and Meaning in Hebrew Narrative", in: R.D. Bergen (ed.), *Biblical Hebrew and Discourse Linguistics*, Winona Lake: Eisenbrauns, 1994, 320–335. This paper is an example of the problems connected with the use of statistics in syntactic analysis.

[33] 1 Sam. 16:23 relates the execution of an instruction imparted in 16:14. It is noteworthy that both instruction and execution employ the same verb form *w^{e}qatal*, clearly with different function. In the instruction *w^{e}qatal* expresses indicative future while in the execution it expresses repetition or habit. The same is found in Ex. 18:25–26 (execution) vs. 18:22 (instruction); see (**12**) below. This is not an isolated phenomenon since it is also found in the parallel sections of Ex. 25–30 (instruction) and 35–40 (execution); see *Syntax* §§ 58–60, and my book review of W. Groß – H. Irsigler – T. Seidl (ed.), *Text, Methode und Grammatik*, St. Ottilien: EOS Verlag, 1991, *Liber Annuus* 44 (1994) 667–692, esp. 689–690. In these texts we see clear cases of verb forms common to historical narrative and to direct speech (§ 7 below).

(b) and placed them as rulers over the people, as rulers of thousands, rulers of hundreds, rulers of fifties, and rulers of tens.	וַיִּתֵּן אֹתָם רָאשִׁים עַל־הָעָם שָׂרֵי אֲלָפִים שָׂרֵי מֵאוֹת שָׂרֵי חֲמִשִּׁים וְשָׂרֵי עֲשָׂרֹת
(c) Now, they used to judge the people at all time:	וְשָׁפְטוּ אֶת־הָעָם בְּכָל־עֵת
(d) every difficult matter they used to bring to Moses	אֶת־הַדָּבָר הַקָּשֶׁה יְבִיאוּן אֶל־מֹשֶׁה
(e) while any small matter they used to judge by themselves.[34]	וְכָל־הַדָּבָר הַקָּטֹן יִשְׁפּוּטוּ הֵם

(**13**) 1 Sam. 26:3 (*wayyiqtol* → non-verbal clause in b)

(a) Saul encamped on the hill of Hachilah (. . .)	וַיִּחַן שָׁאוּל בְּגִבְעַת הַחֲכִילָה (. . .)
(b) while David was staying in the desert.	וְדָוִד יֹשֵׁב בַּמִּדְבָּר

(**14**) Gen. 2:5–7 (*w^{e}x-yiqtol* in a–b.e/*w^{e}qatal* in f → *wayyiqtol*)

(a) Now no shrub of the field was yet in the earth	וְכֹל שִׂיחַ הַשָּׂדֶה טֶרֶם יִהְיֶה בָאָרֶץ
(b) and no herb of the field had yet sprung up,	וְכָל־עֵשֶׂב הַשָּׂדֶה טֶרֶם יִצְמָח
(c) for Yahweh God had not sent rain upon the earth	כִּי לֹא הִמְטִיר יְהוָה אֱלֹהִים עַל־הָאָרֶץ
(d) and there was no man to till the ground.	וְאָדָם אַיִן לַעֲבֹד אֶת־הָאֲדָמָה
(e) Now a moisture used to come up from the earth	וְאֵד יַעֲלֶה מִן־הָאָרֶץ
(f) and water the whole face of the ground.	וְהִשְׁקָה אֶת־כָּל־פְּנֵי־הָאֲדָמָה
(g) Then Yahweh God formed man of dust from the ground.	וַיִּיצֶר יְהוָה אֱלֹהִים אֶת־הָאָדָם עָפָר מִן־הָאֲדָמָה

It is important to note that second-place finite verb forms (*x-qatal* and *x-yiqtol*) as well as *w^{e}qatal* fulfill the same function as the non-verbal clause. They are, of course, different from the point of view of grammar but equivalent from the point of view of syntax for the principle of paradigmatic substitution, since they are capable of filling the same slot in the paradigm. The grammatical difference produces

[34] See previous note on 1 Sam. 16:22–23 (**11**). In (**12**) besides the shift from main-line *wayyiqtol* (a–b) to secondary-line *w^{e}qatal* (c), notice a further shift from *w^{e}qatal* for general information (c) to *(w^e)x-yiqtol* for specification (d–e: "every difficult matter . . . any small matter").

a difference in aspect, i.e. in historical narrative *x-qatal* is used for unique information or action (**7b**) and for anteriority (**6e**), while *x-yiqtol* and *w^eqatal* are used for repeated information or action or habit (**11b–g; 12c–e; 14a–b.e–f**),[35] and the non-verbal clause for contemporaneity (**13b**).

One notes a remarkable correspondence between aspect of information or action, on the one side, and secondary line of communication, on the other. Conversely, tense is tied to the main line of communication. This means that narrative *wayyiqtol* is a tense and exactly corresponds to the narrative tense of modern languages, while the other verb forms and constructions indicate aspect: unity, anteriority, repetition, habit or description, and contemporaneity.[36]

The syntactic equivalence between sentences with second-place finite verb (*x-qatal, x-yiqtol*) and sentences without any finite verb is most noteworthy. The fact that they are paradigmatically interchangeable legitimates for both the designation of "nominal" sentences. Actually, I called "compound nominal" the sentence with a finite verb in the second position, and "simple nominal" the sentence without any finite verb.[37]

The fact that *w^eqatal* constitutes a verbal sentence because it takes the first place in the sentence, and still behaves like a nominal sentence in narrative texts may have two reasons. First, *w^eqatal* is a verb form of the secondary level of communication in historical narrative as I have just indicated. Second, even in discursive texts, where it is at home because it indicates the main line of communication, *w^eqatal* is not found at the very beginning of a direct speech but as a continuation form only.[38]

[35] As reaffirmed by A.F. Rainey, "Further Remarks on the Hebrew Verbal System", *Hebrew Studies* 29 (1988) 35–42, against Z. Zevit, "Talking Funny in Biblical Hebrew and Solving a Problem of the *yaqtul* Past Tense", *Hebrew Studies* 29 (1988), 25–33. *X-yiqtol* and *w^eqatal* are not interchangeable, however, but the first expresses background to the latter as explained in the previous note.

[36] In matter of aspect, Endo, *The Verbal System*, 1996, retains the categories "perfective or non-perfective, complete or non-complete" (32), which I think are inadequate for Biblical Hebrew. Rather, I favor the categories "anteriority-simultaneity-posteriority". On aspect see a recent historical discussion by V. DeCaen, "Ewald and Driver on Biblical Hebrew 'Aspect': Anteriority and the Orientalist Framework", *ZAH* 9 (1996) 129–151.

[37] *Syntax* § 6; *Lettura* § 2. See § 8 below.

[38] An overview of the functions of *w^eqatal* is found in *Syntax* §§ 156–158.

5. *Historical narrative versus direct speech*

A distinction between historical-narrative texts and direct speech texts has come up more than once in my exposition. Indeed, I think that this distinction is necessary in the analysis of Biblical Hebrew.[39] The reason is that these two genres of the prose possess distinctive verb forms, while the verb forms attested in both have a different value.[40]

In earlier studies, I called the two genres "narrative" and "discourse", respectively.[41] Since, however, "discourse" has been used in some circles as a comprehensive term to indicate all kinds of texts, even poetry, there arises a danger of misunderstanding.[42] This is why I speak now of historical-narrative texts and direct-speech texts, or discursive texts—terms which I hope are clear enough.

Having already discussed the verb forms of historical narrative, I will now discuss those of direct speech. In direct speech all the three main temporal axes—present, past and future—are used in contradistinction from historical-narrative texts where only the axis of the past is used.[43]

(**15**) Gen. 42:10–11

(a) (Joseph's brothers) said to him,	וַיֹּאמְרוּ אֵלָיו
(b) "No, my Lord,	לֹא אֲדֹנִי
(c) but your servants have come to buy food.	וַעֲבָדֶיךָ בָּאוּ לִשְׁבָּר־אֹכֶל
(d) All of us,[44]	כֻּלָּנוּ
(e) we are the sons of one man;	בְּנֵי אִישׁ־אֶחָד נָחְנוּ
(f) we are honest;	כֵּנִים אֲנַחְנוּ
(g) your servants have never been spies".	לֹא־הָיוּ עֲבָדֶיךָ מְרַגְּלִים

(**16**) Ex. 7:17–18

(a) Thus says the Lord,	כֹּה אָמַר יְהוָה
(b) "By this you shall know	בְּזֹאת תֵּדַע

[39] This distinction does not contradict H. Weinrich (note 7 above) in any way, *pace* A.J.C. Verheij, *Verbs and Numbers. A Study of the Frequencies of the Hebrew Verbal Tense Forms in the Book of Samuel, Kings, and Chronicles*, Assen and Maastricht: Van Gorcum, 1990, 15, and his book review of my *Syntax* in *BiOr* 49 (1992) 214–217.

[40] See most recently my book review of Dawson, *Text-Linguistics*, *Liber Annuus* 45, esp. § 4.

[41] *Syntax* § 7; *Lettura* § 1.

[42] See "On the Hebrew Verbal System", § 2.

[43] Cf. *Syntax* §§ 52–54; "A Neglected Point of Hebrew Syntax: Yiqtol and Position in the Sentence", *Liber Annuus* 37 (1987) 7–19, § 1; "Essential Hebrew", § 2.

[44] This a *casus pendens* and (e) is the main sentence. The *casus pendens* constitutes a sentence by itself because it paradigmatically interchanges with a complete sentence; see *Syntax* § 120; *Lettura* § 4.4; "Finite Verb", 436–438.

(c) that I am the Lord:	כִּי אֲנִי יְהוָה
(d) Behold, I am about to smite with the rod that is in my hand the waters that are in the Nile,	הִנֵּה אָנֹכִי מַכֶּה בַּמַּטֶּה אֲשֶׁר־בְּיָדִי עַל־הַמַּיִם אֲשֶׁר בַּיְאֹר
(e) and they shall be turned to blood,	וְנֶהֶפְכוּ לְדָם
(f) while the fish that is in the Nile shall die.	וְהַדָּגָה אֲשֶׁר־בַּיְאֹר תָּמוּת
(g) The Nile shall become putrid	וּבָאַשׁ הַיְאֹר
(h) and the Egyptians shall not be (any more) able to drink of the water of the Nile".	וְנִלְאוּ מִצְרַיִם לִשְׁתּוֹת מַיִם מִן־הַיְאֹר

(**17**) Gen. 42:13[45]

(a) (Joseph's brothers) said,	וַיֹּאמְרוּ
(b) "Your servants are twelve,	שְׁנֵים עָשָׂר עֲבָדֶיךָ
(c) we are brothers	אַחִים אֲנַחְנוּ
(d) and the son of one man in the land of Canaan.[46]	בְּנֵי אִישׁ־אֶחָד בְּאֶרֶץ כְּנָעַן
(e) And behold, the youngest is with our father today,[47]	וְהִנֵּה הַקָּטֹן אֶת־אָבִינוּ הַיּוֹם
(f) and one,	וְהָאֶחָד
(g) he is no more".[48]	אֵינֶנּוּ

(**18**) Josh. 9:22

(a) Joshua summoned them,	וַיִּקְרָא לָהֶם יְהוֹשֻׁעַ
(b) and he spoke to them, saying	וַיְדַבֵּר אֲלֵיהֶם לֵאמֹר
(c) "Why did you deceive us, saying,	לָמָּה רִמִּיתֶם אֹתָנוּ לֵאמֹר
(d) 'We are very far from you',	רְחוֹקִים אֲנַחְנוּ מִכֶּם מְאֹד
(e) while you dwell among us?"	וְאַתֶּם בְּקִרְבֵּנוּ יֹשְׁבִים

In direct speech the axis of the present is represented by non-verbal sentence (**15e–f**), the axis of the past by first-place (**15g**, negated *qatal*) or second-place *qatal* (**15c**), and the axis of the future by *yiqtol* (**16b**). These constructions represent the main line of communication in the three respective temporal axes.

In the axis of the present the non-verbal sentence is a main-line construction at the beginning of a direct speech (e.g. **17b; 18d**); in the

45 Compare Gen. 42:32.

46 Sentence (d) comprises the predicate only; the subject ("we") is implied from the previous sentence.

47 This is a "presentative sentence" with word order (grammatical) subject-predicate, introduced by *wᵉhinnēh*. See § 8 below.

48 **17 f–g** consists of two sentences: *wᵉhāʾeḥād* is *casus pendens* with the function of the protasis, and a sentence by itself (see note 44 above), because *ʾênennû* is a complete sentence, being composed of the "quasi-verb" *ʾên* as the predicate and the pronominal suffix as the subject, and is the apodosis.

course of direct speech, it either continues the main line (**17c–g**) or is a secondary-line construction expressing a circumstance (**18e**). Syntax does not always provide sufficient criteria to decide; semantics must be brought in to help.[49]

In the axis of the past, *qatal* is a main-line verb form at the beginning of an oral narrative, while in its development it is a secondary-line verb form. The reason is that, once the oral narrative has begun with *qatal* (or *x-qatal*), it goes on with continuation *wayyiqtol* for the main line of communication (note that *w*^{e}*qatal* is not used with this function!), and with *x-qatal* as well as other non-verbal constructions for the secondary line exactly as the historical narrative (§ 4). Moses' speech in Deuteronomy, for example, begins with *x-qatal* in 1:6 (*yhwh ʾĕlōhênû dibber ʾēlênû*) and goes on with *wayyiqtol*: *wāʾōmar* "I said" (1:9), *wattaʿănû* "you answered" (1:14), *wāʾeqqaḥ* "I took" (1:15), *wāʾăṣawweh* "I commanded" (1:16; 1:18), etc. The narrative chain of *wayyiqtol* is interrupted by secondary-line constructions: *x-yiqtol* (**19c–d**), (*w*^{e})*x-qatal* (**21b–c.e**), and non-verbal clause (**20j–k**).

(**19**) Deut. 3:8–10

(a) At that time we took the land of the two kings of the Amorites — וַנִּקַּח בָּעֵת הַהִוא אֶת־הָאָרֶץ מִיַּד שְׁנֵי מַלְכֵי הָאֱמֹרִי

(b) who were beyond the Jordan, from the valley of the Arnon to Mount Hermon — אֲשֶׁר בְּעֵבֶר הַיַּרְדֵּן מִנַּחַל אַרְנֹן עַד־הַר חֶרְמוֹן

(c) (the Sidonians used to call Hermon Sirion, — צִידֹנִים יִקְרְאוּ לְחֶרְמוֹן שִׂרְיֹן

(d) while the Amorites used to call it Senir), — וְהָאֱמֹרִי יִקְרְאוּ־לוֹ שְׂנִיר

(e) all the cities of the tableland and all Gilead and all Bashan (. . .)[50] — כֹּל עָרֵי הַמִּישֹׁר וְכָל־הַגִּלְעָד וְכָל־הַבָּשָׁן (. . .)

---

[49] In (**18d**) the word order is predicate (*r*^{e}*ḥōqîm*)—subject (*ʾănaḥnû*) while in (**18e**) subject (*w*^{e}*ʾattem*)—predicate (*b*^{e}*qirbēnû yōš*^{e}*bîm*); in other words, (**18d**) shows the normal word order in a predicative sentence and (**18e**) the word order of a circumstantial clause. However, the same word order subject-predicate is also found in presentative sentences. See my "Simple Nominal Clause (SNC) or Verbless Clause in Biblical Hebrew Prose", *ZAH* 6 (1993) 216–227, esp. 220–223, and § 8 below.

[50] Clauses (c–d) literally break the main sentence (a–b) since (e) is an apposition explicating the geographical indication "from the valley of the Arnon to Mount Hermon" of (b). For a geographical analysis of this text see P.A. Kaswalder, *La disputa diplomatica di Iefte (Gdc 11,12–28). La ricerca archeologica in Giordania e il problema della conquista*, Jerusalem: Franciscan Printing Press, 1990, 107–121. Other examples of a parenthetic clause breaking the main sentence are Deut. 3:19 (cf. Josh. 1:14!) and Judg. 20:27–28.

(**20**) Deut. 9:13–15

(a) The Lord spoke to me saying,	וַיֹּאמֶר יְהוָה אֵלַי לֵאמֹר
(b) "I have seen this people,	רָאִיתִי אֶת־הָעָם הַזֶּה
(c) and behold, it is a stubborn people.	וְהִנֵּה עַם־קְשֵׁה־עֹרֶף הוּא
(d) Let me alone,	הֶרֶף מִמֶּנִּי
(e) that I may destroy them	וְאַשְׁמִידֵם
(f) and blot out their name from under heaven,	וְאֶמְחֶה אֶת־שְׁמָם מִתַּחַת הַשָּׁמָיִם
(g) and that I may make of you a nation mightier and greater than they".	וְאֶעֱשֶׂה אוֹתְךָ לְגוֹי־עָצוּם וָרָב מִמֶּנּוּ
(h) Then I turned	וָאֵפֶן
(i) and came down from the mountain,	וָאֵרֵד מִן־הָהָר
(j) while the mountain was burning with fire	וְהָהָר בֹּעֵר בָּאֵשׁ
(k) and while the two tables of the covenant were in my two hands.	וּשְׁנֵי לֻחֹת הַבְּרִית עַל שְׁתֵּי יָדָי

(**21**) Deut. 9:18–20

(a) Then I lay prostrate before the Lord as before, forty days and forty nights	וָאֶתְנַפַּל לִפְנֵי יְהוָה כָּרִאשֹׁנָה אַרְבָּעִים יוֹם וְאַרְבָּעִים לַיְלָה
(b) —bread I did not eat	לֶחֶם לֹא אָכַלְתִּי
(c) nor water did I drink—[51] (. . .)	וּמַיִם לֹא שָׁתִיתִי (. . .)
(d) And the Lord hearkened to me that time also,	וַיִּשְׁמַע יְהוָה אֵלַי גַּם בַּפַּעַם הַהִוא
(e) while the Lord was angry against Aaron as to destroy him.	וּבְאַהֲרֹן הִתְאַנַּף יְהוָה מְאֹד לְהַשְׁמִידוֹ

In the axis of the future, the non-volitive, simply predictive direct speech begins with second-place *yiqtol* (*x-yiqtol*; **16b**) and continues with *w^eqatal* (**16e.g–h**). Note that *w^eqatal* is not found right at the beginning; in fact it is a continuation verb form. Predictive direct speech can also begin with a non-verbal sentence, particularly with a participle (**16d**). In its development, the non-volitive direct speech uses *x-yiqtol* as background construction to a preceding *w^eqatal* (**16f**). Thus, we find a chain of *w^eqatal* and a tense shift "*w^eqatal* → *w^ex-yiqtol*" (**16e–f**) that parallels the chain of *wayyiqtol* and the tense shift "*wayyiqtol* → *w^ex-qatal*" in historical-narrative texts (**7–8**).

---

[51] Note that *leḥem lōʾ ʾākaltî* and *ûmayim lōʾ šātîtî* are two negated *x-qatal* constructions (*wayyiqtol* and first-place *qatal* are both negated with *w^elōʾ* + *qatal*). Though *waw* is missing, they are both circumstantial *x-qatal* constructions with the function of explicating the preceding *wayyiqtol* (background constructions); literally, "Then I prostrate before the Lord . . . *while* I did not eat bread nor drink water".

In direct-speech texts (and in historical narrative as well, **20j**), the participle appears in non-verbal clauses. It has no tense value for itself but assumes that of the dominant finite verb in its environment—future (**16d**), past (**22e**), or present (**18e**).[52]

In direct speech, we also find volitive verb forms—imperative (**20d; 23e–f**), jussive *yiqtol* (**23c**), and *w^eyiqtol* (**20e–g; 23g**). The last verb form is not always recognized as autonomous but I think it should.[53]

(**22**) Josh. 24:16–17[54]

(a) Then the people answered	וַיַּעַן הָעָם
(b) and said,	וַיֹּאמֶר
(c) "Far from us to forsake the Lord to serve other gods;	חָלִילָה לָּנוּ מֵעֲזֹב אֶת־יְהוָה לַעֲבֹד אֱלֹהִים אֲחֵרִים
(d) for the Lord our God,	כִּי יְהוָה אֱלֹהֵינוּ
(e) it is he that brought us and our fathers up from the land of Egypt, from the house of bondage,	הוּא הַמַּעֲלֶה אֹתָנוּ וְאֶת־אֲבוֹתֵינוּ מֵאֶרֶץ מִצְרַיִם מִבֵּית עֲבָדִים
(f) and that did those great signs in our sight,	וַאֲשֶׁר עָשָׂה לְעֵינֵינוּ אֶת־הָאֹתוֹת הַגְּדֹלוֹת הָאֵלֶּה
(g) and preserved us in all the way that we went, and among all the peoples through whom we passed".	וַיִּשְׁמְרֵנוּ בְּכָל־הַדֶּרֶךְ אֲשֶׁר הָלַכְנוּ בָהּ וּבְכֹל הָעַמִּים אֲשֶׁר עָבַרְנוּ בְּקִרְבָּם

[52] For a general treatment of the subject, see *Gesenius' Hebrew Grammar*, ed. A.E. Cowley, E. Kautzsch, Oxford 1910, repr. 1985, § 116, and P. Joüon, *A Grammar of Biblical Hebrew*, Translated and Revised by T. Muraoka, Roma: Pontificio Istituto Biblico, 1991, § 121. From the point of view of syntax, several types of nominal clauses also exist without a participle. There is, however, a difference in terms of aspect. See S.R. Driver, *A Treatise on the Use of the Tenses in Hebrew and Some Other Syntactical Questions*, Oxford: Clarendon, 1892; repr. 1969, Appendix I (*passim*).

[53] I mean that *w^eyiqtol* is not a combination of *waw* plus *yiqtol* but a verb form by itself with a specific morphology and function, just as *wayyiqtol* is not a combination of *waw* and *yiqtol* and *w^eqatal* is not a combination of *waw* and *qatal* but autonomous verb forms, the *waw* being an integral part of them. See my discussion in *Syntax* §§ 132; 159–160; and "A Neglected Point" §§ 1.1–1.2.

[54] Compare (**1**) above. The initial personal pronoun in (**22e**) receives emphasis as in (**1d**). In both cases it is the predicate (or new element of the sentence) as the context convincingly shows. The fact that the subject (or given element) is a qatal (**1d**) or a participle (**22e**) proves that both sentences are "nominal", i.e. the predicate is a noun phrase (a personal pronoun in the two cases under consideration). They inform on *who* did something (since they are cleft sentences), not on the action itself of bringing the Israelites out of Egypt (as if they were plain sentences). Note that the participle with article *hammaʿăleh* in (e) is equivalent to *waʾăšer ʾāśâ* in (f); see *Syntax* § 6. Also note that the LXX clearly translates with a cleft sentence: κύριος ὁ θεὸς ἡμῶν, αὐτὸς θεός ἐστιν, αὐτὸς ἀνήγαγεν ἡμᾶς; see "Marked Syntactical Structures" § 2.

(**23**) Ruth 4:11–13[55]

(a) Then all the people who were at the gate, and the elders, said,	וַיֹּאמְרוּ כָּל־הָעָם אֲשֶׁר־בַּשַּׁעַר וְהַזְּקֵנִים
(b) "We are witnesses.[56]	עֵדִים
(c) May the Lord make the woman, who is coming into your house, like Rachel and Leah,	יִתֵּן יְהוָה אֶת־הָאִשָּׁה הַבָּאָה אֶל־בֵּיתֶךָ כְּרָחֵל וּכְלֵאָה
(d) who together built up the house of Israel.	אֲשֶׁר בָּנוּ שְׁתֵּיהֶם אֶת־בֵּית יִשְׂרָאֵל
(e) May you prosper in Ephrathah	וַעֲשֵׂה־חַיִל בְּאֶפְרָתָה
(f) and be renowned in Bethlehem;	וּקְרָא־שֵׁם בְּבֵית לָחֶם
(g) and may your house be like the house of Perez, whom Tamar bore to Judah, because of the children that the Lord will give you by this young woman".[57]	וִיהִי בֵיתְךָ כְּבֵית פֶּרֶץ אֲשֶׁר־יָלְדָה תָמָר לִיהוּדָה מִן־הַזֶּרַע אֲשֶׁר יִתֵּן יְהוָה לְךָ מִן־הַנַּעֲרָה הַזֹּאת

Biblical Hebrew possesses two sets of verb forms for volitive and non-volitive future, i.e. jussive *yiqtol* and *w*ᵉ*yiqtol*, negated with *ʾal* + *yiqtol*, for volitive future, and indicative *x-yiqtol* and *w*ᵉ*qatal*, negated with *x-lōʾ* + *yiqtol* and *lōʾ* + *yiqtol*, respectively, for non-volitive future.[58]

---

[55] See "Syntactic Analysis of Ruth", *ad l.*

[56] This is a reaction to Boaz's statement: *ʿēdîm ʾattem hayyôm* "you are witnesses this day" (4:10). In (**23b**) the subject "we" is implied.

[57] (**23**) exemplifies a frequent problem with the *ʾăšer* clause. In (d) it can be isolated from the rest of sentence but in (f) it can not because it is followed by a prepositional phrase (*min-hazzeraʿ ʾăšer* . . .) which belongs to the superordinate sentence (*wîhî bêtᵉkā* . . .). See my discussion in *Lettura* § 7.1.

[58] See *Syntax* §§ 61–65; "A Neglected Point" § 1; "Essential Hebrew" § 2.3; and also my book review of Joüon-Muraoka vol. II, *Liber Annuus* 43 (1993) 528–533, esp. 530–532. The exact difference between the so-called "vetitive" *ʾal* + *yiqtol* and "prohibitive" *lōʾ* + *yiqtol* is still to be determined; see *Syntax* § 55. Also see E.J. Revell, "The System of the Verb in Standard Biblical Prose", *HUCA* 60 (1989) 1–37, esp. § 21. Despite the fact that he proceeds in a way partly traditional (e.g. he is interested in the sentence rather than in the text) and partly unconventional (e.g. he speaks of "QTL with no conjunction prefixed", i.e. initial qatal, versus "QTL with prefixed conjunction", i.e. *w*ᵉ*qatal*), Revell makes several interesting points. Among these, the distinction between "modal" (i.e. volitive) and "indicative imperfect", the first being clause-initial, the second non-clause-initial (pp. 17–29). Though he does not identifies *w*ᵉ*yiqtol* as "modal", Revell stresses the non-volitive function of *w*ᵉ*qatal* even in a volitive environment, i.e. when connected with imperative, jussive and cohortative (§§ 1; 17–22). He also recognizes the importance of the first place in the sentence.

6. *From sentence to text*

In Biblical Hebrew narrative two types of sentence are attested (see §§ 3–4 above): type 1: V-x, and type 2: x-V. Type 1 is represented by narrative *wayyiqtol*. It constitutes a verbal sentence and conveys information in general terms. Type 2 comprises categories I–II (N) of § 3 above and constitutes a nominal sentence. It conveys information in specific terms according to the nature of the "x" element on which the emphasis falls (§ 2.3), or signals syntactic dependence (§§ 2.1–2.2).

We discover a coherent development from the level of the sentence to the level of the text, i.e. from the two types of sentence just mentioned to the basic syntactic structures of Biblical Hebrew narrative. These are as follows:

1. (*w*^{e})*x-qatal* → *wayyiqtol*
2. *wayyiqtol* → (*w*^{e})*x-qatal*
3. *wayyiqtol* → *w*^{e}*qatal*/(*w*^{e})*x-yiqtol*
4. *wayyiqtol* → non-verbal clause.

"(*w*^{e})*x-qatal* → *wayyiqtol*" is a shift from a sentence type 2 (x-V) to a sentence type 1 (V-x). This tense shift occurs at the beginning of a text, or of an episode of the text. (*w*^{e})*x-qatal* conveys antecedent information, and *wayyiqtol* marks the main line of narrative (see § 2.1).

"*Wayyiqtol* → (*w*^{e})*x-qatal*" is a shift from a sentence type 1 (V-x) to a sentence type 2 (x-V). This tense shift occurs in the course of a narrative text. *Wayyiqtol* signals the foreground and (*w*^{e})*x-qatal* the background.[59] Besides (*w*^{e}-)*x-qatal*, the background is indicated by (*w*^{e})*x-yiqtol*, *w*^{e}*qatal* and non-verbal clause in historical narrative (§ 4).

Note that in the tense shift "*wayyiqtol* → (*w*^{e})*x-qatal*" both verb forms can be represented by more than one sentence; the same is true for the reversed tense shift "(*w*^{e})*x-qatal* → *wayyiqtol*." E.g., we find in (**9**): once *wayyiqtol* (foreground; a)[60] and twice *x-qatal* (background; b–c); in (**11**): once *wayyiqtol* (a) and six times *w*^{e}*qatal* (b–g); in (**12**): twice *wayyiqtol* (a–b), once *w*^{e}*qatal* (c) and twice *x-yiqtol* (d–e; clauses c–e indicate all background). Similarly, the antecedent information can comprise several clauses (as Gen. 1:1–2 and 2:5–6; see **14**).[61]

---

[59] Some discussion is going on concerning the use of these terms. I'm using "foreground" as equivalent to main line—i.e. *wayyiqtol* in historical narrative—and "background" as secondary line of communication—i.e. *x-qatal*, *x-yiqtol*, *w*^{e}*qatal*, and non-verbal clause. At this point, these terms should be clear enough to the reader.

[60] However, *wayyiqtol* normally appears in a chain of selfsame verb forms.

[61] Contrast Endo, *The Verbal System* 1996, 295: "A chain may be formed by non-

Biblical Hebrew narrative develops by alternating these two tense shifts. Every historical text is generated by various combinations of these basic structures.[62] By alternating main line (*wayyiqtol*) and secondary line (*w^{e}x-qatal/yiqtol*, *w^{e}qatal*, and non-verbal clause), the author shapes his information in a meaningful way according to his strategy of communication.[63]

Direct speech is more varied than historical narrative because all the three temporal axes (past, present, and future) are used as the main line of communication—not only the past as in historical narrative. The following syntactic structures are attested:

5. *(x-)qatal* → continuation *wayyiqtol*
6. continuation *wayyiqtol* → {*x-qatal*/*x-yiqtol*/non-verbal clause}
7. non-verbal clause → non-verbal clause
8. {*x-yiqtol*/non-verbal clause} → main-line *w^{e}qatal*
9. main-line *w^{e}qatal* → background *(w^e)x-yiqtol.*

In the axis of the past, oral narrative begins with *qatal* (**10e; 20b**) or *x-qatal* (Deut. 1:6 in § 5 above) with no difference, i.e. they start the main line of oral narrative. No antecedent-information constructions are used in oral narrative.[64] Once started with *(x-)qatal*, the main line of oral narrative goes on with continuation *wayyiqtol*, which appears in a chain; the chain of *wayyiqtol* is interrupted with secondary-

---

sequential forms (e.g. (*waw*-x-)QATAL, PTC [i.e. a participial clause], Verbless clauses) in the narrative. This chain usually consists of two verbal forms (or two clauses), *but not more than that* (Hence, "two-member chain") (italics mine).

[62] In "Narrative Syntax of Exodus 19–24", the background constructions are indicated by an upwards arrow ↑ while the antecedent-information constructions are placed in level 2 (indented). In his paper, "Clause Types and Textual Structure: An Experiment in Narrative Syntax", in: E. Talstra (ed.), *Narrative and Comment. Contributions Presented to Wolfgang Schneider*, Amsterdam 1995, 166–180, E. Talstra remarks: "For this reason, I think that Niccacci, in his narrative syntax, should allow for more embeddings in a story than only a 'main story line' and 'background information'" (p. 174). In general, I am rather uneasy with Talstra's paper simply because I do not understand it enough. With reference to the passage just quoted, I have established three levels (i.e. main line, secondary line, and direct speech) for practical reasons—to make the outline of the text, which is reproduced in full, practicable. On the one hand, the levels are actually more than three because the constructions marked with ↑ are of a different level from *wayyiqtol* (i.e. background); further, in direct speech I distinguish a main and a secondary level (see § 5 above). On the other hand, from the point of view of syntax *these*, and no more, are the levels of the text. Once this basis has been established, one can further look for literary criteria to identify sub-paragraphs, text-types and compositional devices. Without this basis, the investigation remains uncertain, to say the least.

[63] See *Lettura* § 7.5 and "Analysis".

[64] See my book review of Dawson, *Text-Linguistics*, *Liber Annuus* 45, esp. § 4a.

line constructions, e.g. to express a background information (**19c–d**), a contemporary circumstance (**20j–k**), a specification (**21b–c**), a contrast (**21e**) etc. exactly as in historical narrative.

In the axis of the present, the non-verbal clause is used both at the beginning and in the course of a text. At the beginning it is a main-line construction (**17b; 18d; 23b**); in the course of a text it conveys both main-line (**15e–f; 17c–g**) and background information (**18e**).

In the axis of the future, direct speech begins with indicative *x-yiqtol* (**16b**) or non-verbal sentence (**16d**) and continues with *w^{e}qatal* for the main line (**16e.g–h**) and *(w^e)x-yiqtol* for the secondary line (**16f**). As tense shift "*wayyiqtol* → *(w^e)x-qatal*" is characteristic of narrative, "*w^{e}qatal* → *(w^e)x-yiqtol*" is characteristic of direct speech (**24d–e**).[65]

Characteristic of direct speech is also the use of volitive verb forms. Biblical Hebrew shows two distinct sets of verb forms for volitive versus non-volitive future as indicated in the following table:

Volitive Forms	*versus*	Non-volitive Forms
(x-)yiqtol	*versus*	*x-yiqtol*
w^{e}yiqtol	*versus*	*w^{e}qatal*
imperative (or other volitive forms) → *w^{e}yiqtol* = "do this → *in order that* you may . . ."	*versus*	imperative (or other volitive forms) → *w^{e}qatal* = "do this → *and as a consequence* you will be able to . . ."

Non-volitive forms are present in (**16b–h**), volitive forms in (**20d–g**) and (**23c.e–g**).[66]

All kind of Biblical Hebrew prose, both historical narrative and direct speech, can be analysed with the help of the nine basic syntactic structures listed above.

7. *Verb forms common to historical narrative and to direct speech*

Here is a list the verb forms and constructions that are not specific to historical narrative or to direct speech but are used in both:

---

[65] *Syntax* § 11.

[66] For more information consult *Syntax* §§ 61–65; "A Neglected Point" § 1.

1. *(w^e)x-qatal*
2. continuation *wayyiqtol*
3. indicative *(w^e)x-yiqtol*
4. *w^{e}qatal*
5. non-verbal clause.

(w^e)x-qatal and continuation *wayyiqtol*[67] are used in the same way in historical narrative and in oral narrative, but they are translated differently in languages that have separate sets of verb forms for the two genres of the prose, i.e. with "passé simple", "passato remoto", and "pretérito indefinido", for historical narrative, and with "passé composé", "passato prossimo", and "pretérito perfecto", for oral narrative, in French, Italian and Spanish, respectively.[68]

(w^e)x-yiqtol and *w^{e}qatal* indicate simple future in direct speech (**16e–h**), and repetition or habit in historical narrative where they are translated with the imperfect (**11b–g; 12c–e; 19c–d**).

The non-verbal clause indicates contemporaneity both in the present and in the past but is translated with present tense in direct speech (**18e**) and with imperfect in historical narrative (**13b; 14d; 20j–k**).

Thus, the verb forms and constructions listed above are common to both historical narrative and direct speech, however their value varies from one genre to the other. This fact does not jeopardize the difference between the two genres of the prose, or the existence of a verb system in Biblical Hebrew. It simply attests to the poverty of the language. The Biblical Hebrew situation is comparable to that of a modern language like English, which does not have complete sets of verb forms as compared to Latin languages (see above).

A further important structure common to both historical narrative and direct speech is the "double sentence".[69] It is a two-member construction consisting of a circumstantial clause called "protasis" in the first place, and a main sentence called "apodosis" in the second.[70]

---

[67] "Continuation *wayyiqtol*" contrasts "narrative *wayyiqtol*". The latter both starts and carries on the main line of narrative—the so-called "narrative chain", e.g. (**6b–d**)—and has a fixed tense value, while the first continues a different verb form or construction and has no tense value of its own but assumes that of the preceding verb form or construction (e.g. **6f–g**).

[68] See "On the Hebrew Verbal System", 120, Table 1.

[69] Called "the two-element syntactic construction" in *Syntax*, Ch. 8. I chose this long designation in order to avoid the traditional designation of "construction with *waw apodoseos*" for the simple reason that *waw* is not always present or obligatory. See discussion in *Lettura* § 4.1, and more recently in "Finite Verb", 436–438.

[70] "Protasis" and "apodosis" are intended in broad sense. They are not restricted to the conditional clause but include temporal, causal and comparative clauses. Indeed, all these clauses show the basic syntactic pattern "circumstance—main sentence."

The double sentence may be more at home in direct speech but is also widely used in historical narrative.

(**24**) Gen. 12:12 (instruction, direct speech)

(a) It will happen: when the Egyptians will see you,	וְהָיָה כִּי־יִרְאוּ אֹתָךְ הַמִּצְרִים
(b) they will say,	וְאָמְרוּ
(c) "She is his wife",	אִשְׁתּוֹ זֹאת
(d) and they will kill me,	וְהָרְגוּ אֹתִי
(e) while they will let you live. (. . .)	וְאֹתָךְ יְחַיּוּ (. . .)

versus 12:14 (execution, narrative)

(g) It happened: as soon as Abram entered Egypt,	וַיְהִי כְּבוֹא אַבְרָם מִצְרָיְמָה
(h) the Egyptians saw that the woman	וַיִּרְאוּ הַמִּצְרִים אֶת־הָאִשָּׁה
(i) was very beautiful.[71]	כִּי־יָפָה הִוא מְאֹד

In (**24**) the double sentence is preceded by *w^e^hāyâ* in direct speech (a), to which corresponds *way^e^hî* in historical narrative (g; see also **8c** above). The protasis is *kî* + *yiqtol* in direct speech (a), *k^e^* + infinitive in historical narrative (g). The apodosis is *w^e^qatal* in direct speech (b)—note the tense shift "*w^e^qatal* → (*w^e^-*)*x-yiqtol*" (**24d–e**; see § 6:9 above)—to which corresponds *wayyiqtol* in historical narrative (**24h**).

Remarkably, the double sentence is the only syntactic setting allowing *wayyiqtol*, which is a first-place verb form *per se*, to be preceded by an "x" element. Consider the following examples:

(**25**) Gen. 22:4[72]

(a) On the third day	בַּיּוֹם הַשְּׁלִישִׁי
(b) Abraham lifted up his eyes	וַיִּשָּׂא אַבְרָהָם אֶת־עֵינָיו
(c) and saw the place from afar.	וַיַּרְא אֶת־הַמָּקוֹם מֵרָחֹק

(**26**) Gen. 34:25

(a) Then on the third day,	וַיְהִי בַיּוֹם הַשְּׁלִישִׁי
(b) when they were sore,	בִּהְיוֹתָם כֹּאֲבִים
(c) two sons of Jacob, Simeon and Levi, Dinah's brothers, took each one his sword	וַיִּקְחוּ שְׁנֵי־בְנֵי־יַעֲקֹב שִׁמְעוֹן וְלֵוִי אֲחֵי דִינָה אִישׁ חַרְבּוֹ
(d) and came upon the city unawares,	וַיָּבֹאוּ עַל־הָעִיר בֶּטַח
(e) and killed all the males.	וַיַּהַרְגוּ כָּל־זָכָר

---

[71] Literally, "saw the woman, i.e. that she was very beautiful". See Joüon-Muraoka § 157d.

[72] Consult *Syntax* § 103 where Ex. 16:6b–7 is also quoted as a similar case of a short indication of time (protasis) preceding *w^e^qatal*, another first-place verb form.

(**27**) Ex. 16:22

(a) But on the sixth day וַיְהִי בַּיּוֹם הַשִּׁשִּׁי
(b) they gathered twice as much bread, two omers apiece; לָקְטוּ לֶחֶם מִשְׁנֶה שְׁנֵי הָעֹמֶר לָאֶחָד
(c) then all the leaders of the congregation came וַיָּבֹאוּ כָּל־נְשִׂיאֵי הָעֵדָה
(d) and one told Moses. וַיַּגִּידוּ לְמֹשֶׁה

The "x" element occurs both "nude" (**25a**) and introduced by *way^ehî* (**26a; 27a**). That the "x" element is not part of the sentence is clear from the fact that it is followed by a *wayyiqtol* (**25b; 26c**). Rather, the "x" element constitutes a sentence by itself (in **26b** a second, coordinated "x" element occurs) because it is paradigmatically interchangeable with explicitly complete clauses such as *kî/'im* + *yiqtol/qatal*. Indeed, it is a circumstantial clause with the function of the protasis, and *wayyiqtol* represents the apodosis. Note that in exactly the same sentence pattern a *qatal* is attested instead of *wayyiqtol* in the apodosis (**27b**).[73]

There is evidence to show that the different constructions attested with the function of protasis (i.e. conjunction + finite verb, finite verb in the second position, *w^eqatal*, preposition + infinitive, preposition + noun, adverb and *casus pendens*) occur both preceded by *way^ehî* or *w^ehāyâ* and without such verb forms. When they are "nude", they are secondary-line constructions and as such they break the main line of communication in historical narrative; on the contrary, preceded by *way^ehî* or *w^ehāyâ* they are verbal (rather, the whole double sentence is verbal) and thus they carry on the main line of communication.[74]

Note that the pattern protasis—apodosis is necessary in order to have a double sentence. The reason is that a special relationship exists between the two members precisely when they follow one another in that order. Indeed, not only the protasis cannot stand alone without the apodosis, being a dependent sentence (even when preceded by *way^ehî* or *w^ehāyâ* !), but neither the apodosis, which is the main sentence, can. Ultimately, the reason is that the double sentence is a development of the basic sentence type 2: x-V (§ 6 above) where

[73] The phrase *bayyôm haššiššî lāq^eṭû* could be analysed as a *x-qatal* sentence but the presence of *way^ehî* prevents such an analysis. On the criteria to distinguish a "*x-qatal*" construction (where "x" is part of the sentence) from a double sentence type "*x* | *qatal*" (where "x" is not part of the sentence but the protasis) see *Syntax* §§ 123–125, and *Lettura* § 4.5.

[74] See full discussion in *Syntax* § 127; *Lettura* §§ 4.1–4.4; "Sullo stato sintattico del verbo *hāyâ*", *Liber Annuus* 40 (1990) 9–23, esp. § 6.

both the "x" element and the finite verb are complete sentences. If, on the contrary, the order was reversed—apodosis—protasis—the complex would be a development of the basic sentence type 1: V-x (§ 6 above) where both the finite verb and the "x" element are complete sentences. An example of this is the tense shift "*wayyiqtol* → *w*ᵉ*x-qatal*" (§ 3 above). These facts only confirm the coherent development of the Biblical Hebrew verb system from sentence to the text levels (§ 6).

8. *Non-verbal (verbless) sentence*

It is a sentence without any finite verb, which I called "simple nominal sentence", to distinguish it from the "compound nominal sentence", which has a finite verb in the second place (*x-qatal*, or *x-yiqtol*).

"Verbless clause" is a common but risky designation. It may let people think that the verb is missing. This misunderstanding becomes factual when, e.g., one translates a sentence like *ʾănî yhwh* as "I (am) the Lord", i.e. writing the verb "am" in brackets. The verb "am" is not to be put in brackets because while the English translation needs it, the Hebrew sentence is complete without any form of verb *hāyâ*. It is, therefore, preferable to call this type of sentence "non-verbal", instead of "verbless".

Before coming to a brief description of the non-verbal sentence, a fresh point of view needs to be proposed. One should consider the possibility of classifying the types of sentence in Biblical Hebrew from a more comprehensive point of view than the one presented until now in this paper—i.e. from syntactic predication instead of from the finite verb. As a matter of fact, syntactic predication is not the function of the verb alone. Indeed, it is primarily the function of the verb but every element of the sentence besides the verb—i.e. the grammatical subject, object, indirect complement, or adverb—can become the predicate (see category I in § 3 above). Now, when the verb is the predicate, the sentence is plain, unmarked; when a different grammatical element is the predicate, the sentence is marked. A plain, unmarked sentence conveys information in general terms, precisely because the verb itself is the predicate; a marked sentence, on the contrary, conveys a detail of an information already given.[75] A sen-

[75] See the examples quoted in "Marked Syntactical Structures" § 6.

tence with the finite verb in the second place (*x-qatal, x-yiqtol*) is also marked when the "x" element is not the predicate (see category II in § 3 above).[76] In this case, the marked word order makes the sentence itself dependent on another one with a finite verb in the first place. In both cases (i.e. in categories I and II of § 3 above) the verb is demoted from its role of predicate and from its role of constituting an independent sentence, respectively.

From this point of view we are in a better position to describe the non-verbal sentence. First, in this kind of sentence we have real predication even without any verb form—the participle included. Second, in non-verbal sentences, too, we find plain, or unmarked, and marked structures. The criterion is here "universal" versus "particular" term. That is, a non-verbal sentence is plain, or unmarked, when the predicate is a universal term (adjective, participle, general noun, number; see **15e–f; 17b–d; 18d; 20c; 23b**); it is marked when the predicate is a particular term (a specific character, a proper noun, or a pronoun; see **22e**).[77]

In the predicative sentence, both with and without a finite verb, we distinguish two kinds of predication: grammatical and syntactic. E.g., in (**9b**) *bᵉʾiyyôb* is the predicate and *ḥārâ ʾappô* is the subject; likewise in (**9c**) *ûbišlōšet rēʿāyw* is the predicate and *ḥārâ ʾappô* is the subject. Note that in both sentences the subject is composed of a finite verb and its subject. Consider now the following example of a non-verbal sentence:

(**28**) Jer. 1:11 (same pattern in question and answer; see § 1.2 above)

(a) The word of the Lord came to me, saying,	וַיְהִי דְבַר־יְהוָה אֵלַי לֵאמֹר
(b) "What do you see, Jeremiah?"	מָה־אַתָּה רֹאֶה יִרְמְיָהוּ
(c) I said,	וָאֹמַר
(d) "It is a rod of almond that I see".	מַקֵּל שָׁקֵד אֲנִי רֹאֶה

In (b) *mâ-* is the predicate and *ʾattâ rōʾeh* is the subject; likewise in (d), *maqqēl šāqēd* is the predicate and *ʾănî rōʾeh* is the subject. Here both subjects are composed of an independent personal pronoun and a participle. In other words, the sentence *ʾănî rōʾeh* is embedded in the superordinate sentence *mâ-ʾattâ rōʾeh*; similarly in (**9b–c**) *ḥārâ ʾappô* is embedded in the superordinate sentences *bᵉʾiyyôb ḥārâ ʾappô* and *ûbišlōšet*

[76] "Marked Syntactical Structures" §§ 7.1–7.2.
[77] Consult "Simple Nominal Clause", 218–219.

rēʾāyw ḥārâ ʾappô. I call "syntactic" the components of the superordinate sentence and "grammatical" those of the embedded sentence. See the following diagram:

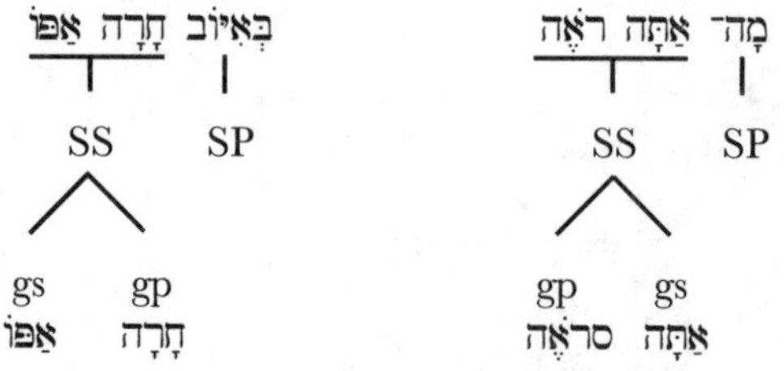

Note: gp = grammatical predicate; gs = grammatical subject
SP = syntactic predicate; SS = syntactic subject

In the non-verbal sentence it is possible to identify a third type of sentence besides the plain, or unmarked, and the marked: the "presentative sentence" (e.g. **17e** above). In a presentative sentence—especially used for self-presentation such as *ʾănî yhwh* "I am the Lord"—there is no syntactic predication but grammatical only; in other words, grammatical subject and predicate are presented as one item in the news.[78]

In predicative independent non-verbal sentence the normal order is predicate-subject (**18d**); conversely, the order is subject-predicate both in circumstantial non-verbal clause (**18e**) and in the presentative sentence.

It is well possible that the *qatal*, or *x-qatal* of report (see § 2.4 above) is the verbal counterpart of non-verbal presentative sentence. But more study is necessary on this issue.

9. *Conclusion*

What emerges from the presentation above is an integrated and coherent system in which both verbal and non-verbal sentences (i.e. with and without a finite verb) find their place and function along the two genres of the prose: historical narrative and direct speech.

[78] See my discussion and examples in "Simple Nominal Clause", 219–222, and in "Marked Syntactical Structures" § 7.3.

9.1 *Tense and aspect in historical narrative*

The Biblical Hebrew verb system comprises both tense and aspect. Main-line constructions are tenses while secondary-line constructions indicate aspect (§§ 4–5 above).

Wayyiqtol is the narrative tense in Biblical Hebrew. *Weex-qatal, weqatal, wex-yiqtol* and the non-verbal sentence indicate aspect, i.e. anteriority, contemporaneity, posteriority, unity, repetition or description according to the particular construction used and the context.

Specifically, *wex-qatal* versus *weqatal* indicate unity versus repetition or description. *Wex-yiqtol* is also used for repetition or description but is not fully interchangeable with *weqatal*; it indicates a secondary line with reference to *weqatal* (specification, contrast; see **12c** *weqatal* → d–e *wex-yiqtol*). Both *wex-qatal* and the non-verbal clause may indicate contemporaneity with reference to a preceding *wayyiqtol* (**7b**) and (**8b.e.g**) for *wex-qatal*; (**13b**) for non-verbal clause. The difference is that the non-verbal clause underlines the aspect of continuity along with contemporaneity.

Wex-yiqtol is also used prospectively in historical narrative to convey posteriority or the prevision of the story.[79]

9.2 *Tense and aspect in direct speech*

In the axis of the past, initial *qatal* (or *x-qatal* with no difference) together with its continuation form *wayyiqtol* is the indicative past tense; *wex-qatal, weqatal, wex-yiqtol* and the non-verbal sentence indicate aspect exactly as in historical narrative.

In the axis of the present, the non-verbal sentence with or without participle is the indicative present tense. It is also used for aspect (contemporaneity). The use of the participle serves to underline continuity.

In the axis of the future, initial *x-yiqtol* together with its continuation form *weqatal* is the indicative future tense. The difference is that *weqatal* is not found at the beginning of a direct speech, while continuation *x-yiqtol* conveys background information to *weqatal* (**16e–f**; § 5 above).[80]

---

[79] See *Syntax* § 88. A more accurate translation of the examples given there is as follows: "... to see *what he would call* (*mah-yyiqrāʾ*) each one of them" (Gen. 2:19b); "... in order to know *what would happen* (*mah-yyēʿāśeh*) to him" (Ex. 2:4).

[80] Some might object that *weqatal* does occur at the beginning of a pericope. The problem is on which criteria we decide where a pericope begins. The safest criterion

Volitive (first-place but sometimes also second-place) *(x-)yiqtol* contrasts indicative (second-place) *x-yiqtol*; similarly, volitive *wᵉyiqtol* contrasts non-volitive *wᵉqatal*.

9.3 *Common verb forms and constructions*

Continuation *wayyiqtol* and *wᵉx-qatal* in direct speech are borrowed from historical narrative, where they are at home; conversely, *wᵉqatal*, *wᵉx-yiqtol* and the non-verbal clause in historical narrative are borrowed from direct speech, where they are at home.[81]

9.4 *Hierarchy of sentences*

Main and dependent sentences are identified not only by the absence or presence, respectively, of subordinating conjunctions such as *kî*, *ʾăšer*, *lᵉmaʿan*, etc. They are also identified by the place of the finite verb: first place in main sentences, second place in subordinate sentences. When subordinating conjunctions are present, the subordination is both grammatical and syntactic; otherwise, it is syntactic only but no less real.

---

is, of course, to consider the direct speeches immediately following a verb of saying used as a quotation formula. In this case, *wᵉqatal* does not appear. (I know one case, Josh. 22:28, where a direct speech begins with *wᵉhāyâ*; however, the speech is divided in two parts by the repetition of the quotation formula *wannōʾmar* in v. 26 and 28; therefore, *wᵉhāyâ* is actually a continuation form.) On the contrary, *wᵉqatal* normally appears in strings in the course of direct speech (1 Sam. 16:14; note 33 above) as well as in historical narrative (**11b–g**).

[81] J. Joosten, "Biblical Hebrew *wᵉqāṭal* and Syriac *hwā qāṭel* Expressing Repetition in the Past", *ZAH* 5 (1992) 1–14, claims that the primary function of both *wᵉqatal* and *yiqtol* is modality (which he understands as indicating mere possibility as opposed to reality, that is the function of the indicative mood), and that the function of expressing repeated action in the past is an extension of that modal function. He also proposes a tentative system of oppositions between indicative constructions (*qatal*, participle + subject, and *wayyiqtol*) and modal constructions (*wᵉqatal*, *yiqtol* and volitive forms), an idea that he has developed in his contribution to the Tilburg conference (in this volume). I think that his theoretical system does not correspond to the syntactic status of *wᵉqatal* and *yiqtol* in Biblical Hebrew. Not distinguishing historical narrative from direct speech, he derives one function of *wᵉqatal* (and *yiqtol*), i.e. repetition, from the other, i.e. modality; however, his proposal is by far too subjective and contrary to plain sense to be a proof. On the other hand, his insistence that the non-verbal sentence expresses indicative present is correct, except for claiming that the participle is a necessary element. Instead, the present tense occurs even without a participle; the participle only adds the aspect of continuity ("cursive present"). One should also note that this holds true for direct speech only. In historical narrative the non-verbal sentence is not a tense but a secondary-line construction expressing aspect.

A sentence with a finite verb in the first place is syntactically verbal; when the finite verb is in the second place the sentence is syntactically nominal. The latter is nominal because it interchanges with (i.e. plays the same function as) the non-verbal sentence (§ 4 above). However, in direct speech initial *x-qatal* and *x-yiqtol* are syntactically verbal because they indicate the main line of communication in the axis of the past and of the future, respectively (§ 9.2 above).

The main criteria of the Biblical Hebrew verb system are, thus, place in the sentence (first or second) and level of communication (main or secondary). If they do not concur, the latter prevails.

Syntactically verbal sentences are main and independent; they signal the foreground or main line of communication both in historical narrative and in direct speech. They are tenses (§§ 9.1; 9.2 above).

Syntactically nominal clauses are dependent although they are grammatically main (i.e. not introduced by any subordinating conjunction); they signal the background or secondary line of communication both in historical narrative and in direct speech. Grammatically they are either verbal or non-verbal, i.e. with or without a finite verb.[82]

In grammatically non-verbal sentences syntactic predication is realized when a general term appears in the first place (§ 8 above). The

---

[82] Talstra, "Clause Types", makes the following remarks: "In Judges 6,33ff., it can be concluded from the absence of new subject noun phrases that the wayyiqtols are secondary to the W-X-Qatal clauses and do not imply a return to the main story line. One can still hold that the wayyiqtols constitute a story line, but deriving its level cannot come from the clause type (wayyiqtol) alone. The lexical and morphological information on clause hierarchy has to be used also" (p. 174). Yes, there are cases where a *wayyiqtol* is not an autonomous, main-line verb form but depends on *wᵉx-qatal* (and on other nominal constructions) which it continues. I call it "continuation *wayyiqtol*"; consult *Syntax* § 146:2, pp. 177–179, or *Lettura*, 259 (*s.v.* "*Wayyiqtol* continuativo"). However, the fact that this *wayyiqtol* depends on *wᵉx-qatal* has nothing to do with "new subject noun phrases" being present or not; what decides is the position of the finite verb, not the presence or absence of the subject. Note that this holds true when the subject *follows* the finite verb; when, on the contrary, the subject *precedes*, we have a "x-finite verb" construction that is definitively different from a "finite verb-x" construction. Indeed, the situation remains exactly the same whether the "x" element is the subject, or the object, or a complement. Therefore, it is not the question of the subject *per se*, except for one's conviction that a change of subject marks a new and more important paragraph than another where no subject is explicitly mentioned—something that can be true but is totally irrelevant at the level of grammar and syntax. In fact, I do not see any justification in assuming that the naming or not naming of the subject, which is a stylistic, semantic or pragmatic phenomenon, might overrule grammar and syntax so as to make a narrative *wayyiqtol* secondary to, or dependent on, *wᵉx-qatal*. Clearly in my view, what is at stake is how we define a sentence. Until we do not agree on this point, we will go similar roads but arrive at different destinations.

result is a plain, unmarked non-verbal predicative sentence; it parallels the syntactically verbal sentence of the type with a finite verb. However, any particular term can be the syntactic predicate in non-verbal sentences; similarly, in grammatically verbal sentences any non-verbal element can be the syntactic predicate. When this happens, we have marked sentences in both types with and without a finite verb.

In predicative sentences, both verbal and non-verbal, the word order is syntactical predicate—subject. In non-predicative sentences (i.e. circumstantial *wᵉx-qatal*, *wᵉx-yiqtol* and circumstantial non-verbal clause) the word order is grammatical subject—predicate.

The word order is grammatical subject—predicate also in the presentative sentence.

9.5 *Coordination and subordination*

Coordination and subordination are based on syntactic independence and dependence. That is, e.g. the tense shifts "*wᵉx-qatal* → *wayyiqtol*" and, conversely, "*wayyiqtol* → *wᵉx-qatal*" do not consist of coordinate but subordinate sentences (*wᵉx-qatal* is subordinate to *wayyiqtol*, of course) despite the presence of waw and the absence of subordinating conjunctions. The same holds true for the other secondary-line constructions in historical narrative (*wᵉx-qatal*, *wᵉx-yiqtol*, *wᵉqatal*, and non-verbal sentence).

Coordination occurs when the verb forms belong to the same level of communication, both main or secondary. Subordination occurs between verb forms of different level.

Coordination exists not only between selfsame verb forms but also between grammatically different forms that syntactically belong to the same linguistic level. E.g. "initial *(x-)qatal* → continuation *wayyiqtol*" as well as "initial *x-yiqtol* → *wᵉqatal*" are coordinate constructions in direct speech.

References

Anbar, M., "La 'reprise'", *Vetus Testamentum* 38 (1988) 385–398.

Bergen, R.D., "Evil Spirits and Eccentric Grammar: a Study of the Relationship Between Text and Meaning in Hebrew Narrative", in: Bergen, R.D. (ed.), *Biblical Hebrew and Discourse Linguistics*, Winona Lake (Ind.): Eisenbrauns, 1994, 320–335.

Cassuto, U., *A Commentary on the Book of Exodus*, Jerusalem: Magnes, 1967.

Chirichigno, G.C., "The Narrative Structure of Exodus 19–24", *Biblica* 68 (1987) 457–479.

Cortese, E., *Da Mosè a Esdra. I libri storici dell'antico Israele*, Bologna: Edizioni Dehoniane, 1985.
DeCaen, V., "Ewald and Driver on Biblical Hebrew 'Aspect': Anteriority and the Orientalist Framework", *Zeitschrift für Althebraistik* 9 (1996) 129–151.
Dozeman, T.B., *God on the Mountain. A Study on Redaction, Theology and Canon in Exodus 19–24*, Atlanta: Scholars, 1989.
———, "Spatial Form in Exodus 19:1–8a and in the Larger Sinai Narrative", *Semeia* 46 (1989) 87–101.
Driver, S.R., *A Treatise on the Use of the Tenses in Hebrew and some Other Syntactical Questions*, Oxford: Clarendon, 1892[3] (reprint 1969).
Endo, Y., *The Verbal System of Classical Hebrew in the Joseph Story: an Approach from Discourse Analysis* (Studia Semitica Neerlandica 32), Assen: Van Gorcum, 1996.
Galbiati, E., *La struttura letteraria dell'Esodo. Contributo allo studio dei criteri stilistici dell'A.T. e della composizione del Pentateuco*, Alba: Cuneo, 1956.
Gesenius, W., Kautzsch, E. & Cowley, E.A., *Gesenius' Hebrew Grammar*, second edition, Oxford: Clarendon, 1910.
Gross, W., "Die Position des Subjekt im hebräischen Verbalsatz, untersucht an den asyndetischen ersten Redesätze in Gen., Ex. 1–19, Jos., 2 Kön.", *Zeitschrift für Althebraistik* 6 (1993) 170–187.
———, "Zur syntaktischen Struktur des Vorfelds im hebräischen Verbalsatz", *Zeitschrift für Althebraistik* 7 (1994) 203–214.
Hendel, R.S., "In the Margins of the Hebrew Verbal System: Situation, Tense, Aspect, Mood", *Zeitschrift für Althebraistik* 9 (1996) 152–181.
Hertog, C. den, "Die invertierten Verbalsätze im hebräischen Josuabuch. Eine Fallstudie zu einem vernachlässigten Kapitel der hebräischen Syntax", in: Mayer, C., Müller, K. & Schmalenberg, G. (eds.), *Nach den Anfängen fragen, Herrn Prof. dr.theol. Gerhard Dautzenberg zum 60. Geburtstag am 30. Januar 1994*, Gießen: Justus-Liebig Universität, 1994, 227–291.
Houtman, C., *Exodus*, Vols. 1–2, Kampen: Kok, 1993–1996.
Joosten, J., "Biblical Hebrew *w^{e}qātal* and Syriac *hwā qātel* Expressing Repetition in the Past", *Zeitschrift für Althebraistik* 5 (1992) 1–14.
Joüon, P. & Muraoka, T., *A Grammar of Biblical Hebrew*, 2 Vols. (Subsidia Biblica 14/I and 14/II), Roma: Pontificio Istituto Biblico, 1991.
Kaswalder, P.A., *La disputa diplomatica di Iefte (Gdc 11,12–28). La ricerca archeologica in Giordania e il problema della conquista*, Jerusalem: Franciscan Printing Press, 1990.
Loza, J., *La palabras de Yahve. Estudio del decálogo*, México, 1989.
Müller, H.P., "Nicht-junktiver Gebrauch von *w-* im Althebräischen", *Zeitschrift für Althebraistik* 7 (1994) 141–174.
Nachmanides, M., (Ramban), *Commentary on the Torah. Exodus*, Chavel, C.B. (ed.), New York: Shilo, 1973.
Niccacci, A., "A Neglected Point of Hebrew Syntax: Yiqtol and Position in the Sentence", *Liber Annuus* 37 (1987) 7–19.
———, "Sullo stato sintattico del verbo *hāya*", *Liber Annuus* 40 (1990) 9–23.
———, *The Syntax of the Verb in Classical Hebrew Prose* (Journal for the Study of the Old Testament, Supplement Series 86), Sheffield: Sheffield Academic Press, 1990.
———, *Lettura sintattica della prosa Ebraico-Biblica. Principi e applicazioni* (Studium Biblicum Franciscanum, Analecta 31), Jerusalem: Franciscan Printing Press, 1991.
———, "Simple Nominal Clause (SNC) or Verbless Clause in Biblical Hebrew Prose", *Zeitschrift für Althebraistik* 6 (1993) 216–227.
———, "Review of Joüon, P. & Muraoka, T.A., *A Grammar of Biblical Hebrew*, Rome: Pontifical Biblical Institute, 1991", *Liber Annuus* 43 (1993) 528–533.
———, "Marked Syntactical Structures in Biblical Greek in Comparison with Biblical Hebrew", *Liber Annuus* 43 (1993) 9–69.
———, "Diluvio, sintassi e metodo", *Liber Annuus* 44 (1994) 9–46.

———, "Review of Gross, W., Irsigler, H. & Seidl, T., *Text, Methode und Grammatik*, St. Ottilien: EOS Verlag, 1991", *Liber Annuus* 44 (1994) 667–692.

———, "Analysis of Biblical Narrative", in: Bergen, R.D. (ed.), *Biblical Hebrew and Discourse Linguistics*, Winona Lake (Ind.): Eisenbrauns, 1994, 175–198.

———, "On the Hebrew Verbal System", in: Bergen, R.D. (ed.), *Biblical Hebrew and Discourse Linguistics*, Winona Lake (Ind.): Eisenbrauns, 1994, 117–137.

———, "Syntactic Analysis of Ruth", *Liber Annuus* 45 (1995) 69–106.

———, "Essential Hebrew Syntax", in: Talstra, E. (ed.), *Narrative and Comment. Contributions Presented to Wolfgang Schneider*, Amsterdam: Societas Hebraica Amstelodamensis, 1995, 111–125.

———, "Organizzazione canonica della Biblia ebraica. Tra sintassi e retorica", *Rivista Biblica* 43 (1995) 9–29.

———, "Review of Dawson, D.A., *Text-linguistics and Biblical Hebrew*, Sheffield: Sheffield Academic Press, 1994", *Liber Annuus* 45 (1995) 543–580.

———, "Finite Verb in the Second Position of the Sentence. Coherence of the Hebrew Verbal System", *Zeitschrift für die alttestamentliche Wissenschaft* 108 (1996) 434–440.

Nicholson, E.W., "The Decalogue as the Direct Address of God", *Vetus Testamentum* 27 (1977) 422–433.

———, *God and His People. Covenant and Theology in the Old Testament*, Oxford: Clarendon, 1986.

Rainey, A.F., "Further Remarks on the Hebrew Verbal System", *Hebrew Studies* 29 (1988) 35–42.

Revell, E.J., "The System of the Verb in Standard Biblical Prose", *Hebrew Union College Annual* 60 (1989) 1–37.

Rosenberg, A.J. (ed.), *Miqra'ot Gedolot. Shemot*, Vol. 1, New York: Judaica Press, 1995.

Sailhamer, J.H., *The Pentateuch as Narrative. A Biblical-Theological Commentary*, Grand Rapids: Zondervan, 1992.

Schneider, W., *Grammatik des Biblischen Hebräisch. Völlig neue Bearbeitung der* "Hebräischen Grammatik für den akademischen Unterricht" *von Oskar Grether*, München: Claudius, 1974.

Silbermann, A.M. & Rosenbaum, M. (eds.), *Chumash, with Targum Onkelos, Haphtaroth and Rashi's Commentary. Shemot*, Jerusalem: Silbermann Family, 1934.

Sonnet, J.P., "Le Sinaï dans l'événement de sa lecture. La dimension pragmatique d'Exode 19–24', *Nouvelle Revue Théologique* 111 (1989) 321–344.

Talstra, E., "Clause Types and Textual Structure: an Experiment in Narrative Syntax", in: Talstra, E. (ed.), *Narrative and Comment. Contributions Presented to Wolfgang Schneider*, Amsterdam, 1995, 166–180.

Van Seters, J., *The Life of Moses. The Yahwist as Historian in Exodus-Numbers*, Kampen: Kok Pharos, 1994.

Verheij, A.J.C., *Verbs and Numbers. A Study of the Frequencies of the Hebrew Verbal Tense Forms in the Book of Samuel, Kings and Chronicles* (Studia Semitica Neerlandica 28), Assen: Van Gorcum, 1990.

———, "Review of Niccacci, A., *The Syntax of the Verb in Classical Hebrew Prose*, Sheffield: Sheffield Academic Press, 1990", *Bibliotheca Orientalis* 49 (1992) 214–217.

Weinrich, H., *Tempus: Besprochene und erzählte Welt*, Stuttgart: Kohlhammer, 1964[1], 1985[4].

Zevit, Z., "Talking Funny in Biblical Hebrew and Solving a Problem of the *yaqtul* Past Tense", *Hebrew Studies* 29 (1988) 35–42.

WORKSHOP: NARRATIVE SYNTAX OF EXODUS 19–24

Alviero Niccacci
(Jerusalem)

In Biblical Hebrew narrative (apart from direct speech), verbal sentences produce a sequence and are main-line constructions, while nominal sentences produce a break and are secondary-line constructions. In Biblical Hebrew narrative, sentences beginning with a finite verb form (i.e. *wayyiqtol*) are verbal, while sentences not beginning with a finite verb form, or not comprising any finite verb form, are nominal.[1]

Thus, we can rephrase H. Weinrich's definition of a text with additions for Biblical Hebrew (in italics) as follows: "A text is a logical (i.e. intelligible and consistent) sequence of linguistic signs, *wayyiqtol in narrative*, placed between two significant breaks in communication, *mainly waw-x-qatal but also non-verbal clauses, w^{e}qatal, and waw-x-yiqtol*".[2]

A break in communication is significant when a change in place, time, characters, etc., takes place that marks a new story. This kind of decision, of course, is taken under different criteria than purely syntactic ones.

1. *Outline of Exodus 19–24*

In the following treatment of Exodus 19–24, I have established three levels of the text called main narrative line, secondary line (antecedent information, or setting of the story), and direct speech, respectively. Main-line verb forms are placed on the right margin of the page, while antecedent (setting) constructions are indented, and background constructions are marked with an arrow (↑). Direct speech is

[1] See my paper, "Basic Facts and Theory of the Biblical Hebrew Verb System in prose", in this volume.

[2] Translation by W.G.E. Watson; see my *Syntax of the Verb in Classical Hebrew Prose*, Sheffield 1990, § 36, p. 56. The original definition in found in H. Weinrich, *Tempus. Besprochene und erzählte Welt*, fourth ed., Stuttgart 1985, 11.

further indented to the left. Each sentence is put in a new line. A sign "÷" indicates that a sentence, being too long for a line, continues in the next line.

1. Exodus 19:1–20:17

19:1	On the third month after the Israelites went out of the land of Egypt,	בַּחֹדֶשׁ הַשְּׁלִישִׁי לְצֵאת בְּנֵי־יִשְׂרָאֵל מֵאֶרֶץ מִצְרָיִם
	on that day	בַּיּוֹם הַזֶּה
	they came to the desert of Sinai.	בָּאוּ מִדְבַּר סִינָי
19:2	In fact they set out from Rephidim,	וַיִּסְעוּ מֵרְפִידִים
	and came into the wilderness of Sinai,	וַיָּבֹאוּ מִדְבַּר סִינַי
	and they encamped in the wilderness.	וַיַּחֲנוּ בַּמִּדְבָּר
	Thus, Israel encamped there, before the mountain,	וַיִּחַן־שָׁם יִשְׂרָאֵל נֶגֶד הָהָר
19:3	while Moses went up toward God.	↑ וּמֹשֶׁה עָלָה אֶל־הָאֱלֹהִים
	Then Yahweh called him from the mountain, saying,	וַיִּקְרָא אֵלָיו יְהוָה מִן־הָהָר לֵאמֹר
	"Thus you will say to the house of Jacob,	כֹּה תֹאמַר לְבֵית יַעֲקֹב
	and tell the Israelites:	וְתַגֵּיד לִבְנֵי יִשְׂרָאֵל
19:4	'You have seen what I did to the Egyptians.	אַתֶּם רְאִיתֶם אֲשֶׁר עָשִׂיתִי לְמִצְרָיִם
	I bore you on eagles' wings	וָאֶשָּׂא אֶתְכֶם עַל־כַּנְפֵי נְשָׁרִים
	and brought you to me.	וָאָבִא אֶתְכֶם אֵלָי
19:5	Therefore, if you will indeed obey my voice	וְעַתָּה אִם־שָׁמוֹעַ תִּשְׁמְעוּ בְּקֹלִי
	and keep my covenant,	וּשְׁמַרְתֶּם אֶת־בְּרִיתִי
	you shall be to me a possession among all the peoples;	וִהְיִיתֶם לִי סְגֻלָּה מִכָּל־הָעַמִּים
	for mine is all the earth	כִּי־לִי כָּל־הָאָרֶץ
19:6	but you shall be to me a kingdom of priests and a holy nation.'	וְאַתֶּם תִּהְיוּ־לִי מַמְלֶכֶת כֹּהֲנִים וְגוֹי קָדוֹשׁ
	These are the words which you shall speak to the Israelites".	אֵלֶּה הַדְּבָרִים אֲשֶׁד תְּדַבֵּר אֶל־בְּנֵי יִשְׂרָאֵל
19:7	So Moses went,	וַיָּבֹא מֹשֶׁה
	called the elders of the people,	וַיִּקְרָא לְזִקְנֵי הָעָם
	and set before them all these words	וַיָּשֶׂם לִפְנֵיהֶם אֵת כָּל־הַדְּבָרִים הָאֵלֶּה
	which the Lord had commanded him.	↑ אֲשֶׁר צִוָּהוּ יְהוָה
19:8	Then all the people answered together	וַיַּעֲנוּ כָל־הָעָם יַחְדָּו
	and said,	וַיֹּאמְרוּ
	"All that the Lord has spoken we will do".	כֹּל אֲשֶׁר־דִּבֶּר יְהוָה נַעֲשֶׂה
	And Moses brought the words of the people back to the Lord.	וַיָּשֶׁב מֹשֶׁה אֶת־דִּבְרֵי הָעָם אֶל־יְהוָה
19:9	The Lord said to Moses,	וַיֹּאמֶר יְהוָה אֶל־מֹשֶׁה
	"Behold, I am coming to you in a thick cloud,	הִנֵּה אָנֹכִי בָּא אֵלֶיךָ בְּעַב הֶעָנָן

Main Narrative line
Secondary line (antecedent information) |
Direct Speech |

	in order that the people may hear when I speak with you,	בַּעֲבוּר יִשְׁמַע הָעָם בְּדַבְּרִי עִמָּךְ
	and in you, too, they may believe for ever".	וְגַם־בְּךָ יַאֲמִינוּ לְעוֹלָם
	Moses, then, told the words of the people to the Lord.	וַיַּגֵּד מֹשֶׁה אֶת־דִּבְרֵי הָעָם אֶל־יְהוָה
19:10	Afterwards the Lord said to Moses,	וַיֹּאמֶר יְהוָה אֶל־מֹשֶׁה
	"Go to the people.	לֵךְ אֶל־הָעָם
	You shall make them holy today and tomorrow.	וְקִדַּשְׁתָּם הַיּוֹם וּמָחָר
	They shall wash their garments	וְכִבְּסוּ שִׂמְלֹתָם
19:11	and shall be ready for the third day;	וְהָיוּ נְכֹנִים לַיּוֹם הַשְּׁלִישִׁי
	for on the third day	כִּי בַּיּוֹם הַשְּׁלִשִׁי
	the Lord will come down upon the Mount Sinai in the sight of all the people.	יֵרֵד יְהוָה לְעֵינֵי כָל־הָעָם עַל־הַר סִינָי
19:12	Thus you shall set bounds for the people round about, saying,	וְהִגְבַּלְתָּ אֶת־הָעָם סָבִיב לֵאמֹר
	'Take heed that you do not go up to the mountain or touch the border of it;	הִשָּׁמְרוּ לָכֶם עֲלוֹת בָּהָר וּנְגֹעַ בְּקָצֵהוּ
	whoever shall touch the mountain	כָּל־הַנֹּגֵעַ בָּהָר
	shall be put to death.	מוֹת יוּמָת
19:13	No hand shall touch him,	לֹא־תִגַּע בּוֹ יָד
	but he shall be in any case stoned	כִּי־סָקוֹל יִסָּקֵל
	or shot;	אוֹ־יָרֹה יִיָּרֶה
	whether beast or man,	אִם־בְּהֵמָה אִם־אִישׁ
	he shall not live.'	לֹא יִחְיֶה
	When the trumpet sounds a long blast,	בִּמְשֹׁךְ הַיֹּבֵל
	they shall come up to the mountain".	הֵמָּה יַעֲלוּ בָהָר
19:14	So Moses went down from the mountain to the people,	וַיֵּרֶד מֹשֶׁה מִן־הָהָר אֶל־הָעָם
	made the people holy,	וַיְקַדֵּשׁ אֶת־הָעָם
	and they washed their garments.	וַיְכַבְּסוּ שִׂמְלֹתָם
19:15	He said to the people,	וַיֹּאמֶר אֶל־הָעָם
	"Be ready for the third day;	הֱיוּ נְכֹנִים לִשְׁלֹשֶׁת יָמִים
	do not go near a woman".	אַל־תִּגְּשׁוּ אֶל־אִשָּׁה
19:16	And on the third day,	וַיְהִי בַיּוֹם הַשְּׁלִישִׁי
	when the day broke,	↑ בִּהְיֹת הַבֹּקֶר
	there were thunders, lightnings, and a thick cloud on the mountain, together with a very loud sound of trumpet.	וַיְהִי קֹלֹת וּבְרָקִים וְעָנָן כָּבֵד עַל־הָהָר וְקֹל שֹׁפָר חָזָק מְאֹד
	Thus the people who were in the camp trembled.	וַיֶּחֱרַד כָּל־הָעָם אֲשֶׁר בַּמַּחֲנֶה
19:17	Then Moses brought the people out of the camp to meet God,	וַיּוֹצֵא מֹשֶׁה אֶת־הָעָם לִקְרַאת הָאֱלֹהִים מִן־הַמַּחֲנֶה
	and they took their stand at the foot of the mountain,	וַיִּתְיַצְּבוּ בְּתַחְתִּית הָהָר
19:18	while Mount Sinai smoked—all of it,	↑ וְהַר סִינַי עָשַׁן כֻּלּוֹ
	because the Lord had come down upon it with fire.	↑ מִפְּנֵי אֲשֶׁר יָרַד עָלָיו יְהוָה בָּאֵשׁ

Main Narrative line
Secondary line (antecedent information) |
Direct Speech |

	Its smoke went up like the smoke of a kiln,	וַיַּעַל עֲשָׁנוֹ כְּעֶשֶׁן הַכִּבְשָׁן
	and the whole mountain trembled greatly.	וַיֶּחֱרַד כָּל־הָהָר מְאֹד
19:19	And the sound of the trumpet grew louder and louder	וַיְהִי קוֹל הַשּׁוֹפָר הוֹלֵךְ וְחָזֵק מְאֹד
	— Moses was speaking,	↑ מֹשֶׁה יְדַבֵּר
	and God was answering him in thunder.	↑ וְהָאֱלֹהִים יַעֲנֶנּוּ בְקוֹל
19:20	Thus the Lord came down upon Mount Sinai to the top of the mountain.	וַיֵּרֶד יְהוָה עַל־הַר סִינַי אֶל־רֹאשׁ הָהָר
	Then the Lord called Moses to the top of the mountain,	וַיִּקְרָא יְהוָה לְמֹשֶׁה אֶל־רֹאשׁ הָהָר
	and Moses went up.	וַיַּעַל מֹשֶׁה
19:21	The Lord said to Moses,	וַיֹּאמֶר יְהוָה אֶל־מֹשֶׁה
	"Go down	רֵד
	and warn the people,	הָעֵד בָּעָם
	lest they break through to the Lord to see,	פֶּן־יֶהֶרְסוּ אֶל־יְהוָה לִרְאוֹת
	because many of them would perish.	וְנָפַל מִמֶּנּוּ רָב
19:22	Even the priests who are allowed to draw near to the Lord, let them behave holy,	וְגַם הַכֹּהֲנִים הַנִּגָּשִׁים אֶל־יְהוָה יִתְקַדָּשׁוּ
	lest the Lord break out upon them".	פֶּן־יִפְרֹץ בָּהֶם יְהוָה
19:23	And Moses said to the Lord,	וַיֹּאמֶר מֹשֶׁה אֶל־יְהוָה
	"The people will not be permitted to come up to Mount Sinai;	לֹא־יוּכַל הָעָם לַעֲלֹת אֶל־הַר סִינָי
	for you charged us saying,	כִּי־אַתָּה הַעֵדֹתָה בָּנוּ לֵאמֹר
	'Set bounds about the mountain,	הַגְבֵּל אֶת־הָהָר
	and thus you shall make it holy'".	וְקִדַּשְׁתּוֹ
19:24	And the Lord said to him,	וַיֹּאמֶר אֵלָיו יְהוָה
	"Go,	לֶךְ־
	get down;	רֵד
	then you shall come up—you and Aaron with you;	וְעָלִיתָ אַתָּה וְאַהֲרֹן עִמָּךְ
	instead, let not the priests and the people break through to come up to the Lord,	וְהַכֹּהֲנִים וְהָעָם אַל־יֶהֶרְסוּ לַעֲלֹת אֶל־יְהוָה
	lest he break out against them".	פֶּן־יִפְרָץ־בָּם
19:25	So Moses went down to the people	וַיֵּרֶד מֹשֶׁה אֶל־הָעָם
	and told them.	וַיֹּאמֶר אֲלֵהֶם
20:1	God spoke all these words, saying,	וַיְדַבֵּר אֱלֹהִים אֵת כָּל־הַדְּבָרִים הָאֵלֶּה לֵאמֹר
20:2	"I am the Lord your God,	אָנֹכִי יְהוָה אֱלֹהֶיךָ
	who brought you out of the land of Egypt, out of the house of slaves.	אֲשֶׁר הוֹצֵאתִיךָ מֵאֶרֶץ מִצְרַיִם מִבֵּית עֲבָדִים
20:3	You shall have no other gods in front of me.	לֹא יִהְיֶה־לְךָ אֱלֹהִים אֲחֵרִים עַל־פָּנָיַ
20:4	You shall not make for you any graven image, or any likeness	לֹא תַעֲשֶׂה־לְךָ פֶסֶל וְכָל־תְּמוּנָה
	that is in heaven above,	÷ אֲשֶׁר בַּשָּׁמַיִם מִמַּעַל
	that is in the earth beneath,	÷ וַאֲשֶׁר בָּאָרֶץ מִתָּחַת
	and that is in the water under the earth.	÷ וַאֲשֶׁר בַּמַּיִם מִתַּחַת לָאָרֶץ

Main Narrative line

Secondary line (antecedent information) |

Direct Speech |

20:5 You shall not bow down to them | לֹא־תִשְׁתַּחֲוֶה לָהֶם
or serve them, | וְלֹא תָעָבְדֵם
for I the Lord | כִּי אָנֹכִי יְהוָה אֱלֹהֶיךָ אֵל קַנָּא פֹּקֵד עֲוֺן אָבֹת עַל־בָּנִים
your God am a jealous God, who visits the iniquity of the fathers upon the children,
upon the third and the fourth | ÷ עַל־שִׁלֵּשִׁים וְעַל־רִבֵּעִים לְשֹׂנְאָי
generation for those who hate me,
20:6 and who bestows mercy | וְעֹשֶׂה חֶסֶד לַאֲלָפִים לְאֹהֲבַי וּלְשֹׁמְרֵי מִצְוֺתָי
upon thousands for those who love me and keep my commandments.
20:7 You shall not take the name of | לֹא תִשָּׂא אֶת־שֵׁם־יְהוָה אֱלֹהֶיךָ לַשָּׁוְא
Yahweh in vain;
for the Lord will not | כִּי לֹא יְנַקֶּה יְהוָה אֵת אֲשֶׁר־יִשָּׂא אֶת־שְׁמוֹ לַשָּׁוְא
hold guiltless the one who takes his name in vain.
20:8 Remember the sabbath day to make | זָכוֹר אֶת־יוֹם הַשַּׁבָּת לְקַדְּשׁוֹ
it holy.
20:9 Six days you shall work, | שֵׁשֶׁת יָמִים תַּעֲבֹד
and do all your job; | וְעָשִׂיתָ כָּל־מְלַאכְתֶּךָ
20:10 but the seventh day is a sabbath to | וְיוֹם הַשְּׁבִיעִי שַׁבָּת לַיהוָה אֱלֹהֶיךָ
the Lord your God.
You shall do no job—you, your | לֹא־תַעֲשֶׂה כָל־מְלָאכָה אַתָּה וּבִנְךָ־וּבִתֶּךָ
son and your daughter, | ÷ עַבְדְּךָ וַאֲמָתְךָ וּבְהֶמְתֶּךָ וְגֵרְךָ אֲשֶׁר בִּשְׁעָרֶיךָ
your manservant and your maidservant, your cattle and your sojourner who is within your gates;
20:11 for it is in six | כִּי שֵׁשֶׁת־יָמִים עָשָׂה יְהוָה אֶת־הַשָּׁמַיִם וְאֶת־הָאָרֶץ אֶת־הַיָּם
days that the Lord made heaven and earth, the sea,
and all that is in them, | וְאֶת־כָּל־אֲשֶׁר־בָּם
and rested the seventh day; | וַיָּנַח בַּיּוֹם הַשְּׁבִיעִי
therefore the Lord blessed the | עַל־כֵּן בֵּרַךְ יְהוָה אֶת־יוֹם הַשַּׁבָּת
sabbath day
and made it holy. | וַיְקַדְּשֵׁהוּ
20:12 Honor your father and your mother, | כַּבֵּד אֶת־אָבִיךָ וְאֶת־אִמֶּךָ
that your days may become long in | לְמַעַן יַאֲרִכוּן יָמֶיךָ עַל הָאֲדָמָה
the land
which the Lord your God shall give you. | אֲשֶׁר־יְהוָה אֱלֹהֶיךָ נֹתֵן לָךְ
20:13 You shall not kill. | לֹא תִּרְצָח
20:14 You shall not commit adultery. | לֹא תִּנְאָף
20:15 You shall not steal. | לֹא תִּגְנֹב
20:16 You shall not testify against your neighbour | לֹא־תַעֲנֶה בְרֵעֲךָ עֵד שָׁקֶר
as a false witness.
20:17 You shall not covet your neighbour's house; | לֹא תַחְמֹד בֵּית רֵעֶךָ
you shall not covet | לֹא־תַחְמֹד אֵשֶׁת רֵעֶךָ וְעַבְדּוֹ וַאֲמָתוֹ וְשׁוֹרוֹ וַחֲמֹרוֹ
your neighbour's wife, his manservant and his maidservant, his ox and his ass
and anything that belongs to your neighbour. | וְכֹל אֲשֶׁר לְרֵעֶךָ

Main Narrative line
Secondary line (antecedent information) |
Direct Speech |

2. Exodus 20:18–23:33

20:18	Now all the people were seeing the thunders, the lightnings, the sound of the trumpet and the mountain smoking.	| וְכָל־הָעָם רֹאִים אֶת־הַקּוֹלֹת וְאֶת־הַלַּפִּידִם | ÷ וְאֵת קוֹל הַשֹּׁפָר וְאֶת־הָהָר עָשֵׁן
	Thus the people saw,	וַיַּרְא הָעָם
	were in disarray,	וַיָּנֻעוּ
	and stood afar off.	וַיַּעַמְדוּ מֵרָחֹק
20:19	They said to Moses,	וַיֹּאמְרוּ אֶל־מֹשֶׁה
	"You speak to us	| דַּבֵּר־אַתָּה עִמָּנוּ
	and we will obey;	| וְנִשְׁמָעָה
	but let not God speak to us	| וְאַל־יְדַבֵּר עִמָּנוּ אֱלֹהִים
	lest we die".	| פֶּן־נָמוּת
20:20	And Moses said to the people,	וַיֹּאמֶר מֹשֶׁה אֶל־הָעָם
	"Do not fear,	| אַל־תִּירָאוּ
	for it is to prove you that God came,	| כִּי לְבַעֲבוּר נַסּוֹת אֶתְכֶם בָּא הָאֱלֹהִים
	and in order that the fear of him be before your eyes,	| וּבַעֲבוּר תִּהְיֶה יִרְאָתוֹ עַל־פְּנֵיכֶם
	that you may not sin".	| לְבִלְתִּי תֶחֱטָאוּ
20:21	Thus the people stood afar off,	וַיַּעֲמֹד הָעָם מֵרָחֹק
	while Moses drew near to the thick darkness	↑ וּמֹשֶׁה נִגַּשׁ אֶל־הָעֲרָפֶל
	where God was.	↑ אֲשֶׁר־שָׁם הָאֱלֹהִים
20:22	Yahweh said to Moses,	וַיֹּאמֶר יְהוָה אֶל־מֹשֶׁה
	"Thus you shall say to the children of Israel. . . ."	| כֹּה תֹאמַר אֶל־בְּנֵי יִשְׂרָאֵל

<COVENANT CODE (20:22–23:33)>

3. Exodus 24:1–18

24:1	Now to Moses he said,	| וְאֶל־מֹשֶׁה אָמַר
	"Come up to the Lord, you and Aaron, Nadab and Abihu, and seventy of the elders of Israel.	| עֲלֵה אֶל־יְהוָה אַתָּה וְאַהֲרֹן נָדָב וַאֲבִיהוּא וְשִׁבְעִים מִזִּקְנֵי יִשְׂרָאֵל
	You shall worship afar off.	| וְהִשְׁתַּחֲוִיתֶם מֵרָחֹק
24:2	Then Moses alone shall draw near to the Lord,	| וְנִגַּשׁ מֹשֶׁה לְבַדּוֹ אֶל־יְהוָה
	while they shall not draw near	| וְהֵם לֹא יִגָּשׁוּ
	and the people shall not come up with him".	| וְהָעָם לֹא יַעֲלוּ עִמּוֹ
24:3	Then Moses went	וַיָּבֹא מֹשֶׁה
	and told the people all the words of the Lord and all the ordinances.	וַיְסַפֵּר לָעָם אֵת כָּל־דִּבְרֵי יְהוָה וְאֵת כָּל־הַמִּשְׁפָּטִים
	All the people answered with one voice,	וַיַּעַן כָּל־הָעָם קוֹל אֶחָד
	and said,	וַיֹּאמְרוּ

Main Narrative line

Secondary line (antecedent information) |

Direct Speech |

"All the words which the Lord has spoken we shall do". | כָּל־הַדְּבָרִים אֲשֶׁר־דִּבֶּר יְהוָה נַעֲשֶׂה

24:4 Then Moses wrote all the words of the Lord. וַיִּכְתֹּב מֹשֶׁה אֵת כָּל־דִּבְרֵי יְהוָה
He rose early in the morning, וַיַּשְׁכֵּם בַּבֹּקֶר
and built an altar at the foot of the mountain, וַיִּבֶן מִזְבֵּחַ תַּחַת הָהָר
and twelve pillars for the twelve tribes of Israel. ÷ וּשְׁתֵּים עֶשְׂרֵה מַצֵּבָה לִשְׁנֵים עָשָׂר שִׁבְטֵי יִשְׂרָאֵל

24:5 Then he sent young men of the Israelites, וַיִּשְׁלַח אֶת־נַעֲרֵי בְּנֵי יִשְׂרָאֵל
and they offered burnt offerings וַיַּעֲלוּ עֹלֹת
and sacrificed peace offerings to the Lord consisting of oxen וַיִּזְבְּחוּ זְבָחִים שְׁלָמִים לַיהוָה פָּרִים

24:6 Then Moses took half of the blood וַיִּקַּח מֹשֶׁה חֲצִי הַדָּם
and put it in basins, וַיָּשֶׂם בָּאַגָּנֹת
while half of the blood he threw against the altar. ↑ וַחֲצִי הַדָּם זָרַק עַל־הַמִּזְבֵּחַ

24:7 Then he took the book of the covenant, וַיִּקַּח סֵפֶר הַבְּרִית
and read it in the hearing of the people. וַיִּקְרָא בְּאָזְנֵי הָעָם
They said, וַיֹּאמְרוּ
"All that the Lord has spoken we will do | כֹּל אֲשֶׁר־דִּבֶּר יְהוָה נַעֲשֶׂה
and will obey". | וְנִשְׁמָע

24:8 Moses took the blood וַיִּקַּח מֹשֶׁה אֶת־הַדָּם
and threw it upon the people, וַיִּזְרֹק עַל־הָעָם
and said, וַיֹּאמֶר
"Behold the blood of the covenant | הִנֵּה דַם־הַבְּרִית
which the Lord has made with you on the basis of all these words". | אֲשֶׁר כָּרַת יְהוָה עִמָּכֶם עַל כָּל־הַדְּבָרִים הָאֵלֶּה

24:9 Then Moses and Aaron, Nadab, and Abihu, and the seventy of the elders of Israel went up. וַיַּעַל מֹשֶׁה וְאַהֲרֹן נָדָב וַאֲבִיהוּא וְשִׁבְעִים מִזִּקְנֵי יִשְׂרָאֵל

24:10 They saw the God of Israel וַיִּרְאוּ אֵת אֱלֹהֵי יִשְׂרָאֵל
—now under his feet there was as it were a pavement of sapphire stone, and like the very heaven for clearness — ↑ וְתַחַת רַגְלָיו כְּמַעֲשֵׂה לִבְנַת הַסַּפִּיר וּכְעֶצֶם הַשָּׁמַיִם לָטֹהַר

24:11 while against the nobles of the Israelites he did not stretch his hand: ↑ וְאֶל־אֲצִילֵי בְּנֵי יִשְׂרָאֵל לֹא שָׁלַח יָדוֹ
in fact, they beheld God, וַיֶּחֱזוּ אֶת־הָאֱלֹהִים
ate וַיֹּאכְלוּ
and drank. וַיִּשְׁתּוּ

24:12 Then the Lord said to Moses, וַיֹּאמֶר יְהוָה אֶל־מֹשֶׁה
"Come up to me on the mountain, | עֲלֵה אֵלַי הָהָרָה
and be there, | וֶהְיֵה־שָׁם
and I will give you the tables of stone, and the law and the commandment, | וְאֶתְּנָה לְךָ אֶת־לֻחֹת הָאֶבֶן וְהַתּוֹרָה וְהַמִּצְוָה
which I have written to instruct them". | אֲשֶׁר כָּתַבְתִּי לְהוֹרֹתָם

24:13 Moses rose with his servant Joshua. וַיָּקָם מֹשֶׁה וִיהוֹשֻׁעַ מְשָׁרְתוֹ
Thus Moses went up to the mountain of God, וַיַּעַל מֹשֶׁה אֶל־הַר הָאֱלֹהִים

24:14 while to the elders he said, ↑ וְאֶל־הַזְּקֵנִים אָמַר
"Tarry here for us, | שְׁבוּ־לָנוּ בָזֶה

Main Narrative line
Secondary line (antecedent information) |
Direct Speech |

	until we come back to you.	עַד אֲשֶׁר־נָשׁוּב אֲלֵיכֶם
	And behold, Aaron and Hur are with you;	וְהִנֵּה אַהֲרֹן וְחוּר עִמָּכֶם
	whoever has a case,	מִי־בַעַל דְּבָרִים
	shall draw near to them".	יִגַּשׁ אֲלֵהֶם
24:15	Thus Moses went up to the mountain,	וַיַּעַל מֹשֶׁה אֶל־הָהָר
	and the cloud covered the mountain.	וַיְכַס הֶעָנָן אֶת־הָהָר
24:16	The glory of the Lord settled on Mount Sinai,	וַיִּשְׁכֹּן כְּבוֹד־יְהוָה עַל־הַר סִינַי
	and the cloud covered it six days.	וַיְכַסֵּהוּ הֶעָנָן שֵׁשֶׁת יָמִים
	On the seventh day he called Moses from the midst of the cloud,	וַיִּקְרָא אֶל־מֹשֶׁה בַּיּוֹם הַשְּׁבִיעִי מִתּוֹךְ הֶעָנָן
24:17	while the appearance of the glory of the Lord was like a devouring fire on the top of the mountain in the sight of the Israelites.	↑ וּמַרְאֵה כְּבוֹד יְהוָה כְּאֵשׁ אֹכֶלֶת בְּרֹאשׁ הָהָר לְעֵינֵי בְּנֵי יִשְׂרָאֵל
24:18	Moses then entered the cloud,	וַיָּבֹא מֹשֶׁה בְּתוֹךְ הֶעָנָן
	and went up on the mountain.	וַיַּעַל אֶל־הָהָר
	Moses remained on the mountain forty days and forty nights.	וַיְהִי מֹשֶׁה בָּהָר אַרְבָּעִים יוֹם וְאַרְבָּעִים לָיְלָה

Main Narrative line
Secondary line (antecedent information) |
Direct Speech |

1.1 *Narrative proper*

From the point of view of the verb forms used, Exodus 19–24 is divided into three sections:

1. 19:1–20:17
2. 20:18–23:33[3]
3. 24:1–18.[4]

The beginning of Exodus 19 is marked by a nominal construction (i.e. without a finite verb form in the first position of the sentence). It is a double sentence with protasis ("On the third month after the people of Israel went out of the land of Egypt, on that day"), and

[3] In 21:1 we find the title of a new collection of laws ("These are the ordinances which you shall set before them"), but from the point of view of syntax it continues the main line of direct speech.

[4] Until the end of the Book of Exodus, no nominal construction breaks the chain of narrative *wayyiqtol* forms and the flow of communication although we distinguish different pericopes (see § 2.2 below). The *w^eqatal* found in 36:1 conveys background information (begun in 35:34) to the preceding main-line *wayyiqtol* in 35:31. The fact that from the point of view of syntax there is no break in communication means that the different pericopes are intentionally linked one to the other. The interpretation shall have to consider this fact. On the possible import of syntactic analysis on the interpretation of the Hebrew Bible as a whole, see my "Organizzazione canonica della Bibbia ebraica. Tra sintassi e retorica", *Rivista Biblica* 43 (1995) 9–29.

apodosis ("they came to the desert of Sinai").[5] It gives the setting of a new text (the date, in this case).[6] The main line begins in 19:2 and continues until the next break in 20:18.

A non-verbal clause marks the beginning of a new episode of the story in 20:18. The main line of the narrative starts soon after with *wayyiqtol*, which resumes the information already given as a circumstance: "*Now all the people were seeing* the thunders. . . . *Thus the people saw*, were in disarray (or: moved backwards) and stood afar off".[7]

The third break is represented by a *wᵉx-qatal* construction in 24:1: *wᵉʾel-mōšeh ʾāmar*. This is the only narrative information after 20:22 where a similar phrase is found with a *wayyiqtol: wayyōʾmer yhwh ʾel-mōšeh*. The phrase in 20:22 introduces a series of precepts for the people through Moses, while the one in 24:1 introduces a command for Moses himself. This change is also marked by a change in the verb form used.[8]

---

[5] Ramban comments on the unusual order in the narrative (arrival at Sinai; departure from Rephidim) as follows: "The chapter should have commenced: They journeyed from Rephidim, and they encamped in the desert of Sinai in the third month of their departure from the land of Egypt, similar to what is stated in Ex. 17:1 in reference to their entry into the desert of Sin. The Israelites' entry into the Sinai desert was placed at the beginning of the chapter to emphasize that it was an occasion of great joy and celebration" (*Miqraʾot Gedolot. Shemot*, ed. A.J. Rosenberg, Vol. 1, New York: Judaica Press 1995, 279).

[6] "The passage begins, *On the third ḥōdheš*, without preceding *wayᵉhī* ['And it came to pass'], and without any link with the previous context . . .": U. Cassuto, *A Commentary on the Book of Exodus*, Jerusalem: Magnes, 1967, 223. Jewish traditional commentators, including Cassuto, distribute the facts of Exodus 19 along the scheme of a week and date the proclamation of the Torah on the sixth day of the third month. "It is clear, however, that the text of Exodus 19 does not preclude a spreading of the events over a longer period of time. Aside from the time of preparation (19:10f., 14f.), the writer/redactor does not seem to have worked with a particular chronology. Rather, presenting Moses as repeatedly going up and going down, he manages to spread the events. It makes for a lively story in which, step by step, he leads his readers to the climax of his account: the speaking of God (20:1)": C. Houtman, *Exodus*, Vol. 2: Chapters 7:14–19:25, Kampen 1996, 460–461.

[7] The same resumptive technique is attested in 19:1–2 for the coming to the Sinai desert, and in 19:18,20 for the God's descent on the holy mountain. Note that the participle *rōʾīm* "were seeing" underlines contemporaneity with the proclamation of the Ten Commandments by God; compare Cassuto, *A Commentary*, 1967, 252. Ramban thinks differently, against "the opinion of the commentators" (in his own words): "All this happened before the Revelation . . .": Ramban (Nachmanides), *Commentary on the Torah. Exodus*, ed. C.B. Chavel, New York Shilo 1973, 324. The reason is that Ramban harmonizes this passage with the account of Deuteronomy 5 (*ibid.*, 323).

[8] This was noted by Ramban in a remarkable passage, where he also concisely expounds his understanding of the dynamics of Exodus 19–24: "*And unto Moses He said.* The reason for this kind of expression [when it should have said, as elsewhere, *And the Eternal spoke unto Moses*], is that up till now the commandments and

Inside the three pericopes listed above we find other nominal constructions, which however do not break the flow of communication but rather convey background information to a preceding main-line *wayyiqtol* (indicated with ↑).

The main narrative line is represented by a chain of *wayyiqtol* forms, each one conveying a piece of information that is on the same linguistic level with the previous one, and normally subsequent to it. The chain of *wayyiqtol* goes on uninterrupted until the need is felt of shifting to a secondary level. In this case the piece of information is not subsequent but rather antecedent, circumstantial, posterior, contrastive, or descriptive according to the construction used.[9] Anteriority, contemporaneity, posteriority, contrast, and description are aspects of an action or information, not tenses. They are conveyed in a secondary line of communication and are indicated by nominal clauses with a finite verb in the second position, *w^{e}qatal*, or without any finite verb.[10]

Biblical Hebrew narrative develops by alternating main-line, or foreground, *wayyiqtol* and secondary-line, or background, nominal constructions. This alternation gives the narrative the desired relief.[11]

A tense shift "*wayyiqtol* → *w^{e}x-qatal*", characteristic of Biblical Hebrew narrative, is found in 19:2–3 where Israel's encamping before Mount Sinai is related with a main-line *wayyiqtol* in contrast with Moses' ascending towards God: "Thus, Israel encamped (*wayyiḥan*) there, before the mountain, *while Moses went up* (*ûmōšeh ʿālâ*) toward God".[12]

---

the ordinances were addressed to the children of Israel, therefore Scripture said here that this particular commandment was given to Moses, that he alone should do it; thus He commanded him: 'After you have set before them the commandments and the ordinances, and have made with them the covenant, come up to Me.' This was why Moses fulfilled the first command [i.e., of telling the people the section beginning with *Ye yourselves have seen*—above 20:29—up to *for they will be a snare unto thee*—23:33], on the sixth day of Sivan, [following the Revelation which took place on that morning], and on the seventh he rose up early in the morning and made with them the covenant, and after that he went up to the mountain, he and those that were asked to come, as they were commanded": Ramban, ed. Chavel, 422.

[9] "Basic Facts" § 2.

[10] "Basic Facts" § 3.

[11] See the main structures listed in "Basic Facts" § 6.

[12] If we had twice *wayyiqtol* (*wayyiḥan*—**wayyaʿal*) the two pieces of information were unrelated (i.e. not tied together as foreground and background) and subsequent one to the other, that is: "Thus Israel encamped there, **and then Moses went up* to God". The presence of the article in *hāhār* "*the* mountain" in v. 2 and the peculiar expression in v. 3, "Moses went up *toward God*" (LXX: "to the mountain of God"), clearly refer back to the pericope of Moses' call in Exodus 3. The mountain intended is the same, though designated with different names (Horeb, Sinai), and so Moses knew well the place where to find God; for this reason only here he goes up

Note that *wayyiḥan* resumes *wayyaḥănû* of 19:2 precisely in order to add the information concerning Moses.[13] Therefore it does not indicate a second encampment of the people.[14]

A similar case is found in 20:21: "Thus the people stood (*wayyaʿămōd*) afar off, *while Moses drew near* (*ûmōšeh niggaš*) to the thick darkness".[15] *Wayyaʿămōd* resumes *wayyaʿamdû* of v. 18, again in order to inform on the different stand of the people and of Moses.

Tense shift "*wayyiqtol* → *wᵉx-qatal*" in 19:17b–18 conveys contemporaneity: "and they took their stand (*wayyityaṣṣᵉbû*) at the foot of the mountain *while Mount Sinai smoked* (*wᵉhar sînay ʿāšan*)".

The same tense shift occurs in 24:6b in order to mark a difference in the handling of the two halves of the blood: "Then Moses took half of the blood (*wayyiqqaḥ . . . ḥāṣî haddām*) and put it (*wayyāśem*) in basins, *while half of the blood he threw* (*waḥăṣî haddām zāraq*) against the altar".

Finally, a "*wayyiqtol* → *wᵉx-qatal*" tense shift is found in 24:13b–14: "Moses went up (*wayyaʿal*) to the mountain of God, *while to the elders he said* (*wᵉʾel-hazzᵉqēnîm ʾāmar*)". This *wᵉx-qatal* construction and the following command to the elders constitute a pause in the flow of the main line of narrative. Afterwards, in 24:15 a resumptive *wayyiqtol* takes up again the same verb form of v. 13 and renews the main line: "*Thus Moses went up* (*wayyaʿal*) to the mountain of God".

---

without being first called by God. Actually Exodus 3 contains a number of connections, both parallel to and divergent from, our passage; e.g. a theophanic phenomenon is found in both; Moses' movement toward God is stopped in Exodus 3 (as is that of the people in Ch. 19) while it is encouraged in Exodus 19–20 and 24; a call and a mission of Moses towards the people as well as a self-presentation of God are found in both; in both Moses first addresses the elders of the people, etc.

[13] It is a resumptive repetition, a literary technique usually called with its German name of *Wiederaufnahme*. See note 7 above; *Syntax*, 201, note 33; "Basic Facts" § 2.1 (Ex. 6). Also consult Cassuto, *A Commentary*, 1967, 225–226. The naming of the subject (Israel) in 19:2b, despite the fact that this is not needed grammatically, and the position of the geographical specification that is split before and after the subject ("there . . . before the mountain") suggest an intentional contrast between Israel and Moses. Medieval Jewish exegetes noted that in the double mention of the encampment the verb is first in the plural, then in the singular, a fact which they interpreted in a spiritual way with reference to the unity of the people at Sinai (*Miqraʾot Gedolot. Shemot*, Vol. 1, 279–280). Note that the terms *bᵉnê yiśrāʾēl* and *yiśrāʾēl* are used as synonymous in the Pentateuch; however, when it is the subject of a finite verb, *yiśrāʾēl* is mostly treated as singular (e.g. Ex. 14:30–31; 17:11; Num. 17:21; 21:1).

[14] *Pace* J.H. Sailhamer, *The Pentateuch as Narrative. A Biblical-Theological Commentary*, Grand Rapids: Zondervan, 1992, 281, note 39.

[15] In 19:22 the verb *niggaš* is used for the priests who are allowed to "draw near to" the Lord. In 24:2 it appears together with verb *ʿālâ*: "*Come up*. . . . Then Moses alone *shall draw near to* the Lord, while they *shall not draw near*, and the people shall not *come up* with him".

Another tense shift besides "*wayyiqtol* → *wᵉx-qatal*" is "*wayyiqtol* (foreground) → non-verbal clause (background)." This second tense shift also expresses contemporaneity but stresses the aspect of continuity—it indicates a contemporaneous continuous action or a description. We have two examples of this tense shift in Exodus 24: "They saw the God of Israel—*now* under his feet there was as it were a pavement of sapphire stone . . ." (24:10); and "On the seventh day he called Moses from the midst of the cloud, *while* the appearance of the glory of the Lord was like a devouring fire . . ." (24:16b–17).

A third tense shift, and perhaps the most abrupt one, is "*wayyiqtol* (foreground) → *(wᵉ)x-yiqtol* (background)" found twice in 19:19: "And the sound of the trumpet grew (*wayᵉhî*) louder and louder—*Moses was speaking, and God was answering him* (*mōšeh yᵉdabbēr wᵉhāʾelōhîm yaʿănennû*) in thunder". Note that *wayᵉhî* is a *wayyiqtol* as any other such verb form.[16]

1.2 *Direct speech*

Until now, I have tried to explain the line of communication of the narrative proper, i.e. what is called main narrative line and secondary line (antecedent information) in the outline of the text. I have left aside the third level of the text, the direct speech, although it occupies a large part of Exodus 19–24. The reason is that the direct speech requires a different approach; in it the verb forms are used differently from historical narrative, and the levels of the text are distinguished in a specific way.[17]

Understandably, in narrative the axis of the past alone is used as the main level of communication, because narrative is concerned with past events. Instead, in direct speech all the three temporal axes—past, present and future—are used as the main level of communication. That is, one can report orally a past event, or communicate present information, or predict the future. For each temporal axis, specific verb forms are used—*qatal* for the past (e.g. 19:4), non-verbal clause for the present (e.g. 20:2), *yiqtol* and *wᵉqatal* for the future (e.g. 19:5). Other verb forms are used both in narrative and in direct speech although in a different way.[18] In direct speech, we also find volitive verb forms, which are of course not found in narrative proper.

---

[16] See my paper "Sullo stato sintattico del verbo *hāyâ*", *Liber Annuus* 40 (1990) 9–23.

[17] "Basic Facts" § 5.

[18] "Basic Facts" § 7.

A debated issue of direct speech concerns the verb forms of the future, which can be volitive and not volitive, or simply predictive. Volitive future is indicated by jussive *yiqtol*, mostly placed in the first position of the sentence, but sometimes in the second, while non-volitive, predictive future is indicated by indicative *yiqtol* placed in the second position, not in the first. Jussive yiqtol is continued by volitive *wᵉyiqtol* while indicative *yiqtol* is continued by non-volitive *wᵉqatal*.[19]

A good example is 24:1–2: "Come up (*ʿălēh*, imperative) to the Lord, you and Aaron, Nadab and Abihu, and seventy of the elders of Israel. You shall worship (*wᵉhištaḥăwîtem, wᵉqatal*) afar off. Then Moses alone shall draw near (*wᵉniggaš, wᵉqatal*) to the Lord, while they shall not draw near (*wᵉhēm lōʾ yiggāšû, wᵉx-yiqtol*) and the people shall not come up (*wᵉhāʿām lōʾ yaʿălû, wᵉx-yiqtol*) with him". We find here an interplay of different forms both volitive (imperative) and non-volitive (*wᵉqatal* and negative *wᵉx-lōʾ* + *yiqtol*). The two *wᵉqatal wᵉhištaḥăwîtem* and *wᵉniggaš* do not carry on the volitive force of the preceding imperative; they communicate instructions, not commands.[20]

Further, in direct speech *wᵉqatal* is normally found in a chain of selfsame verb forms for the main line of communication (as is *wayyiqtol* in historical narrative). The chain of *wᵉqatal* is only interrupted when the author wishes to shift from the main-line to a secondary line of communication in order to convey contemporaneity, contrast, or description. In the passage under discussion, the two *wᵉqatal* forms convey two subsequent instructions, both in the main level of communication: "You shall worship. . . . *Then* Moses alone shall draw near" (24:1–2). The fact that after these two *wᵉqatal* we find *wᵉx-yiqtol*, and not another *wᵉqatal*, means that the new information is not conveyed in the main line but in a secondary line: "*while* they shall not draw near, *and* the people shall not come up with him" (24:2b). Clearly the tense shift "*wᵉqatal* → *wᵉx-lōʾ* + *yiqtol*" is intended to establish a contrast between what concerns Moses, on the one side, and what concerns his companions and all the people, on the other.

---

[19] "Basic Facts" § 6.

[20] The paper by E.J. Revell, "The System of the Verb in Standard Biblical Prose", *HUCA* 60 (1989) 1–37, is remarkable for its treatment of the indicative (non-volitive) versus the modal (volitive) system of Biblical Hebrew. Among other things he writes: "One imperative is followed by another where the command is urgent, or is addressed to someone who is inferior in status, or is despised. Where an imperative is followed by a perfect with *waw* consecutive, the situation is not urgent, and the command is given to someone who is esteemed" (24). In the first sentence just quoted, one should add "or a *wᵉyiqtol*" after "by another [i.e. imperative]". Unfortunately, Revell does not recognise *wᵉyiqtol* as an autonomous, volitive verb form.

A seemingly intriguing case is found in 19:3 where we find a parallel pair of constructions,[21] the second of which is a *w^e^yiqtol: kōh tōʾmar (x-yiqtol) l^e^bêt yaʿăqōb w^e^taggēd (w^e^yiqtol) libnê yiśrāʾēl* "(God said to Moses) Thus you will (or: must) say to the house of Jacob, and tell the Israelites". Based on clear cases, one has to say that *w^e^yiqtol* conveys an injunction, not an instruction (which is expressed with *w^e^qatal*; e.g. 19:10–12). As a consequence, the initial *x-yiqtol* (*kōh tōʾmar*) is also volitive, not indicative.[22] This grammatical feature underlines the urgency of the divine injunction.

A similar case is present in the people's reply in 24:7b: "All that the Lord has spoken we will (or: promise to) do (*kōl ʾăšer-dibber yhwh naʿăśeh, x-yiqtol*)[23] and will obey (*w^e^nišmaʿ, w^e^yiqtol*).

A clear example of this volitive structure is found in 20:19 where the *w^e^yiqtol* is preceded by an imperative: "You speak (*dabbēr*) to us and we will (or: promise to) obey (*w^e^nišmaʿ*)".[24]

2. *Narrative analysis*

I'll try now to understand the state of affairs presented by the author, or the text. This state of affairs cannot be *sic et simpliciter* identified with the *ordo rerum*, or the actual course of events. In fact, an author may deliberately modify the *ordo rerum* for a specific purpose. At the level of the text, only the state of affairs intended by the author can be recovered and is meaningful. A common mistake is to confuse the two levels. I would say that the historical-critical study runs precisely this risk (see § 3 below).

---

[21] As Cassuto, *A Commentary*, 1967, 226 observes: "The Divine utterance is composed in true poetic style, having the rhythm of verse and being marked by parallelism between its parts". Indeed, elevated, solemn prose as the passage under consideration and pure poetry converge.

[22] On the one side, a *w^e^x-yiqtol* construction is jussive when it is followed by a *w^e^yiqtol*; see *Syntax* § 64:4; and "A Neglected Point of Hebrew Syntax: Yiqtol and Position in the Sentence", *Liber Annuus* 37 (1987) 7–19, § 1.3.2. On the other side, all the cases of *w^e^yiqtol* of the root *ngd* "to tell" in prose texts are preceded by clear volitive forms (imperatives, or jussive forms): Gen. 46:31; 49:1; Judg. 14:15; 1 Sam. 15:16; 25:8; 2 Kgs. 7:9; Jer. 42:2–3.

[23] The "x" element comprises here a clause with *ʾăšer* that is embedded in the superordinate *x-yiqtol* sentence.

[24] The tense shift "imperative → *w^e^yiqtol*" is a well established volitive structure; see *Syntax* § 64:2; "A Neglected Point" § 1.2.

2.1 *Exodus 19–20*

The analysis presented above, based on the verb forms used, is only the first step although the basic one. The second step consists in applying to Exodus 19–24 what we can call a narrative syntax in order to evaluate the texture of the pericopes identified in the first step. In this way, we hope to understand the development inside the text.

One of the main problems of Exodus 19 concerns Moses' multiple going up and down the mountain and approaching God. Let us review the evidence and try to interpret it.

19:2–3 "Thus, Israel encamped there, before the mountain, while Moses went up toward God". This first time Moses' ascending is not preceded by a specific command (with an imperative) or instruction (with *w^{e}qatal*). The ensuing divine commission to Moses takes place on the mountain. Moses then goes down to the people (19:7) and tells them the words that God has commissioned him to relay, and they accept them.

19:8b "And Moses brought the words of the people back to the Lord". This suggests that Moses went up again to the mountain. The Lord then announces his coming to Moses in order that the people may hear him speaking to their leader and may believe also in him (19:9). The text communicates two goals of the divine revelation: obedience to God and belief in Moses. At this point we read:

19:9b "Moses, then, told the words of the people to the Lord". Is it a resumptive repetition (*Wiederaufnahme*) of the information of 19:8b, or is it a new event? Though the verbs used are different—*wayyāšeb* and *wayyaggēd*, respectively—the event may be one, related twice for a certain purpose. In other words, *wayyāšeb* may mean "Moses went to report," but did not carry out his intention at once because God forestalled him with a new announcement (19:9a).[25] The literary

[25] Similarly Ramban: "'And Moses brought the words of the people back to the Lord' . . . means that Moses ascended Mount Sinai prepared to report to God that the Israelites were willing to accept the Torah. Since everything is revealed before God, He did not ask Moses what the people had said. When he said to Moses, 'Behold, I am coming to you in the thickness of the cloud, in order that the people hear when I speak to you, and they will also believe in you forever' (verse 9), then Moses replied, 'O Lord of the universe, Your children are believers, and they accept upon themselves whatever You will say'" (*Miqra'ot Gedolot. Shemot*, Vol. 1, 1995, 289). This is a charming way of saying that first Moses came back and said nothing but later he reported to God the people's reply. Ramban finds support for his interpretation in Num. 13:26–27: "They [i.e. the spies] went their way and came to Moses and Aaron and to all the congregation of the people of Israel in the wilderness of

repetition may have the effect of including Moses in the positive reply of the people (19:8)—as if they accepted both God and Moses at the same time.[26]

The rest of Exodus 19 is composed according to a pattern "instruction or command—execution", as shown in the following diagram:

	Instruction/command	Execution
(I)	10 וַיֹּאמֶר יְהוָה אֶל־מֹשֶׁה	14 וַיֵּרֶד מֹשֶׁה מִן־הָהָר
	לֵךְ אֶל־הָעָם	אֶל־הָעָם
	וְקִדַּשְׁתָּם הַיּוֹם וּמָחָר	וַיְקַדֵּשׁ אֶת־הָעָם
	וְכִבְּסוּ שִׂמְלֹתָם	וַיְכַבְּסוּ שִׂמְלֹתָם
		15 וַיֹּאמֶר אֶל־הָעָם
	11 וְהָיוּ נְכֹנִים לַיּוֹם הַשְּׁלִישִׁי	הֱיוּ נְכֹנִים לִשְׁלֹשֶׁת יָמִים
		אַל־תִּגְּשׁוּ אֶל־אִשָּׁה
	כִּי בַּיּוֹם הַשְּׁלִשִׁי	16 וַיְהִי בַיּוֹם הַשְּׁלִישִׁי בִּהְיֹת הַבֹּקֶר
	יֵרֵד יְהוָה לְעֵינֵי כָל־הָעָם	וַיְהִי קֹלֹת וּבְרָקִים וְעָנָן כָּבֵד עַל־הָהָר
	עַל־הַר סִינָי	וְקֹל שֹׁפָר חָזָק מְאֹד
		וַיֶּחֱרַד כָּל־הָעָם אֲשֶׁר בַּמַּחֲנֶה
	12 וְהִגְבַּלְתָּ אֶת־הָעָם סָבִיב לֵאמֹר	
	הִשָּׁמְרוּ לָכֶם עֲלוֹת בָּהָר וּנְגֹעַ בְּקָצֵהוּ	
	כָּל־הַנֹּגֵעַ בָּהָר מוֹת יוּמָת	
	לֹא־תִגַּע בּוֹ יָד כִּי־סָקוֹל יִסָּקֵל	
	13 אוֹ־יָרֹה יִיָּרֶה	
	אִם־בְּהֵמָה אִם־אִישׁ לֹא יִחְיֶה	
	בִּמְשֹׁךְ הַיֹּבֵל הֵמָּה יַעֲלוּ בָהָר	17 וַיּוֹצֵא מֹשֶׁה אֶת־הָעָם לִקְרַאת הָאֱלֹהִים
		מִן־הַמַּחֲנֶה
		וַיִּתְיַצְּבוּ בְּתַחְתִּית הָהָר
		18 וְהַר סִינַי עָשַׁן כֻּלּוֹ
	cf. 19:11	מִפְּנֵי אֲשֶׁר יָרַד עָלָיו יְהוָה בָּאֵשׁ
		וַיַּעַל עֲשָׁנוֹ כְּעֶשֶׁן הַכִּבְשָׁן
		וַיֶּחֱרַד כָּל־הָהָר מְאֹד
		19 וַיְהִי קוֹל הַשֹּׁופָר הוֹלֵךְ וְחָזֵק מְאֹד
	cf. 19:9	מֹשֶׁה יְדַבֵּר וְהָאֱלֹהִים יַעֲנֶנּוּ בְקוֹל
(II)	20 וַיֵּרֶד יְהוָה עַל־הַר סִינַי אֶל־רֹאשׁ הָהָר	
	וַיִּקְרָא יְהוָה לְמֹשֶׁה אֶל־רֹאשׁ הָהָר	
	21 וַיַּעַל מֹשֶׁה וַיֹּאמֶר יְהוָה אֶל־מֹשֶׁה	
	רֵד הָעֵד בָּעָם פֶּן־יֶהֶרְסוּ אֶל־יְהוָה לִרְאוֹת	

Paran, at Kadesh, and brought back (*wayyāšîbû*) word to them and to all the congregation, and showed them the fruit of the land. Then they reported (*waysapprû*) to him and said... (direct speech follows)". For Ibn Ezra, Moses actually reported the people's reply already the first time, and the second mention is a literary repetition (he quotes other cases in the Bible) (*ibid.*, 286; 288, Hebrew). Finally, Rashi dates the two mentions in different days—the third and the fourth of the month, respectively (*Chumash, with Targum Onkelos, Haphtaroth and Rashi's Commentary. Shemot*, eds. A.M. Silbermann – M. Rosenbaum, Jerusalem: Sibermann Family, 1934, 99). Cassuto, *A Commentary*, 1967, 228–229, follows Rashi.

[26] This literary interpretation may look overcomplicated to someone. Note, however, that the historical-critical solution—i.e. that the final text is the result of joining

וְנָפַל מִמֶּנּוּ רָב
22 וְגַם הַכֹּהֲנִים הַנִּגָּשִׁים אֶל־יְהוָה יִתְקַדָּשׁוּ
פֶּן־יִפְרֹץ בָּהֶם יְהוָה
23 וַיֹּאמֶר מֹשֶׁה אֶל־יְהוָה
לֹא־יוּכַל הָעָם לַעֲלֹת אֶל־הַר סִינָי
כִּי־אַתָּה הַעֵדֹתָה בָּנוּ לֵאמֹר
הַגְבֵּל אֶת־הָהָר וְקִדַּשְׁתּוֹ

(III)
24 וַיֹּאמֶר אֵלָיו יְהוָה
לֶךְ־רֵד וְעָלִיתָ אַתָּה וְאַהֲרֹן עִמָּךְ
וְהַכֹּהֲנִים וְהָעָם אַל־יֶהֶרְסוּ לַעֲלֹת
אֶל־יְהוָה פֶּן־יִפְרָץ־בָּם
25 וַיֵּרֶד מֹשֶׁה אֶל־הָעָם וַיֹּאמֶר אֲלֵהֶם

The basic pattern is clear enough though some problems remain. One of these consists in the doubling, even tripling, God's command to Moses to go down and warn the people with regard to the mountain. In fact, the execution of 19:10–13 is related in 19:14–19 (this is unit I in the diagram above).[27] But therewith[28] a new command to Moses follows to go up again and then down and warn the people in similar terms (unit II in the diagram above). Indeed, Moses protests that the people has already been warned (19:23) but this is not explicitly stated in the text, which only tells that the people "took their stand at the foot of the mountain" (19:17). In 19:24 God, then, repeats the command to go down (19:21), not yet executed (unit III in the diagram above). He also repeats the warning about the mountain, this time with a variation: it concerns the priests besides the people. Between the command to go down and the warning to the people, we read an instruction (with *w^eqatal*) for Moses to go up together with Aaron, once completed his mission. This instruction looks

together different sources—is hardly satisfactory. In fact, it is not easy to accept that the redactor overlooked the repetition, or did not care about it. See § 3 below.

[27] God's descent in 19:18 marks a new phase for the mountain. Earlier there were upon it thunders, lightnings and a sound of trumpet (19:16); after, smoke and fire. These phenomena usually accompany a theophany or a God's intervention on earth (e.g. Gen. 15;17; 2 Sam. 22:9; Isa. 9:17; Ps. 18:9; 68:3). As Cassuto observes, "there is no reference here, as many have supposed, to volcanic phenomena . . . the fire of the volcanoes goes upward and does not descend from the sky" (*A Commentary*, 1967, 232). Further, the terms *šōpār* "trumpet" (Ex. 19:16,19) and *yōbēl* "ram's horn, trumpet" (19:3) are used together, both in construct state and as variants, in Josh. 6:4–13.

[28] God's descent on Mount Sinai is taken up again in 19:20, after it had been mentioned in a circumstantial clause in 19:18 in order to explain the smoking of the mountain. Thus the main line of the story is resumed; rightly so Cassuto, *A Commentary*, 1967, 233. Note that also in 19:3 and in 24:16 Moses' call by God is tied to some kind of coming close of one to the other.

forward since it is executed later in the next chapter (20:21), although Aaron is not mentioned there.[29]

The triple repetition of the warning (units I–III) may be a compositional device aiming at inculcating God's awe upon the people. It accords with 20:20: "And Moses said to the people, 'Do not fear, for it is to prove you that God came, and in order that fear of him be before your eyes, that you may not sin'".[30]

As commanded, Moses goes down and speaks to the people (19:25). His words are not related but of course he tells God's repeated warning concerning the holy mountain.[31]

In the meantime, while Moses is at the feet of the mountain with the people, God pronounces the Ten Words (20:1–17). This time only does God speak directly to the people;[32] later on, he always

[29] This fact does not seem to constitute a problem because a similar procedure is found in 24:13 where we read, first, "Moses rose with his servant Joshua"; then, "Thus Moses went up to the mountain of God", i.e. in the actual going up the companions of Moses are not mentioned any more.

[30] As Cassuto aptly comments, "It may also be added that the triple reference to an important subject (*vv.* 12–13; 21–22; 24) accords with a common literary practice": *A Commentary*, 1967, 233.

[31] In another place at least the verb *ʾāmar* is not followed by a speech: "Cain spoke (*wayyōʾmer*) to Abel his brother. And when they were in the field, Cain rose up . . ." (Gen. 4:8). True, the LXX supplies the expected words: διέλθωμεν εἰς τὸ πεδίον "Let us go out to the field", which are also present in other ancient versions, while some manuscripts leave a blank space (see BHS). However, Rashi comments on the passage: "There are Midrashic explanations of these words, but this is the plain sense of the text" (*Chumash, with Targum Onkelos, Haphtaroth and Rashi's Commentary. Bereshit*, ed. A.M. Silbermann – M. Rosenbaum, Jerusalem 1934, 18). In another case, 2 Sam. 21:2–3, a quotation formula with verb *ʾāmar* is not followed by a speech but by a parenthetic explanatory clause; afterwards the same quotation formula is repeated (as *Wiederaufnahme*, or resumptive repetition; see notes 7 and 13 above), and this time a direct speech follows: "The king (David) called the Gibeonites and spoke (*wayyōʾmer*) to them. (Now the Gibeonites were not of the people of Israel, but of the remnant of the Amorites, and the Israelites had made an oath to them, but Saul had sought to slay them in his zeal for the Israelites and Judah.) Thus David said (*wayyōʾmer*) to the Gibeonites . . ." (direct speech follows).

[32] In Deut. 5:22(19)–31(28) we find similar information, i.e. the Ten Words are spoken to all of Israel; afterwards, the people asks Moses that God may not speak directly to them; during the proclamation of the Ten Commandments the people stays outside the camp. Finally, also in Deuteronomy 5 the distinction between the Ten Words and the Covenant Code is clearly marked because after the proclamation of the Ten Words the people is instructed to go back to their tents while Moses has to remain with God to receive all the precepts. The historical-critical implications of this fact have been studied by E.W. Nicholson, "The Decalogue as the Direct Address of God", *VT* 27 (1977) 422–433. A full comparison between Exodus 19–20 and Deuteronomy 4–5 has been done by J. van Seters, *The Life of Moses. The Yahwist as Historian in Exodus-Numbers*, Kampen: Pharos, 1994, 270ff. (however, the author's late dating of the Exodus material contradicts sound critical study).

speaks to Moses, and Moses relates God's words to the people, as the people itself requests (20:19). In fact, the people stays afar off while Moses draws near to God (20:21) as instructed earlier (19:24); and the following Covenant Code (20:22–23:33) is spoken by God to Moses and then relayed by Moses to the people (24:3).

Before coming to Exodus 24, we briefly discuss the phraseology concerning the people's going up to the mountain. On the one side, there is a tension between 19:13b: "When the trumpet sounds a long blast, they (i.e. the people)[33] shall come up to the mountain (*hēmmâ yaʿălû bāhār*)", and 19:23 (cf. 19:12): "The people will not be permitted to come up to Mount Sinai (*lōʾ-yûkal hāʿām laʿălōt ʾel-har sînāy*)". On the other side, in 19:17 we read what seems to be the execution of 19:13b: after a very loud sound of the trumpet, "Moses brought the people out of the camp to meet God, and they took their stand at the foot of the mountain". One concludes, therefore, that after the sound of the trumpet the people has to move from the camp toward the mountain, but is not allowed even to touch its border (19:12), and must remain far from it.[34]

Finally, a note on 19:19–20 is in order. During the sounding of a trumpet that became louder and louder, "Moses was speaking, and God was answering him in thunder (*bᵉqôl*)"; afterwards, God came down to the top of the mountain and called Moses to go up there. How are we to understand this information? It seems that the unusual, majestic "dialogue" between Moses, who is down with the people, and God fulfills the promise of 19:9:[35] "Behold, I am coming to you in a thick cloud, in order that the people may hear when I speak with you, and in you, too, they may believe for ever". What counts here is not the content of the speech, because the divine "voice" (*qôl*) is the thunder, but the fact that God solemnly approves Moses in face of the people.[36]

---

[33] Thus Rashi and Rashbam (*Miqraʾot Gedolot. Shemot*, Vol. 1, 292). Rashi gives a spiritual reading of the passage on the basis of 19:17: "This (the word *lqrʾt*, 'to meet', which is used when two persons are approaching one another) tells us that the Shechina was going forth to meet them, as a bridegroom who goes forth to meet his bride" (*Chumash. Shemot*, 100). However, Ibn Ezra quotes with approval the opinion of Rabbi Shemuel ben Hofni, who thought that those allowed to go up to the mountain were Aaron, his sons and the seventy elders of 24:1 (*ibid.*, 290, Hebrew).

[34] "The Israelites went forth *from the camp* and went as far as they were permitted to go, *and they took their stand at the foot of the mountain.* They stood there and waited": Cassuto, *A Commentary*, 1967, 232.

[35] Thus explicitly Ibn Ezra (*Miqraʾot Gedolot. Shemot*, Vol. 1, 294, Hebrew).

[36] There is no consensus among traditional Jewish commentators about whether

2.2 *Exodus 24*

As noted earlier, the beginning of Exodus 24 is marked by a nominal *w^{e}x-qatal* construction, which opposes the following instruction said for Moses to the preceding Covenant Code said for the people. Moses is commanded to go up to the Lord[37] together with Aaron, Nadab, and Abihu, and seventy elders (24:1). It is a new ascent to the holy mountain, different from those preceding. This command is followed by a series of instructions for the whole group, then for Moses alone and finally for the people: "You shall worship afar off. Then Moses alone shall draw near to the Lord, while they shall not draw near and the people shall not come up with him" (24:1b–2).

Before executing this order and the instructions, Moses went down to the people, and therefore to the foot of the mountain (19:17), and told them all the words and ordinances of the Lord, i.e. the Covenant Code, and the people accepted them (24:3) as they did with the Ten Words (19:8). Moses, then, wrote the book of the covenant, and performed a covenant rite with victims and blood. Half of the blood was thrown against the altar,[38] and half upon the people, after they had again and officially accepted all the words of God read to them by Moses from the book of the covenant: "Behold the blood of the covenant which the Lord has made with you on the basis of all these words" (24:8).

The execution of the initial order and instructions is related in 24:9–11. Moses went up with the group; they saw God, ate and

---

or not this passage implies the proclamation of the Torah (*Miqra'ot Gedolot. Shemot*, Vol. 1, 294; 295–296). However, this does not seem to be the point of the passage because both the Ten Commandments and the Covenant Code are proclaimed later on (*pace* Cassuto, *A Commentary*, 1967, 233, who thinks that the content of the dialogue is represented by the following paragraph 19:20–25).

[37] Two stylistic observations by traditional Jewish commentators are worth mentioning. Ramban comments as follows on the fact that the Lord speaks of himself in the third person in Ex. 24:1: "*Come up to the Eternal.* In line with the simple meaning of Scripture, the reason for this expression [when it should have said: 'Come up unto Me'], is because it is the Scriptural style to mention the proper name instead of the pronoun . . ." (examples follow; Ramban, ed. Chavel, 422–423). Further, Ibn Ezra explains the shift, concerning Moses, from second to third person in 24:1–2 as follows: "Do not be surprised that (God) said at the beginning, 'Come up to the Lord', and then, 'And Moses alone shall draw near', because such is the use of the language" (*Miqra'ot Gedolot, ad l.*). However, Ramban object to this that it was necessary to mention Moses in order to make it clear that he alone, and not Aaron and the others mentioned in v. 1, were to draw near to the Lord.

[38] The building of the altar executes the instruction of 20:24–26 as noted by Ibn Ezra (*Miqra'ot Gedolot, ad* 24:4).

drank[39] without anything evil happening to them. All this executes the instruction, "You shall worship afar off" (24:1b).

A new command to go up to the mountain follows—clearly to the very top of the mountain (24:12). As God says to Moses, "Come up to me on the mountain . . . and I will give you the tables of stone, and the law and the commandment, which I have written to instruct them". This is a new writing on tables of stone by God himself, different form the writing by Moses in 24:4. The latter was the basis for the covenant at Sinai; the first is for the instruction of the people.[40]

The execution of the command for Moses to go up to the mountain is presented in contrast with an order for the elders that came with Moses[41] to wait there and settle their disputes with Aaron and Hur (24:13). The news of Moses' going up is then resumed after the parenthesis of the elders in order to move on the narrative (24:15). The cloud covered the mountain, and the glory of God settled on the mountain for six days. Finally, on the seventh day "Moses entered the cloud and went up to the mountain".

---

[39] For Ibn Ezra and Ramban eating and drinking happened afterwards, when the "nobles" full of joy went down from the mountain and joined the celebration of the people; as for Rashi, he finds it difficult to explain that eating and drinking (*Miqra'ot Gedolot, ad* 24:11). Thus the event was not seen as a covenant meal by traditional Jewish exegetes as is by modern commentators; see, e.g., T.B. Dozeman, *God on the Mountain. A Study on Redaction, Theology and Canon in Exodus 19–24*, Atlanta: Scholars, 1989, 113–115. The opinion of Cassuto, *A Commentary*, 315, is significant in this respect: "(They) were worthy that God should reveal Himself to them . . . and, nevertheless, *they ate and drank* at the sacred meal of the peace offerings when they returned to the camp. Perhaps there is an allusion here to the fact that Aaron and his sons and the elders did not attain to the spiritual level of Moses . . . for during the forty days of his stay on Mount Sinai 'he neither ate bread nor drank wine' (xxxiv 28; compare Deut. ix 9, 18)". It seems clear, though, that the rapid succession of the three verbs ("They saw God and ate and drank") suggests that everything happened on the spot, i.e. the ate and drank before God.

[40] Here we can see, perhaps, different stages of putting into writing the oral revelation—first by Moses for the immediate purpose of making the covenant, then by God in a more durable form, to instruct future generations. In fact, the (second) tables of the law were kept inside the ark of the covenant (Deut. 10:5; 1 Kgs. 8:9; 2 Chr. 5:10). Is this writing by God a way of expressing the inspiration of the Scriptures, which transmits the original revelation to future believers?

[41] Rashi comments on *wᵉʾel-hazzᵉqēnîm ʾāmar* as follows: "when he left the camp", and therefore he interprets the text as: "Now to the elders *he had said*" (*Chumash. Shemot*, 131). However, it seems clear that the text refers to the seventy who had come up with Moses (24:1), as Ibn Ezra notes: "*To the elders*, i.e. to those known, who saw the Glorious Name" (*Miqra'ot Gedolot, ad l.*). Rashi's interpretation is also rejected by Ramban. Because of Moses' long staying away from the group, problems could arise jut as it happened among the people at the foot of the mountain (Ex. 32:1).

Thus, with a three-stage going up—Moses went up with the chosen group (24:9), with Joshua (24:13, 15), and finally alone (24:18)—the command of 24:1 is fully executed. The delaying effect of the narrative is powerful and the tension becomes higher and higher. The inaccessibility of God and the mediatorial role of Moses are forcibly stressed.

From the text also emerges that the multiple going up by Moses to the mountain is connected with the revelation of different codes of precepts by God. The Covenant Code is revealed after the fourth ascension (20:21), and the code of Chs. 25–29, concerning the sacred tent and the organization of the cult, after the seventh ascension (24:18).[42]

In sum, from the point of view of narrative syntax, and despite some problems of detail, Exodus 19–24 is a straightforward complex. It comprises the following main points: a promise by the God of the exodus from Egypt of establishing a special relationship with Israel on the condition of keeping the divine will; a theophany aimed at inspiring on the people the awe of God and of Moses his envoy; the Ten Words and the Covenant Code as the basis of the covenant; and finally the ratification of the covenant.[43]

The end of Exodus 24 is not the end of the text. The main line of communication goes on with a chain of narrative *wayyiqtol* introducing a series of instructions and commands communicated by God to Moses during his stay on the top of the mountain for forty days and forty nights (Exodus 25–31). Thereafter some events are described

---

[42] This fact has been noted by T. Dozeman, "Spatial Form in Ex. 19:1–8a and in the larger Sinai Narrative", *Semeia* 46 (1989) 87–101. He concludes: "Thus, the canonical form of the Sinai narrative follows the progress of Moses up and down the mountain as he mediates each successive legal code to Israel . . . Moses' ascents provide the narrative context for the promulgation of distinct legal codes, which are now all anchored in the one revelation on Mount Sinai and the giving of the Torah there" (95–97). On the occasion of the second covenant (§ 2.3), however, Moses went up only once to the mountain (Ex. 34:4).

[43] Add to this that both the narrative Exodus 19 and 24 and the non-narrative section of the Book of Covenant show a careful composition as shown by E. Galbiati, *La struttura letteraria dell'Esodo. Contributo allo studio dei criteri stilistici dell'A.T. e della composizione del Pentateuco*, Alba: Cuneo, 1956. This is an accurate, and unfortunately ignored, investigation on the literary structure of all the Book of Exodus according to established stylistic canons of the Ancient Near Eastern literatures. According to Galbiati by paying attention to style, the historical critical problems of the text can be better solved. See more recently G.C. Chirichigno, "The Narrative Structure of Exodus 19–24", *Biblica* 68 (1987) 457–479; and J.P. Sonnet, "Le Sinaï dans l'événement de sa lecture: La dimension pragmatique d'Exode 19–24", *Nouvelle Revue Théologique* 111 (1989) 321–344.

that prepare the ratification of a new covenant, presented as second—a kind of repetition of the first (Exodus 32–33, and then 34–35). From the syntactic point of view, there is no break from the beginning of Chapter 24 to the end of the Book of Exodus. It is a continuous text centered around Mount Sinai.[44]

After the second covenant has somehow saved the first from total failure,[45] a long section describes the execution of the instructions given to Moses in the forty days and forty nights of the first covenant (Exodus 25–30), and someway epitomized in 35:4–19.[46] The execution (Exodus 36–40) is related almost with the same words, only changing the verb forms from command or instruction with imperative or *w*ᵉ*qatal*, respectively, to execution with *wayyiqtol*.[47]

3. *Narrative analysis and historical-critical study*

The historical-critical study runs the risk of taking for a different source what actually is a literary device, such as resumptive repetition,

---

[44] Indeed, the Sinai narrative reaches far beyond the Book of Exodus. In fact, after the Book of Exodus closes with the erection of the Tent of meeting, Leviticus consists almost entirely of a series of speeches by God to Moses from the Tent of meeting; and the beginning of Numbers refers back to the end of Exodus only a month later (compare Num. 1:1 with Ex. 40:17). Israel's departure from Sinai does not occur before Num. 10:11, nineteen days after the beginning of Numbers. See "Organizzazione canonica" § 2.

[45] Between the first and the second covenant there are many similarities and also some peculiarities. In both we find a connection between the wonders done by God and the people's obedience to his commands (19:4–5; 34:10–11). In both the covenant is made on the basis of specific prescriptions by God (24:8; 34:27). Among the peculiarities we note that the wonders done by God are different; they are the exodus from Egypt in the first covenant (19:4–5), and the conquest of the promised land in the second (34:10–11). God's prescriptions, constituting the basis of the covenant, change, too. One could further ask about the relationship between these Sinaitic covenants and the Deuteronomic one established on the land of Moab (compare Deut. 28:69–29:8 = 29:1–9 RSV). But this subject cannot be pursued here.

[46] These random observations are made from the perspective of the final text. For historical-critical research, of course, the two covenants are doublets, or variants of the same event: the one of Ex. 24 is traditionally ascribed to the Elohist writer, the one of Ex. 34 to the Yahwist one; and the story of the golden calf (Ex. 32) was introduced to link them together. However, E.W. Nicholson, *God and His People. Covenant and Theology in the Old Testament*, Oxford: Clarendon, 1986, holds a different view (see § 6, "Apostasy and Renewal of the Covenant at Sinai [Ex. 34:10–28]").

[47] See *Syntax* § 57–60, and my book review of W. Groß – H. Irsigler – T. Seidl (ed.), *Text, Methode und Grammatik*, St. Ottilien 1991, *Liber Annuus* 44 (1994) 667–692, § 6, as well as that of D.A. Dawson, *Text-Linguistics and Biblical Hebrew*, Sheffield 1994, *Liber Annuus* 45 (1995) 543–580, § 8.

inclusion, parallelism, etc. In other words, if one disregards the syntactic and literary texture of the biblical texts, one may easily interpret on the level of the *ordo rerum* an element that actually belongs to the state of affairs of the text (see § 2 above).[48]

The following comparison with the historical-critical analysis of Exodus 19–24[49] intends to show, on the one side, that different methodologies are used in the diachronic and in the synchronic study, and to suggest, on the other side, that the first needs to be based on the second and to come after it from the point of view of time.

In Exodus 19–24, literary critics detect additions of different periods (notably E and dtr) to the old J narrative. This narrative was interspersed with parallel E material (preparation of the people, theophany and Covenant Code) and later additions; as a consequence, from Exodus 19 J continues in Exodus 24. The Decalogue was originally placed in 24:3 for some authorities, or after 19:9 for others; however, for most critics it did not originally belong to the Sinai narrative. When the Covenant Code (of E origin since J has its counterpart in Exodus 34) was inserted, the Decalogue was transferred to, or inserted in, Exodus 20. At the same time, other redactional adjustments were made. In the critics' opinion, the difficulties of the text are the result of various redactions and of the use of the Sinai pericope in Israel's liturgy during the ages.

The difference in approach is to be stressed first. Diachronic study takes for granted that the text underwent a series of redactions and preserves traces of them; it therefore looks for inconsistencies, doublets, grammatical harshness or even errors. On the contrary, synchronic study assumes that the text is readable as it is, even if it underwent different redactions. Diachronic study is interested in isolating the original account and the successive additions, while the synchronic

---

[48] I have discussed this issue apropos the flood narrative, which is a favorite piece of the historical-critical research in: "Diluvio, sintassi e metodo", *Liber Annuus* 44 (1994) 9–46.

[49] I benefited from critical remarks by my colleague prof. Enzo Cortese, who also helped me with some bibliography; however, the responsibility for the position held here is mine. As representatives of the historical-critical view I quote the following: E. Cortese, *Da Mosè a Esdra. I libri storici dell'antico Israele*, Bologna 1985 (second ed. in preparation); J. Loza, *La palabras de Yahve. Estudio del decálogo*, México 1989 (a fresh study by the author on the same subject is to be published soon); and Nicholson, *God and His People*. These are among the few works that display a sound critical evaluation of the traditions as they demonstrate the basic antiquity of the covenant and of the Decalogue in Exodus 19ff. against the view, unfortunately fashionable today, which holds everything as post-exilic.

study aims at understanding the meaning of the text in its final form. Both approaches have their advantages and disadvantages.

A major anomaly is seen by historical critics in the sequence of 19:25 "Moses went down to the people and told them", and 20:1 "God spoke all these words saying". However, unless one wishes to exasperate the problem, the text is understandable in the way indicated above, i.e. Moses went down to the people and repeated God's warning as commanded earlier by God. Thus the Ten Words were pronounced by God from the mountain while Moses was down with the people.

Another anomaly is found in the sequence from 23:33 to 24:1. However, Moses' going up in 24:1 is different from that of 20:21. The first starts a new series of ascensions, after those of Chapters 19–20, which culminate in the giving of the instructions concerning the tabernacle and the cult (Chapters 25–30), while the second is tied to the revelation of the Covenant Code (20:22–23:33). Indeed, in the logic of the text every revelation—except that of the Ten Words—is connected with a special ascension of Moses, who acts as the mediator between God and Israel (§ 2.1–2.2 above). It seems that the anomaly seen by the critics depends on their conviction that Chapter 19 and Chapter 24 represent two versions (E and J, respectively) of the same theophany. Although a similar opinion had already been propounded by Rashi,[50] it does not seem to represent the logic of the text.

This does not mean that the historical-critical study is impossible, or unnecessary; on the contrary, it is legitimate and necessary. However, the synchronic study must come first in order to help the critic not to misinterpret the information of the text. Indeed, understanding the final text helps the critic not to exaggerate its problems. Further, the diachronic study needs to refine its method in order to achieve more convincingly its goal, which is, among other things, to illustrate the historical dimension and growth of the revelation.

[50] Commenting on Ex. 24:1, *wᵉʾel-mōšeh ʾāmar*, Rashi notes: "This section was spoken before the Ten Commandments *were given* (i.e. *ʾmr* is the pluperfect); it was the fourth of Sivan when 'Come up' was said to him". In a similar vein he comments on 24:16, 'And He called unto Moses' on the seventh day of Sivan: to utter the Ten Commandments"; see *Chumash. Shemot*, 128; 131. However, Ramban disagrees (in his comment on 24:1): "But if so, the sections of the Torah are not in chronological order, nor even in their ordinary sense" (Ramban, ed. Chavel, 419).

A better appreciation of biblical narrative on the part of modern scholars, including the literary critics, is urgent. In fact, the more we study the text of the Bible, the more we see that it is everything but incoherent and chaotic. An intelligent perusal of the traditional Jewish exegetes, who tried their best to understand the biblical text, can help in this endeavor.

Time has come to speak of "authors", rather than of redactors, or glossators, of the Bible. To say, for instance, that the multiple Moses' ascensions in Exodus 19–24 are the result of successive redactions, shifts the problem rather than solving it. It does not explain why a sophisticated author did not notice the inconsistencies of the traditions he used and/or left them in the text.

THE ALLEGED FINAL FUNCTION OF THE BIBLICAL HEBREW SYNTAGM <*WAW* + A VOLITIVE VERB FORM>

Takamitsu Muraoka
(Leiden)

Classical Hebrew possesses a great variety of lexical and syntactic means for the purpose of expressing the purpose of an action.[1] Among these formal means we may distinguish three basic categories: 1. the infinitive construct with or without the preposition *Lamed* attached, 2. a variety of particles, prepositions or conjunctions, whether simplex or compound, and whether combined with the preposition *Lamed* or not, e.g. פן, לבלתי, יען, למען, על דברת, בעבור, אשר, ש, ש, and 3. according to many authorities, a volitive[2] form of the prefix conjugation with the proclitic conjungtion *waw*. All these linguistic resources which speakers of Ancient Hebrew had at their disposal have been recently subjected to an illuminating investigation by Fassberg.[3] In the present paper we shall deal with only the third category.

To be more precise, the third category takes the form of a syntagm: <a volitive form of a verb + a simple *waw*, i.e. not vocalised with a *patach* + a volitive form of a verb>, and it is widely believed that the second verb (or any other further subsequent verb[4] also prefixed with the conjunction *waw*) in such a syntagm indicates the purpose of the action denoted by the first verb. This is the basic position indicated in my revision of Joüon's grammar,[5] shared by many other Hebraists.[6]

---

[1] Under "purpose" we also include "intended result." We believe that the term "resultative" or "consecutive" is to be restricted to cases where something has actually resulted.

[2] We refer the term "volitive" to "modal," for the latter can, in theory, include the indicative, which is certainly not meant here. To add to this terminological ambiguity, the term "modal" is also used in the current literature to refer to nuances such as "can, must, may" which the prefix conjugation is believed to possess.

[3] Fassberg 1994:74–142.

[4] In the following we shall, in the interest of succinct expression, use the term "the second verb" to include possible third or more, coordinated volitive verb.

[5] Joüon-Muraoka 1991 (1993): § 116, although I have added a footnote of mine (§ 116 *b*, note 1) to indicate my reservations and doubts.

[6] Driver 1892: § 59–65; Gibson 1994: § 126; Fassberg 1994: 74–142; Waltke-O'Connor 1990: 575; Lambdin 1973: 118f. Endo (1996: 226) is unable to choose between the two opposing interpretations.

By way of definition, let me also state at the start that by "modal forms" we mean the jussive, cohortative and imperative. Here we naturally ought to bear in mind that not every category of a prefix conjugation verb form in Hebrew is capable of unambiguously marking it as modal, namely cohortative or jussive.[7] For example, יִשְׁמְרוּ and אֶבְנֶה are unmarked in this respect. For the purpose of our paper we have examined all the prefix conjugation verb forms with a simple *waw* as second (and third etc. as the case may be) form in our syntagm of verbs whose root begins with one of the letters of the Hebrew alphabet from *Aleph* to *Yod* inclusive. Having regard to the theme of our congress we have focused on the narrative, though some examples in Job have been left out of account as well as the book of Daniel, the verb syntax of which latter book seems to call for a separate enquiry. We have further looked at cases where the second verb only is clearly marked as volitive,[8] whereas the first is an unmarked prefix conjugation form.

Unlike the so-called *waw* consecutive, or inversive according to Joüon-Muraoka (§ 117 *a*), what Joüon-Muraoka call energic *waw* of allegedly firnal force is not phonetically different in shape from its counterpart called by them simple *waw*. In both categories the conjunction is basically vocalised with a *shewa*, not a *patach*, nor is the following prefix conjugation prefix geminated. The distinction is first and foremost semantic: the verb prefixed with such an energic *waw* is said to be logically subordinate to the preceding finite verb[9] and to indicate the purpose of the action denoted by the preceding verb. On this currently prevailing view we have some reservations.

---

[7] An oft-quoted study by Orlinsky (1940–42) attempts to establish that a prefix conjugation followed by an imperative and joined to the conjunction *waw* must be volitive. He is not concerned with the function of the syntagm, or rather his supposition is that the syntagm is a juxtaposition of two volitives. Thus he proposes emending 1 Kgs. 18:5 לֵךְ וְנַעֲבֹר to לךְ ונַעַבְרָה, which he renders "Come, let us pass through" (p. 371). He further states that the second verb is cohortative-jussive "not only in function, but also in form" (p. 379).

[8] Gibson 1994: § 126 mentions Gen. 24:14 הַטִּי־נָא כַדֵּךְ וְאֶשְׁתֶּה "let down your pitcher that I may drink" as illustrative of this syntagm. He must have used a criterion other than purely morphological in order to identify the second verb as modal.

[9] A few exceptions are mentioned by Fassberg 1994: 79 top.

1. *Logical parallelism*

Although the definition of the syntagm in morphological terms appears at first sight to be objective and clear-cut, an element of interpretive ambiguity does arise, for both verbs are defined as volitive, which means that both can be of same morphological category. In such and many other cases the decision as to whether the syntagm indicates a purpose would depend solely on general, contextual consideration. A case in point would be Gen. 11:3 נִלְבְּנָה לבנים וְנִשְׂרפה לִשׂרפה "Let us make bricks and burn them thoroughly."[10] See also Job 23:5 אדעה... . ואבינה; Ec. 11:9 שְׂמַח . . . בילדוּתֶיךָ וִיטִיבְךָ לבך בימי בחורותיך "Delight in your youth, young man, make the most of your early days" (Revised English Bible); 1 Sam. 18:17 אל תהי בו ידי ותהי בו יד פלשתים; Ps. 144:5 הַט שָׁמֶיךָ ותרד גַע בהרים ויעשנו; Num. 23:3 התיצב על עֹלָתֶךָ ואלכה, hardly "so that I may go away"; 1 Sam. 17:8 בְּרוּ לכם איש וְיֵרֵד אלי (L: et descendat; G καὶ καταβήτω) where the notion of purpose is implausible because the grammatical subject of the second verb, introduced in the first clause, is indefinite. These all appear to us to be cases of juxtaposition, there being hardly any thought of logical subordination evident between the two clauses. One may include here cases in which the first verb is a prefix conjugation form, though not marked as volitive and yet followed by a volitive: Ps. 96:11 יִשְׂמְחוּ השמים וְתָגֵל הארץ "Let the heaven be glad and the earth rejoice" ("intensive" in Kelly's classification); Is. 44:17 יסגוד לו וישתחו ויתפלל אליו ויאמר; Num. 6:25 יָאֵר יהוה פניו אליך וִיחֻנֶּךָּ.

Because of this difficulty in distinguishing between the two kinds of *waw*, Joüon-Muraoka (§ 115 *c*) mentions three ways which could help resolve this ambiguity: context, syntax and comparison with Arabic. Let us leave Arabic out for the moment. The syntactic factor has been described above in terms of the constituents of the syntagm in question. The remaining factor, general context, proves to be most intractable. Fassberg (1994: 77), by contrast, maintains that the logical subordination is in most cases in no doubt, although he illustrates (1994: 76) the ambiguity and possible conflicting interpretations by quoting ancient and modern translations of a few Bible passages.[11]

[10] An example which should be assigned to the category called coordinate by Kelly 1920: 3.

[11] He also questions the interpretation by Kelly (1920), who sees a coordinating *waw* in Gen. 31:37 שׂים כה נגד אַחַי ואחיך וְיוכיחו בין שנינו ". . . and let them decide", which Fassberg would correct to "that they may decide".

2. *Grammatical, syntactic parallelism*

Joüon-Muraoka (§ 116 *b*), quoting Ex. 3:3 אָסֻרָה־נָּא וְאֶרְאֶה, state that
the final meaning of the syntagm is confirmed by סָר לִרְאוֹת in the
following verse, a highly interesting observation. One may also note
Is. 5:19b וְתִקְרַב וְתָבוֹאָה עֲצַת קְדוֹשׁ יִשְׂרָאֵל וְנֵדָעָה where נדעה is parallel
to נראה combined with an explicitly final לְמַעַן in the first half of the
verse—יָחִישָׁה מַעֲשֵׂהוּ לְמַעַן נִרְאֶה. Contrast also 1 Chr. 21:22 ... תְּנָה־לִּי
לִקְנוֹת ... וְאִבְנֶה ... וְהֵעָצֵר הַמַּגֵּפָה with its parallel in 2 Sam. 24:21 ... לִקְנוֹת
לִבְנוֹת ... וְתֵעָצַר הַמַּגֵּפָה with a final infinitive construct, לִבְנוֹת. This
sort of grammatical parallelism, however, is by itself no absolute proof
that the two parallel syntagms possess an identical syntactic function.
It is not impossible that we have here to do with a series of actions
viewed from different perspectives expressed by different syntactic
means. There is no certainty that in altering the explicitly final syntagm
(לבנות), which he found in his source document, to ואבנה the chronicler introduced a merely stylistic modification. This interpretive
ambiguity can be further illustrated by means of the famous story in
Genesis 27, which contains a stock example quoted by many to demonstrate the alleged final force of our syntagm (v. 4 הָבִיאָה לִּי וְאֹכֵלָה), but
which, in the following verses, presents this utterance recast in a great
variety of forms:

v. 4	עֲשֵׂה־לִי מַטְעַמִּים כַּאֲשֶׁר אָהַבְתִּי וְהָבִיאָה לִּי וְאֹכֵלָה בַּעֲבוּר תְּבָרֶכְךָ נַפְשִׁי	

(Isaac to Esau)

| v. 7 | ... הָבִיאָה לִּי צַיִד וַעֲשֵׂה־לִי מַטְעַמִּים וְאֹכֵלָה וַאֲבָרֶכְכָה | (Rebecca passes
on her husband's above instruction to her favourite son) |

| v. 10 | ... וְהֵבֵאתָ לְאָבִיךָ וְאָכָל בַּעֲבֻר אֲשֶׁר יְבָרֶכְךָ | (Rebecca's instruction
to Jacob) |

| v. 19 | קוּם־נָא שְׁבָה וְאָכְלָה מִצֵּידִי בַּעֲבוּר תְּבָרֲכַנִּי נַפְשֶׁךָ | (Jacob speaking to
Isaac) |

| v. 25 | הַגִּשָׁה לִּי וְאֹכְלָה מִצֵּיד בְּנִי לְמַעַן תְּבָרֶכְךָ נַפְשִׁי | (Isaac to Jacob) |

| v. 31 | יָקֻם אָבִי וְיֹאכַל מִצֵּיד בְּנוֹ בַּעֲבוּר תְּבָרֲכַנִּי נַפְשֶׁךָ | (Esau to Isaac) |

In v. 4 our syntagm is immediately followed by a lexical means explicitly marked as final (בעבור), and the verb of the clause clearly
indicates a purpose of not only the immediately preceding verb, but
of the complex instruction consisting of multiple components. In v. 7
the verb which was explicitly marked as final in the original utterance by Isaac is couched in a less explicit syntagm. Did Rebecca just
choose a synonymous syntagm for the sake of stylistic variation? Is
the last verb subordinate to the immediately preceding or to the

preceding whole complex? Where does the indication of purpose set in? In v. 10 there is no relationship of purpose between the first two verbs, which in v. 7 allegedly did involve such a relationship. The same consideration applies in comparing v. 19 and v. 31. Here, the twin brothers, moreover, varied the modus of the verbs: imperative versus possibly jussive (revocalising יָקֻם to יָקֹם). The syntagm in v. 25 is basically the same as in v. 4 with the added lexical variation (למען instead of בעבור).

In fact, such a grammatical, syntactic parallelism turns out to be a double-edged sword. Consider the following cases: Ex. 3:10 ועתה לכה ואשלחך אל פרעה והוצא את עמי בני ישראל // ib. 3:11 מי אנוכי כי אלך אל פרעה וכי אוציא את בני ישראל;[12] ib. 4:4 שְׁלַח ידך וֶאֱחֹז בזנבו וַיִּשְׁלַח ידו וַיַּחֲזֶק בו; Gen. 24:57 נִקְרָא לַנַּעֲרָ וְנִשְׁאֲלָה את פיה וַיִּקְרְאוּ לרבקה ויאמרו אליה הֲתֵלְכִי עם האיש הזה. In all these cases, which can be extensively multiplied, the first verb gives a command or a proposal, and the second its execution in the *indicative* in the form of a prefix conjugation with the inversive *waw*. In Josh. 4:16 צַוֵּה את הכהנים . . . וְיַעֲלוּ מן הירדן the verb יעלו is hardly final, for it is what the priests were to be commanded to do, as becomes apparent in its sequel—וַיְצַו יהושע . . . לאמר עֲלוּ . . . .[13]

3. *Identity or otherwise of the subjects of the two verbs*

What does not seem to have been noticed so far is the fact that in the great majority of our examples the subject of the leading verb is not identical with that of the allegedly subordinate, second verb. In this respect our syntagm is markedly different from the other two types of final constructions. In the case of the infinitive construct its logical subject is almost always identical with that of the main verb: e.g. Gen. 4:11 האדמה אשר פצתה את פיה לקחת את דמי אחיך "the earth that opened its mouth to take the blood of your brother." The only

[12] Fassberg (1994: 76, note 16) prefers "that you may bring out", instead of which Kelly would have "and bring out" (coordinate). In general we question the wisdom of including the imperative as the second verb. Lambdin (1973: 119) does not include the imperative.

Here Moses recast God's command as two independent coordinate clauses (. . . כי . . . וכי). Are we to conclude that Moses' Hebrew was not up to the mark and he failed to get God's intention right?

[13] Cf. Brockelmann (1960: § 146, c): "So kann auch der Inhalt eines Befehls nach dem Imperativ im Apokopatus stehen, wie مره يات "befiehl ihm zu kommen".

example of identical subject is Jdg. 13:8 יבוא נא . . . ויוֹרֵנוּ, supposing that the second verb is subordinate to the first (V: veniat iterum et doceat; G ἐλθέτω καὶ φωτισάτω/συμβιβασάτω). In Ps. 144:5 הט שָׁמֶיךָ ותרד we hardly have an expression of purpose. This appears to be the reason why one is often not quite certain whether one is having to do with a truly final clause or a juxtaposition of multiple volitive clauses which express a wish of the speaker. This is particularly true where a noun constituent of the leading clause happens to be a constituent of the allegedly final clause also as in 1 Sam. 27:5 יתנו לי מקום . . . ואשבה שם (V: ut habitem ibi; G καὶ καθήσομαι ἐκεῖ); ib. 28:7 בַּקְשׁוּ לי אשת בעלת אוב ואלכה אליה (V: . . . et vadam; G: καὶ πορεύσομαι). In the case of a final particle למען with a prefix conjugation form we find 35 cases of identical subjects[14] as against 84 of different subjects. From these statistics one may conclude that our syntagm is at least less final than that with למען, for instance.

4. *Position of final expressions within a sentence*

Another syntactic consideration which seems to speak against the current view is that, whereas clauses which can be said to be final on morphological as well as contextual grounds can precede the main clause, our syntagm, by definition, does not occupy the initial slot. Examples of the former are 1 Sam. 17:28 למען ראות המלחמה ירדת; Ez. 40:4 למען הראוֹתְכָה הֻבָאתָה הנה; Gen. 42:9 לראות את עֶרְוַת הארץ באתם.

5. *Asyndesis*

Fassberg (1994: 81) justly mentions several examples of asyndetic construction in which the verb of allegedly final force lacks the conjunction *waw*. These, as Fassberg points out, are, with a single exception, all found in poetic passages: e.g., Ex. 7:9 קח את מטך והשלך לפני פרעה יהי לתנין; Hos. 10:12 זִרְעוּ לכם לצדקה קִצְרוּ לפי חסד where it is not clear what Fassberg would make of the immediately following, equally asyndetic imperatival clause נִירוּ לכם ניר "Break up your fallow ground"; Ps. 118:19 פִּתְחוּ לי שערי צדק אבא בם; Prov. 20:13 אל תאהב

[14] E.g., Ps. 119:11 בלבי צפנתי אמרתך למען לא אחטא לך.

שנה פן תִּוָּרֵשׁ פְּקַח עיניך שְׂבַע לחם where the first hemistich has an explicitly (negative) final conjunction, פן. Fassberg thinks that this is typical of the poetic idiom which makes sparing use of conjunctions, subordinate or coordinate. However, nearly 70 out of a total of 190 examples of למען with a verb occur in poetic passages.[15]

6. *A semantic aspect*

Since the issue at hand seems to have a great deal to do with semantics, it is important to underline a striking difference in the range of meanings of leading verbs between our alleged "final" syntagm and the explicitly and frequently used syntagm <למען + participle>. Fassberg (1994: 90) confirms the insight gained by Kuhr as early as 1929 (Kuhr 1929: § 41) that none of the verbs occurring commonly in the first syntagm, viz. those of giving, whether physically or verbally (such as נתן, לקח, קרא, דבר) or those of physical movement (עלה, קום, בוא, שלח) occurs in any למען-clause. On the other hand, Fassberg (1994: 90) mentions as the most frequent lexemes as the first verb preceding למען such verbs as היה (10×), עשׂה (9×), ידע (6×), נתן (5×). There is thus clearly a semantic mismatch between the two syntagms.

7. *Ancient versions*

It is true that some of the ancient versions, especially the Vulgate and the Septuagint, often make use of a final construction with *ut* and ἵνα or ὅπως respectively: Gen. 27:4 הָבִיאָה לי ואֹכֵלָה > *adfer ut comedam* and ἔνεγκέ μοι, ἵνα φάγω; ib. 23:4 תנו . . . ואקברה > *date . . . ut sepeliam* and δότε . . . καὶ θάψω. However, they are never consistent nor do they always agree among themselves: see 1 Sam. 27:5 . . . יִתְּנוּ לִי מָקוֹם וְאֵשְׁבָה שָּׁם: Vulg. *detur mihi locus . . . ut habitem ibi* vs. LXX δότωσάν δή μοι τόπον . . . καὶ καθήσομαι ἐκεῖ.[16]

---

[15] The Peshitta, which, as far as our question is concerned, generally follows the Hebrew syntax of the source text, attests, however, cases of deviation where the Hebrew syndesis is replaced by asyndesis: Gen. 27:25 הַגִּשָׁה לִּי וְאֹכְלָה > ܩܪܶܒ ܠܝ ܐܶܟܘܠ; ib. 27:4 הָבִיאָה לִי ואֹכֵלָה > ܐܰܝܬܳܐ ܠܝ ܐܶܟܘܠ; ib. 30:25 שַׁלְּחֵנִי וְאֵלְכָה > ܫܰܪܳܝܢܝ ܐܶܙܶܠ.

[16] Another possibility of translation besides that agreeing with the current view

We have also looked into Saadia's Arabic translation, his *tafsir*, of the Pentateuch. Since Joüon had mentioned Arabic as a possible aid to our enquiry, we were curious how Saadia dealt with this question. To this end we checked eleven representative examples in Genesis. The picture is mixed. (a) In three cases he uses the final conjunction حتي (27:25; 30:26; 42:34).[17] Since at 30:26 we find a form marked as subjunctive امضي, one may assume that the subjunctive is used in the other two cases as well despite the absence of vocalisation. (b) In six cases he uses asyndetic construction. In two of them we find a form clearly marked as jussive, امض (24:56 and 30:25).[18] This is in keeping with Arabic syntax, an imperative followed by a jussive.[19] One might safely posit the jussive in the remaining four cases as well (Gen. 27:4, 27:9, 29:21, 49:1).[20] (c) In the remaining two cases (12:1f., 23:4)[21] Saadia uses a prefix conjugation form with the conjunction *waw*, despite the fact that in the latter case the Hebrew text has a form explicitly marked as cohortative. Or is it possible to postulate here also a subjunctive in accordance with Classical Arabic syntax, which does allow the use of *wa* with a subjunctive when the simultaneity of both actions is to be stressed (Reckendorf 1921: § 231)? There is no question of simultaneity, however, in Gen. 12:1f. Although the extent of our enquiry is nothing but limited, we see that Saadia identified in most of these eleven passages final clauses. We find it all the same striking that not a single case of *fa* has turned up, despite the fact that the particle in conjunction with a subjunctive

---

on our syntagm as in *let a place be given me ... so that I may live there* (New Revised Standard Version) is indicated in *... qu'on me donne une place ... où je puisse résider* (Bible de Jérusalem); *Grant me a place ... where I may settle* (Revised English Bible). Mr. Martin Baasten, a Leiden student of mine, draws my attention to yet another possibility, this time in an ancient version: Gen. 18:21 ארדה־נא ואראה, for which the LXX shows καταβὰς οὖν ὄψομαι.

[17] Gen. 27:25 הגשה לי ואכלה ... למען תברכך > قدم لي حتي اكل ... لكي تباركك; 30:26 תנה ... ואלכה > اعطني ... حتي امضى; 42:34 והביאו ... ואדעה > اتوني ... حتي اعلم.

[18] 24:56 שלחוני ואלכה > اطلقوني امض ; 30:25 שלחני ואלכה > اطلقني امض.

[19] Brockelmann 1960: § 153 and 146, Anm. c. Incidentally in the former paragraph Brockelmann speaks of "Folge" and in the latter of "Absicht", though in both paragraphs he is discussing the same syntagm. This terminological ambiguity is not peculiar to Semitic language. See Muraoka 1973. In Blass-Debrunner (1954: § 391) one notices an extraordinary degree of subtlety: "tatsächliche Folge", "wirklliche oder mögliche Folge", "beabsichtigte Folge".

[20] 27:4 והביאה לי ואכלה > واتني به اكل منه; 27:9 קח לי ... ואעשה אתם > خذ لي ... اصلحهما; 29:21 הבה ... ואבואה > اعطني ... ادخل; 49:1 האספו ואגידה > اجتمعو اخبركم.

[21] 12:1f. לך לך ... ואעשך > امض ... واصنع منك ...; 23:4 תנו ... ואקברה > اعطوني ... وادفن.

does express "ein eventuelles Ziel, das die Folge einer supponierten Handlung bildet" (Reckendorf 1921: § 230, 1). Let us note, however, that in Arabic the syntagm <*fa* + subjunctive> can have the leading verb not only as an imperative, but also a plain indicative, even of preterital meaning: see a great variety of examples quoted by Reckendorf (1921: § 230). Indeed the ambiguity of our syntagm is partly due to the fact that the leading verb is also modal. The analogy of Arabic becomes even more complicated when we realise that the language allows even the use of the indicative with a *fa* of final meaning: see Reckendorf 1921: § 230, 2. Even so, one must ask whether this is a sufficient ground for assigning a distinct function to this particular syntagm. And even if in very many places such a translation, not only in the ancient versions, but also in modern European languages, reads well and elegantly, the question still remains whether or not it is essentially a question of translation expedience. The Arabic evidence, which Joüon adduced, namely its particle *fa*, must be seen from the perspective of the structure of Arabic as a whole, namely Arabic possesses two distinct conjunctions, *wa* for simple linkage and *fa* for energic linkage, whereas Hebrew, though in possession of two distinct allomorphs (three, in fact, which are two) [w^e and *wa* + gemination or accent shift], shows a different distribution. Our difficulty is precisely due to the fact that the same allomorph, namely w^e, is attested in clause sequences consisting of volitive verb forms, though some of such clauses can be interpreted as containing final expression.

8. *Complex inner hierarchy*

Though this is not strictly a reservation against the current view, we would like to mention here another kind of ambiguity, an ambiguity which arises where the syntagm in question consists of more than two verbs and one needs to decide which of the second and subsequent verbs indicates a purpose of the action denoted by the first verb. In Neh. 5:2 נקחה דגן ונאכלה ונחיה the advocates of the current view would have to argue that both the second and third verbs indicate a purpose ("... so that we may have something to eat and survive"), whereas in Gen. 43:8 שִׁלְחָה הנער . . . ונקומה ונלכה ונחיה ולא נמות they would say that a purpose clause begins only with the fourth verb, though the last verb is not marked as volitive and it is hardly the case that נחיה indicates a purpose of not only שלחה, but also ונלכה נקומה. In Ex. 8:4 הַעְתִּירוּ אל יהוה וְיָסֵר הצפרדעים ממני . . . וַאֲשַׁלְּחָה את העם ויזבחו ליהוה is Pharaoh encouraging the practice of his troublesome Gastarbeiters' religion? In 1 Kgs. 21:2 תנה לי את כרמך ויהי לי לגן יָרָק . . . ואתנה לך תחתיו . . . one might argue that the second clause indicates a purpose of the first, but hardly the third. In 1 Sam. 28:22 ועתה שמע נא גם אתה בקול שפחתך ואשׂימה לפניך פת לחם וֶאֱכֹל ויהי בך כח כי תלך בדרך we seem to have a rather complex case where ואשׂימה is definitely not final, and it is followed by another imperative parallel to the leading verb, also an imperative, but ויהי can be said to be final in relation to this second imperative only. Equally complicated is Gen. 42:16f. שִׁלְחוּ מכם אחד ויקח את אחיכם ואתם הֵאָסְרוּ וְיִבָּחֲנוּ דבריכם האמת אתכם where יקח could be said to be subordinate to שלחו, whereas האסרו is coordinate with שלחו, thus not subordinate to what precedes, whereas יבחנו could be considered to be subordinate to all that precedes it, but hardly to the immediately preceding הֵאָסְרוּ. More complex is Jer. 9:16f. קִרְאוּ (1) לַמְקוֹנְנוֹת ותבואינה (2) ואֶל החכמות שִׁלְחוּ (3) ותבואנה (4) ותמהרנה (5) ותִשֶּׂנָה (6) עלינו נהי ותרדנה (7) עינינו דמעה ועפעפינו יִזְּלוּ (8) מים possibly with the following structure:

```
                3 — — 1
               /       /
          (5 + 4)     2
            /
           6
          /
      (8 + 7)
```

The oblique line indicates that a verb underneath can be said to be logically subordinate to the one immediately above, the plus sign indicates that the two adjacent verbs are in the relationship of juxtaposition,[22] whereas the broken, horizontal line between (1) and (3) signifies that the two verbs introduce each its own syntagm of allegedly final force. The non-clause-initial position of the last verb, incidentally, shows that it and the immediately preceding verb are merely juxtaposed (parallelism). This is partial justification of our thesis that the syntagm in question is basically that of juxtaposition, a series of juxtaposed, coordinate volitive forms with no notion of purpose marked

[22] Verb 5 is clearly subordinate to verb 4, but not in a relationship of purpose.

as its *function*. Likewise in Gen. 22:5 שְׁבוּ לָכֶם פֹּה... ואני והנער נֵלְכָה ונשתחוה וְנָשׁוּבָה where the multiple subject of the second verb נלכה is fronted by virtue of a contrast of the subject with the embedded one, "you", of the preceding imperative. Whereas the third verb may be said to indicate a purpose of the second, the concluding נשובה hardly indicates a purpose of any of the preceding verbs. It is simply independent. It can be said to be subordinate to the preceding two, but then not indicating a purpose, but an action chronologically subsequent to them, which is not a function we are discussing here.[23]

Conclusion

We may not have *demonstrated* that the consensus view is wrong, but we hope to have adduced enough evidence tending to show that such an interpretation does not necessarily follow, and it is more than likely that two or more conjoined volitive verbs are essentially a series of expressions of the speaker's wish. Where the speaker or writer wishes explicitly to mark a logical relation of subordination to indicate a purpose, he availed himself of one of several lexical or syntactic means. Otherwise he was content with a simple, non-committing juxtaposition of verb forms, which may sound a shade too vague to some people's liking. Surveying the versional evidence, it strikes me that precisely those versions in the languages that are genetically and structurally closest to Hebrew, namely Aramaic and Syriac, turn out to be the most indifferent to this alleged nuance of the syntagm. Although we did not check these two versions systematically for the purpose of this presentation, we have mentioned a couple of cases of minor accomodation by means of asyndetic structure displayed by the Peshitta, which also has one instance where we find a case of real transformation into a final structure: 1 Sam. 7:8 אַל תַּחֲרֵשׁ ממנו מִזְּעֹק אל יהוה... וְיֹשִׁעֵנִי > ܠܐ ܬܫܬܐܩ ܡܢܢ ܠܡܩܥܐ ܩܕܡ ܡܪܝܐ ܕܢܦܪܩܢ. We are inclined to regard this apparent insensitivity to the alleged subtlety and elegance of Hebrew syntax not as an indication of those translators' incompetence or inepititude. That there was a measure of fluidity possible in our biblical writers' mode of thinking is manifest in the various linguistic patterns used in Genesis 27 in casting and

[23] This is close to the second usage translatable with "then" as identified by Kelly 1920: 3.

recasting the arrangement that the ageing Isaac made regarding the future of his twin sons. The occasional difficulty indicated (Joüon-Muraoka § 116 *b*) as to whether the intended nuance is that of purpose or consecution (result) may be better understood against this background.

In summing up we would say that the syntagm in question does not have a *function* of formally indicating a purpose. A sequence of volitive verb forms is a series of so many expressions of the speaker's or writer's wish and will.[24] The fact that in some cases the second verb can be more elegantly[25] translated as indicating a purpose of the first is essentially a question of pragmatics and translation techniques, and not of descriptive grammar and syntax.[26] Where one and the same syntagm or linguistic form appears to possess multiple translation values, but the choice boils down in the last analysis to the question of aesthetics, one becomes disinclined to assign those distinct patterns of translation as so many grammatical, syntactic functions, unless one is able to demonstrate that the choice between those different patterns of translation is conditioned by another grammatical, syntactic, or semantic factor.

Finally, this study shows by implication that there are features of the Biblical Hebrew syntax which cannot be meaningfully discussed within the current framework of text linguistics or discourse linguistics.

---

[24] Kuhr (1929: 47, note 2), who is inclined towards the current view, does indicate the alternative possibility: "Dagegen dürfte wohl in allen denjenigen Fällen psychologische Koordination vorliegen, wo der pluralische Koh.[ortativ] eine an das Sub.[ekt] des Imp.[erativs] gerichtete Aufforderung zu gemeinsamem Handeln ausdrückt . . ." This concession is all the more significant since it is going against his entire thesis, "konjunktionslose Hypotaxe".

[25] Cf. Driver (1892: 64): "This weak וְ is used with the imperfect . . . in order to express the design or purpose of a preceding act, which it does in a less formal and circumstantial manner than בעבור, למען etc., but with greater conciseness and elegance"; Joüon-Muraoka (1991: 168 *b*): "Finality or purpose is expressed in a light and elegant way by means of the *Waw with an indirect volitive* (§ 116). . . ."

[26] This consideration equally applies when it is sometimes said (e.g., Joüon-Muraoka 1991: § 167) that a protasis and an apodosis in a conditional expression can be asyndetically juxtaposed as in Prov. 18:22 מצא אשה מצא טוב. One may observe a similar phenomenon in the sphere of semantics. In translating a Dutch text into Hebrew and coming across *schoonvader* one would need to choose between חָם "husband's father" and חֹתֵן "wife's father". This, however, does not mean that the Dutch noun has two distinct *senses*: it has only one *sense*, namely, "spouse's father", which has two *applications*, and Hebrew possesses two distinct lexemes for the two applications of which Dutch is capable. Anthropological implications of such a difference between the two languages belong to a dimension other than purely linguistic.

References

Blass, F., Debrunner, A. & Rehkopf, F., 1954⁹, *Grammatik des neutestamentlichen Griechisch*, Göttingen: Vandenhoeck & Ruprecht.

Brockelmann, C., 1960[14], *Arabische Grammatik*, Leipzig: VEB Verlag Enzyklopädie.

Brown, F., Driver, S.R. & Briggs, Ch.A., 1907, *A Hebrew and English Lexicon of the Old Testament*, Oxford: Oxford University Press.

Driver, S.R., 1987[3], *A Treatise on the Use of the Tenses in Hebrew and some Other Syntactical Questions*, Oxford: Clarendon.

Ehrlich, A.B., 1908, *Randglossen zur hebräischen Bibel. Textkritisches, sprachlliches und sachliches*, Band 1: Genesis und Exodus, Leipzig: J.C. Hinrich.

Endo, Y., 1996, *The Verbal System of Classical Hebrew in the Joseph Story: an Approach from Discourse Analysis* (Studia Semitica Neerlandica 32), Assen: van Gorcum.

Fassberg, S.E., 1994, *Studies in Biblical Syntax*, Jerusalem: Magnes.

Gibson, J.C.L., 1994, *Davidson's Introductory Hebrew Grammar. Syntax*, Edinburgh: T&T Clark.

Hosoe, I., 1932, *An Enquiry into the Meaning of Tense in the English Verb*, Tokyo: Taibundo.

Joüon, P. & Muraoka, T., 1991, *A Grammar of Biblical Hebrew*, 2 Vols. (Subsidia Biblica 14/I and 14/II), Roma: Pontifico Istituto Biblico.

Kelly, F.T., 1920, "The Imperfect with Simple *Waw* in Hebrew", *Journal of Biblical Literature* 39:1–23.

Kuhr, E., 1929, *Die Ausdruksmittel der konjunktionslosen Hypotaxe in der ältesten hebräischen Prosa* (Beiträge zur semitischen Philologie und Linguistik 7), Leipzig: J.C. Hinrich.

Lambdin, T.O., 1973, *Introduction to Biblical Hebrew*, London: Darton, Longman & Todd.

Longacre, R.E., 1994, "*Weqatal* Forms in Biblical Hebrew Prose: A Discourse-Modular Approach", in: Bergen, R.D. (ed.), *Biblical Hebrew and Discourse Linguistics*, Winona Lake (Ind.): Eisenbrauns, 50–98.

Moulton, J.P., 1908[3], *A Grammar of New Testament Greek*, Edinburgh: T&T Clark.

Muraoka, T., 1973, "Purpose or Result? ὥστε in Biblical Greek", *Novum Testamentum* 15:205–219.

———, 1985, *Emphatic Words and Structures in Biblical Hebrew*, Jerusalem/Leiden: Magnes/E.J. Brill.

Orlinsky, H.M., 1940–42, "On the Cohortative and Jussive after an Imperative or Interjection in Biblical Hebrew", *The Jewish Quarterly Review* 31:371–382; 32: 191–205 & 273–277.

Paul, H., 1920[5] (= 1960[6]), *Prinzipien der Sprachgeschichte*, Tübingen: Niemeyer.

Qimron, E., 1987, "Consecutive and Conjunctive Imperfect: the Form of the Imperfect with War in Biblical Hebrew", *The Jewish Quarterly Review* 77:149–161.

Reckendorf, H., 1921, *Arabische Syntax*, Heidelberg: Carl Winter's Universitätsbuchhandlung.

Swete, H.B., 1909[3] (repr. 1956), *The Gospel According to St. Mark*, Grand Rapids: Eerdmans.

Taylor, V., 1952, *The Gospel According to St. Mark*, London: Macmillan.

Verheij, A.J.C., 1990, *Verbs and Numbers. A Study of the Frequencies of the Hebrew Verbal Tense Forms in the Book of Samuel, Kings and Chronicles* (Studia Semitica Neerlandica 28), Assen: van Gorcum.

Wackernagel, J., 1924–26[2] (repr. 1950–57), *Vorlesungen über Syntax mit besonderer Berücksichtigung von Griechisch, Lateinisch und Deutsch*, 2 Vols., Basel: Birkhäuser.

Waltke, B.K. & O'Connor, M., 1990, *An Introduction to Biblical Hebrew Syntax*, Winona Lake (Ind.): Eisenbrauns.

WORKSHOP: NOTES ON THE USE OF HEBREW TENSES IN EXODUS 19–24

Takamitsu Muraoka
(Leiden)

Exodus 19

1. The first verse of the chapter is a chronological note as background against the events now to be told: three months had elapsed since the exodus. Hence this unusual syntax: there is no familiar initial *waw* and the verse begins with an initial temporal phrase lacking the familiar ויהי.

2. Here begins actually the narrative with the usual *waw* inversive. Perhaps the *athnach* marks the mid-point between two utterance units: A new unit begins with ויחן in the singular, restating ויחנו (with בני ישראל as its subject), and this last clause of the verse would then form a syntactic unit with v. 3a, the S-V indicating contrast in the subject (Moses versus Israel). Others take עלה as a pluperfect, making Moses start his ascent on the second day (Rashi). Ehrlich's (1908: 336) "Moses schickte sich an, hinaufzusteigen" (German Imperfect) is unlikely: no such use of the suffix conjugation is known elsewhere.

3. וְתַגֵּיד, vocalised as jussive, but clearly coordinate with תאמר, not final (parallelism; so Ehrlich 1908: 336).

5. והייתם: the preceding *athnach* marks this clause as the beginning of the apodosis; there is otherwise no *formal* means to tell where the apodosis begins, here or with ושמרתם.

6. ואתם תהיו: the tense is on a par with והייתם (5), a suffix conjugation with a *waw* inversive. It could have been והייתם here too but for the intruding pronoun stressing the unique position of Israel among the earthly nations, a notion continued from v. 5: סגלה מכל העמים.

7. ויבא: continues ויקרא (v. 3) after a long interlude.

9. ויגד: "on the following, i.e. fourth, day" (Rashi). Rashi, apparently guided by the *athnach*, makes this the beginning of the new narrative unit, followed by ויאמר (v. 10a). Moses apparently reported again on the people's response.

13. המה: contrast with Moses, now it is their turn to ascend. The address is mixed: partly put in the mouth of Moses, and partly in God's mouth.

18. עָשַׁן: an unusual tense. One expects a sort of circumstantial clause. Likely a haplography for יֶעְשַׁן, or revocalise: עָשֵׁן (so 20:14). Cf. V *fumabat*, G ἐκαπνίζετο, S ܬܢܢ ܗܘܐ.

19. משה ידבר והאלהים יעננו: a typical circumstantial clause with an iterative, habitual prefix conjugation in the non-initial position. Cf. V *Moses loquebatur et dominus respondebat ei* (but the preceding verbs also in the imperfect: e.g. *eratque mons omnis terribilis*), G Μωυσης ἐλάλει, ὁ δὲ θεὸς ἀπεκρίνατο αὐτῷ (but same as in V), S ܘܡܘܫܐ ܡܡܠܠ ܗܘܐ ܘܐܠܗܐ ܡܦܢܐ ܠܗ.

22. יתקדשו: modal on a par with רד העד (v. 21). In the non-initial position on account of גם, which tends to take the clause-initial position.

23. אתה: a mark of protest and confrontation.

24. הכהנים והעם: initial position in contrast with אתה ואהרון (v. 23).

Exodus 20

4. פֹּקֵד (so also עֹשֶׂה, v. 5): indicates a permanent quality and attribute just as קַנָּא.

7. זָכוֹר: an infinitive absolute in commandments of general applicability, not specific actions, corresponding with לא, and not אל, in the prohibitive commands.[1] The other positive commandment is כבד (11: no imperative).[2] Thus the elaboration of the third commandment on the sabbath is couched in the prefix conjugation: תעבד ועשית . . . לא תעשה.

14. וכל העם ראים, a circumstantial clause in relation to v. 1 וידבר אלהים.

עָשֵׁן, lacking the definite article, is not attributively used (G τὸ ὄρος τὸ καπνίζον), but it is an object complement: "they saw the mountain, as it smoked."

15. ונשמָעָה, hardly final.

17. ומשה נִגַּשׁ, contrast, not a pluperfect.

Exodus 21

2. כי "if", "broadly, after which special cases are introduced by אם" (BDB, s.v. כי 2.b).[3] Likewise v. 8, 9, 10, 11 corresponding to כי

[1] See Joüon-Muraoka 1991: § 123 *u* and Muraoka 1985: 84f.

[2] *Pace* Longacre 1994: 96, note 6.

[3] So also Longacre 1994: 91, though he does not mention BDB. This significant lexical distinction is evident in an embedded conditional clause such as Ex. 21:18 וכי יְרִיבֻן אנשים והִכָּה איש את רעהו באבן או באגרף ולא ימות ונפל למשכב אם יקום והתהלך בחוץ על משענתו וְנִקָּה הַמַּכֶּה "when individuals quarrel and one strikes the other with a stone or fist so that the injured party, though not dead, is confined to bed, but

in v. 7; v. 19 in relation to v. 18; v. 23 in relation to v. 22; v. 27 in relation to v. 26; v. 29, 30, 32 in relation to v. 28, etc. אשר also functions like אם in this context: e.g. v. 13.

שש שנים יעבד: on the fronting of the adverbial and especially the end-position of the verb, cf. Muraoka 1985: 40f. (where the SOV is being discussed). Such or similar examples are to be found at, e.g., 22:17, 20, 21, 24, 27, 28, 29, 30; 23:7, 8, 9, 13.

When an apodosis begins with a verbum finitum itself, and not any other element including the negative particle, it is usually introduced by a *waw* apodosis and a suffix conjugation form: the apodosis introduced by אם—3b, 6, 8 וְהֶפְדָּהּ, 11 ויצאה, 19 וְנִקָּה, 23 ונתתה, 30 ונתן, 22:2b ונמכר, 7 ונקרב), 23:23 (ואיבתי); introduced by כי—21:35 (ומכרו). Where the main verb of the apodosis does not take the clause-initial position, no apodotic *waw* is used: v. 9, 10, 21, 26, 27, 29 (השור יסקל), 32, 22:1, 2a, 3: exceptions 22:6, 11, 12, 13. Joüon-Muraoka (1991: § 176 *d*) have noted this use of the apodotic *waw* as typical of casuistic legal codes. *Pace* Longacre (1994: 94), it is not the semantic choice, namely choice between different functions of various verb forms, that determines which verb form is to be used in the apodosis, but it is rather a case of complementary distribution conditioned by the word class of the initial clause constituent. For example, in v. 3 אִם־בְּגַפּוֹ יָבֹא בְּגַפּוֹ יֵצֵא אִם־בַּעַל אִשָּׁה הוּא וְיָצְאָה אִשְׁתּוֹ עִמּוֹ the יָצְאָה is no less modal than the יֵצֵא, if the former is at all modal. Nor has Longacre explained the use of *w^e^qatal* in a protasis as in 21:26 וכי יַכֶּה אִישׁ אֶת־עֵין עַבְדּוֹ . . . וְשִׁחֲתוֹ.

12. וָמֵת, a suffix conjugation form in the light of 16 וּמְכָרוֹ וְנִמְצָא. Since this formula appears to be analogous to a conditional כי-clause, the clause-initial participle in these cases must have the tense/aspect value of the prefix conjugation. The use of a suffix conjugation form with the *waw* inversive also supports this analysis. This is in spite of the status constructus form of the participle: it is thus rather verbal than nominal.

13. והאלהים אִנָּה: the fronted subject is in focus—"it is God that . . ." The *waw* inversive with the suffix conjugation—ושמתי—confirms the conditional force of the אשר here.

(if he) recovers and walks around outside with the help of a staff, then the assailant shall be free of liability".

Exodus 22

10. ולקח cannot be preterital, for one would expect ויקח after שָׁלַח. It must be inversive following תהיה, an interpretation supported also by the *athnach*.

14. בָּא, striking, whether it be a participle or a suffix conjugation form: יבא is expected. But the suffix conjugation is attested in the apodosis, "expressing the certainty and suddenness with which the result immediately accompanies the occurrence of the protasis" (Driver 1892:176). Driver (ib.) also mentions two cases where a participle occurs in the apodosis: Gen. 4:7 and Lev. 21:9. The question is whether such certainty and suddenness are intended in our case.

30. תהיון: quite a few cases of the *nun* paragogicum in this legal corpus: יאריכון (20:12); תעשׂון (20:23); יריבֻן (21:18); יֶחֱצוּן (21:35); יַרְשִׁיעֻן (22:8); תְעַנּוּן (22:21); תשִׂימוּן (22:24); תשליכון (22:30). A stylistic feature? Solemnity?[4]

Exodus 23

4. תֹּעֶה: an object complement as in Num. 11:10 וישמע משה את העם בֹּכֶה (Joüon-Muraoka 1991: § 126 *b*). Cf. רֹבֵץ in the following verse.

7. אל: for the first time, instead of the usual לא.

12. וינפש, a simple *waw* and the verb is coordinate with ינוח.

Exodus 24

6. וחצי הדם זָרַק על המזבח, emphasising the contrast with the other half.

11. The first half is a parenthetical commentary.

14. Moses did not say this to the elders after his ascent, but prior to it. This proteron husteron was necessary in order to say in the preceding verse that he did what he had been told to do: עֲלֵה . . . וַיַּעַל.

15. ויעל with Moses as its subject occurs three times in this pericope (v. 12–18). Not that he made three ascents, but it only shows that a series of actions indicated by the narrative forms with the inversive *waw* do not have to mean that those actions took place in that order one after another. This important event is presented from three different angles: Moses' obedience to God's call to ascend (v. 13), the

[4] Mr. A. Warren of Cambridge draws my attention to Joüon-Muraoka 1991: § 44 *e*—". . . no long form occurs with the prohibitive אל and extremely rarely with the inversive Waw". The examples mentioned accord with this description.

mount was enveloped in a thick cloud of partition for an intimate communication (v. 15), Moses actually penetrated the screen into the divine presence for a prolonged communication (v. 18).

17. A circumstantial clause.

Some concluding remarks

1. Longacre (1994: 95), concluding his study of "juridical discourse" in Exodus 21, writes:

> Juridical discourse (casuistry) resolves into a series of minidiscourses in which *w^eqatal* forms are presumably basic. But the positing of hypothetical cases via conditional sentences blocks the occurrence of the *w^eqatal* in many syntactic situations. All of this, it seems to me, points towards a functional explanation of *w^eqatal* in the law codes that may prove to be preferable to the traditional explanation in terms of consecution of tenses as such.

This prompts us to make the following observations.

a. Contrary to Longacre (1994: 92) the use of the tenses in our legal pericope (Ex. 21:2–23:19) shows no feature which can be considered truly unique in relation to that which one finds in other literary genres. There is no question of "a special and restricted development" in the law codes. The only significant feature we would mention is the pregnant use of the participle having the value of introducing a protasis without a usual conditional particle. To say that *w^eqatal* forms "occur in non-initial verb clauses within a protasis or an apodosis" (Longacre 1994: 92) amounts to belabouring the obvious. The statement that "they occur as initial in an apodosis where there is no semantic reason to prepose a noun or to choose an infinitival absolute construction" (ib.) ignores the exceptions mentioned above under 21:2: for instance, 22:6 אם יִמָּצֵא הַגַּנָּב יְשַׁלֵּם שְׁנָיִם. The use of a *w^eqatal* form is certainly not unique to legal codes: see Judg. 4:8 אם תלכי עִמִּי והלכתי. All these considerations render his notion of "functional explanation" as uniquely applicable to law codes rather vague and unconvincing.

b. In our juridic pericope (21:2–23:19) there are found 54 examples of casuistic law, namely those containing a protasis introduced by כי, אם or אשר. Of those 54 the table below shows the frequency of various types of the first constituent of the apodosis:

w^eqatal	11×: 21:3b, 5f., 8, 11, 13, 19, 23, 30, 35; 22:2, 7
+ pc[5]	18×: 21:2, 3a, 4, 9, 10, 14, 26, 27, 29, 31, 32, 33f., 37; 22:3, 4, 9, 16, 25
לא-pc	4×: 21:7, 21; 22:14, 24
inf. abs.-pc	14×: 21:12, 15, 16, 17, 20, 22, 28; 22:5, 13, 15, 18, 22; 23:4, 5
pc[6]	4×: 22:6, 11, 12, 19
ptc	1×: 22:14b
NC[7]	2×: 22:1, 2.

c. From the above table we note that the apodotic *waw* in a conditional sentence is always joined to an inversive perfect.[8] Joüon-Muraoka (1991: § 176 *d*) have already noted that in casuistic legal codes no such *waw* is attested before a noun or negator. They also add the infinitive absolute to the list of such avoided constituents, a feature not confined, however, to legal codes: idem 1991: § 177 *m*.

d. Within a protasis or apodosis we meet with the inversive *waw* familiar throughout Classical Hebrew: e.g., 21:4 אם אדניו יתן לו אשה . . . כי יתן . . . וְיָלְדָה־לו בנים . . .; 22:9 שְׁבֻעַת יהוה תהיה . . . וְלָקַח בעליו ולא ישלם.

2. Some practioners of text linguistics seem to raise the distinction between historical narrative and direct speech on one hand, and the assignment of various tenses to these two kinds of speech form on the other, to the level of language universals. Thus Niccacci (1994: 119) writes: "This distinction . . . is based on the fact that practically every language uses separate sets of verb forms for these two genres . . . is particularly clear in French, Spanish, Italian and other such languages that possess a rich variety of verb forms". One such rich language is, of course, Classical Greek. The following passage, randomly chosen from Homer, however, appears to defy such a neat distinction.

> ὣς ἔφατ' (impf.) εὐχόμενος, τοῦ δ' ἔκλυε (impf.) Φοῖβος Ἀπόλλων,
> βῆ (aor.) δὲ κατ' Οὐλύμποιο καρήνων χωόμενος κῆρ,

---

[5] An apodosis introduced by an element other than a verb (the negator excluded) and then followed by a prefix conjugation form (pc = prefix conjugation).

[6] An apodosis opening directly with a prefix conjugation form.

[7] Nominal clause.

[8] That these perfects are inversive may be concluded from 21:13 וְשַׂמְתִּי with an ultima accent. Note also cases of the inversive *waw* with the prefix conjugation of other types of apodosis as in 1 Sam. 15:23 יען מָאַסְתָּ דְּבַר יהוה וַיִּמְאָסְךָ מִמֶּלֶךְ "because you rejected the word of *yhwh*, he has denied you kingship".

τόξ' ὤμοισιν ἔχων ἀμφηρεφέα τε φαρέτρην,
ἔκλαγξαν (aor.) δ' ἄρ' ὀϊστοὶ ἐπ' ὤμων χωομένοιο,
αὐτοῦ κινηθέντος· ὁ δ' ἤιε (impf.) νυκτὶ ἐοικώς.
ἕζετ' (impf.) ἔπειτ' ἀπάνευθε νεῶν, μετὰ δ' ἰὸν ἕηκεν· (aor.)
δεινὴ δὲ κλαγγὴ γένετ· (aor.) ἀργυρέοιο βιοῖο.
οὐρῆας μὲν πρῶτον ἐπῴχετο (impf.) καὶ κύνας ἀργούς,
αὐτὰρ ἔπειτ' αὐτοῖσι βέλος ἐχεπευκὲς ἐφιεὶς
βάλλ'· (impf.) αἰεὶ δὲ πυραὶ νεκύων καίνοντο (impf.) θαμειαί.

(Iliad 1: 43–52)

We see that two of the four preterital tenses which Classical Greek has at its disposal are freely but skilfully mixed, and one of them, the imperfect, Niccacci would assign to the sphere of the present, and the other, the aorist, to the domain of the past. The choice between them in this epic pericope, a Greek equivalent of the biblical historical narrative, is conditioned by the well-known tense values of these two verb categories.

This situation remains essentially[9] unaltered even in the New Testament:

Καὶ ὄντος τοῦ Πέτρου κάτω ἐν τῇ αὐλῇ ἔρχεται (historical pres.) μία τῶν παιδισκῶν τοῦ ἀρχιερέως καὶ ἰδοῦσα τὸν Πέτρον θερμαινόμενον ἐμβλέψασα αὐτῷ λέγει (hist. pres.)· καὶ σὺ μετὰ τοῦ Ναζαρηνοῦ ἦσθα τοῦ Ἰησοῦ. ὁ δὲ ἠρνήσατο (aor.) λέγων· οὔτε οἶδα οὔτε ἐπίσταμαι σὺ τί λέγεις. καὶ ἐξῆλθεν (aor.) ἔξω εἰς τὸ προαύλιον καὶ ἀλέκτωρ ἐφώνησεν. (aor.) καὶ ἡ παιδίσκη ἰδοῦσα αὐτὸν ἤρξατο (aor.) πάλιν λέγειν τοῖς παρεστῶσιν ὅτι οὗτος ἐξ αὐτῶν ἐστιν. ὁ δὲ πάλιν ἠρνεῖτο (impf.). καὶ μετὰ μικρὸν πάλιν οἱ παρεστῶτες ἔλεγον (impf.) τῷ Πέτρῳ· . . . ὁ δὲ ἤρξατο (aor.) ἀναθεματίζειν καὶ ὀμνύναι . . . καὶ εὐθὺς ἐκ δευτέρου ἀλέκτωρ ἐφώνησεν (aor.) καὶ ἀνεμνήσθη (aor.) ὁ Πέτρος τὸ ῥῆμα ὡς εἶπεν αὐτῷ ὁ Ἰησοῦς . . . καὶ ἐπιβαλὼν ἔκλαιεν (impf.).

(Mark 14: 66–72)

[9] The significant difference lies in the highly frequent use of the historical present. That this usage was already at home in Homer, however, is pointed out in Hosoe 1932: 38 where reference is made to Paul 1920: 276. See further Wackernagel 1924: I, 47, 158, 162ff.

The subtle shift between the aorist and the imperfect has been picked up by some sensitive New Testament scholars: "repeated denials" on ἠρνεῖτο (v. 70) (Taylor 1952: 575); "the weeping continued some while; Mt.'s and Lc.'s ἔκλαυσεν . . . is less suggestive" on ἔκλαιεν (v. 72) (Swete 1956: 366); "the compound [ἐπιβαλὼν ἔκλαιεν] expresses with peculiar vividness both the initial paroxysm and its long continuance, which the easier but tamer word of the other evangelists fails to do (Moulton 1908: 131f.).

3. It is highly desirable to revise at one point the terminology currently in use, not only in text-linguistic studies on the Hebrew tenses: whereas the label *wayyiqtol* with an energic *waw* is distinct from *w^{e}yiqtol* with a simple *waw, w^{e}qatal* is ambiguous. One should use *w^{e}qataltí* with ultima accent, thus energic, consecutive *waw*, and *w^{e}qatálti* with penultima accent, thus simple, copulative *waw*, as Joüon-Muraoka (§ 115 *c*, 117) do. Verheij (1990: 107–109), for instance, discusses the two distinct forms as if they were one: his *w^{e}qatal* in 1 Chr. 19:12 וְהוֹשַׁעְתִּיךָ with an apodotic *waw* prefixed and following יֶחֶזְקוּ, and וּבָא at 2 Chr. 24:11 following a frequentative,[10] preterital *yiqtol* (יָבִיא) are clearly cases of *w^{e}qataltí*, whereas another *w^{e}qatal* at 2 Chr. 34:4 וְהֵדַק, juxtaposed with שִׁבַּר is undoubtedly a *w^{e}qatálti* form.

[10] Verheij (1990: 108) mentions this example as a case of the chronicler's *w^{e}qatal* corresponding to *wayyiqtol* in his source, וַיַּעַל at 2 Kgs. 12:11. It appears that the computer software which was at Verheij's disposal was not yet capable of picking up a significant grammatical difference in perspective between the two texts, namely whereas the chronicler's source presents the chain of events as punctiliar, the chronicler himself highlights the frequentative aspect, as is evident from the tense of the introductory verb, יָבִיא, followed by two more prefix conjugation forms of equally frequentative/iterative force (וְיָעֲרוּ וְיִשָּׂאוּ), and reinforced by כֹּה עָשׂוּ לְיוֹם בְּיוֹם. Although the sequence in this verse (2 Chr. 24:11) is rather complex and unique, the underlying principle is clear and by no means surprising: a frequentative, preterital *yiqtol* followed by an energic *waw* prefixed to an equally frequentative, preterital *qatal*, thus a *w^{e}qataltí*, which in turn is followed by another energic (sequential) *waw* prefixed to two still frequentative, preterital *yiqtol*s joined by a simple *waw*. See also Driver 1897: 35, 90.

BIBLIOGRAPHY

Althaus, H.P., Henne, H. & Wiegang, E. (eds.), *Lexicon der germanistischen Linguistik*, Tübingen: Niemeyer, 1980.

Anbar, M., "La 'reprise'", *Vetus Testamentum* 38 (1988) 385–398.

Andersen, F.I., *The Hebrew Verbless Clause in the Pentateuch* (Journal of Biblical Literature Monograph Series XIV), Nashville: Abingdon, 1970.

———, *The Sentence in Biblical Hebrew* (Janua Linguarum, Series Practica 231), The Hague: Mouton, 1974.

———, "Salience, Implicature, Ambiguity and Redundancy", in: Bergen, R.D. (ed.), *Biblical Hebrew and Discourse Linguistics*, Winona Lake (Ind.): Eisenbrauns, 1994, 99–116.

Andrews, E., *Markedness Theory. The Union of Asymmetry and Semiosis in Language* (The Roman Jakobson Series in Linguistics and Poetics), Durham and London: Duke University Press, 1990.

——— & Tobin, Y. (eds.), *Toward a Calculus of Meaning. Studies in Markedness, Distinctive Features and Deixis* (Studies in Functional and Structural Linguistics 43), Amsterdam/Philadelphia: John Benjamins, 1996.

Bakker, E.J., "Foregrounding and Indirect Discourse: Temporal Subclauses in a Herodotean Short Story", *Journal of Pragmatics* 16 (1991) 225–247.

Bandstra, B.R., *The Syntax of the Particle ky in Biblical Hebrew and Ugaritic*, Ph.D. diss., Yale University, 1982.

———, "Word Order and Emphasis in Biblical Hebrew Narrative: Syntactic Observations on Genesis 22 from a Discourse Perspective", in: Bodine, W.R. (ed.), *Linguistics and Biblical Hebrew*, Winona Lake (Ind.): Eisenbrauns, 1992, 109–123.

Bar-Asher, M. (ed.), *Language Studies*, Jerusalem: Magnes Press, 1985.

Barr, J., *The Semantics of Biblical Language*, Oxford: Oxford University Press, 1961.

———, "The Image of God in the Book of Genesis—A Study in Terminology", *Bulletin of the John Rylands Library of Manchester* 51 (1968) 11–26.

Bartelmus, R., *HYH. Bedeutung und Funktion eines hebräischen* "Allerweltswortes"—*zugleich ein Beitrag zur Frage des hebräischen Tempussystems* (Arbeiten zu Text und Sprache im Alten Testament 17), St. Ottilien: EOS, 1982.

———, *Einführung in das Biblische Hebräisch. Mit einem Anhang Biblisches Aramäisch*, Zürich: Theologischer Verlag, 1994.

Bauer, H. & Leander, P., *Historische Grammatik der hebräische Sprache des Alten Testaments*, Halle: Niemeyer, 1922 (reprint Hildesheim: George Olms, 1962).

Benveniste, E., *Problèmes de linguistique générale*, Paris: Gallimard, 1966.

Bergen, R.D. (ed.), *Biblical Hebrew and Discourse Linguistics*, Winona Lake (Ind.): Eisenbrauns, 1994.

———, "Evil Spirits and Eccentric Grammar: a Study of the Relationship Between Text and Meaning in Hebrew Narrative", in: Bergen, R.D. (ed.), *Biblical Hebrew and Discourse Linguistics*, Winona Lake (Ind.): Eisenbrauns, 1994, 320–335.

Bergsträsser, G., *Hebräische Grammatik. Mit Benutzung der von E. Kautzsch bearbeiten 28. Auflage von Wilhelm Gesenius' hebräischer Grammatik*, Leipzig: J.C. Hinrichs, 1929 (reprint Hildesheim: George Olms, 1962).

Berns, M., *Contexts of Competence. Social and Cultural Considerations in Communicative Language Teaching*, New York: Plenum, 1990.

Beyerlin, W., *Herkunft und Geschichte der ältesten Sinaitraditionen*, Tübingen: Mohr, 1961.

Blakemore, D., *Semantic Constraints on Relevance*, Oxford: Basil Blackwell, 1987.

Blass, F., Debrunner, A. & Rehkopf, F., *Grammatik des neutestamentlichen Griechisch*, Göttingen: Vandenhoeck & Ruprecht, 1954[9], 1976[20].

Blass, R., "Are There Logical Relations in a Text?", *Lingua* 90 (1993) 91–110.

Bodine, W.R. (ed.), *Linguistics and Biblical Hebrew*, Winona Lake (Ind.): Eisenbrauns, 1992.

———, "The Study of Linguistics and Biblical Hebrew", in: Bodine, W.R. (ed.), *Linguistics and Biblical Hebrew*, Winona Lake (Ind.): Eisenbrauns, 1992, 1–5.

———, "How Linguists Study Syntax", in: Bodine, W.R. (ed.), *Linguistics and Biblical Hebrew*, Winona Lake (Ind.): Eisenbrauns, 1992, 89–107.

——— (ed.), *Discourse Analysis of Biblical Literature. What It Is and What It Offers*, Atlanta: Scholars, 1995.

Brinker, K., "Zum Textbegriff in der heutigen Linguistik", in: Sitta, H. & Brinker, K. (eds.), *Studien zur Texttheorie und zur deutschen Grammatik*, Düsseldorf: Schwann, 1973, 9–41.

Brockelmann, C., *Hebräische Syntax*, Neukirchen-Vluyn: Neukirchener, 1956.

———, *Arabische Grammatik*, Leipzig: VEB Verlag Enzyklopädie, 1960[14].

Brown, F., Driver, S.R. & Briggs, Ch.A., *A Hebrew and English Lexicon of the Old Testament*, Oxford: Oxford University Press, 1907.

Buber, M., *Die fünf Bücher der Weisung. Verdeutscht von Martin Buber gemeinsam mit Franz Rosenzweig*, Heidelberg: Schneider, 1981[10].

Buth, R., *Word Order in Aramaic from the Perspectives of Functional Grammar and Discourse Analysis*, Ph.D. diss., Los Angeles, 1987.

———, "The Hebrew Verb in Current Discussions", *Journal of Translation and Textlinguistics* 5 (1992) 91–105.

———, "Methodological Collision Between Source Criticism and Discourse: The Problem of 'Unmarked Overlay' and the Pluperfect *wayyiqtol*", in: Bergen, R.D. (ed.), *Biblical Hebrew and Discourse Linguistics*, Winona Lake (Ind.): Eisenbrauns, 1994, 138–154.

———, "Functional Grammar, Hebrew and Aramaic: An Integrated, Exegetically Significant Textlinguistic Approach to Syntax", in: Bodine, W.R. (ed.), *Discourse Analysis of Biblical Literature. What It Is and What It Offers*, Atlanta: Scholars, 1995, 77–102.

Cassuto, U., *A Commentary on the Book of Exodus*, Jerusalem: Magnes, 1967.

Childs, B.S., *Exodus. A Commentary* (Old Testament Library), London: SCM, 1974.

Chirichigno, G.C., "The Narrative Structure of Exodus 19–24", *Biblica* 68 (1987) 457–479.

Chomsky, N., *Syntactic Structures*, The Hague: Mouton, 1957.

Chvany, C.V., "Foregrounding, Saliency, Transitivity", *Essays in Poetics* 10 (1985) 1–23.

Closs Traugott, E. & Pratt, M.L., *Linguistics for Students of Literature*, New York: Jovanovich, 1980.

Cohen, D., *La phrase nominale et l'évolution du système verbal en sémitique. Etudes de syntaxe historique*, Leuven: Peeters, 1984.

Comrie, B., *Aspect: An Introduction to the Study of Verbal Aspect and Related Problems* (Cambridge Textbooks in Linguistics), Cambridge: Cambridge University Press, 1976.

Cortese, E., *Da Mosè a Esdra. I libri storici dell'antico Israele*, Bologna: Dehomiane, 1985.

Couper-Kuhlen, E., "Temporal Relations and Reference Time in Narrative Discourse", in: Schopf, A. (ed.), *Essays on Tensing in English. Time, Text and Modality*, Vol. 1, Tübingen: Niemeyer, 1987, 7–25.

———, "Foregrounding and Temporal Relations in Narrative Discourse", in: Schopf, A. (ed.), *Essays on Tensing in English. Time, Text and Modality*, Vol. 2, Tübingen: Niemeyer, 1989, 7–29.

Daneš, F., "Zur semantische und thematischen Struktur des Kommunikats", in: Daneš, F. & Viehweger, D. (eds.), *Probleme der Textgrammatik*, Berlin: Akademieverlag, 1976, 29–40.

——— & Viehweger, D. (eds.), *Probleme der Textgrammatik*, Berlin: Akademieverlag, 1976.
Dawson, D.A., *Text-linguistics and Biblical Hebrew* (Journal for the Study of the Old Testament, Supplement Series 177), Sheffield: Sheffield Academic Press, 1994.
De Beaugrande, R. & Dressler, W., *Einführung in die Textlinguistik*, Tübingen: Niemeyer, 1981.
———, "Text Linguistics and Discourse Studies", in: Dijk, T.A. van (ed.), *Handbook of Discourse Analysis*, Vol. 1: Disciplines of Discourse, London: Academic Press, 1985, 41–70.
DeCaen, V., *On the Placement and Interpretation of the Verbs in Standard Biblical Hebrew Prose*, Ph.D. diss., University of Toronto, 1995.
———, "Ewald and Driver on Biblical Hebrew 'Aspect': Anteriority and the Orientalist Framework", *Zeitschrift für Althebraistik* 9 (1996) 129–151.
Dijk, T.A. van, *Some Aspects of Text Grammars*, The Hague: Mouton, 1972.
———, Ihwe, J., Petöfi, J. & Rieser, H. (eds.), *Zur Bestimmung narrativer Strukturen auf der Grundlage von Textgrammatiken*, Hamburg: Buske, 1972.
———, *Text and Context*, London: Longman, 1977.
——— & Petöfi, J. (eds.), *Research in Texttheory/Untersuchungen in Texttheorie: Grammars and Descriptions*, Berlin: De Gruyter, 1977.
———, *Facts: The Organization of Proposition in Discourse Comprehension*, Amsterdam: University of Amsterdam Institute for General Literature Studies, 1978.
———, *Handbook of Discourse Analysis*, Vol. 1: Disciplines of Discourse, London: Academic Press, 1985.
Dik, S.C., *Functional Grammar*, Amsterdam: North Holland, 1978.
———, *Studies in Functional Grammar*, London: Academic Press, 1980.
———, *The Theory of Functional Grammar*, Dordrecht: Foris, 1989.
Disse, A., *Informationsstruktur im Biblischen Hebräisch. Sprachwissenschaftliche Grundlagen und exegetische Konsequenzen einer Korpus Untersuchung zu den Büchern Deuteronomium, Richter und 2Könige*, Ph.D. diss., Tübingen: Universität Tübingen, 1996.
Dozeman, T.B., *God on the Mountain. A Study on Redaction, Theology and Canon in Exodus 19–24*, Atlanta: Scholars, 1989.
———, "Spatial Form in Exodus 19:1–8a and in the Larger Sinai Narrative", *Semeia* 46 (1989) 87–101.
Dressler, W. (ed.), *Textlinguistik*, Darmstadt: Wissenschaftliche Buchgesellschaft, 1978.
———, "Textsyntax", *Lingua e Stile* 5 (1970) 191–213.
Driver, S.R., *A Treatise on the Use of the Tenses in Hebrew and some Other Syntactical Questions*, Oxford: Clarendon, 1987[3].
Dry, H.A., "The movement of Narrative Time", *Journal of Literary Semantics* 12 (1983) 19–53.
Ehrlich, A.B., *Randglossen zur hebräischen Bibel. Textkritisches, sprachliches und sachliches*, Band 1: Genesis und Exodus, Leipzig: J.C. Hinrich, 1908.
Endo, Y., *The Verbal System of Classical Hebrew in the Joseph Story: an Approach from Discourse Analysis*, Ph.D. diss., University of Bristol, 1993.
———, *The Verbal System of Classical Hebrew in the Joseph Story: an Approach from Discourse Analysis* (Studia Semitica Neerlandica 32), Assen: van Gorcum, 1996.
Eskhult, M., *Studies in Verbal Aspect and Narrative Technique in Biblical Hebrew Prose* (Acta Universitatis Upsaliensis, Studia Semitica Upsaliensia 12), Uppsala: Almqvist & Wiksell, 1990.
———, "The Old Testament and Text Linguistics", manuscript, 1996.
Exter Blokland, A.F. den, *In Search of Text Syntax. Towards a Syntactic Segmentation Model for Biblical Hebrew*, Amsterdam: VU University Press, 1995.
Fassberg, S.E., *Studies in Biblical Syntax*, Jerusalem: Magnes, 1994.
Fleisch, H., "Arabic Linguistics", in: Lepschy, G. (ed.), *History of Linguistics. The Eastern Traditions of Linguistics*, Vol. 1, London: Longman, 1994, 164–179.
Fleischmann, S., *Tense and Narrativity. From Medieval Performance to Modern Fiction*, Austin (Texas): University of Texas Press, 1990.

Fokkelman, J.P., *Narrative Art and Poetry in the Books of Samuel. Vol. IV. Vow and Desire.* (Studia Semitica Neerlandica), Assen: van Gorcum, 1993.

Follingstad, C.M., "*Hinneh* and Focus Function with Application to Tyap", *Journal of Translation and Textlinguistics* 7 (1995) 1–24.

Foolen, A., *De betekenis van Partikels. Een dokumentatie van de stand van het onderzoek met bijzondere aandacht voor* "maar", Nijmegen: A. Foolen, 1993.

Fox, A., "Topic Continuity in Biblical Hebrew", in: Givón, T. (ed.), *Topic Continuity in Discourse: Quantified Cross-Language Studies* (Typological Studies in Language 3), Amsterdam/Philadelphia: John Benjamins, 1983, 215–254.

Fradkin, R., "Typologies of Person Categories in Slavic and Semitic", in: Andrews, E. & Tobin, Y. (eds.), *Toward a Calculus of Meaning. Studies in Markedness, Distinctive Features and Deixis* (Studies in Functional and Structural Linguistics 43), Amsterdam/Philadelphia: John Benjamins, 1996, 319–345.

Galbiati, E., *La struttura letteraria dell'Esodo. Contributo allo studio dei criteri stilistici dell' A.T. e della composizione del Pentateuco*, Alba: Cuneo, 1956.

Gesenius, W., Kautzsch, E. & Cowley, E.A., *Gesenius' Hebrew Grammar*, second ed., Oxford: Clarendon, 1910.

Gibson, J.C.L., *Davidson's Introductory Hebrew Grammar. Syntax*, Edinburgh: T&T Clark, 1994.

Givón, T. (ed.), *Discourse and Semantics* (Syntax and Semantics 12), New York: Academic Press, 1979.

———, *Topic Continuity in Discourse: A Quantitative Cross-Language Study* (Typological Studies in Language 3), Amsterdam/Philadelphia: John Benjamins, 1983.

———, "Introduction", in: Givón, T. (ed.), *Topic Continuity in Discourse* (Typological Studies in Language 3), Amsterdam/Philadelphia: John Benjamins, 1983, 1–42.

———, "Beyond Foreground and Background", in: Tomlin, R.S., *Coherence and Grounding in Discourse* (Typological Studies in Language 11), Amsterdam/Philadelphia: John Benjamins, 1987, 175–188.

———, *Mind, Code and Context. Essays in Pragmatics*, Hillsdale (NJ) and London: Erlbaum, 1989.

———, *Syntax. A Functional-Typological Introduction*, 2 Vols., Amsterdam/Philadelphia: John Benjamins, 1984: 1990.

———, *Functionalism and Grammar*, Amsterdam/Philadelphia: John Benjamins, 1995.

Goldenberg, G., "Verbal Category and the Hebrew Verb". In: Bar-Asher, M. (ed.), *Language Studies* 1 (1985) 295–348.

———, "On Direct Speech and the Hebrew Bible", in: Jongeling, K. et al. (eds.), *Studies in Hebrew and Aramaic Syntax. Presented to Professor J. Hoftijzer on the Occasion of his Sixty-Fifth Birthday*, Leiden: E.J. Brill, 1991, 79–96.

———, "Aramaic Perfects", in: *Israel Oriental Studies* 12 (1992) 113–137.

Greenberg, J.H., *Universals of Language. Report of a Conference Held at Dobbs Ferry, New York, April 13–15, 1961*, Cambridge (Mass.): MIT Press, 1963[1], 1973[2].

Greimas, A.J., *Sémantique Structurale*, Paris: Larousse, 1966.

Grice, H.P., "Logic and Conversation", in: Cole, P. & Morgan, J.L. (eds.), *Syntax and Semantics 3: Speech Acts*, London: Academic Press 1975, 41–58.

Grimes, J., *The Thread of Discourse*, The Hague: Mouton, 1975.

Groppe, D., "Progress and Cohesion in Biblical Hebrew Narrative: the Function of *ke/be* + the Infinitive Construct", in: Bodine, W.R. (ed.), *Discourse Analysis of Biblical Literature. What It Is and What It Offers*, Atlanta: Scholars, 1995, 183–192.

Gross, W., "Das nicht substantivierte Partizip als Prädikat im Relativsatz hebräischen Prosa", *Journal of Northwest Semitic Languages* 4 (1975) 23–47.

———, Irsigler, H. & Seidl, T. (eds.), *Text, Methode und Grammatik: Wolfgang Richter zum 65. Geburtstag*, St. Ottilien: EOS, 1991.

———, "Die Position des Subjekt im hebräischen Verbalsatz, untersucht an den

asyndetischen ersten Redesätze in Gen., Ex. 1–19, Jos., 2 Kön.", *Zeitschrift für Althebraistik* 6 (1993) 170–187.
———, "Zur syntaktischen Struktur des Vorfelds im hebräischen Verbalsatz", *Zeitschrift für Althebraistik* 7 (1994) 203–214.
———, *Die Satzteilfolge im Verbalsatz alttestamentlicher Prosa*, Tübingen: J.C.B. Mohr, 1996.
Gülich, E., *Makrosyntax der Gleiderungssignale im gesprochenen Französisch*, München: Fink, 1970.
———, & Raible, W., "Überlegungen zu einer makrostrukturellen Textanalyse: J. Thurber, 'The Lover and His Lass'", in: Dijk, T.A. van & Petöfi, J. (eds.), *Research in Texttheory/Untersuchungen in Texttheorie: Grammars and Descriptions*, Berlin: De Gruyter, 1977.
Haiman, J., *Natural Syntax. Iconicity and Erosion*, Cambridge: Cambridge University Press, 1985.
Hardmeier, C., *Prophetie im Streit vor dem Untergang Judas. Erzählkommunikative Studien zur Enstehungssituation der Jesaja- und Jeremiaerzählungen in II Reg 18–20 und Jer 37–40* (Beiheft zur Zeitschrift für die alttestamentliche Wissenschaft 187), Berlin/New York: De Gruyter, 1989.
Harris, Z., "Discourse Analysis", *Language* 28 (1952) 1–30.
Harweg, R., *Pronomina und Textkonstitution*, München: Fink, 1968.
Heinemann, W. & Viehweger, D., *Textlinguistik. Eine Einführung*, Tübingen: Niemeyer, 1991.
Hendel, R.S., "In the Margins of the Hebrew Verbal System: Situation, Tense, Aspect, Mood", *Zeitschrift für Althebraistik* 9 (1996) 152–181.
Hertog, C. den, "Die invertierten Verbalsätze im hebräischen Josuabuch. Eine Fallstudie zu einem vernachlässigten Kapitel der hebräischen Syntax", in: Mayer, C., Müller, K. & Schmalenberg, G. (eds.), *Nach den Anfängen fragen, Herrn Prof. dr.theol. Gerhard Dautzenberg zum 60. Geburtstag am 30. Januar 1994*, Gießen: Justus-Liebig Universität, 1994, 227–291.
Hillers, D.R., "Some Performative Utterances in the Bible", in: Wrights, D.P. et al. (eds.) *Pomegranates and Golden Bells, Fs J. Milgrom*, Winona Lake (Ind.): Eisenbrauns, 1995, 757–766.
Hoftijzer, J., *Verbale vragen*, Leiden: E.J. Brill, 1974.
———, *A Search for Method: A Study in the Syntactical Use of the H-locale in Classical Hebrew*, Leiden: E.J. Brill, 1981.
———, "A Preliminary Remark on the Study of the Verbal System in Classical Hebrew", in: Kaye, A.S., *Semitic Studies in Honour of Wolf Leslau*, Wiesbaden: Harrassowitz, 1991, 645–651.
———, "Überlegungen zum System der Stammesmodifikationen im klassischen Hebräisch", *Zeitschrift für Althebraistik* 5 (1992) 117–134.
———, *The Function and Use of the Imperfect Forms with Nun-paragogicum in Classical Hebrew* (Studia Semitica Neerlandica 21), Assen: van Gorcum, 1985.
Hopper, P.J., "Aspect and Foregrounding in Discourse", in: Givón, T. (ed.), *Discourse and Semantics* (Syntax and Semantics 12), New York: Academic Press, 1979, 213–241.
——— & Thompson S.A., "Transitivity in Grammar and Discourse", *Language* 56 (1980) 251–299.
Hosoe, I., *An Enquiry into the Meaning of Tense in the English Verb*, Tokyo: Taibundo, 1932.
Houtman, C., *Exodus*, Vols. 1–2, Kampen: Kok, 1993–1996.
Hwang, S.J.J., "A Cognitive Basis for Discourse Grammar", *Southwest Journal of Linguistics* 7 (1984) 133–156.
Irsigler, H., *Ps. 73—Monolog eines Weisen* (Arbeiten zu Text und Sprache im Alten Testament 20), St. Ottilien: EOS, 1984.
Isenberg, H., *Texttheorie und Gegenstand der Grammatik*, Berlin: Akademie, 1974.

Israelit-Groll, S. (ed.), *Pharaonic Egypt—the Bible and Christianity*, Jerusalem: Magnes, 1985.

Jakobson, R., "Shifters, Verbal Categories and the Russian Verb", in: Jakobson, R., *Selected Writings II*, The Hague: Mouton, 1957/1991, 130–147.

———, "Implications of Language Universals for Linguistics", in: Greenberg, J.H. (ed.), *Universals of Language. Report of a Conference Held at Dobbs Ferry, New York, April 13–15, 1961*, Cambridge (Mass.): MIT Press, 1963[1], 1973[2], 263–278.

———, "Zur Struktur des Russischen Verbums", in: Jakobson, R., *Form und Sinn. Sprachwissenschaftliche Betrachtungen*, München: Fink, 1974, 55–67.

———, *Form und Sinn. Sprachwissenschaftliche Betrachtungen*, München: Fink, 1974.

Jenni, E., *Die Hebräischen Präpositionen. Band 1: Die Präposition beth*, Stuttgart: Kohlhammer, 1992.

———, *Die Hebräischen Präpositionen. Band 2: Die Präposition caph*, Stuttgart: Kohlhammer, 1994.

Jespersen, O., *Essentials of English Grammar*, London: Allen & Unwin, 1933.

Jongeling, K., Murre-Van den Berg, H.L. & van Rompay, L. (eds.), *Studies in Hebrew and Aramaic Syntax: Presented to Professor J. Hoftijzer on the Occasion of his Sixty-fifth Birthday*, Leiden: E.J. Brill, 1991.

Joosten, J., "The Predicative Participle in Biblical Hebrew", *Zeitschrift für Althebraistik* 2 (1989) 128–159.

———, "Biblical Hebrew *w^eqāṭal* and Syriac *hwā qāṭel* Expressing Repetition in the Past", *Zeitschrift für Althebraistik* 5 (1992) 1–14.

———, "Tekstlinguïstiek en het Bijbels-Hebreeuwse werkwoord: een kritische uiteenzetting", *Nederlands Theologisch Tijdschrift* 49 (1995) 265–272.

Joüon, P., *Grammaire de l'Hebreu biblique*, Roma: Pontificio Istituto Biblico, 1923.

——— & Muraoka, T., *A Grammar of Biblical Hebrew*, 2 Vols. (Subsidia Biblica 14/I and 14/II), Roma: Pontificio Istituto Biblico, 1991.

Kallmeyer, W. & Meyer-Hermann, R., "Textlinguistik", in: Althaus, H.P., Henne, H. & Wiegang, E. (eds.), *Lexikon der germanistischen Linguistik*, Tübingen: Niemeyer, 1980[2] (1973[1]), 242–258.

Kaswalder, P.A., *La disputa diplomatica di Iefte (Gdc 11,12–28), La ricerca archeologica in Giordania e il problema della conquista*, Jerusalem: Franciscan Printing Press, 1990.

Kaye, A.S., *Semitic Studies in Honour of Wolf Leslau*, Wiesbaden: Harrassowitz, 1991.

Kelly, F.T., "The Imperfect with Simple *Waw* in Hebrew", *Journal of Biblical Literature* 39 (1920) 1–23.

Kirsner, R., "The Human Factor and the Insufficiency of Invariant Meanings", in: Andrews, E. & Tobin, Y. (eds.), *Toward a Calculus of Meaning. Studies in Markedness, Distinctive Features and Deixis* (Studies in Functional and Structural Linguistics 43), Amsterdam/Philadelphia: John Benjamins, 1996, 83–107.

König, F.E., *Historisch-kritisches Lehrgebäude der hebräischen Sprache*, Leipzig: J.C. Hinrich, 1881–97 (reprint Hildesheim: George Olms, 1979).

Kuhr, E., *Die Ausdruksmittel der konjunktionslosen Hypotaxe in der ältesten hebräischen Prosa* (Beiträge zur semitischen Philologie und Linguistik 7), Leipzig: J.C. Hinrich, 1929.

Kuppevelt, J. van, "Main Structure and Side Structure in Discourse", *Linguistics* 33 (1995), 809–833.

Kuryłowicz, J., "Verbal Aspect in Semitic", *Orientalia* 42 (1973) 114–120.

Labov, W., "The Transformation of Experience in Narrative Syntax", in: Labov, W., *Language in the Inner City*, Philadelphia: University of Pennsylvania Press, 1972, 354–396.

——— & Waletzky, J., "Narrative Analysis: Oral Versions of Personal Experience", in: Helm, J. (ed.), *Essays on the Verbal and Visual Arts*, Seattle: University of Washington Press, 1967, 12–44.

Lambdin, T.O., *Introduction to Biblical Hebrew*, London: Darton, Longman & Todd, 1973.

Leitner, G., "English Grammatology", *International Review of Applied Linguistics* 23 (1984) 199–215.

Lepschy, G. (ed.), *History of Linguistics. The Eastern Traditions of Linguistics*, Vol. 1, London: Longman, 1994.

Levinson, S.C., *Pragmatics* (Cambridge Textbooks in Linguistics), Cambridge: Cambridge University Press, 1983.

Ljungberg, B.-J., "Tense, Aspect and Modality in Some Theories of the Biblical Hebrew Verbal System", *Journal of Translation and Textlinguistics* 7 (1995) 82–96.

Lode, L., "Postverbal Word Order in Biblical Hebrew. Structure and Function", *Semitics* 9 (1984) 113–164.

Loewe, R., "Hebrew Linguistics", in: Lepschy, G. (ed.), *History of Linguistics, The Eastern Traditions of Linguistics*, Vol. 1, London: Longman, 1994, 97–163.

Longacre, R.E., "Some Fundamental Insights of Tagmemics", *Language* 41 (1965) 65–76.

———, *The Grammar of Discourse*, New York: Plenum, 1983.

———, "Vertical Threads of Cohesion in Discourse", in: Neubauer, F. (ed.), *Coherence in Natural Language Texts*, Hamburg: Helmut Buske, 1983.

———, *Joseph: A Story of Divine Providence: A Text Theoretical and Textlinguistic Analysis of Genesis 37 and 39–48*, Winona Lake (Ind.): Eisenbrauns, 1989.

———, "Discourse Perspective on the Hebrew Verb: Affirmation and Restatement", in: Bodine, W.R., *Linguistics and Biblical Hebrew*, Winona Lake (Ind.): Eisenbrauns, 1992, 177–190.

———, "*Weqatal* Forms in Biblical Hebrew Prose: A Discourse-Modular Approach", in: Bergen, R.D. (ed.), *Biblical Hebrew and Discourse Linguistics*, Winona Lake (Ind.): Eisenbrauns, 1994, 50–98.

———, "Building for the Worship of God: Exodus 25:1–30:10", in: Bodine, W.R. (ed.), *Discourse Analysis of Biblical Literature. What It Is and What It Offers*, Atlanta: Scholars, 1995, 21–49.

——— & Hwang, S.J.J., "A Textlinguistic Approach to the Biblical Hebrew Narrative of Jonah", in: Bergen, R.D. (ed.), *Biblical Hebrew and Discourse Linguistics*, Winona Lake (Ind.): Eisenbrauns, 1994, 336–358.

Loprieno, A., "The Sequential Forms in Late Egyptian and Biblical Hebrew: a Parallel Development of Verbal Systems", *Afroasiatic Linguistics* 7 (1980) 1–20.

Lowery, K.E., "The Theoretical Foundations of Hebrew Discourse Grammar", in: Bodine, W.R. (ed.), *Discourse Analysis of Biblical Literature. What It Is and What It Offers*, Atlanta: Scholars, 1995, 213–253.

Loza, J., *La palabras de Yahve. Estudio del decálogo*, México, 1989.

Lyons, J., *Introduction to Theoretical Linguistics*, Cambridge: Cambridge University Press, 1968.

———, *Language and Linguistics. An Introduction*, Cambridge: Cambridge University Press, 1981.

———, *Linguistic Semantics. An Introduction*, Cambridge: Cambridge University Press, 1995.

MacKay, K.L., "Repeated Action, the Potential and Reality in Ancient Greek", *Antichthon* 15 (1981) 36–46.

Mann, W.C. & Thompson, S.A., "Rhetorical Structure Theory: Towards a Functional Theory of Text Organization", *Text* 8 (1988) 243–281.

———, *Discourse Description: Diverse Linguistic Analysis of a Fund-raising Text* (Pragmatics & Beyond 16), Amsterdam/Philadelphia: John Benjamins, 1992.

———, Matthiessen, M.I.M. & Thompson, S.A., "Rhetorical Structure Theory and Text Analysis", in: Mann, W.C. & Thompson, S.A. (eds.), *Discourse Description: Diverse Linguistic Analysis of a Fund-raising Text* (Pragmatics & Beyond 16), Amsterdam/Philadelphia: John Benjamins, 1992, 39–78.

Mayer, C., Müller, K. & Schmalenberg, G. (eds.), *Nach den Anfängen fragen, Herrn Proff.dr.theol. Gerhard Dautzenberg zum 60. Geburtstag am 30. Januar 1994*, Gießen: Justus-Liebig Universität, 1994.
McFall, L., *The Enigma of the Hebrew Verbal System; Solutions from Ewald to the Present Day*, Sheffield: Almond, 1982.
Merwe, C.H.J. van der, "The Vague Term 'Emphasis'", *Journal for Semitics* 1 (1989) 118–132.
———, "Pragmatics of the Translation Value of *gam*", *Journal for Semitics* 4 (1992) 181–199.
———, "Particles and the Interpretation of Old Testament Texts", *Journal for the Study of the Old Testament* 60 (1993) 27–44.
———, "Discourse Linguistics and Biblical Hebrew Grammar", in: Bergen, R.D. (ed.), *Biblical Hebrew and Discourse Linguistics*, Winona Lake (Ind.): Eisenbrauns, 1994, 13–49.
———, "Reconsidering Biblical Hebrew Temporal Expressions", *Zeitschrift für Althebraistik* (forthcoming).
———, "The Concept 'Reference Time' and Biblical Hebrew Temporal Expressions", *Biblica* (forthcoming).
———, Naudé, J.A., & Kroeze, J., "A Biblical Hebrew Reference Grammar for Students", University of Stellenbosch, 1996, manuscript.
Mettinger, T.N.D., "The Hebrew Verbal System: a Survey of Recent Research", *Annual of the Swedish Theological Society* 9 (1974) 64–84.
Mey, J.L., *Pragmatics. An Introduction*, Oxford: Blackwell, 1993.
Meyer, R., *Hebraische Grammatik III. Satzlehre* (Sammlung Göschen, Band 5765), Berlin: De Gruyter, 1972[3].
Michel, D., *Tempora und Satzstellung in den Psalmen*, Bonn: Bouvier, 1960.
Miller, C.L., *The Representation of Speech in Biblical Hebrew Narrative. A Linguistic Analysis*, Atlanta: Scholars Press, 1996.
Moulton, J.P., *A Grammar of New Testament Greek*, Edinburgh: T&T Clark, 1908[3].
Müller, H.P., "Nicht-junktiver Gebrauch von *w*- im Althebräischen", *Zeitschrift für Althebraistik* 7 (1994) 141–174.
Muraoka, T., *Emphasis in Biblical Hebrew*, Ph.D. diss., Hebrew University Jerusalem, 1969.
———, "Purpose or Result? ὥστε in Biblical Greek", *Novum Testamentum* 15 (1973) 205–219.
———, *Emphatic Words and Structures in Biblical Hebrew*, Jerusalem/Leiden: Magnes/ E.J. Brill, 1985.
Nachmanides, M., (Ramban), *Commentary on the Torah. Exodus*, Chavel, C.B. (ed.), New York: Shilo, 1973.
Niccacci, A., "A Neglected Point of Hebrew Syntax: Yiqtol and Position in the Sentence", *Liber Annuus* 37 (1987) 7–19.
———, "Sullo stato sintattico del verbo *haya*", *Liber Annuus* 40 (1990) 9–23.
———, *The Syntax of the Verb in Classical Hebrew Prose* (Journal for the Study of the Old Testament, Supplement Series 86), Sheffield: Sheffield Academic Press, 1990.
———, *Lettura sintattica della prosa Ebraico-Biblica. Principi e applicazioni* (Studium Biblicum Franciscanum, Analecta 31), Jerusalem: Franciscan Printing Press, 1991.
———, "Simple Nominal Clause (SNC) or Verbless Clause in Biblical Hebrew Prose", *Zeitschrift für Althebraistik* 6 (1993) 216–227.
———, "Review of Joüon, P. & Muraoka, T.A., *A Grammar of Biblical Hebrew*, Rome: Pontifical Biblical Institute, 1991", *Liber Annuus* 43 (1993) 528–533.
———, "Marked Syntactical Structures in Biblical Greek in Comparison with Biblical Hebrew", *Liber Annuus* 43 (1993) 9–69.
———, "Diluvio, sintassi e metodo", *Liber Annuus* 44 (1994) 9–46.

———, "Review of Gross, W., Irsigler, H. & Seidl, T., *Text, Methode und Grammatik*, St. Ottilien: EOS, 1991", *Liber Annuus* 44 (1994) 667–692.
———, "On the Hebrew Verbal System", in: Bergen, R.D. (ed.), *Biblical Hebrew and Discourse Linguistics*, Winona Lake (Ind.): Eisenbrauns, 1994, 117–137.
———, "Analysis of Biblical Narrative", in: Bergen, R.D. (ed.), *Biblical Hebrew and Discourse Linguistics*, Winona Lake (Ind.): Eisenbrauns, 1994, 175–198.
———, "Syntactic Analysis of Ruth", *Liber Annuus* 45 (1995) 69–106.
———, "Essential Hebrew Syntax", in: Talstra, E. (ed.), *Narrative and Comment. Contributions Presented to Wolfgang Schneider*, Amsterdam: Societas Hebraica Amstelodamensis, 1995, 111–125.
———, "Organizzazione canonica della Biblia ebraica. Tra sintassi e retorica", *Rivista Biblica* 43 (1995) 9–29.
———, "Review of Dawson, D.A., *Text-linguistics and Biblical Hebrew*, Sheffield: Sheffield Academic Press, 1994", *Liber Annuus* 45 (1995) 543–580.
———, "Finite Verb in the Second Position of the Sentence. Coherence of the Hebrew Verbal System", *Zeitschrift für die alttestamentliche Wissenschaft* 108 (1996) 434–440.
Nicholson, E.W., "The Decalogue as the Direct Address of God", *Vetus Testamentum* 27 (1977) 422–433.
———, *God and His People. Covenant and Theology in the Old Testament*, Oxford: Clarendon, 1986.
Noth, M., *Das 2. Buch Mose. Exodus*, Göttingen: Vandenhoeck & Ruprecht, 1978.
Orlinsky, H.M., "On the Cohortative and Jussive after an Imperative or Interjection in Biblical Hebrew", *Jewish Quarterly Review* 31 (1940–42) 371–382; 32 (1940–42) 191–205 & 273–277.
Paul, H., *Prinzipien der Sprachgeschichte*, Tübingen: Niemeyer, 1920^5, 1960^6.
Petöfi, J., "Eine Textgrammatik mit einer nicht-linear festgelegten Basis", in: Dijk, T.A. van, *Some Aspects of Text Grammars*, The Hague: Mouton, 1972, 77–129.
Pike, K.L., *Language and Its Relation to a Unified Theory of the Structure of Human Behaviour*, The Hague: Mouton, 1967.
Polotsky, H.J., "The Coptic Conjugation System", *Orientalia* 29 (1960) 392–422.
———, "A Note on the Sequential Verb-form in Ramesside Egyptian and in Biblical Hebrew", in: Israelit-Groll, S. (ed.), *Pharaonic Egypt, the Bible and Christianity*, Jerusalem: Magnes, 1985, 157–161.
Qimron, E., "Consecutive and Conjunctive Imperfect: the Form of the Imperfect with Waw in Biblical Hebrew", *Jewish Quaterly Review* 77 (1987) 149–161.
Rainey, A.F., "Further Remarks on the Hebrew Verbal System", *Hebrew Studies* 29 (1988) 35–42.
Reckendorf, H., *Arabische Syntax*, Heidelberg: Carl Winter's Universitätsbuchhandlung, 1921.
Regt, L. de, *A Parametric Model for Syntactic Studies of a Textual Corpus, Demonstrated on the Hebrew of Deuteronomy 1–30* (Studia Semitica Neerlandica 24), Assen: van Gorcum, 1988.
———, "Devices of Participant Reference in Some Biblical Hebrew Texts: Their Importance in Translation", *Jaarbericht* "Ex Oriente Lux" 32 (1991–92) 150–171.
———, "Domains and Subdomains in Biblical Hebrew Discourse", in: Talstra, E. (ed.), *Narrative and Comment. Contributions Presented to Wolfgang Schneider*, Amsterdam: Societas Hebraica Amstelodamensis, 1995, 147–161.
———, "Rules and Conventions of Participant Reference in Biblical Hebrew and Aramaic", manuscript, 1996.
———, Waard, J. de, Fokkelman, J.P. (eds.), *Literary Structure and Rhetorical Strategies in the Hebrew Bible*, Assen/Winona Lake (Ind.): van Gorcum/Eisenbrauns, 1996.
Reinhart, T., "Principles of Gestalt Perception in the Temporal Organizations of Narrative Texts", *Linguistics* 22 (1984) 779–809.

Revell, E.J., "The System of the Verb in Standard Biblical Prose", *Hebrew Union College Annual* 60 (1989) 1–37.

———, *The Designation of the Individual. Expressive Usage in Biblical Narrative*, Kampen: Kok Pharos, 1996.

Richter, W., *Grundlagen einer althebräischen Grammatik. A. Grundfragen einer sprachwissenschaftlichen Grammatik. B. Beschreibungsebene: Bd. I. Das Wort, Bd. II. Die Wortfügung (morphosyntax), Bd. III. Der Satz* (Arbeiten zu Text und Sprache im Alten Testament 8.10.13), St. Ottilien: EOS, 1978–1980.

———, *Untersuchungen zur Valenz althebräischer Verben 1* (Arbeiten zu Text und Sprache im Alten Testament), St. Ottilien: EOS, 1985.

———, *Biblia Hebraica Transcripta. 1 und 2 Samuel* (Arbeiten zu Text und Sprache im Alten Testament), St. Ottilien: EOS, 1991.

Rosenberg, A.J. (ed.), *Miqra'ot Gedolot. Shemot*, Vol. 1, New York: Judaica Press, 1995.

Rundgren, F., *Das althebräische Verbum. Abriss der Aspektlehre*, Uppsala: Almqvist & Wiksell, 1961.

———, *Erneuerung des Verbalaspekts im Semitischen: funktionell-diachronische Studien zur semitischen Verblehre* (Acta Societas Linguisticae Upsaliensis, Nova Series 1:3), Uppsala: Almqvist & Wiksell, 1963.

———, *Integrated Morphemics. A Short Outline of a Theory of Morphemics* (Acta Societas Linguisticae Upsaliensis, Nova series 3:1), Uppsala: Almqvist & Wiksell, 1976.

Sailhamer, J.H., *The Pentateuch as Narrative. A Biblical-Theological Commentary*, Grand Rapids (Mich.): Zondervan, 1992.

Schiffrin, D., *Discourse Markers*, Cambridge: Cambridge University Press, 1987.

———, *Approaches to Discourse*, Oxford: Blackwell, 1994.

Schleppegrel, M.J., "Paratactic Because", *Journal of Pragmatics* 16 (1991) 323–337.

Schmidt, S.J., *Grundriß der empirischen Literaturwissenschaft. Teilband 1*, Braunschweig: Vieweg, 1980.

Schneider, W., *Grammatik des Biblischen Hebräisch. Völlig neue Bearbeitung der* "Hebräischen Grammatik für den akademischen Unterricht" *von Oskar Grether*, München: Claudius, 1974[1], 1982[5].

Schopf, A. (ed.), *Essays on Tensing in English. Time, Text and Modality*, 2 Vols., Tübingen: Niemeyer, 1987–1989.

Schweizer, H., *Metaphorische Grammatik A. Grundfragen einer sprachwissenschaftlichen Grammatik. B. Beschreibungsebene: Bd. I. Das Wort, Bd. II. Die Wortfügung (morphosyntax), Bd. III. Der Satz* (Arbeiten zu Text und Sprache im Alten Testament 8.10.13), St. Ottilien: EOS, 1981.

———, *Biblische Texte verstehen*, Stuttgart: Kohlhammer, 1986.

Silbermann, A.M. & Rosenbaum, M. (eds.), *Chumash, with Targum Onkelos, Haphtaroth and Rashi's Commentary. Shemot*, Jerusalem: Silbermann Family, 1934.

Sinclair, M., "Fitting Pragmatics into the Mind. Some Issues in Mentalist Pragmatics", *Journal of Pragmatics* 23 (1995) 509–539.

Sitta, H. & Brinker, K. (eds.), *Studien zur Texttheorie und zur deutschen Grammatik*, Düsseldorf: Schwann, 1973.

Sonnet, J.P., "Le Sinaï dans l'événement de sa lecture. La dimension pramatique d'Exode 19–24", *Nouvelle Revue Théologique* 111 (1989) 321–344.

Sperber, D. & Wilson, D., *Relevance, Communication and Cognition*, Cambridge (Mass.): Harvard University Press, 1986 (1995[2]).

Stipp, H.J., "*Wehaya* für nichtiterative Vergangenheit? Zu syntaktischen Modernisierungen im masoretischen Jeremiabuch", in: Gross, W., Irsigler, H. & Seidl, T. (eds.), *Text, Methode und Grammatik: Wolfgang Richter zum 65. Geburtstag*, St. Ottilien: EOS, 1991, 521–547.

Swete, H.B., *The Gospel According to St. Mark*, Grand Rapids: Eerdmans, 1909[3] (repr. 1956).

Talstra, E., "Text Grammar and Hebrew Bible 1: Elements of a Theory", *Bibliotheca Orientalis* 35 (1978) 168–175.

———, "Text Grammar and Hebrew Bible 2: Syntax and Semantics", *Bibliotheca Orientalis* 39 (1982) 26–38.

———, *2 Kön. 3: Etüden zur Textgrammatik*, Amsterdam: VU University Press, 1983.

———, "Towards a Distributional Definition of Clauses in Classical Hebrew: a Computer-assisted Description of Clauses and Clause Types in Deut. 4:3–8", *Ephemerides Theologicae Lovanienes* 63 (1987) 95–105.

———, "Biblical Hebrew Clause Types and Clause Hierarchy", in: Jongeling, K. et al. (eds.), *Studies in Hebrew and Aramaic Syntax: Presented to professor J. Hoftijzer on the Occasion of his Sixty-Fifth Birthday*, Leiden: E.J. Brill, 1991, 180–193.

———, "Text Grammar and Biblical Hebrew: The Viewpoint of Wolfgang Schneider", *Journal of Translation and Textlinguistics* 5 (1992) 269–287.

———, *Narrative and Comment. Contributions Presented to Wolfgang Schneider*, Amsterdam: Societas Hebraica Amstelodamensis, 1995.

———, "Clause Types and Textual Structure: an Experiment in Narrative Syntax", in: Talstra, E. (ed.), *Narrative and Comment. Contributions Presented to Wolfgang Schneider*, Amsterdam: Societas Hebraica Amstelodamensis, 1995, 166–180.

———, "Tense, Aspect and Clause Connections, The Syntax of Joshua 23", *Journal of Northwest Semitic Languages* (forthcoming).

Taylor, V., *The Gospel According to St. Mark*, London: Macmillan, 1952.

Thompson, S., "'Subordination' and Narrative Event Structure", in: Tomlin, R.S. (ed.), *Coherence and Grounding in Discourse* (Typological Studies in Language 11), Amsterdam/Philadelphia: John Benjamins, 1987, 435–454.

Tobin, Y., "Process and Result and the Hebrew Infinitive: A Study in Linguistic Isomorphism", in: Jongeling, K. et al. (eds.), *Studies in Hebrew and Aramaic Syntax: Presented to professor J. Hoftijzer on the Occasion of his Sixty-Fifth Birthday*, Leiden: E.J. Brill, 1991, 194–209.

———, *Invariance, Markedness and Distinctive Feature Analysis. A Contrastive Study of Sign Systems in English and Hebrew* (Current Issues in Linguistic Theory 111), Amsterdam/Philadelphia: John Benjamins, 1994.

———, "Invariance, Markedness and Distinctive Feature Theory. The Modern Hebrew Verb", in: Andrews, E. & Tobin, Y. (eds.), *Toward a Calculus of Meaning. Studies in Markedness, Distinctive Features and Deixis* (Studies in Functional and Structural Linguistics 43), Amsterdam/Philadelphia: John Benjamins, 1996, 347–379.

Tomlin, R.S., *Basic Word Order: Functional Principles*, London: Croom Helm, 1986.

Trubetzkoy, N.S., "Die phonologischen Systeme", *Travaux du Cercle Linguistique de Prague* 4 (1931) 96–116.

Van Peer, W., *Stylistics and Psychology: Investigations of Foregrounding*, London: Croom Helm, 1986.

Van Seters, J., *The Life of Moses. The Yahwist as Historian in Exodus-Numbers*, Kampen: Kok Pharos, 1994.

Verheij, A.J.C., *Verbs and Numbers. A Study of the Frequencies of the Hebrew Verbal Tense Forms in the Book of Samuel, Kings and Chronicles* (Studia Semitica Neerlandica 28), Assen: van Gorcum, 1990.

———, "Review of Niccacci, A., *The Syntax of the Verb in Classical Hebrew Prose*, Sheffield: Sheffield Academic Press, 1990", *Bibliotheca Orientalis* 49 (1992) 214–217.

Verschueren, J., Östman, J.-O. & Blommaert, J. (eds.), *Handbook of Pragmatics, Manual*, Amsterdam/Philadelphia: John Benjamins, 1995.

Wackernagel, J., *Vorlesungen über Syntax mit besonderer Berücksichtigung von Griechisch, Lateinisch und Deutsch*, 2 Vols., Basel: Birkhäuser, 1924–1926[2] (repr. 1950–57).

Waltke, B.K. & O'Connor, M., *An Introduction to Biblical Hebrew Syntax*, Winona Lake (Ind.): Eisenbrauns, 1990.

Weber, J.-J., "The Foreground-Background Distinction: A Survey of Its Definitions and Applications", *Language in Literature* 8 (1983) 1–15.

Weinrich, H., *Tempus: Besprochene und erzählte Welt*, Stuttgart: Kohlhammer, 1964[1], 1985[4].

———, "Die Textpartitur als heuristische Methode", in: Dressler, W. (ed.), *Textlinguistik*, Darmstadt: Wissenschaftliche Buchgesellschaft, 1978, 391–412.

———, *Textgrammatik der deutschen Sprache*, Mannheim: Duden, 1993.

Werlich, E., *A Text Grammar of English*, Heidelberg: Quelle & Meyer, 1983.

Wheatley-Irving, L., "Semantics of Biblical Hebrew Temporal Subordinate Clauses in 1 Samuel and 1 Kings: When You Say 'When'?" Paper Read at Seminar "Biblical Hebrew and Discourse Linguistics", Dallas (Tex.): Texas Summer Institute, 1993.

Winther-Nielsen, N., *A Functional Discourse Grammar of Joshua. A Computerassisted Rhetorical Structure Analysis* (Coniectanea Biblica. Old Testament Series 40), Stockholm: Almqvist & Wiksell, 1995.

——— & Talstra, E., *A Computational Display of Joshua. A Computer-assisted Analysis and Textual Interpretation* (Applicatio 13), Amsterdam: VU University Press, 1995.

Wolde, E.J. van, *Words Become Worlds, Semantic Studies of Genesis 1–11* (Biblical Interpretation Series 6), Leiden: E.J. Brill, 1994.

———, "Who Guides Whom? Embeddedness and Perspective in Biblical Hebrew and in 1 Kings 3:16–28", *Journal of Biblical Literature* 114 (1995) 623–642.

———, "The Text as an Eloquent Guide. Rhetorical, Linguistic and Literary Features in Genesis 1", in: de Regt, L.J., de Waard, J., Fokkelman, J. (eds.), *Literary Structure and Rhetorical Strategies in the Hebrew Bible*, Assen/Winona Lake (Ind.): van Gorcum/Eisenbrauns, 1996, 134–151.

———, "The Verbless Clause and its Communicative Function", in: Miller, C. (ed.), *The Verbless Clause in Biblical Hebrew*, Winona Lake (Ind.): Eisenbrauns, 1998 (in press).

Wright, D.P. et al. (eds.), *Pomegranates and Golden Bells, Fs J. Milgrom*, Winona Lake (Ind.): Eisenbrauns, 1995.

Zevit, Z., "Talking Funny in Biblical Hebrew and Solving a Problem of the *yaqtul* Past Tense", *Hebrew Studies* 29 (1988) 35–42.

Zuber, B., *Das Tempussystem des biblischen Hebräisch* (Beiheft zur Zeitschrift für die alttestamentliche Wissenschaft 164), Berlin: De Gruyter, 1986.

INDEX OF BIBLICAL TEXTS

INDEX OF AUTHORS